A World in
Flux

'For a better understanding of India's economic challenges and the needed policies, the writings and advice of Shankar Acharya have been the lodestar throughout my years of working with the government and later as an outside observer. Dr Acharya is endowed with an exceptionally sharp analytical mind and a profound understanding of India's complex political economy. This wonderful Festschrift, featuring essays by some of the best contemporary policy economists, is a gem—a must-read for policymakers and serious scholars alike.'

Vijay Laxman Kelkar
Vice President, Pune International Centre, and
Former Finance Secretary of India

'Economic policy reforms resulted in a sharp upturn in India's economic growth after 1991. Shankar Acharya was a key reformer and has been an outstanding analyst of the country's performance. These essays assess India's current position in a turbulent world and the needed policy reforms. They are a well-deserved tribute to Shankar Acharya and a valuable source for those wishing to understand the economy and its potential.'

Anne O. Krueger
Emeritus Professor, Stanford University, and Former Deputy
Managing Director, International Monetary Fund (IMF)

'I have long considered Shankar Acharya to be India's finest macroeconomist, with his conservative judgments reflecting his personality. This collection of engaging essays is a worthy celebration of a distinguished economist.'

T.N. Ninan
Former Chairman and Editor of *Business Standard*

'Much like Shankar Acharya's immensely consequential career, *A World in Flux* delves deep into a diverse and complex set of topics. It speaks directly to our current moment, addressing our need for a full understanding of the world order in transition and its implications for India. Highly recommended, particularly to scholars and policymakers of the Global South.'

Y.V. Reddy
Former Governor, Reserve Bank of India, and Chairman,
Fourteenth Finance Commission

A World in Flux

Flux

INDIA'S ECONOMIC PRIORITIES

ESSAYS IN HONOUR OF SHANKAR ACHARYA

Edited by AMITA BATRA
and A.K. BHATTACHARYA

RUPA

Published by
Rupa Publications India Pvt. Ltd 2025
7/16, Ansari Road, Daryaganj
New Delhi 110002

Sales centres:
Bengaluru Chennai
Hyderabad Jaipur Kathmandu
Kolkata Mumbai Prayagraj

P-ISBN: 978-93-6156-646-2
E-ISBN: 978-93-6156-538-0

First impression 2025

10 9 8 7 6 5 4 3 2 1

The moral right of the authors has been asserted.

Printed in India

Contents

Uday Kotak   *vii*
Foreword: My Friend, Philosopher and Guide

Amita Batra and A.K. Bhattacharya   *xi*
Introduction

Section I: Global Dynamics

Martin Wolf   3
Whither the World Economy? Implications for India

Amita Batra   24
The Global Trade Reset in the 2000s and India's Trade Policy Priorities

Montek Singh Ahluwalia   47
Climate Change in India: An Agenda for the Next 10 Years

Emmanuel Jimenez   77
People Power: Human Capital Development in India and Other Asian Economies

Roberto Zagha   93
Latin America's Failure to Catch Up: The Examples of Argentina and Brazil

Shyam Saran   118
Moving China from the Margins to the Centre of Global Finance

Ajay Chhibber   137
Reforming the Bretton Woods Institutions for the Twenty-First Century

Section II: India: The Domestic Economy

Sajjid Z. Chinoy   155
  Getting Rich before Getting Old: India's Macroeconomic
  Imperatives in a Post-Pandemic World

Michael Debabrata Patra   194
  Monetary Policy Challenges and Choices in Heightened
  Uncertainty

Sudipto Mundle and Manish Gupta   212
  Fiscal Performance in a Soft State: A Review of Central and
  State Government Finances in India

Radhicka Kapoor   242
  India's Quest for Productive Employment and the Role of
  MSMEs

Rakesh Mohan   261
  Indian Urbanization Is Slowing Down: What Can Be
  Done about It?

Deepak Mishra and Mansi Kedia   294
  Digitalization and Development: India's Journey from the
  Backwaters to the High Seas of Digital Revolution

S. Mahendra Dev   320
  Priorities for Indian Agriculture: A Case for Cooperative
  Federalism to Improve Incomes and Livelihoods

A.K. Bhattacharya   345
  Waiting for Consensus: How India's Political Economy
  Impacts Its Economic Reforms

List of Contributors   370
Notes   372
Index   405

Uday Kotak

Foreword
My Friend, Philosopher and Guide

I had the pleasure of meeting Dr Shankar Acharya in the mid-1990s when he was the chief economic adviser (CEA) in the government. Shankar is a man of amazing intellect. He is forthright, open to an alternative point of view, and a very good listener.

In the 1990s, after Kotak entered into a joint venture with Goldman Sachs, I would visit Delhi frequently to discuss with the government raising capital in the international markets for public sector companies since domestic capital markets did not have the depth. Further, the non-banking financial (NBFC) sector was going through a difficult phase, with a tight monetary policy and the consequences of the securities scam of 1992. Shankar was among the few persons with whom I could freely discuss macro issues and their impact on the micro financial sector. The seeds of the possibility of a deeper engagement with him began to be sown in my mind then.

Shankar worked as the CEA with successive finance ministers (Manmohan Singh, P. Chidambaram and Yashwant Sinha) and I do believe that his contribution to the Indian economy and the financial sector is under-appreciated. He was a key catalyst in the policymaking process between the government, the Reserve Bank of India (RBI) and a relatively newly formed Securities and Exchange Board of India (SEBI). A significant amount of the transformation of the Indian financial sector that we are witnessing today has its roots in those years when Shankar was the CEA.

I was appointed on the board of the Indian Council for Research on International Economic Relations (ICRIER) in 2000 at the instance of its then director and chief executive Dr Isher Judge Ahluwalia. I was always interested in the area of economic policy and its correlation with the world of finance. This increased my interaction with economists and policymakers. I started meeting Shankar more frequently on my trips to Delhi. I began to learn how to blend economics and finance. I have no doubt that this has helped shape Kotak into a better institution over the years.

In March 2003, I reached out to Shankar to join the board of the newly approved Kotak Mahindra Bank. Shankar readily agreed. That was one of the finest decisions the bank took.

Shankar joined our board in May 2003 and became chairman in 2006. The twelve years from 2006 to 2018 saw the growth of our bank from a fledgling to an institution of reasonable stature and size under Shankar's chairmanship. He, as chairman, was always available for our top leadership and me. He, at times, cautioned us on some areas which turned out to be right most of the time.

His own memoirs, *An Economist at Home and Abroad*, has a chapter on his years with our bank. It is a wonderful read. Under Shankar's chairmanship, the relationship between the board and the management was always transparent and based on trust on both sides. To quote from his book, 'KMB was not run as a "Lala company" but as a wholly professional one.'

One of the least known aspects of Shankar is that behind the economist lurks an entrepreneurial spirit, which related wonderfully to the Kotak DNA. I wish many policymakers in different fields would take a leaf from Shankar to embrace policy, process and professionalism, combined with an openness to creativity.

Over the past twenty years plus, I have been a regular reader of Shankar's columns in *Business Standard*, and greatly value his views. His sustained and eloquent advocacy for the critical need for fiscal prudence and consolidation, greater openness in India's foreign trade policies, and a stronger pursuit of employment generation and human resource development to ensure the rapid, job-full growth of India's economy have been a hallmark of his writings, which have been invaluable for both policymakers and others like myself.

Some of Shankar's friends think that he is sometimes too cautious in predicting growth rates and the future. I disagree. He is a great risk manager for the country's economic thinking, who has consistently posed relevant but difficult questions regarding our economic policies and their impact on our economic and social development.

As this book's title indicates, we live at a time of immense change and uncertainty about the world's economy, its geopolitics and the trends in technological change, which pose both challenges and opportunities for India. The editors, Professor Amita Batra of Jawaharlal Nehru University and A.K. Bhattacharya of *Business Standard*, have done a wonderful job of marshalling a glittering cast of thinkers and policymakers to shed light on what needs to be done, both in India and the world outside, to bring about better outcomes for all. Each of the talented contributors has had significant interaction with Shankar at some stage in his professional life.

This book is a fitting tribute to one of India's finest policy economists in the last forty years. I wish it great success. Shankar will always be my friend, philosopher and guide!

October 2024

Amita Batra and A.K. Bhattacharya

Introduction

In the realm of economic policymaking in India, Shankar Acharya has few peers. For well over two decades, when there were few voices advocating economic reforms, he played a stellar role in shaping India's economic policies and continued to influence their evolution in subsequent years through his writings, research and contributions as a member of various government committees. His is a voice that all governments, irrespective of their political affiliations, have been keen to hear. A Festschrift in his honour has been long overdue. That gap is now being filled.

About Shankar Acharya

With a global education from top universities in the UK and the US, Shankar Acharya is among the rare economists who have come back to their roots and had an exceptional career across domains of policymaking, think tanks, finance and banking. Having completed his high school from the Highgate School in England, Shankar Acharya went on to do his undergraduate studies in Philosophy, Politics and Economics (PPE) from Oxford University. This was followed by a PhD in development economics from Harvard University at the end of which, in 1971, he joined the World Bank.

At the Bank, after a couple of years of working on the research side, he moved to country economic work on East Africa, where he led the Tanzania Basic Economic Mission which produced an eight-volume report on Tanzania's economy in 1977. Soon after this, he was picked to be a part of the team of the World Bank's first World Development Report (WDR) in 1978.

In the second year of the WDR, at 33 years of age, Shankar Acharya was chosen to be the director of the report which was on structural transformation and development policies. The report laid out policy priorities to assist developing countries in confronting the challenges of structural transformation. Among other policies, the report highlighted how the continued reliance on supportive measures like tariff protection could prove to be self-defeating in advancing manufacturing capabilities—an insight which is still relevant today.

Notwithstanding his being clearly among the rising stars at the Bank, his desire to return to his roots in India and contribute to the economic policymaking there remained intact. In 1982, after a little over a decade in the World Bank, which, taken together with his student days, meant a sojourn of over 23 years, he came back to India, initially on leave from the Bank and as senior fellow at the National Institute of Public Finance and Policy (NIPFP) in New Delhi. It is here that he wrote the pathbreaking report 'Aspects of the Black Economy in India' for the Ministry of Finance, Government of India, in 1984.

The black money study was commissioned by the Central Board of Direct Taxes, and it appropriately focused on tax-evaded income. The report was submitted to the newly elected government under Rajiv Gandhi in 1985, and expectedly triggered a healthy debate on the size and nature of India's black money and what needed to be done to tackle that menace. The report had estimated that tax-evaded income ranged between 70 per cent and 140 per cent of total income assessed to tax, which led to a broader estimate of the black income at about 18 to 21 per cent of the gross domestic product (GDP) in 1983–84.

To its credit, Dr Acharya's report made no suggestions on demonetization or voluntary disclosure schemes to deal with the problem—ploys that governments would experiment with but neither of which would work out. Instead, the measures recommended by his report included the reduction of the high direct tax rates on income and wealth, the simplification and rationalization of excise and customs duties, and a shift away from direct controls on prices and quantities to move towards greater freedom of the market system and prices. Indeed, in subsequent years, most of these recommendations found their way into government policy.

Soon after this, he joined the Ministry of Finance as economic adviser. In this capacity, he had the primary responsibility of drafting the pathbreaking long-term fiscal policy (LTFP) document. The trigger for the report came from the finance minister Vishwanath Pratap Singh who, in his first budget in 1985, announced the government's decision to release a long-term fiscal policy to provide a road map for the future direction of the government's taxation policy. Bimal Jalan, the chief economic adviser, chose Dr Acharya to be the man to steer the exercise through consultation and discussion among officials and experts, and draft the report. In just about 10 months, the LTFP document was finalized and presented to Parliament; it was a report that provided a medium-term fiscal policy strategy, embedding the tax policy intentions of the government within a broad macro-fiscal framework, and promising reforms of indirect taxes including a recommendation for the introduction of a value-added tax system.

In effect, the LTFP report committed the government to sweeping reforms of both central excise and customs duties. For the former, it recommended the phased introduction of VAT principles in excise taxation, conferring the name MODVAT (modified value added tax) on the new system. For customs duties, the LTFP argued the case for a uniform tariff for all commodities, citing not only its advantage in terms of the simplification it would imply for industry, trade and customs administration, but also the fact that it would help ensure uniform, effective protection that would assist the process of specialization based on comparative advantage.

With political uncertainty deepening in the late 1980s and the momentum of reforms slowing, Shankar Acharya—who by then had become a senior economic adviser—decided to return to the World Bank in November 1990 as the chief of the public economics division. But this turned out to be a short stint. In early 1993, the P.V. Narasimha Rao government invited Shankar Acharya to become the chief economic adviser (CEA). He accepted the offer and became part of the legendary economic reforms team led by the then finance minister Dr Manmohan Singh. As is well established, the consequent liberalization of the economy marked a turning point in India's economic history. India has since experienced sustained progress in overall economic growth and prosperity of its people. Dr Acharya served in the capacity of the CEA through the 1990s with three different governments under the Congress, the United Front and NDA-1, and thus played a significant role in maintaining the continuity of economic reforms throughout the decade. With his technical expertise being highly valued across political parties and regimes, Dr Acharya went on to become the longest serving CEA in India.

After 15 years in the MoF, with the last eight as CEA, Shankar Acharya decided to take another sabbatical from the government in 2001. Persuaded by his close friend, the very dynamic Isher Judge Ahluwalia, he joined the Indian Council for Research on International Economic Relations (ICRIER) as honorary professor and member, Board of Governors. In 2002, when he turned 56, he quit government service and has since been with ICRIER.

Over these last two decades, he has been a most prolific author, having written 11 books—mostly on Indian economic issues and policies, and numerous scholarly articles in academic journals. Among these, *The Essays on Macroeconomic Policy and Growth in India* (published by Oxford University Press in 2006) provides rare insights into India's macroeconomic policies and performance during the crucial decade of the 1990s. The essays on macroeconomic management and external sector policies in particular are a combination of an insider's perspective, analytical rigour, and clear and precise exposition. The book also includes an authoritative account of tax reforms over three decades from 1975 to 2005 in one of the chapters. His two latest books published in 2021 are *India's Economy, 2015–2020: Contemporary Commentary* (Academic Foundation) and *An Economist at Home and Abroad: A*

Personal Journey (HarperCollins). The last, his memoir, provides an interesting account of his peripatetic life across continents, and true to his character, remains almost entirely an account of his personal journey without any self-eulogization as a top policymaker.

Since 2003, he has been a regular columnist for *Business Standard,* a leading financial daily in India. Writing a monthly column for over 20 years is some impressive feat! His columns are a reflection of a wealth of experience, acute intellect and immense common sense. His ability to be unbiased and steer clear of extremes stands out particularly in them.

Shankar Acharya was non-executive chairman of Kotak Mahindra Bank—one of India's newest and most successful private commercial banks—for 12 years (2006–18). He also served as member of the Securities and Exchange Board of India (1997–2000), member, Twelfth Finance Commission (2004), member, National Security Advisory Board (2009–13), and member, Technical Advisory Committee on Monetary Policy (2005–16). Incidentally, this excludes the offers for senior positions in successive governments over the last two decades that he has refrained from accepting.

About This Volume

This volume is a collection of essays invited from distinguished economists, academics and policy practitioners who have been closely associated, in some capacity or the other, with Shankar Acharya over different points of time in his life and career. The overarching thought and theme in this volume has been to get some of the best minds from India and abroad to reflect on fast-evolving global dynamics, and to delineate opportunities and policy priorities for India in this context. Except for indicating the broad underlying theme and the title of the volume, the contributing authors were not given any specific or detailed guidelines. The volume, therefore, remains eclectic and the essays are varied, but they all deliberate on important issues arising from the global context and the macroeconomic developments and policy priorities for India.

For convenience, the 15 essays in the volume are divided into two parts: 'Global Dynamics' and 'India: The Domestic Economy'. In the first part, the first three essays address broad issues related to global growth and a multilateral rules-based order, global trade reset, and climate change, followed by three essays on the development experience of Latin America, human capital development in East Asia, and financial sector developments in China; the last essay relates to reforms in the multilateral institutions. In the second part of the volume, the first three essays focus on India's macroeconomic imperatives, and monetary policy and public finance issues; the next two discuss employment and urbanization-related issues; the last set of three essays are devoted to digitalization, agriculture and political economy.

Contours and Challenges of a Changing World

In the first essay, Martin Wolf discusses the relevance of a multilateral rules-based order in an increasingly protectionist and inward-looking world with diminishing respect for the erstwhile framework, especially among its influential founding members. Using the 10-year moving averages measure for the period starting from 2007 and going into the 2020s, Wolf presents evidence of a global slowdown during this period. He also highlights the fall in the rate of 'catch-up', which he defines as the difference in the growth of GDP per head between advanced and developing and emerging market economies. Causal factors for the slowdown are discussed in detail, with a focus on the set of economies contributing a major share of global growth. On the likely future scenario, Wolf leans towards a greater possibility of a continued downturn in growth. Proceeding to discuss the transition from hyperglobalization—a phase of heightened trade and economic integration in the world—to that of 'slowbalization' marked by increased protectionism, Wolf presents some alternative scenarios of a world that is likely to be far less open. In this context, he identifies the challenges for the Indian economy. Notably, Wolf points at how there might be opportunities for India to take advantage of even in this inward-looking global environment. He considers 'China-Plus-One' as the core plank of the available opportunity for India.

Wolf is emphatic about the need for India to adopt a more outward-looking growth orientation. On the basis of available literature, he argues on the fallacy of India's belief in its 'large' market as a sufficient driver of economic growth. In this context, therefore, he brings out the relevance of the global market for India, and the need and necessity for it to remain open.

Several factors contribute to India's special advantage in the China-Plus-One world according to Wolf. These include India's favourable placement, politically, in relation to both the West as well as the Global South, its large and thriving diaspora, and human capital that, being large in size, should be capable of contributing to its export potential. Wolf hopes that by using these advantages and adopting appropriate policies, including a more open and outward growth orientation, India will strive for a higher growth rate, and thereby help bring about a positive change in the world.

Presenting a detailed account of evolving global trade dynamics and multilateral trade order over more than two decades in the current century, Amita Batra,. in the following essay, reflects on the necessary trade policy priorities for India. According to Batra, the first decade saw a multifold increase in global trade led by global value chains (GVCs), China's accession to the WTO and its emergence as the 'factory of the world', and the launch of the Doha Development Agenda (DDA) in 2001 as the first round of the WTO. However, the decade ended with a slowdown in the rate of growth of global trade consequent upon the global financial crisis in 2008. This was followed by a period of political compulsions reflected most distinctly in the 'bring back jobs to America' slogan early in the next decade. In 2011, natural disasters in East Asia led to a disruption in regional value chains. As a result, a process of reshoring, nearshoring and restructuring of the GVCs was initiated. This process of GVC diversification—also referred to as 'China-Plus-One'—gathered further momentum at the end of the decade when the world was struck by the pandemic. In the wake of the Ukraine war, both GVC diversification and trade trends are increasingly being guided by geopolitical proximity among nations.

The more profound shifts, according to Batra, are evident at the institutional level. While the WTO was already at a difficult juncture with negligible progress in the DDA in the first decade, it is the turnaround in the US trade policy and the increasing use of trade instruments in bilateral contexts violating the multilateral norms since 2017 that has hastened the retreat of the multilateral rules-based trade order in the global economy. Simultaneously, she observes that there has been a dramatic rise in the number and depth of preferential trade agreements (PTAs) to facilitate global trade and GVCs.

Notwithstanding these adverse trends, global trade has remained resilient and GVC-led trade has continued to be the predominant component therein. In the light of these developments, Batra emphasizes the need for India to adopt a more open trade policy in order to take advantage of the opportunities presented by the altered trade context.

The following essay by Montek Singh Ahluwalia deals with the most critical challenge confronting humanity in the present times, that is, climate change. Highlighting the significance of climate change for India, Ahluwalia discusses why it is imperative for India to work on an action programme with a sense of urgency. Differentiating between adaptation and mitigation, Ahluwalia puts forth the challenge of mitigation in terms of collective action that requires cooperation across countries. For India, he presents a set of detailed commitments that would be consistent with its international commitments to achieving its net-zero objective by the target date of 2070.

Bringing out the challenges of implementing policies in the face of conflicting interests, Ahluwalia presents a national agenda of possible steps in the direction of managing climate change in the medium term. Among other suggestions, he emphasizes the need to quantify a 10-year action programme that would enable India to achieve the net-zero goal by 2070. Primarily, Ahluwalia suggests that the actions should be focused in the areas of a shift from coal-based power to renewable energy, electrification of road and rail transport, and the pursuit of using electricity for industrial heating. Each of these areas has been dealt with in great detail, with clear targets indicated in the specific action area, advantages and disadvantages of the specified action programme, challenges of implementation and critical inputs as well as supporting action to achieve set targets. The tasks involved would require technical expertise and design capabilities. Over and above that, Ahluwalia stresses the need to build national consensus for effective implementation as well as appropriately address and reconcile diverse and conflicting interests along the way. In this context, he highlights the need to design separate but consistent action plans at the Centre and the State levels—both contributing to the larger agenda in each area of action in this respect. Impressively, Ahluwalia, with his unmatchable policy experience in the Indian context, lays out a possible mechanism and an institutional structure to achieve the desirable outcomes with remarkable specificity and clarity.

The Development Experience of East Asia and Latin America

Emmanuel Jimenez, in his essay, brings forth the significance of human capital development for a country like India where the demographic profile can potentially yield a positive dividend. However, the author warns at the outset that the opportunity to exploit this dividend is limited in time and does not extend infinitely into the future. Jimenez undertakes an analysis of India's progress on human development relative to that made by its Asian counterparts. Using the World Bank's Human Capital Index (HCI) and its various subcomponents, he discusses the progress that India has made in many aspects of human capital development over the last 50 years. Acknowledging that India has seen progress on several fronts, the author, however, points to the many dimensions of the HCI where India continues to lag behind its comparator set of middle-income Southeast Asian economies like Vietnam, Thailand and such others.

The provision of basic services like education and health—which ultimately determine the productive potential of the workforce in any country—remain wanting in India. Among the priority areas that require focus, according to Jimenez, are improving the nutritional status of young children, reducing the number of children and youth who remain out of school, and providing better-quality basic education and skills training and better health services.

An important point that Jimenez makes is that corrective action and appropriate policies and programmes in this context are not any more difficult to design or implement. The availability of a large number of studies providing robust analytical evidence and insights relating to the policy set that can assist India in achieving the demographic dividend makes it simpler for India. In addition to these studies from other regions that are replicable, the author also points to India having the wherewithal to undertake and conduct relevant research on its own. Simultaneously, he says that India also has the ability to attract the best international researchers to identify the unfinished agenda. Essentially, the author belabours the point that there is no dearth of evidence, existing research or potential to undertake fresh research in this context. The most important driver here has to be the 'will' to change the course of human development in India.

Roberto Zagha, in the next essay, discusses the factors that have limited the progress of Latin American countries. Recounting the initial advantages in terms of their freedom from colonization, early efforts in industrialization and developing educational systems, Zagha discusses how, with a higher per capita income in the 1960s in comparison with their South and East Asian peers, many of the Latin American economies were considered to have significantly better growth prospects. However, he goes on to lament how the early growth advantage has either significantly narrowed or completely disappeared for most Latin American economies that have registered growth rates of two per cent or less over a period of more than four decades.

Among factors that Zagha considers responsible for the disappointing growth experience of these economies, the four that he draws attention to include unequal income distribution, intervention by the United States in establishing favourable political regimes, the impact of maintaining a high exchange rate on industrial development, and an excessive focus on macroeconomic stabilization relative to long-term development. Against this background, Zagha presents a detailed account of Argentina and Brazil—two economies that were expected to have a bright future at one point of time but have, in contrast, experienced four decades of economic stagnation.

In case of Argentina, he highlights the lack of economic diversification away from agriculture and the inability to reduce the dependence on external capital as major factors contributing to long-term economic stagnation. A series of 'orthodox' reform programmes, according to Zagha, left the Argentine economy in frequent external debt crises. In case of Brazil, notwithstanding the successes and strong economic performance in the early decades of the twentieth century, its economy has been in a prolonged phase of dismal growth since 1980. Zagha discusses Brazil's economic decline over five time periods: 1973–80, 1980–94, 1994–99, 1999–2015, with the last having started in 2015 and still ongoing. The excessive trade protectionism and, later in the mid-1990s, the excessive obsession with keeping interest rates high have limited its growth trajectory.

Based on the decade-wise account of the two economies, Zagha outlines nine lessons emphasizing, among others, the importance of well-paced context-specific reforms, exchange rate valuation, carefully calibrated capital account liberalization and a focus on manufacturing sector growth with an export orientation.

Tracing the evolution of China's financial industry and its integration in international financial markets, Shyam Saran addresses some of the key issues that have both geopolitical and economic ramifications. Having started with building the domestic financial industry and its subsequent consolidation, China undertook a gradual and incremental upgradation to integrate with the international financial market. The consequent expansion in the size and scale of its operations across financial instruments accords it a profitable lure as well as opportunities that, according to Saran, few would want to miss. Interestingly, Saran states that China has continued to evolve its financial sector in several ways in order to navigate the geopolitical pressures from the West. He discusses the Chinese efforts towards the internationalization of its currency and the increasing use of the RMB in trade settlement in this context. China has been among the first countries to introduce a digital currency that assists it in overcoming its partial capital account convertibility limitations. The success of the China International Payment System (CIPS), even if limited, does provide an alternative to the West-created and dominated Society for Worldwide Interbank Financial Telecommunication (SWIFT) system of international payments that has also been their channel for imposing and implementing sanctions on Iran, and more recently, Russia. Saran also discusses interesting contrasts as evident in China developing alternative systems to bypass the US in its actions against friendly nations while simultaneously adopting a collaborative approach with West-dominated institutions to further its own programmes—be it the Asian Infrastructure Investment Bank (AIIB), or the creation of a digital cross-border payment system or reserve liquidity arrangement for the Asia-Pacific economies. Possibly, according to Saran, this could also be a step towards China learning to develop modern practices. In Saran's view, China—while yet some distance away from becoming a major player in global finance—has been successful in developing and providing financial alternatives, instruments and institutions, and in the process has enabled, to an extent, the diminution of the Western dominance of the financial world. Saran concludes his essay with a cautionary note, saying that the lack of realization or consideration in India about important questions relating to participation in China-led financial initiatives or their impact on the global financial landscape may not bode well for the nation, even in the limited regional context.

Reforming Multilateral Institutions

In his essay, Ajay Chhibber reviews the role of multilateral development banks and the scope for their reform. According to

Chhibber, the Bretton Woods (BW) institutions and the original vision of an open rules-based trade and financial architecture were successful—through their policy advice and programmes—in impacting the development processes of many countries. However, given the challenges of the evolving present context, it is increasingly difficult to view the BW institutions as effective. Chhibber draws attention to two main issues that may be limiting the capabilities of the multilateral institutions. The first is the size and leverage, and the second the mandate and effectiveness of the multilateral institutions (MIs). In particular, Chhibber highlights the shortfall in the climate fund as critical evidence in this context. As for the mandate, Chhibber discusses in detail how the IMF has overextended itself and underperformed in areas like its surveillance function, especially of advanced economies. As for the World Bank, its slow and bureaucratic structure has impacted its ability to be effective. The Bank has also been at the receiving end of criticism on its index of doing business. The need for reforming these institutions is therefore obvious.

Chhibber also considers that this may be the most appropriate time to discuss the reform path of MIs. Starting with the global financial crisis (GFC), the increasingly frequent adverse events of the recent past, such as the pandemic, the Russia-Ukraine war, the Israel-Hamas conflict and the existential threat of climate change, reinforce the urgency of initiating the reform process without any further delay. Chhibber suggests building on existing structures and working towards their reform, particularly with respect to the voting shares reflecting the global shifts in the economic weight of the emerging market economies. On the issue of the remit and resources of the World Bank and the IMF, Chhibber lays out a fairly detailed outline, with the former restricted to ensuring macroeconomic policy and financial stability and the latter to work for a 'livable planet and shared prosperity'. On resources, while recommending an enlargement of the base, he also underlines the importance of better utilization.

Growth, Monetary Policy and the Fisc

In an extensively researched essay, Sajjid Z. Chinoy examines the macroeconomic imperatives that would be needed to sustain the Indian economy's growth to a higher level in the coming years. Chinoy's thesis is that the surprise growth of 9.2 per cent in 2023–24 rode on a public investment drive, a relatively healthy banking sector, an upturn in real estate and a rise in services exports. But looking ahead, can this growth momentum be sustained on its own, asks Chinoy.

His findings have shed light on at least three significant fault lines. India's growth in 2023–24 continues to be below its pre-pandemic path. In other words, the adverse impact of Covid-19 on the basic factors of production has left its mark on the economy. The Indian economy's debt sustainability continues to pose challenges to achieving higher growth. And the need for creating jobs to take advantage of the demographic transition in the economy and ensuring higher growth is paramount.

How can all these be achieved? Chinoy lucidly lists out three macroeconomic imperatives in the given situation. Job creation must receive priority attention from policymakers. Unless labour is made into an attractive factor of production through appropriate labour market reforms, both domestic consumption and export competitiveness are likely to be a casualty. A key recommendation Chinoy makes is to place exports at the centre of India's growth strategy. His clinching argument is that no major economy in the last many years has grown sustainably without recording strong export growth.

Finally, policymakers cannot afford to ignore the importance of boosting government revenues through a ramp-up in disinvestment and asset monetization—an initiative that has slowed down in recent years, and through increased tax mobilization. These resources would be needed to boost investment but more importantly to bring down government deficits so that the larger goal of macroeconomic stability could be achieved. Chinoy's analysis and recommendations for securing higher growth can be ignored only to the Indian economy's peril.

In his essay, Michael Debabrata Patra dwells on how the Reserve Bank of India (RBI) managed its policy interventions and approach during the Covid-19 pandemic and the post-Covid years. But at the very start, he introduces an important qualifier. The conduct of monetary policy across the world entered into uncharted territory even before the Covid-19 outbreak, he notes. Apart from the pandemic, geopolitical conflicts in Ukraine and Gaza proved to be a testing time for the conduct of monetary policy. There were shocks on both growth and inflation fronts. But with an extraordinary response, central banks decided to bring down interest rates to unusually low levels, even into the negative zone, and released a substantial amount of liquidity to address concerns over a contraction in economic activity during the pandemic. In contrast, central banks engaged in the most synchronized and aggressive monetary policy tightening in response to the global inflation surge in the aftermath of the Ukraine conflict.

India was no exception, even though Patra argues in his paper that there were some differences. And it is in the context of these differences that the author studies the Indian monetary policy response and its defining features. Patra embarks on a highly perceptive assessment of the importance of measuring uncertainty, the correlation of monetary policy and supply shocks, the coordination between monetary and fiscal policies, the impact of regime shifts on monetary policy, and the importance of modelling monetary policy processes and effectively communicating monetary policy implementation. With the help of these assessments, Patra concludes that the Indian experience shows how monetary policy choices could be country-specific even when the nature and contours of uncertainty are globally pervasive and overwhelming. This is a lesson that few monetary policymakers can ignore.

What is Patra's recommendation for the future conduct of monetary policy? Significantly, in response to the pandemic, India did not lower its policy rate as steeply as was done in many advanced countries. Instead, the rate was brought down to the level of the inflation target. The flexibility built into the inflation targeting regime had its own advantages—allowing the monetary policy to ensure price stability even while being conscious of promoting growth. The policy of having an inflation tolerance band around a target paid rich dividends, just as the system of making inflation management a shared responsibility—under which the government sets the target and the RBI achieves it—served the desired purpose. Policymakers should wait and watch while guiding inflation down to the goal, but there can be no letting down of the guard as far as monetary policy is concerned.

In their essay, Sudipto Mundle and Manish Gupta analyze the fiscal performance of India's Union and State governments against the backdrop of a complex set of conditions where decision-making and implementation suffer on account of attempts to accommodate the demands and aspirations of different interest groups in spite of the limited capacity and resources of a weak state. What makes these complexities even more complicated is India's federal structure in which the States compete with the Union government for a larger share of resources. In this race, States often use their resources to deliver many private goods at subsidized rates—which are unwarranted—even as they fall short in the delivery of public goods like basic education, public health or security.

It is in this context that the paper reviews India's recent fiscal performance at both the Central and the State levels, and what it brings out is quite interesting. At 27 per cent of gross state domestic product (GSDP), the level of debt or outstanding liabilities of the States is well below the target set by the 15th Finance Commission, but the Centre's debt is substantially higher, inflating total public debt to 89 per cent in 2019–20 and slightly lower at 80 per cent as budgeted for 2024–25. This constrains the government's ability to spend adequately in areas such as health, education and infrastructure.

Rounding off their analysis of fiscal performance by governments, Mundle and Gupta focus on the Centre, which, according to them, has consistently raised capital expenditure even while displaying a commitment to fiscal consolidation. Of course, buoyant tax revenues have helped the Centre to stay committed to high capex, fiscal consolidation and restraint on revenue expenditure. The main concern for the Centre, according to them, is the high level of debt. The way forward, therefore, should be for the Centre to reduce its debt and for the more economically developed States to focus on raising expenditure on capex and social spending. The economically less developed States, on the other hand, need to raise their share of spending on capex and social services, along with focusing on reversing the declining share of their own revenue receipts and their rising levels of public debt.

Labour Markets and Urbanization

A notable shift in employment towards the agricultural sector has been one of the widely noticed trends in India's labour market after the outbreak of the Covid-19 pandemic. Employment in agriculture rose from 42.4 per cent in 2019–20 to 45.7 per cent in 2022–23, thereby adding an estimated 61.2 million people to the workforce in this sector. This was, therefore, bad news for India's structural transformation. But Radhicka Kapoor notes that even before the pandemic, India's structural transformation had remained sluggish with the manufacturing sector failing to emerge as an engine of productive job creation.

Going beyond this, Kapoor presents four empirical findings on the state of India's industrial sector with special emphasis on how it plays on the labour market. These findings bring out how India's firm landscape is dominated by informal microenterprises, even as the distribution of employment among enterprises has been dominated by microenterprises. Given this background, the role of MSMEs in creating jobs can hardly be over-emphasized. MSMEs in labour-intensive industries not only create jobs but also help enhance productivity and competitiveness. Kapoor believes that policy recommendations must recognize this and, therefore, proposes a new policy in her essay, advocating for a shift away from indefinitely subsidizing subsistence entrepreneurs.

Kapoor argues that encouraging and supporting robust enterprise growth is essential for generating well-paying and productive jobs to meet the aspirations of a rising working-age population. In India, therefore, empowering and encouraging MSMEs are of immense importance, particularly because the country's labour-intensive industries are mostly run by smaller enterprises and not by capital-intensive ones.

In his essay, Rakesh Mohan delves deep into the issues that trouble the urbanization journey in India. Citing the fact that a little more than half the world became urban only around 2007, he notes that the experience of living in towns and cities is relatively new and yet, he regrets, there is no 'exceptional attention' being paid to urbanization. The bigger surprise is that in spite of the unprecedented increase in the urban population over the last three decades without any focused policy effort, the world, including the emerging economies, has managed to cope with this transformation. Mohan posits that India's urbanization journey going forward can be managed because rapid urbanization is accompanied by industrial and economic growth. The worry, if any, is on account of slow industrial development in terms of both value-added and employment, particularly in urban areas.

Mohan brings out another worrying feature of the urbanization experience in India. While Indian urbanization has been slow over the last 50 years, the experience of this process itself has been anomalous. For instance, the share of manufacturing in the GDP has been stagnating; urban manufacturing employment growth has also been sluggish; the share of net rural-urban migration in urban population growth has been static at 20 per cent, and so on. This strange phenomenon of industrialization and urbanization in India which is inconsistent with the historical experience of other fast-growing countries needs to be studied in depth, argues Mohan.

Reflecting on the future of urbanization in India, he raises two very important issues. One, there is a need to think about the kind of urban patterns that could emerge as a result of rapid technological changes, particularly after the pandemic, and which have already affected the nature of human behaviour, like physical shopping, eating at restaurants or working from office. Two, Indian cities must prepare to manage the impact of the imminent climate change. Already, they are suffering from the ills of pollution from industrialization and transportation. Mohan, however, is an optimist. He believes that despite the many ills that trouble the living experience in Indian cities, policies can be framed in a way that the country can look forward to more livable cities.

Digitalization, Agriculture and Political Economy

In their essay on digitalization, Deepak Mishra and Mansi Kedia raise an important issue with regard to the correlation between digital initiatives and economic growth. They note that India's digitalization—driven by its investments in creating a robust digital public infrastructure—has helped the country deliver welfare benefits and improve financial inclusion among the poor and underprivileged. The essay also examines whether the adoption of digital technologies helped accelerate India's development through higher economic growth, job creation and efficient services delivery. The authors concede that the impact of digitalization on productivity and growth is not easy to determine, but aver that there are many examples indicative of potential growth.

However, there are challenges. The unconnected and under-connected are mostly marginalized people. Even though mobile phone penetration is at almost 99 per cent, internet usage is at less than 70 per cent of the population. This gap—mainly on account of affordability, literacy and digital skills—needs to be solved through an ecosystem approach that includes policies both on the supply and the demand sides, the authors argue. The spread of infrastructure will be as important as making both data connections and devices affordable and secure.

No less important is the role of India's big information technology companies in ensuring a comprehensive and resilient growth of the digital economy. A robust system to manage the risks of privacy breaches, data misuses and cyber-related financial crimes will have to be built along with the creation of an effective grievance redressal mechanism. The final message from Mishra and Kedia in this regard is that digitalization in India needs to be steered competently to avoid risks resulting in counterproductive outcomes for the economy.

S. Mahendra Dev devotes his essay to underlining the basic imperatives for allowing the country's farm sector to realize its inherent potential and help the economy grow at a faster pace. Although agriculture's contribution to the GDP is less than 20 per cent, it provides employment to 46 per cent of the Indian workforce. Dev, therefore, pulls no punches in noting that India's storied economic reforms of 1991 focused on reforms of trade, industrial, fiscal and financial sector policies, but had no package specifically designed for agriculture. The belief was that the liberalization of industry would improve the terms of trade for agriculture, which did happen, but the fact is that agriculture is yet to undergo any major economic reform in India. The need for major direct reforms of Indian agriculture, therefore, is urgent, argues Dev.

The reforms agenda for agriculture, according to the author, has to be set in the context of three broad interconnected goals: achieving an annual growth rate of four per cent for agriculture and raising the incomes of farmers, ensuring inclusion, and maintaining the sustainability of farming by addressing environmental and climate change concerns. Quite clearly, raising productivity, improving incomes, ensuring diversification with the help of technology, and achieving climate resilience are among the priorities that Dev lists in his essay. Increasing total factor productivity, marketing reforms, providing remunerative prices to farmers, reducing subsidies and increasing investments, encouraging startups for invitations, embracing digital technology, and focusing on water management are also among the key areas that cannot be ignored. The author makes two more specific recommendations for the agricultural sector. One, the government should set up an Agriculture and Food Marketing (AFM) council on the lines of the Goods and Services Tax (GST) Council to discuss Centre-State issues on food and agriculture. Two, since the States allocate a significant amount of funds to agriculture in their budgets, the Centre should work closely with them in a spirit of cooperative federalism for improving the incomes and livelihoods, and promoting inclusive growth and sustainability in agriculture.

Taking a deep dive into India's economic policy evolution since Independence, A.K. Bhattacharya examines the lessons that emanate from the interplay of reforms and political economy. The presence of a political and economic environment supportive of reforms, according to him, is a key attribute that enables the political economy to make a meaningful impact on the roll-out of the desired economic policy changes. This was particularly so in the first four decades after India's Independence.

The situation changed somewhat when the Indian economy was in trouble from the late 1980s. The willingness to consider pursuing some of the long overdue reforms in industrial policies became evident. And when the economy was in dire straits facing its worst crisis, the political establishment went along with the reforms even when they were implemented by a minority government. That was in 1991.

Ironically, the fervour for reforms slowed considerably as the Indian economy averted the crisis and was back on the growth path. The major reform steps that were taken during the crisis years were continued, but the appetite for fresh and decidedly more difficult reforms was missing. Instead, there were disruptive moves like demonetization, a gradual increase in import tariffs, and the reintroduction of import-substitution policies like the production-linked incentive (PLI) scheme.

Bhattacharya concludes that India's political economy is yet to become so mature as to recognize the importance of economic reforms and encourage their implementation with serious commitment. The only way to take the process of economic reforms forward is by not underestimating the importance of building an environment for reforms. This is because even a political majority is not a guarantee for economic reforms. India's political economy must also learn the importance of consensus-building, involving Opposition political parties, State government representatives and industry leaders.

▪

The 15 essays in this volume present a vast menu of perspectives and policy suggestions in the global and Indian context for the reader. Undoubtedly, these perspectives will serve as an important tool in enhancing the overall understanding of these global and Indian policy concerns. They highlight many problems and challenges, but also offer a way out for policymakers. The broad message is of hope that not all is lost, if only policy fixes can be applied and the right economic priorities receive due attention.

Section 1

Global Dynamics

Martin Wolf

Whither the World Economy? Implications for India

I have had the pleasure of knowing Shankar Acharya since September 1971 when we met as young professionals assigned to work in the Domestic Finance Division of the World Bank. He had just finished his studies in economics at Harvard University, and I had done the same at Oxford. The deputy chief of that division was Montek Singh Ahluwalia.

Shankar, Montek and I became lifelong friends, as did our wives Gayatri, Isher and Alison. These relationships began some three years before my own with India, which started in 1974, when I was lucky to be appointed senior economist in the Indian Division of the World Bank. My first book *India's Exports*, published in 1981 by the World Bank, was on India's trade policies.[1]

Much later in my life, after I had started to write for the *Financial Times*, I was lucky enough to follow the transformation of Indian policy in which Montek and Shankar played leading roles as senior officials in the Ministry of Finance, under the direction of the then finance minister, Manmohan Singh.

By virtue of his intellect, integrity, education and experience, Shankar was the ideal chief economic adviser. After his official career ended, he became the most authoritative commentator on the Indian economy. Whenever I have needed a balanced, precise and well-informed view of what was going on, I always turned to his columns in *Business Standard*. I have admired him as a consummate professional and treasured him as a friend over more than half a century.

■

I approach the subject of this chapter in two minds. I have long believed that an open world economy supported by a system of agreed-upon rules is the best way to organize international economic relations. The question is whether this is still a relevant framework for a world characterized by nationalism, protectionism, interventionism and disdain, even among its founding powers, for the notion of a rules-based multilateral order. If not, what is likely to replace it? And, not least, what obstacles and opportunities might this create for India, a rising power that might become a superpower in time, but is not one yet?

The argument below will begin with a discussion of the slowdown in global economic growth. The second section will focus on prospects for global growth, especially the chance of a re-acceleration against that of a continued slowdown, concluding with the greater likelihood of the latter. The third section will look at the shift in the world economy from hyperglobalization to 'slowbalization' over the past one and a half decades, and consider what might happen next. The final section will examine what this changing global environment might imply for India's prospects, stressing that taxing circumstances might offer not only challenges but also opportunities.

The Slowdown in Global Economic Growth

The 10-year moving average of growth rates of the world economy peaked at a rate of 4.2 per cent in the decade up to and including 2007, the year when what should properly be called the transatlantic financial crisis began (see Figure 1).[2] If the International Monetary Fund (IMF) forecasts through 2029 prove to be correct, global growth would average a whole percentage point lower than in the 2000s. In advanced economies, the 10-year average growth is forecast to fall by more than a percentage point between the decade up to and including 2007, and the 2020s.[3]

In emerging and developing countries, the 10-year average growth peaked at 6.5 per cent in 2012 and is forecast to fall to 3.8 per cent in the 2020s. In emerging and developing Asia, the world's most dynamic region (and home to about half of the world's population), the 10-year average growth peaked at the extraordinary rate of 8.4 per cent in the decade up to and including 2012, and is forecast to fall to just 4.6 per cent in the 2020s. (Note that growth has fallen by less in the world as a whole than in regional components because faster growing regions inevitably have rising shares in the global total.)

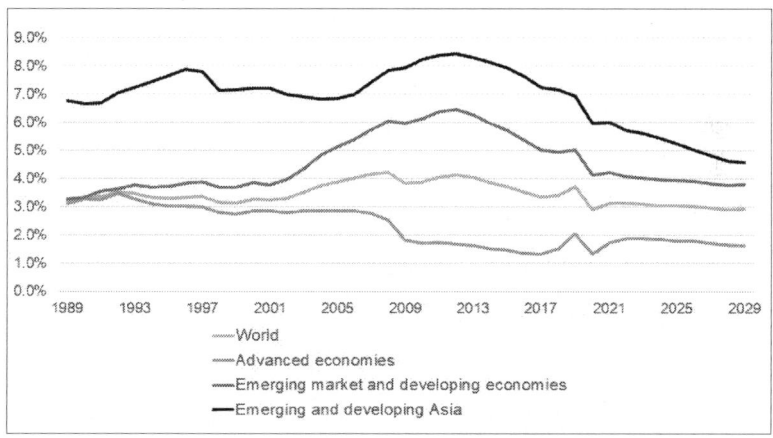

Figure 1: Growth of GDP in Constant Prices
(10-year Moving Average Placed in the Final Year)

Source: IMF WEO database.

This picture of sharp slowdowns is far from the result of falling population growth alone. In advanced countries, the 10-year average growth in gross domestic product (GDP) per head fell by a percentage point in the decade after the financial crisis of 2007–09 from just over two per cent, and is forecast to remain well below pre-financial-crisis levels throughout the 2020s. For emerging and developing countries, the decline in the average growth of GDP per head from its pre-2012 peak has been by two percentage points. For emerging and developing countries in Asia, the fall is forecast to be even more dramatic, from an average of 7.1 per cent in the 10 years to 2012, to a forecast of a mere four per cent in the decade up to and including 2029 (see Figure 2).

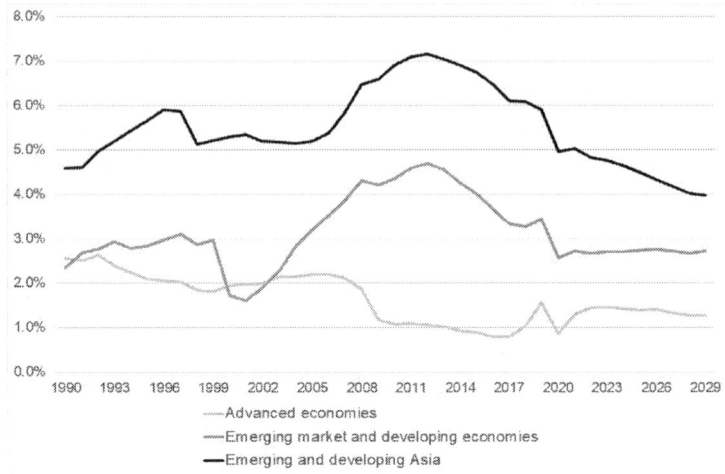

Figure 2: Growth of GDP Per Head of Developing and Advanced Countries (10-year Moving Average at Constant Prices Placed in the Final Year)

Source: IMF WEO database.

Why Have These Sharp Falls in Growth Rates Occurred?

Global growth is driven by the rate of innovation in the economies at the frontier and the speed with which the rest of the world catches up. Both have changed for the worse since 2007 in the case of high-income countries, and 2012 in the case of China. Meanwhile, the rate of growth of GDP per head in high-income economies is also a rough indicator of the rate of growth of productivity at the frontier.[4] This has fallen by about a percentage point a year, according to IMF data.

The rate of catch-up can be defined as the difference between the growth of GDP per head in emerging and developing countries, and that in advanced economies. This has fallen from a peak of around 3.5 percentage points to a little less than half that rate in IMF forecasts for the 2020s. In other words, both fundamental engines—progress at the frontier and catch-up by less advanced economies on the economies at the frontier—have slowed significantly, a point made in the IMF's *World Economic Outlook* for April 2024[5] (see Figure 3).

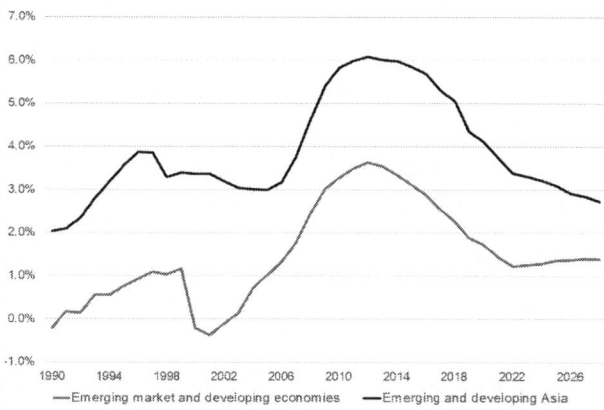

Figure 3: Gap between Growth of GDP Per Head in Developing and Advanced Countries (10-year Moving Average at Constant Prices Placed in the Final Year)

Source: IMF WEO database.

This is not the first such sharp slowdown. There was also a marked slowdown after the 1970s.[6] One plausible explanation for that advanced by Robert Gordon of Northwestern University is that fundamental innovation slowed.[7] While progress in digital technologies has been impressive, its impact has (so far) been narrower and less fundamental than that of the wide range of new technologies introduced during the Second Industrial Revolution, roughly from 1870 to 1920. Another explanation is the fact that many of the profound economic and social changes that followed—in energy systems, transport, urbanization, education and, not least, the organization of business—were one-offs. Their benefits could not be repeated.

Yet another explanation is that activities in which productivity growth is the fastest and whose prices also tend to fall most quickly make up a declining share of the GDP relative to activities dependent on largely unchanged amounts of increasingly expensive labour. The rising share of services relative to manufacturing in GDP is, in part, a consequence of this change. Moreover, while one can raise productivity relatively easily in services whose output can be converted into 'bits', it has been hard to do so in those dependent on the direct application of human labour, especially skilled human labour. Against this pessimism on productivity growth, some argue that we are understating the true impact of new technologies because much of their output is poorly measured. This is plausible. But it is quite unlikely that mismeasurement fully explains the long-term productivity slowdown.

What, however, caused the further slowdown in the growth of GDP per head in high-income countries since the financial crisis? One plausible explanation is that the pre-crisis credit boom exaggerated sustainable growth in GDP and GDP per head. Another is that after the efficacy of monetary policy was largely exhausted with the fall in central bank intervention rates to (or even below) zero, post-crisis fiscal policy proved insufficiently powerful to take up the slack. The failure to use fiscal policy adequately was particularly evident in the eurozone where a combination of financial-cum-fiscal crises crippled the economies of Greece, Ireland, Italy, Portugal and Spain, while the rules applicable to all members prevented countervailing fiscal expansion elsewhere. But in the US too, fiscal policy was arguably tightened too soon after the crisis. The resulting weakness in demand undermined capital formation and thus both the growth of the capital stock and the pace of adoption of innovations embodied within it.

Another factor behind the general post-crisis slowdown was the impact of the crisis on the supply of finance, further reinforced by the countercyclical tightening of financial regulation. A more general factor, no doubt, has been uncertainty. This was an inevitable result of a big financial crisis. But it was further exacerbated by the Covid pandemic of 2020 and the subsequent surge in price levels caused by the interaction of expansionary fiscal and monetary policies with post-pandemic disruptions to supply, and the impact of Russia's February 2022 invasion of Ukraine upon the prices of energy and food.[8]

Uncertainty was exacerbated, once again, by the war in West Asia that followed the attack on Israel by Hamas on 7 October 2023. Above all, it was worsened by the deterioration in relations between the US and China. Inevitably, this uncertainty has slowed decision-making and consequently, innovation, investment and the required reallocation of resources.[9]

Emerging and developing countries tend to be particularly vulnerable to financial crises and similar global upheavals. It has, however, not been the bigger and more successful among them but the smaller and weaker that have been hit the hardest.[10] A more direct cause of the slowdown in growth in emerging and developing countries, and consequently the deceleration in the catch-up process, has been the sharp decline in China's rate of growth. The impact is not surprising, since China generated 32 per cent of the GDP of all emerging and developing countries (at purchasing power parity) in 2022. India generated another 12.5 per cent. Add in Russia (five per cent), Indonesia (4.2 per cent), Brazil (four per cent), Turkey (3.5 per cent) and Mexico (3.2 per cent), and one then has 64 per cent of the total output of emerging and developing countries.[11] So it is on these economies that one must focus.

For some three decades, China's growth averaged close to 10 per cent a year—an incredible performance for almost any country, let alone one this large. Average growth remained at that level in the decade up to and including 2014. By 2023, however, China's 10-year average growth rate fell to six per cent. Furthermore, by 2029, according to IMF forecasts, it will have fallen to some four per cent (see Figure 4).

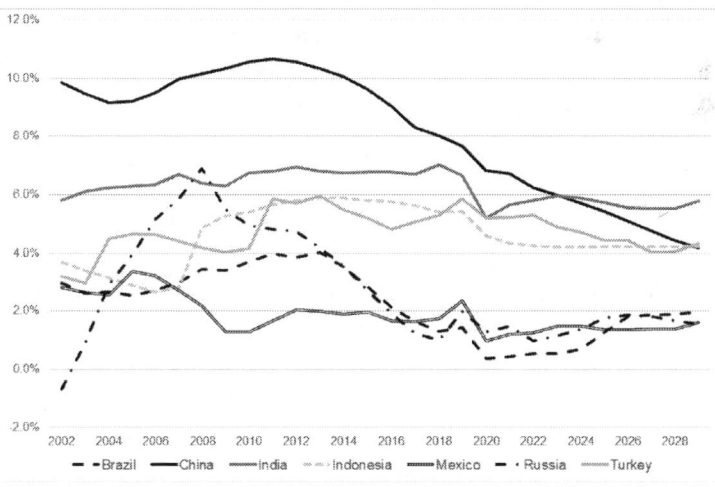

Figure 4: Growth of the Seven Largest Emerging Countries, in Constant Prices (10-year Moving Average at Constant Prices Placed in the Final Year)

Source: IMF WEO database.

The growth rates of other large emerging economies including India have been more consistent than China's over the last decade or so (the other exception being Russia, which has suffered a precipitous decline in average rates of growth since the financial crisis). India's growth has been relatively stable and fast. But it shows no sign of achieving China's erstwhile rate of 10 per cent; six per cent looks more likely. Indonesia and Turkey are moving towards an average of about four per cent, while Brazil, Mexico and Russia have been stuck at two per cent or less for a long time. In all, given China's dramatic decline in growth and the lack of any offsetting growth accelerations elsewhere, it is no surprise that the average growth of large emerging and developing countries has been slowing sharply.

The picture of the growth of GDP per head is naturally worse, except in countries where the population has stopped growing. India is forecast to enjoy a growth rate of GDP per head of close to five per cent in the decade up to 2029, which is in line with similar averages since the 1990s. This is also forecast to be higher than China's over that period. Despite its slowdown, China's growth is still forecast to be higher than in the other large emerging economies, with the exception of India. Indonesia and Turkey are forecast to slow to a 10-year average in the growth of GDP per head, of a little over three per cent in the decade up to 2029, with Brazil, Russia and Mexico down to two per cent or less over the same decade (see Figure 5).

A complementary way of looking at what has happened in the world economy is to focus on the sources of growth. In its *World Economic Outlook* published in April 2024, the IMF concluded that 'a significant and broad-based slowdown in total factor productivity growth accounted for more than half of the growth decline.'[12] Moreover, it argued, 'this deceleration was driven in part by increased misallocation of capital and labor across firms.' In addition, a 'widespread drop in postcrisis private capital formation' as well as slower growth in the working-age population as a result of demographic shifts (namely, ageing and past declines in fertility) exacerbated the slowdown.

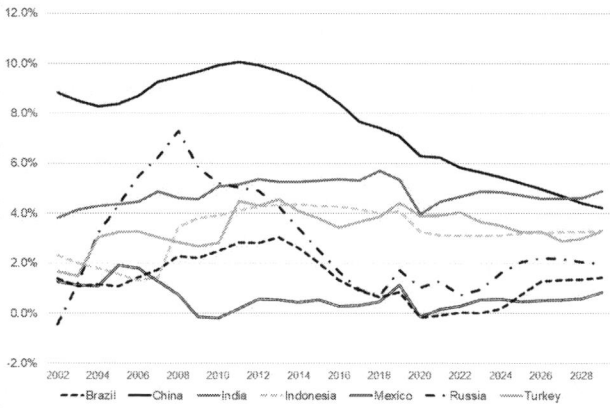

Figure 5: Growth of GDP Per Head of the Seven Largest Emerging Countries, in Constant Prices (10-year Moving Average at Constant Prices Placed in the Final Year)

Source: IMF WEO database.

Prospects for Global Economic Growth

Now turn to the future. Is growth performance likely to improve or worsen over the next couple of decades? We do not know. But there are some factors we do know with some certainty. We know a substantial amount about the fundamental forces of demography, the global environment, technology, and prospects for global political and economic relations. We also know about possible shocks which are rarely true surprises; a financial crisis, a pandemic, a war, or a revolution might come as a shock, but we know that such things can happen. What we do not know is their likelihood.

Three possible developments might accelerate growth in the years ahead. The first is a cessation of shocks. Over the past 15 years, the world economy has been buffeted by a series of big shocks. We may have just been unlucky—the dice of history has come up unfavourably for a while. Maybe the next few decades will be relatively quiet.

The second development is accelerated technological change. The continued improvement in digital technologies and conceptual breakthroughs, notably artificial intelligence (AI), along with advances in the life sciences, might deliver extraordinary advances in productivity and thus growth in the years ahead. The most significant development is AI. The emergence of thinking machines could enormously increase the productivity of human labour, especially the productivity of human thinking.

The third possible development is a reversal of malign policy trends noted in the IMF analysis of the growth slowdown. Instead, governments might decide to improve policy and strengthen global cooperation. Desperation has improved policy in many countries in the past; India's reforms in 1991 are a good example. Sooner or later, there could be a similar reaction against continued low growth.

Unfortunately, there are also powerful arguments against such optimism. First, there are several identifiable fragilities which seem to make further shocks disturbingly likely. One is that indebtedness—both public and private—is extremely high going by past standards. If real and nominal interest rates also remain high, the chances of further financial shocks are likely to remain elevated relative to what we assumed in the halcyon years between the end of the Cold War and the global financial crisis.

Another is the shift in the balance of power away from the West, especially the US, towards Asia and, above all, China. The shift is made more significant by the cultural and ideological differences of the main protagonists. This is creating complex political and economic changes. These are also emerging in the form of new alliances (notably, that between China, Russia and Iran, but also in a more assertive 'Global South', of which Iran is also a part), in new stresses (notably between the US and China), in the progressive fragmentation of the world economy, and in the decline in the authority of Western-dominated but supposedly global institutions such as the World Trade Organization (WTO), the IMF and the World Bank. Yet another fragility consists in the decay of liberal democracy in many parts of the world, including leading Western powers, and its replacement by demagogic populism.

Second, there is the threat of climate change. One danger here is simply a failure to mitigate the threat of continuing rises in the concentration of greenhouse gases (GHGs) in the atmosphere, which would force not just persistent rises in temperatures, but also the very real possibility of passing thresholds for accelerated changes in temperatures and the global environment, including rises in sea levels, desertification and similar disasters. An opposite danger is that the costs of mitigation and adaptation would prove to be high and thus would divert a significant part of investible resources away from growth towards defending the global environment against its consequences. Either way, it seems likely that climate change itself—or the costs of managing it—will slow economic growth significantly.

Third, we know that the combination of rising longevity with low fertility rates will slow the growth of the labour force in many economies over the next two decades, and in many countries, the labour force will actually shrink. Not only was the global fertility rate barely above the replacement level in 2021, but it was also far below that level in high-income and upper-middle-income countries (which includes China).

Moreover, the fertility rate was already below replacement in high-income and upper-middle-income countries as far back as 2000.[13] The weight of these economies in the world economy is so large that their relatively slow growth, simply for this reason, is bound to slow aggregate growth. With ageing, the labour force will grow more slowly than the population. This automatically means that GDP per head would grow more slowly than GDP.

Fourth, there is good reason to be sceptical about the impact of technological change on growth. As noted above, the impact of the digital revolution, including the internet—which was a bona fide transformation—is not strongly visible in the data on economic growth. It is quite likely that artificial intelligence will also not be as transformative as people currently imagine. It is also worth noting that if it is as transformative as people suppose, it will transform society as well as politics. That is quite likely to be disruptive in ways that would affect the economies as well.

Finally, in a world with so many threats, it is likely to be hard for policymakers to take on some of the difficult challenges needed to accelerate growth. These are likely to include fiscal tightening, planning reform and transforming existing institutions. Meanwhile, the populist demagogues who are so successful today are unlikely to take on the more difficult and sensitive tasks of reform and market opening.

On the contrary, they have a depressing tendency towards blaming unscrupulous foreigners for everything that has gone wrong in their societies, even though the principal explanations are domestic policy failures and the predatory behaviour of domestic elites.[14] The result has been the rising protectionism, to which the discussion will turn in the next section.

In all, then, it is highly likely that global growth will continue to disappoint in the years ahead. If this is to turn out to be mistaken, it might be because of far faster growth in India itself and the rather more unlikely prospect of an African economic renaissance. These are the countries with burgeoning populations and 'catch-up' opportunities that could make a big difference to the global picture over the next generation. Unfortunately, there is also the possibility of a true disaster—war among the great powers, for example, or a disruptive decoupling between the US and China.

From Hyperglobalization and 'Slowbalization' to What?

The environment is indeed likely to be difficult. But among the leading determinants of the opportunities available will be the prospects for economic integration. Self-sufficiency is not a good strategy: India's own history since Independence shows that. For India to choose self-sufficiency would be a blunder. To have self-sufficiency forced upon it by the outside world would be a tragedy.

So what are the prospects for global economic integration? This question can be linked to our brief discussion earlier on the causes of the slowdown in growth since the global financial crisis. One cause of the 'misallocation' of resources analysed by the IMF is the slowdown in the growth of world trade relative to that of output. The era of what Arvind Subramanian, former chief economic adviser to the government of India, and Martin Kessler of the Peterson Institute for International Economics called 'hyperglobalization' in a paper published in 2013 has been replaced by what is now called 'slowbalization'.[15]

The story of what has happened is shown in the ratio of gross exports of goods to world output since 1820 (see Figure 6). There are three points: first, the openness of the world economy measured in this simple way varies in both directions over time, with two particularly big upswings, one in the late nineteenth and early twentieth centuries, and another in the second half of the twentieth century and the early years of the twenty-first, but also a collapse in the 1930s and early 1940s as the Great Depression and the Second World War took hold; second, the openness of the world economy reached unprecedented levels in the early 2000s, partly because the unbundling of production across frontiers meant intense trade in intermediate goods, which raised gross trade relative to value-added; third, since 2008, the ratio of trade to GDP has oscillated but not collapsed. By historical standards, on this simple measure, the world economy is no longer globalizing, but it is not obviously deglobalizing either, remaining very open by historic standards.

Figure 6: World Exports over World Output (per cent)

Source: Fouquin and Hugot (CEPII 2016) to 1979, and IMF from 1980.

To understand what has happened, it is necessary to grasp the forces at work. The most fundamental are economic opportunities: reductions in costs of transport and communication, shifts in comparative advantage, and changing opportunities for exploiting economies of scale and learning by doing. Also important are changes in economic ideologies and geopolitical realities.

Finally, shocks—wars, crises and pandemics—also shift the perceptions of business, peoples and politicians of the risks, costs and benefits of trade. The history of trade over the past two centuries reflects the interactions of these forces.[16]

The period from the fall of the Soviet Union to the global financial crisis was the era of hyperglobalization, because this was when all these forces came together. Thus, close to one and a half centuries of divergent economic growth had created huge gaps in productivity and labour costs between the advanced economies and those that were behind. The invention of the container ship and the jumbo jet, together with advances in information and communication technology, also allowed unprecedented integration of business organizations and the unbundling of supply chains across borders. In addition, a worldwide shift towards a belief in market-oriented and open economies transformed policies.

Subsequently, in the period of slowbalization, the main drivers weakened or went into reverse. The opportunity for the exploitation of differences in labour costs diminished as costs converged, especially vis-à-vis China. Moreover, as its economy grew, its opportunities for commerce shifted away from the world towards its own rapidly growing internal economy. There have also been ideological shifts, among them the rise in protectionism and nationalism notably in the US, triggered partly by the economic rise of China and the 'China shock' to US industrial employment.

Not dissimilar ideological changes have occurred in Xi Jinping's China as well. There, too, policy has shifted from reliance on the free market and private business towards greater government intervention and a more nationalist perspective on relations with outside countries. Perhaps most importantly, the succession of crises—notably including the pandemic and the wars—combined with rising great power tensions have transformed trust into suspicion and risk-taking into 'de-risking'.

Given all this, it is not surprising that the number of trade restrictions imposed annually has risen rapidly since 2010.[17] This has— as Dev Patel, Justin Sandefur and Arvind Subramanian compellingly argue—not been costless for emerging and developing countries.[18] The era of hyperglobalization, they note, was one of the rapid convergence of average incomes in many developing countries towards those in high-income countries. This convergence has now slowed sharply and possibly even ended.

The obvious question is not whether large-scale trade liberalization will recommence in the foreseeable future. That seems unlikely since there has been no globally significant trade liberalization in goods since China joined the WTO in 2001. The question is, rather, whether the world will remain on the slowbalization path or move, instead, into a sharp retreat from integration and, if so, what could such a retreat look like?

A likely path, it now seems, is one of divisions into blocs centred on the US and its allies on the one hand, and on China and its allies on the other, while many countries, especially emerging and developing ones, strive to avoid making such choices. A recent analysis from the WTO concludes that 'trade flows have become more sensitive to geopolitical distance since the start of the war [in Ukraine].'[19]

More precisely, 'Trade in goods between hypothetical East and West blocs has grown 4 per cent slower than intra-bloc trade since the start of the war. On the other hand, we find no evidence of an increased regionalisation of world trade since the shock of the COVID-19 pandemic or the war in Ukraine. Therefore, our results suggest that near-shoring strategies did not have a large impact on world trade. Finally, our results confirm that increased trade tensions between the world's two largest economies have significantly reduced their bilateral trade'[20] (see Figure 7).

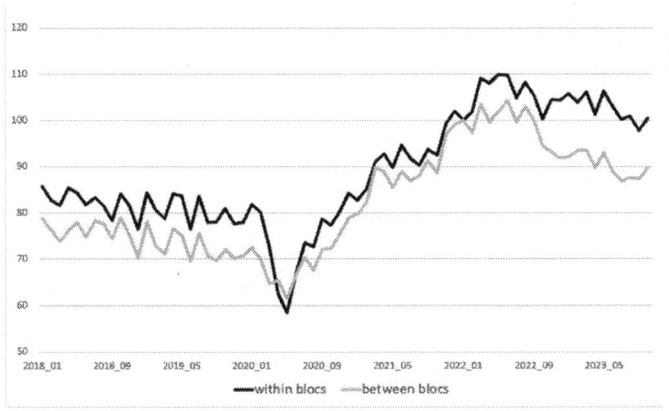

Figure 7: Relative Decline of Trade between Blocs ($ Index)
Source: Blanga-Gubbay and Rubínová (2023).

Even so, it is possible that the move into blocs and even the reduction in direct trade between the US and China will, on balance, divert trade more than it will substantially reduce it. But if Donald Trump is elected president and imposes, as he threatens, 10 per cent tariffs on all US imports and 60 per cent tariffs on imports from China, slowbalization might, after the inevitable retaliation, be replaced by a rapid retreat.[21]

In all, prospects for growth in world trade, at least in goods, seem to be stuck somewhere between poor and dreadful, partly because of a vicious downward spiral from rising protectionism towards decelerating economic growth, the slowing growth of trade, especially in manufactures, and so back to rising protectionism.

At the same time, trade in services might, some argue, prove relatively more robust.[22] But some services are face-to-face and thus depend on the movement of people. Given the rising hostility to immigration, even on a temporary basis, such services might not be that dynamic. Moreover, over the 2010–22 period, the value of world trade in services grew at five per cent a year according to the WTO, against the four per cent growth for merchandise.[23] So any recent difference in favour of services has not been big.

Implications for India

How can India best navigate the world described above—a world of slower economic growth, slower growth of trade, rising great-power friction and environmental constraints? The short answer is that it must recognize constraints, exploit opportunities, and seek to play a leadership role as its place in the world becomes more important. To its credit, India did play a valuable role as host of the G20, especially in commissioning an important report on the vital task of financing the climate transition in developing countries, prepared under the direction of the former senior official N.K. Singh and the former US treasury secretary Lawrence Summers.[24] But far more than this will be needed in the years ahead.

Its starting point must be economic growth. That is the foundation upon which India's prosperity, security and influence must be built. In his Independence Day speech in 2023, Prime Minister Narendra Modi referred to 'the dream of a developed India by 2047'.[25] So what might this mean?

Figure 8 provides a simple answer. According to the IMF, Greece was the poorest advanced country in 2022. In that year, India's GDP per head at purchasing power parity (PPP) was also just 22 per cent of that of Greece. This is already a big improvement on the relative position in 1990 when India's GDP per head at PPP was 7.5 per cent of that of Greece. Now assume that the GDP per head of Greece continues to grow at its 1990–2029 trend rate (including IMF forecasts) of just 0.6 per cent a year until 2047, while the GDP per head of India continues to grow at its 1990–2029 trend rate of 4.8 per cent a year. Would India catch up by 2047? The answer is no. India's GDP per head would still be only 62 per cent of the Greek level at that time.

If India is to catch up by 2047, its GDP per head would need to grow at a compound rate of 7.5 per cent a year after 2029. That would be a big acceleration above the earlier and already substantially improved rate of growth achieved after the reforms of the 1990s. It would imply sustained growth at around eight per cent a year. That would not be far below China's rate of growth before the deceleration over the last 12 years or so. Is that likely? The answer is no. It would mean a more than 50 per cent increase in the trend rate of growth of GDP per head. Achieving this would require a big rise in the rate of investment in physical and human capital, and a marked acceleration of productivity growth. It would certainly require radical reform.

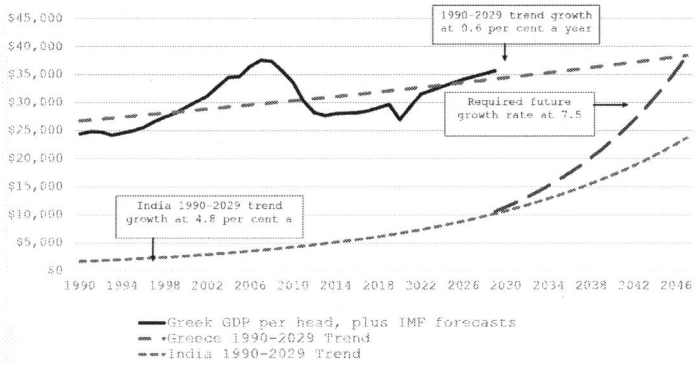

Figure 8: How India Might Become an 'Advanced Country' by 2047
(GDP Per Head at Purchasing Power Parity at Constant 2017 $s)

Source: IMF WEO database, plus author's calculations.

These domestic challenges are not the focus of this chapter. But achieving anything close to the objective Modi has set for India does raise two sets of questions about India's economic relationship with the rest of the world. The first concerns how the world might adjust to its rise, and the second, what the best relationship for India itself would be.

On the first, the most important point is that India has a relatively big economy simply because at over 1.4 billion, it has the largest population in the world. Yet, it is currently ranked by the World Bank as only a lower-middle-income country.

According to the IMF, India's GDP per head at market prices was 144th, and its GDP per head at purchasing power parity 131st in the world in 2022, though its GDP at market prices was ranked fifth and its GDP at PPP third, globally. [26] It follows that India's impact on the rest of the world would inevitably be large if its economy continued to grow faster than the world economy over an extended period.

According to IMF forecasts, India's share in the world GDP at PPP will rise from 3.8 per cent in 1990 to 9.2 per cent by 2029. If its post-1990 rate of growth continues, the share is likely to reach around 14 per cent by 2047. If the far faster rate of growth needed to achieve advanced country status by 2047 were achieved, its share would be around 24 per cent. It would then have become an economic colossus.

Similarly, if India continued to grow rapidly, it would have a 'bow wave' impact on global commerce and capital flows unless its economic openness shrank dramatically. Fortunately, that effect need not prove a significant constraint on India's economic growth since its share in world exports of merchandise was only 14th in the world in 2022 (if intra-EU trade was excluded). Even in world exports of commercial services, it was only eighth in 2021. [27] Therefore, there is plenty of room for further expansion, provided India creates opportunities for the exports of its trading partners in parallel with the expansion of its own exports. India's actual share in world exports, for example, was a mere 2.2 per cent in 2022 against China's 18.4 per cent. Even its exports of commercial services were only four per cent of the world total in 2021—well below the US share of 12.9 per cent and the Chinese share of 6.5 per cent. [28]

In an outstanding paper published in 2020, Shoumitro Chatterjee of Pennsylvania State University and Arvind Subramanian, then at Ashoka University, argued that the turning away from trade that they observed in the policies of the Modi government was a mistake, arguing that 'abandoning export orientation is akin not just to killing the goose that has laid golden eggs. It is akin to killing the *only* goose that can lay eggs.'[29]

The evidence for this was strong: it rested on the simple fact that the acceleration in India's growth rate from the 1990s coincided with a rise in the ratio of trade to GDP from 19 per cent in 1991 to close to 60 per cent (on the old data series) in 2012. But by 2020, it had fallen back by some six percentage points (on the new series). Without further liberalization, this decline in the trade ratio might continue (see Figure 9).

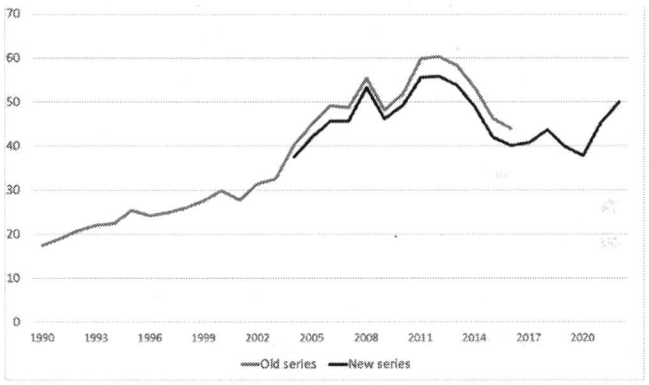

Figure 9: India's Ratio of Trade to GDP (per cent)

Source: CSO, India.

Chatterjee and Subramanian argued that reversing India's openness rested on three big mistakes. The first was assuming that India was a large country with a large market. But, as they noted, India's market size was partly an illusion because its middle class was far smaller relative to its population. They argued that the true market size for tradeable, especially more sophisticated, goods and services was somewhere between 15 and 45 per cent of the GDP, less than 20 per cent of

China's and a mere 1.5–5 per cent of the world market. They also argued against a second mistake, which was making the assumption that exports had not played an important role in India's growth over the last three decades. On the contrary, they argued, exports had been an important driver of relatively fast post-reform economic growth. They argued, finally, that it was yet another big mistake to believe that global opportunities were disappearing.

One reason for countervailing optimism is that India enjoys some special advantages. One is that in a China-Plus-One world, India—properly organized with the right policies and rapidly improving infrastructure—is an obvious 'plus one'. A second advantage is that India is politically quite close to the West and many countries of the Global South. It is also big enough and important enough to be treated with respect by much of the world. A third advantage, rightly stressed by Chatterjee and Subramanian, is the size and success of the Indian diaspora, especially in the US. Fourth, while India's size means that its exports might meet market limits in some sectors, its human and physical resources should also give it the ability to diversify and upgrade exports with huge success, as China has done.

A fifth consideration, powerfully argued by Richard Baldwin of the International Institute for Management Development (IMD) in Lausanne, is that even if trade in manufactures is likely to grow relatively slowly in the years ahead, the reverse is likely to be the case for services. This is partly because it is more difficult to block (even tax) disembodied (internet-enabled) trade in services than it is to block the movement of physical objects. It is also because improvements in communications technology plus artificial intelligence could simultaneously dramatically shorten the effective distance between foreign and domestic labour, and increase their substitutability. Thus, argues Baldwin, globalization is not dying. It is merely changing. Moreover, one can add, this shift towards the globalization of services is unambiguously favourable to a country with India's human resources and potential.[30]

Finally, a rising India will have the ability to shape the global economic environment in its interests, including on economic openness, managing climate and preserving global peace. India must not, in self-defeating pessimism, merely reconcile itself to the environment it sees around it. It can seek to change it for the better. It should embrace the implications of its need to grow at least twice as fast as the world economy, and ideally considerably faster than that. It must therefore develop a long-run policy designed to use its resources and influence to shape the world in its favour. This is not just desirable, but, in my opinion, also feasible.

When I first worked on India for the World Bank in the 1970s, I was frequently told that the far faster growth we were seeing in South Korea, for example, was irrelevant to a giant country like India. We were also told that the Indian market was large enough to provide a basis for growth. Both propositions were wrong. As a result of the policies taken in this spirit of defeat, the people of India lost decades of faster potential growth and are now far poorer than they need to be.

Then it was China that seized the opportunity that India did not. Some 40 years ago, they had much the same average standards of living. Today, according to the IMF, India's real GDP per head is 40 per cent of China's levels (see Figure 10). It would be a tragedy if, in another bout of defeatism, India failed to seize the opportunities now in front of it. Yes, it will be difficult. Yes, there are dangers. But a huge country with vast potential can and must not only seize them, but also act to create them.

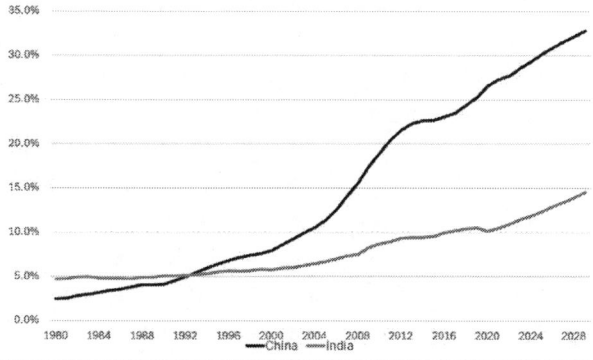

Figure 10: GDP Per Head at Purchasing Power Parity Relative to the US (per cent)

Source: IMF World Economic Outlook Database.

Amita Batra

The Global Trade Reset in the 2000s and India's Trade Policy Priorities

The 2000s have been witness to some of the most significant and transformative trends in global goods trade and the global trade order. The first decade saw a multi-fold increase in global trade led by the unbundling of production across nations in the form of global value chains (GVCs), and a predominance of trade in intermediate goods. The process was interrupted by the global financial crisis (GFC) in 2008, subsequent to which political compulsions reflected in 'bring back jobs to America', coupled with the natural disasters in East Asia in 2011, initiated a process of reshoring, nearshoring and restructuring of GVCs. While the second decade started with a slowdown, the rate of growth of global trade recovered in 2017, only to be interrupted again by the pandemic in 2020.

The pandemic brought forth the need to develop resilient GVCs and reduce the dependence on a single, concentrated source of imports. Diversification away from China (China-Plus-One) has, in this third decade, become the dominant strategy of large corporations in their effort to ensure GVC resilience. A more significant shift in the structure of GVCs has occurred in the aftermath of the Ukraine crisis as geopolitical alignments have led to a convergence of the objectives of economic security and national security into a singular defining parameter of global trade, often at the expense of efficiency.

Trade is increasing among countries closer to each other in terms of geopolitical distance, rather than the empirically proven, theoretical precept of physical distance. Regional trade blocs such as North America and the European Union (EU), earlier seen as regional GVC hubs with high intensity of intra- and inter-regional trade, especially with East Asia, are now becoming selectively protectionist and more inward-looking. The protectionist tendencies are getting further reinforced by the challenge of climate change. Notwithstanding these factors, GVC-engendered trade in intermediate goods continues to contribute about half of world trade.

The more profound shifts are evident at the institutional level. There has been a gradual erosion of multilateral trade norms and the World Trade Organization (WTO), and a simultaneous and dramatic rise in the number, depth and role of the preferential trade agreements as facilitative instruments for GVC-led trade. The turnaround in the US trade policy since the first Trump presidency in 2017 stands out as a critical contributory factor to the retreat of trade multilateralism. A further intensification of protectionism and undermining of the global multilateral trade order is likely in the next few years, with President Trump assuming office in January 2025 and his announcements in the first month imposing 'reciprocal tariffs' on US trade partners.

This essay presents the defining aspects of trends in global goods trade and institutional evolution and transformation, as evident over the last two and a half decades in this century. In light of these developments, this essay reflects on the nature of India's trade policy responses and priorities going into the future.

The First Decade, 2000–10: GVC Take-off, Multifold Increase in Trade, and China's Centricity to GVCs[1]

The first decade of this century witnessed the 'take-off' moment for GVCs. The rise in the share of GVC-led trade and intermediate goods trade really picked up momentum in and after 2002, till it peaked in 2006, contributing more than half (56.1 per cent) of global trade—its highest level since 1989. The unprecedented annual growth rate in intermediate goods trade registered during these years in the first decade reflected an acceleration in the GVC functions of offshoring and outsourcing.

Trade in intermediate goods was led mainly by developing countries which, by 2006, were contributing a little over 36 per cent to global intermediate goods trade. Among developing countries, Mexico and China were the lead economies in terms of both absolute value of intermediate goods trade and the rate of growth. Among regions, developing East Asia emerged as the most GVC-intensive region in the first decade of the century. In fact, the East Asian economies, with the exception of South Korea,[2] exhibited relatively fast growth in intermediate goods exports—both as a reflection of their role as important trans-shipment hubs of intermediate goods trade and their participation in intermediate goods trade or GVCs in the most trade-dynamic manufactured goods sectors. China was the primary driver of this activity within the region. With a higher rate of growth and absolute value, China ranked third after the US and Germany in 2006—all within five years of its accession to the WTO in 2001. In fact, by the end of the first decade, China had already displaced the US and Germany as lead exporters, and emerged as the major or lead trading partner for almost all economies in the world.

The first decade also saw the East Asian region evolve from Japan-led triangular trade into network trade involving the Southeast Asian economies, with China's centricity to the East Asian value chain hub getting firmly established. This was most evident in the electronics sector. While the change was evident after the Plaza Accord—as Japanese multinational corporations (MNCs) relocated their electronics parts and components (P&C) factories in Korea and Taiwan, and later, as wages started to increase in these NIEs, to Association of Southeast Asian Nations (ASEAN) economies like Malaysia, Thailand and the Philippines in the 1990s—things really changed when China acceded to the WTO in 2001. From then on, P&C flows from East Asia started to move into China. China's exports surged multiple times post 2001 and grew more rapidly than its imports, especially after 2005. In volume terms, the East Asia and Southeast Asian exports of electronics P&C increased rapidly over the first decade of the twenty-first century.

The electronics sector dominated the intermediate goods trade, reflecting the high levels of GVC dynamism. The architecture of 'modularity' of the electronics sector—owing to standardization, codification and computerization—allowed for a high degree of interoperability of parts and components, and hence fragmentation of production across different locations. Other factors contributing to the high intensity of trade and value chain activity of the electronics industry included the high value-to-weight ratio of products that made the transportation of intermediates and final goods across long distances cost-effective.

The Asian electronics GVC hub also developed strong links with the North American and European hubs, the former being stronger than the latter. Most lead firms in the sector were from developed economies in Europe, Japan, the US and Korea, while countries like Mexico, China and Thailand were able to have large numbers of contract manufacturers. Both lead firms and contract manufacturers were important players in the electronic GVCs, though their operation varied across nations depending on whether they were in the category of original equipment manufacturers (OEMs) or original design manufacturers (ODMs).

This first decade, it is worth mentioning, also witnessed some shifts in sectors that had been early entrants into the process of value chain production, such as textiles and clothing (T&C). After the end of the quota system,[3] the apparel GVC restructured such that factory production shifted to developing countries—such as Bangladesh, Sri Lanka, Vietnam and Cambodia—that were not any more restricted by quotas, and countries like Korea and Taiwan, having exhausted their quotas, moved to higher value products given their increasing wages and income levels. In 2008, prior to the GFC, the US, Japan and the EU were the largest apparel consumers, and together accounted for about three-fourths of global apparel imports. In 2008, China had already emerged as the lead exporter with its export share doubling from 15.2 per cent to 33.4 per cent from 1995 to 2008, and witnessing a fivefold increase in the value of its exports. Other emerging market economies that also gained export share in the first half of the 2000s included Bangladesh, Turkey, India, Indonesia, Mexico and Vietnam. Together, these economies accounted for only 15.4 per cent of world exports.

Institutional Developments: China's Accession to the WTO and the Start of DDA

The first decade of the twenty-first century saw two momentous developments—both in 2001—at the multilateral level. The first was the accession of China to the WTO after a prolonged period of negotiations, and second, the start of the Doha Development Agenda (DDA) after a long struggle by the developing world to steer the WTO negotiations towards a more inclusive, development-oriented agenda.

China, with a context-specific trade and FDI policy, emerged as the 'factory of the world' by the end of the first decade of the 2000s. The rapid pace of trade liberalization in China was supplemented by preferential tariffs in intermediate goods in trade-dynamic sectors such as automobiles and electronics. With the additional benefit of lower wage rates, it was able to take advantage of production offshoring and intensify its backward integration with GVCs.

The DDA was initiated after a long hiatus since the Uruguay Round ended in 1994. The seven years in the interim saw resistance from developing economies against the inclusion of 'non-trade' issues.[4] The signing of the DDA in 2001, the first round of the WTO, was a major breakthrough for developing countries as it set out a clear objective of serving the trade interests of developing countries at the multilateral forum. However, the negotiations on the DDA were slow to progress and entered a deadlock soon afterwards, owing to the differential positions of the developed and developing economies on issues of market access, trade facilitation, liberalization of services, and such others. As the rapid pace of trade continued during this period, preferential trade agreements as per Article XXIV of GATT (General Agreement on Tariffs and Trade) assumed significance as the alternative mode of facilitating trade—especially GVC-led trade—in intermediate goods. The number of trade agreements (regional trade agreements in force) more than doubled from less than 100 in 2000 to 211 by 2010 (see Table 1).

Table 1: Number of Regional Trade Agreements (RTAs) (in force)

Year	Cumulative Number of RTAs in force
2000	99
2010	211
2015	274
2020	314
2023	367
2024	369

Source: www.wto.org

The Second Decade: Trade Slowdown, China's Upstream GVC Evolution and Deeper Trade Agreements

After a quick post-GFC rebound in 2010, global trade growth remained below the pre-GFC average rate of seven per cent in subsequent years from 2012 to 2014, and turned negative in 2015. However, in 2017, global trade recovered, recording its highest growth in volume and value terms since 2011.

The share of developing countries in total global trade continued to increase in the second decade as well. By 2018, over half (58 per cent) the exports from developing countries were to other developing countries. Within this growing South–South trade, intra-regional trade in East Asia was the fastest growing and also the most resilient component. Notably, intra-regional trade for most East Asian economies was predominantly conducted with China, while for the latter, extra-regional trade was a relatively important component of its total trade.

The electronics sector maintained its dominant dynamism in GVCs, and the East Asian region continued to rank the highest in total trade of intermediate goods in the electronics sector. The major contributors to this trade in the region were China, Hong Kong, Korea and Malaysia. Notably, China's progression in the electronics value chain was already underway. By 2018, China's value-added in exports in the sector had increased to 67 per cent from 55 per cent in 2003.[5] In addition to this, a growing number of Chinese firms such as Huawei and Lenovo had, by this time, emerged as lead firms in the sector.

The T&C GVCs also saw a further consolidation in the second decade of this century. Manufacturing T&C GVCs were now concentrated in mainly three regions: China, the Southeast Asian economies of Vietnam, Indonesia and Cambodia, and South Asian countries like India, Sri Lanka and Bangladesh. Within this, there was a further regional shift over the years. While China retained its lead share of over 30 per cent of global T&C exports, the share of apparel exports in China's total exports declined during this period. The increase in wages in China led to other regional economies like Bangladesh and Vietnam, and to some extent, Cambodia, gaining from the consequent GVC shifts. India, however, was unable to capitalize on this shifting dynamic in the labour-intensive T&C GVC, and therefore registered a fall in its share of global exports in this sector during this period.

China's Economic Reorientation and Upstream GVC Participation

It is interesting to note that the prevalent view in China at this time was already tending towards evolving to the next stage of enhancing manufacturing capabilities. While low-end, labour-intensive assembly production had been at the core of China's emergence as the lead exporter of the world, the need to advance to the next stage of 'make in China' was already being recognized and discussed by the end of the first decade.

The increase in domestic value addition (DVA) content in Chinese exports and the fact that imported inputs were increasingly being substituted by domestic components in China were already evident early in the second decade of the twenty-first century. In fact, China had become more upstream since 2005, and foreign inputs contained in its exports declined by three per cent. The trend continued to hold even beyond 2012, and the decline in imported inputs or the foreign value addition (FVA) to DVA ratio was higher in the later period of 2012–16 relative to that in 2005–12.[6]

In 2015, China released its 'Made in China 2025' plan that adopted innovation as its central focus, and spelt out its intention to specialize in high-tech export production away from labour-intensive manufactures. The plan aimed at increasing the domestic content of core components by 40 per cent by 2020 and 70 per cent by 2025.[7] Targeted investments were envisioned in research and development, and towards achieving leadership in artificial intelligence (AI) and robotics.

The shifts in the Chinese growth process intensified over the decade, and were later reflected in the 'dual circulation' strategy 2020 that was aimed at a reduction of China's dependence on imports. The strategy was incorporated in China's 14th Five-Year Plan for the period 2021–25 wherein the emphasis was on innovation and industrial modernization, having shifted from traditional areas like infrastructure and urbanization. The strategy was designed primarily in response to the US's efforts to decouple from China-led supply chains. While this was not an explicit move towards import-substitution, China was already in pursuit of economic resilience.

Institutional Developments: The Increasing Scope and Coverage of PTAs

The deadlock in DDA negotiations at the WTO rendered the multilateral organization incapable of evolving in response to the transformation that global trade had undergone in the previous decade. The increasing complexity of production fragmentation and the necessity to facilitate the movement of intermediate goods across multiple borders made it imperative that new and advanced standards and trade measures be developed. As multiple countries were involved in complex GVCs, a coordinated and complementary approach towards trade policy, investment and the accompanying transfer of technology or know-how across borders was required. Preferential trade agreements (PTAs)—allowed under GATT Article XXIV—became the obvious alternative instruments for GVC-led global trade.

While PTAs have been there for a long time—the US-Canada Auto Pact of 1965 being among the first ones—they evolved significantly in the second decade of the 2000s in terms of scope and coverage, going beyond the traditional areas of tariffs and customs liberalization to include subsidies, TBTs and regulatory standards as well as environment and sustainable governance (ESG) issues. The US and the EU countries were in the lead in moving towards deep trade agreements in the 2010s. Asian economies like Japan and Korea also signed some deep trade agreements during this decade.

Specifically, the increased number and coverage of provisions on investment liberalization, intellectual property and ESG contributed to greater depth in the PTAs in the second decade of the century. The investment provisions in PTAs, unlike bilateral investment treaties (BITs), had the advantage of specifying exclusions from the MFN (most favoured nation) in their applicability and were not time-limited, thereby assisting member economies in creating a more conducive business environment for foreign investors. In addition to this, the focus of investment provisions was on the removal of any restrictive performance requirements[8] and the arbitral mechanism which increasingly included a combination of state-state and investor-state dispute settlement (ISDS) mechanisms.[9]

As more and more developing countries sought to integrate with GVCs as a means to specialization and manufacturing competitiveness, the emphasis on granting assurance to MNCs (or advanced economies) for the protection of their intellectual property (IP) in the countries integrated across GVCs (invariably developing economies) became an almost essential component of PTAs. Hence, over time and across GVCs, a strengthening of intellectual property rights (IPR) to 'TRIPS plus' was increasingly evident in deep trade agreements in the second decade. While the US and the EU led the way for IP-related provisions, some Asian countries, even those that were earlier known to have rather shallow agreements, are now at par with them, having signed the Comprehensive and Progressive Agreement for Trans-Pacific Partnership (CPTPP), which has the highest-level TRIPS-plus IPR chapter.[10]

While broad trends on PTAs with environment-related provisions (ERPs) are idiosyncratic,[11] it is observed that the ERPs' inclusion is higher in the second decade, and in the North–North and North–South PTAs—the latter essentially following the rationale to raise the regulatory levels of partner economies.[12] Environment-related provisions have also been included in the broader category of ESG provisions in some free trade agreements (FTAs). The EU FTAs, for example, include a trade and sustainable development (TSD) chapter covering both—the ERPs and provisions relating to labour or worker conditions. The EU and the US are in the lead in this context, with the EU having signed more PTAs with labour provisions (LPs), and the US having more labour provisions in its PTAs.[13] While the North American Free Trade Agreement (NAFTA) set the precedent in this context, the inclusion of the provisions as side agreements in the NAFTA provided a more accommodative and cooperative framework in terms of implementation. The United States-Mexico-Canada Agreement (USMCA)—that is the renegotiated NAFTA—has increased the coverage and the detail of LPs, thus setting a more difficult precedent and standard for future trade agreements with the US.[14]

The North–South PTAs, with a comprehensive inclusion of labour provisions, are viewed by many to be driven by a protectionist motivation as well, even if concerns about labour or worker conditions may be the primary driver. The emphasis on the inclusion of labour provisions as core provisions rather than side agreements—as was true for the earlier PTAs (such as the NAFTA)—has much to do with perceptions in the US vis-à-vis China and the trade imbalance argument following the GFC. The shift of blue collar jobs to the developing world, mostly to China, that had accompanied the production unbundling created a political narrative and constituency in the US, and to some extent, in the developed world as a whole. The growing sentiment was that China was able to work the multilateral trade rules to its advantage and, hence, it was necessary to rein in its growing trade surplus vis-à-vis the US and others by developing a rules-based trade order that espoused standards and norms higher than or beyond those of the WTO. US participation in the Trans-Pacific Partnership (TPP), a mega-regional trade agreement in 2012, was seen as a means towards accomplishing this objective.

With the membership accounting for over 40 per cent of US exports and 40 per cent of global GDP and open to further expansion, the TPP negotiated by the US with 11 like-minded countries was envisioned by the Obama administration as the most ambitious and promising instrument of Asia-Pacific trade integration, and a means to achieve economic growth and trade resurgence for the US. The idea of a mega-regional trade agreement in which China could gain entry only by abiding by the high standards specified in areas such as state-owned enterprises (SoEs), intellectual property, and environment and labour standards that were considered especially difficult for China, was perceived as a means for containing the 'rogue' economy.[15] Staying out of the TPP would imply China losing out on the potential gains in trade and investment that the TPP was expected to yield for its members. The Trans-Pacific Partnership was thus signed by 12 Pacific Rim countries[16] in February 2016.

Ironically, however, in less than a year, in January 2017, the US withdrew from the TPP. This was the first trade policy action taken by the Trump presidency, followed by the imposition of tariffs on a select set of 200 imports from China in 2018, thus initiating selective and discriminatory bilateralism as a means to conduct its trade policy, and as a consequence, violating the norms of the multilateral rules-based trade order. Thus began the erosion of the institution of the WTO by an economy that was thus far considered the leader of liberal capitalism and its representative supra-national institutions. This was over and above the fact that the WTO was ineffective in resolving the standstill in DDA negotiations over the preceding decade and a half. The further emaciation of an already inadequate institution happened when, in the last few years of the second decade of the century, the US stalled the working of the dispute settlement mechanism (DSM) by not making appointments to the appellate body. As a unique pillar of the WTO, the DSM, with its appellate body, was the most significant administrative reform in the transformation from the GATT to the WTO. The established procedure for dispute settlement had gone a long way in ensuring stability in the global trade system.

The 2020s: The Pandemic, the Ukraine Crisis and the Spillover Implications for Global Trade and GVCs

The 2020s have been witness to a series of unprecedented global events as a consequence of which the contours of global trade and GVCs are undergoing a significant shift. The trade tensions that were triggered by the unilateral imposition of tariffs by the United States on select imports from China in 2018 have been intensified following the pandemic and the Russian invasion of Ukraine in 2022. While the imposition of higher tariffs played out largely as a bilateral phenomenon and had limited implications for other economies, the pandemic brought forth the risks of single-source dependence and China's centricity to GVCs. The Ukraine crisis hit harder by bringing the energy crisis to the foreground as well as through the ensuing geopolitical ramifications. Both the events have had significant consequences for GVCs that have been the fundamental mechanism of global trade over the preceding two decades.

The pandemic's wave-like spread, and the timing and severity of the lockdowns, most significantly the zero-Covid policy in China, led to an unravelling of GVCs. The need to build more resilient supply chains through diversification was therefore a natural outcome, and has been reflected by the accelerated pace of the China-Plus-One strategy of large corporations that was initiated in the aftermath of the global financial crisis, but that progressed at a slow pace in the first decade of the century. In addition to this, in the aftermath of the Ukraine crisis, alternative investment locations are being identified on the basis of geopolitical considerations, and friendshoring or allyshoring has become the dominant trend, often at the expense of efficiency and low-cost production—the two guiding principles of production unbundling and GVCs in the first decade.

National security and strategic autonomy are defining the design and use of trade policy instruments in the present time. This involves reduced single-source dependence, particularly in sectors classified as 'critical' and of strategic importance such as high technology, energy and the environment. The Inflation Reduction Act (IRA) in the United States and the Carbon Border Adjustment Mechanism (CBAM) in the EU, as passed in 2022, are prime examples of such strategies. While ensuring diversification away from 'concentrated risk' or single source of imports, these trade policies are aimed at increasing trade and economic integration in respective regional blocs and among friendly alliances that are increasingly inward-looking. Simultaneously, they violate multilateral norms and the rules-based trade order, and adversely impact the growth and development potential of less developed economies.

The CBAM—ostensibly an attempt to align trade rules with climate change mitigation and to make prices more accurate indicators of the carbon content of imported products—effectively implies that trade is among countries with similar high-grade climate policies and EU-compatible climate regulatory frameworks. The imposition of tariffs on carbon-intensive imports in product groups like cement, electricity, aluminium, iron and steel, fertilizers and hydrogen, while enabling diversification away from 'concentrated risk' countries (China and Russia, among others), also leaves other developing and the least developed economies at an inherent disadvantage given their lower technological, institutional and administrative capabilities to fulfil the carbon emission requirements and/or less stringent climate policies. The EU does not include a special and differential treatment (S&DT) clause in the application of the CBAM either. Furthermore, there is no provision in the CBAM for financing a green transition in less developed economies through sharing the revenue earned from the CBAM import tariffs. This is in contradiction with the CBDR-RC (common but differentiated responsibilities and respective capabilities) principle and Paris Agreement norms that the EU is committed to and otherwise includes in the trade and sustainable development chapter of its FTAs.[17] The inherently discriminatory nature of the CBAM, in apparent contradiction with the MFN principle of the WTO, also creates possibilities of retaliatory protectionist trade measures by the affected exporters.

Similarly, the IRA in the US addresses environmental concerns and supports energy security through the subsidy programme for the production of electric vehicles (EVs). However, the local content requirements (LCR) provisions in the act reveal the underlying motivation to favour domestic manufacturing in the US, and encourage nearshoring and friendshoring of supply chains towards a further deeper integration in North America, and diversification away from sources classified as 'concentrated risk'. North American producers in the electric vehicles (EVs) sector are favoured with the specified rules of origin (ROOs) such that the tax credits on EVs are linked to (a) the mineral content of the batteries that is extracted in the US or its FTA partners, or recycled in the US, and (b) the components' value being assembled in North America. It is also indicated that the percentage requirements for both—the mineral content and the component value—being linked to tax credits will increase over time. Notably, tax credits will not be applicable for components coming from 'foreign entities of concern'. Clearly a means to strengthen the North American value chain in the EV sector, the IRA undermines the rules-based multilateral order not just in terms of the MFN principle but also on the WTO criteria for preferential trade agreements under Article XXIV.

The About-Turn in US Trade Policy

The US trade policy in the last decade reveals a series of contradictions vis-à-vis its position as the leader of liberal capitalism and the rules-based multilateral trade order in the preceding decades.

The underlying rationale for the US's unilateral, protectionist trade policies, more recently coupled with inward-looking industrial policies, has been punitive with regard to China for violating the rules-based multilateral trade order. However, the US seems to be doing much the same and in a larger measure. The big difference, of course, is greater transparency in the imposition of trade barriers by the US. In the period 2017–23, the United States made the maximum (5,198) contribution to harmful trade and industrial policy interventions, while China followed in the second place with a smaller number (3,469) of interventions.[18]

The incongruities are similarly apparent in the reported US-led informal talks—held earlier in 2024—on reforms of the DSM. The lack of interest on the part of the US to revive the DSM with a functional appellate body as an integral component is well established by now. The US's proposal to normalize the bilateral settlement of disputes as a means towards achieving the June 2022 ministerial commitment to restoring a fully functioning DSM does not augur well for the rules-based trade order. Bilateralism and a reduced precedential status, as desired by the US, will bring in an element of uncertainty and arbitrariness in dispute resolution, and hence, adversely impact global trade.

In this context, it is interesting to note that having rendered the established procedures and precedents at the WTO DSM ineffective, the EU and the US initiated an investigation into the production of electric vehicles (EVs), overcapacity and subsidies in China, while simultaneously also raising tariffs on imports of EVs from there. This unilateral action undertaken as a response to Chinese EVs flooding the EU market will produce the inevitable consequence of a further intensification of bilateral trade tensions and deterioration in the global trade context. The normal course of action should have been taking recourse to the DSM at the WTO with a 'dumping' complaint against China. A fair and timely investigation would follow, with due process and actionable judgement.

While the US and the EU are leading the way in the unilateral implementation of protectionist trade policies in combination with industrial policy measures, friendly allies have followed suit with similar trade restrictions and protectionist measures. For example, in 2023, in the chip-making industry which is at the heart of US-China trade and technology competition, the Netherlands announced export restrictions on certain advanced semi-conductor equipment, and Japan on some chip-making metals, as part of a three-way deal with the US to protect national security. The UK followed the EU and announced, though with prospective implementation, a carbon border tax on select carbon-intensive imports.

The US Trade Policy Alternative That Is Not Really an Alternative

On a positive note, the only major trade initiative taken by the Biden administration over the last four years is the US-led Indo-Pacific Economic Framework for Prosperity (IPEF) that has the underlying motivation of containing China by establishing a rules-based economic order. The IPEF comprises four pillars. The agreement on one of these, the supply chain pillar, was signed in November 2023 on the sidelines of the APEC summit in Washington, thereby signalling the keenness of the member economies to move forward with the idea of creating resilient supply chains in a more constructive manner. The agreement entered into force in February 2024.

The constituent provisions of the agreement, while ensuring a comprehensive coverage of preventive measures against supply chain disruptions, are, however, non-binding, thus providing no guarantees towards the achievement of the stated objectives. This is a key difference as compared to standard FTAs. The provisions also allow for several flexibilities, especially in situations where a country deems fit to apply measures or not provide information to protect its essential security interests. Considering that this has been the rationale for the imposition of most trade-restrictive and inward-looking industrial policy measures over the last few years, the agreement may fall short in ensuring a rules-based trade order in the region and consequently, the broader strategic objective of the IPEF.

Finally, the November 2023 meeting of trade ministers held in the US failed to arrive at an agreement on the most crucial of the four pillars of the IPEF, the trade pillar. This pillar had been expected to build on the rules-based multilateral trading system and extend it to cooperation in newer areas of labour, environment and digital trade. Of course, with President Trump having assumed office in January this year, the question of the survivability of the IPEF remains open given his dislike for institutional arrangements and trade agreements. President Trump has been emphatic about 'knocking out' the IPEF during his election campaign.

Global Trade and GVCs since 2018: Early Trends

Even as the global trade context has undergone significant shocks and the multilateral trade order stands substantially weakened, it is noteworthy that global trade has remained remarkably resilient, recording the highest rate of growth in 2022 after several years of slow growth, followed by positive though modest growth in 2023. Global trade has hit a record high of $33 trillion in 2024. Evidence of the impact of trade shocks and the inward trade orientation of the lead economies on trade in intermediate goods is as yet scant. The share of intermediate goods trade in total merchandise trade remains close to 50 per cent, indicative, therefore, of the continued importance of GVCs.

However, there is an evident reconfiguration of GVCs—particularly in Asia—even though China continues to maintain its centrality in the global intermediate goods trade. Also, trade is increasingly being driven by geopolitical compulsions, getting concentrated within major trade relationships, and there is a decline in the diversification of trade partners. US-China trade is observed to be growing at a slower rate since 2018, relative to their trade with the world. The trade intensity within the European and North American GVC hubs, though, has been maintained. Mexico is observed to be the largest single-country source of imports for the US.[19]

Early and emerging trends indicate that even though China's share of US imports in the tariffed category of products has fallen since 2018, there is little evidence of the reshoring of production back to the US. A majority share of US imports has just shifted their country of origin away from China. The shift away from China as a source of imports happened to countries which have the deepest supply chain linkages with China. This is especially true for the major beneficiaries of this shift, that is, countries that gain the most in terms of their export share to the US, such as Vietnam in the area of electronics. In strategic sectors, the expansion of exports to the US also leads to increased supply chain integration with China for these major beneficiary economies. So while the US's dependence on direct imports from China has seen a decline, indirect imports may be the same or greater than earlier. The reconfiguration of supply chains as a consequence of US import tariffs is thus not in line with the policy objective of reduced import dependence on China. In case of strategic sectors, in addition to this, supply chain integration with China increased as exports to the US from the beneficiary economies increased. In fact, it has been observed that the integration with Chinese supply chains is among the strongest indicators for identifying the 'plus one' economy for friendshoring GVCs.[20]

The other important aspect of the global trade context is the intensification of ASEAN–East Asia economic integration through WTO-compatible trade agreements, the Regional Comprehensive and

Economic Partnership (RCEP), and membership of the CPTPP. The RCEP, operationalized in January 2022 with common, cumulative ROOs, has built-in provisions towards deeper integration over time. Furthermore, with the overlapping membership of seven of its members with the more rigorous and higher-order CPTPP that is already in force in the region, the Asian trade bloc seems to have geared up for enhanced and deeper economic integration. The expanding membership of the CPTPP, along with the RCEP, is evidence of a large number of economies' willingness to pursue economic integration on WTO-prescribed norms and rules. The UK attended its first CPTPP meeting as a member in November 2023, and six more formal applicants await the consideration of their requests. East Asian regionalism, therefore, has been a beacon of some hope in a global trade context increasingly driven by unilateral trade policies that are getting progressively more protectionist.

Trade Policy Priorities for India

India's share in global merchandise exports has remained stagnant at less than two per cent for over a decade now. This has been true even during the early years of the last decade when trade as a share of the GDP was on the rise in India. The share of manufacturing in India's total exports has consistently been on the decline.[21] This is worrisome given the contribution that manufacturing can make towards employment creation. For a large, low-skilled and labour-abundant economy like India, employment creation continues to be a challenge. Just as some Southeast Asian economies (Malaysia, Thailand and Vietnam) and Eastern and Central European economies (Poland, Hungary and the Czech Republic) have, in the last two decades, developed their manufacturing sector specialization and export competitiveness through integration with GVCs and regional GVC hubs, India should also aim at enhancing its integration with GVCs, particularly with the proximate regional East Asian GVC hub. Having thus far benefitted only to a limited extent from the earlier shifts in GVCs, India needs to prioritize the formulation and implementation of a more open and stable trade policy that will help enhance its attractiveness as an alternative investment location for MNCs in their China-Plus-One strategy.

To realize this objective, India would need, among other economic reforms, a more open trade policy. As a necessary first step in that direction, India needs to bring down its average applied MFN tariffs in the manufacturing sector and specifically in the trade and GVC-dynamic sectors. India has followed a relatively protectionist trade policy in recent years. The average MFN tariffs in the manufacturing sector and the number of tariff lines in the higher tariff (>15%) category have been progressively increased over the last few years. Apart from the fact that this introduces an element of unpredictability in its trade policy, India is considered a relatively more inward-looking and protectionist economy in comparison with other EMEs such as Vietnam, which offer a far more liberal trade regime.[22] The outward-looking, export-oriented foreign investor would much rather opt for a more open and predictable trade environment, such as is available in comparator emerging market economies like Vietnam, Malaysia, Mexico and others. India should, therefore, accord immediate priority to reducing its average applied manufacturing sector MFN tariffs. Some reduction in tariffs has been undertaken in the last two budgets. However, in most cases where a reduction of the basic customs duty has been announced in Budget 2025, the effective tariffs have remained unchanged due to an additional levy of a cess. A more systematic and broad-based reduction in tariffs needs to be undertaken such that there is a close alignment of India's tariff rates with the ASEAN levels. This should be done with a specified time schedule. This will help infuse predictability in the trade policy as well as attract export-oriented foreign direct investment.

India's objective of building complete supply chains within the country under the production-linked incentive (PLI) scheme may not be the most optimal means for achieving manufacturing competitiveness either. Apart from the fact that building complete supply chains is a time-consuming process and not necessarily the most efficient one, PLI, introduced in 2020, is spread across 14 sectors, many of which (such as textiles, white goods, automobiles and food processing) are hard to justify as strategic from the viewpoint of deserving financial incentives. In addition to this, financial incentives, when combined with protectionist policies such as high tariffs, will not ensure efficient outcomes. Higher tariffs do not ensure the availability of domestic inputs that can substitute imported, more efficient inputs. This has already been evident in case of mobile phones where the local content remains small relative to imports, despite the relative success of the sector in terms of exports.

India also needs to ensure an early conclusion of its FTAs with the EU and review the FTA with ASEAN (ASEAN-India Trade in Goods Agreement, AITIGA). FTA commitments are a means to lock in reforms and the upgradation of the domestic regulatory framework to international standards, thereby ensuring policy predictability. Deeper FTAs signal a higher-level trade policy commitment and an environment conducive to business. So far, India's FTAs have been shallow with limited offers of tariff line liberalization. India's FTAs with developed economies like the UK and the EU have seen successive postponements of their deadlines, while those with regional economies like ASEAN and Korea have been long under review. India, therefore, needs to focus on the successful and early conclusion of deeper trade agreements and also delineate policy steps for participation in higher-grade, mega-regional trade agreements like the CPTPP.

In this context, India needs to reorient its negotiating strategy that is presently based on viewing FTAs narrowly and only through the lens of bilateral trade deficits, to one based on an understanding of FTAs as instruments of GVC integration. The FTA review with ASEAN, in particular, should be seen as a means to integrate with a proximate regional GVC hub and an opportunity to make good the loss of staying out of the RCEP. This would be timely as the centrality of ASEAN to the regional value chains (RVCs) or GVCs has been getting reinforced in the wake of the China-Plus-One diversification strategy, reorienting along the lines of allyshoring. Regional economies like Japan and Korea are actively subsidizing friendshoring to Indonesia, Thailand and Vietnam, among other ASEAN economies. Vietnam is emerging as the new semiconductor manufacturing friendshoring location for the US.

Furthermore, as discussed above, ASEAN–East Asia is the only trade bloc that continues to follow the rules-based trade order in the regional trade agreements. This is important for a country like India that does not have an FTA with the US or the EU yet. Apart from the fact that India will find it hard to overcome the adverse impact of the CBAM, the traditional export markets like the EU and the US are also projected to have a slower growth of less than three per cent in the next few years. Southeast-East Asia continues to be resilient in terms of economic growth, and is projected to significantly contribute to global trade in the near future.

It may therefore be useful if India were to evolve its FTA strategy as well—from laying emphasis on procedurally cumbersome, excessively complex, dual-criteria-based ROOs, to making them more facilitative of GVC or RVC integration. Accepting some form of region-wide cumulation in the ROOs will be useful for India in overcoming the limitation of staying out of the RCEP and assist in its negotiation with the ASEAN in the FTA review process. Another aspect of the FTA that calls for careful reconsideration by Indian negotiators is the investment chapter where India needs to evolve its stance on the investor-state dispute settlement mechanism beyond the one based on its highly restrictive model Bilateral Investment Treaty (BIT) of 2016. In this context, the reduction in the period for the exhaustion of domestic remedies under the India-UAE FTA in 2024 is a forward-looking policy measure. Also, the review of the model BIT—as announced in the 2025 budget—should be undertaken at the earliest.

It may also be useful for India if future FTA negotiations were undertaken on a simultaneous and comprehensive basis—inclusive of goods, services and investment liberalization. Further, in the context of the liberalization of services, India has to think beyond Mode 4 liberalization to consider sectors which—when combined with manufacturing—will contribute to export competitiveness. This includes areas of comparative advantage for India, such as repair and maintenance as well as digital services—a sector that has received special focus in the ASEAN vision towards establishing the regional economic community.

Finally, good logistics helps in the efficient movement of goods within and across borders, reduces trade costs, and facilitates GVC operations. In the World Bank's Logistics Performance Index (LPI), while India has made considerable progress in its rank, score and almost all subcomponents over the last five years, it continues to lag behind its ASEAN peers in areas such as customs clearance and trade infrastructure (refer to Table 2). While investing in trade infrastructure such as warehouses and ports is already being planned in India, the introduction and use of electronic data interchange, as in ASEAN, will help contribute to more efficient customs clearance procedures and overall trade facilitation.

Table 2: Logistics Performance Index and Subcomponents, 2023

Score/Country	India	Thailand	Vietnam	Malaysia
LPI	3.4	3.5	3.3	3.6
Customs	3	3.3	3.1	3.3
Infrastructure	3.2	3.7	3.2	3.6
International Shipments	3.5	3.5	3.3	3.7
Logistics Competence	3.5	3.5	3.2	3.7
Tracking and Tracing	3.4	3.6	3.4	3.7
Timeliness	3.6	3.5	3.3	3.7

Source: World Development Indicators, World Bank, 2023.

Therefore, as global trade growth proceeds in an increasingly protectionist environment, India will need to look beyond its traditional export markets and undertake substantive steps towards establishing a more investment-conducive and predictable trade policy. This objective assumes even greater relevance in the evolving global trade context since President Trump assumed office in January 2025. Given the element of increased uncertainty under Trump 2.0 with respect to both the magnitude and the targets of selective protectionism, especially the 'reciprocal tariffs', it may be useful for India to focus on developing a strategy for the diversification of its export basket and markets. Even though it is still hard to ascertain how reciprocal tariffs will be evaluated and administered, it would be opportune and useful for India to undertake a systematic reduction of its applied tariffs and align these with its comparator Asian economies.

Like some other countries (the EU, Mexico and the UK), India could also accelerate the pace of its FTA negotiations to secure alternative export markets. In particular, the early conclusion of deep trade agreements with the EU and the UK and a review of the FTA with ASEAN will be beneficial for India. This is relevant since it has been observed that deep mega-regional trade agreements offer the advantage of stability of trade during periods of adverse global shocks and uncertainties. While the membership of the RCEP should be rethought, India should also apply for membership in the CPTPP and actively initiate preparation towards early participation in this open and multilateral rules-abiding trade agreement.

On the multilateral front too, it may be time to accept that the revival of the WTO with a fully functional DSM may not be possible anymore. Collective alternatives suited to the evolving trade contours and challenges need to be designed and debated within and among developed and developing countries. Plurilaterals, wherein like-minded countries come together to formulate rules on critical issues of global trade, are one such alternative. India has thus far stayed out of plurilaterals and, in fact, questioned their legal status. It may now be time for India to reconsider its position and develop a perspective on appropriate structures of these alternative trade formulations of 'variable geometry'. There is a need and necessity to ensure that principles of openness, fairness and equity continue to direct global trade. India should take the lead in this direction.

Overall, India needs to design a multipronged strategic trade policy to confront and combat the varied challenges of the present-day global trade environment.

Montek Singh Ahluwalia

Climate Change in India: An Agenda for the Next 10 Years[1]

I have known Shankar Acharya for over six decades, which makes it a very special pleasure to contribute to this Festschrift in his honour. We first met as students at Oxford in 1964, and then overlapped for several years in Washington, D.C., where we both worked for the World Bank. I returned to Delhi in 1979 and we resumed our friendship when Shankar returned shortly thereafter.

At first, I thought this piece in his honour should be on India's fiscal problems in the years ahead, because that is the area in which we both worked together when he was chief economic adviser in the Ministry of Finance and I was secretary, economic affairs. However, on further reflection, I decided to devote this chapter to something entirely different: climate change, which wasn't anywhere on the agenda when we worked together but has since moved to the centre stage.

This chapter is structured as follows: **Section I** summarizes why climate change is important for India and why global cooperation is necessary to solve the problem. **Section II** provides a summary of the evolution of the global agreement on climate change and the current state of play in this area, which provides the backdrop within which India must chart its future course of action. **Section III** outlines a credible agenda for the next 10 years, consistent with its stated longer-term objective of getting to net zero by 2070. **Section IV** discusses the conflicts of interests which arise in the course of managing climate change and which make its implementation especially difficult. **Section V** summarizes the recommendations emerging from this essay.

I. Climate Change and Its Impact on India

The science of climate change is now well understood.[2] We know that global temperatures have been rising since the start of the Industrial Age, mainly because the burning of fossil fuels has produced steadily rising emissions of greenhouse gases (GHGs). Since these gases decay only over a very long period, their concentration in the atmosphere has risen steadily, producing a 'greenhouse effect' leading to global warming which, in turn, has triggered wide-ranging climate change.

Although both developed and developing countries will be adversely affected by climate change, countries in the tropics will be the worst affected. India is a member of this group and will be affected in many ways. Global warming will affect ocean currents, leading to unpredictable changes in the monsoons. Total precipitation may not change, but the regional distribution could change significantly, and we are also likely to see a greater frequency of concentrated rainfall.[3] This will lead to an increased 'runoff' of fresh water, reducing the rate of recharge of underground aquifers, which will reduce water availability.

Rising temperatures will lead to a fall in crop yields, with negative effects on rural incomes. Heat stress will also reduce labour productivity, especially in the construction sector. Greater heat and humidity could also lead to an increase in disease vectors and possibly induce new pandemics, all of which have implications for the health policy. It is also easy to see that the burden of all these changes will fall most heavily on the poor.

All this highlights the fact that managing climate change should be a high priority for India, and this calls for action in two areas: mitigation and adaptation. Mitigation refers to steps to reduce the emissions of GHGs with a view to limiting global warming, and adaptation refers to action that needs to be taken to cope with the effects of climate change, which have already occurred and are likely to continue for some time.

Mitigation and adaptation pose very different challenges. Mitigation calls for global cooperation because the only way to stop global warming is to stabilize the concentration of GHGs in the atmosphere and this requires every country to cooperate in curtailing its own emissions.

Cooperation is essential because individual countries are unlikely to take sufficient action since they bear all costs of the mitigation action they take but don't get all the benefits. Adaptation does not require collective action in the same sense because countries can take adaptation action individually, and the benefits of such action in one country are independent of actions taken by other countries.

This chapter deals primarily with mitigation, mainly because adaptation, though equally important, is too vast a subject to cover in the space available. However, some problems of adaptation are touched upon in Section IV.

II. The State of the Global Compact on Mitigation

The search for a global solution to manage climate change has been underway for more than 30 years. It started with the Earth Summit in Rio in 1992, when it was first formally acknowledged that global warming was being caused by the burning of fossil fuels and that cooperation was needed to stop the process. The United Nations Framework Convention on Climate Change (UNFCCC) was established to provide a framework for negotiating an agreed-upon pattern of cooperation.

Since then, the Conference of the Parties (COP) to the convention has met 29 times to evolve a workable global consensus on this issue. These meetings have had a mixed record at best. They have certainly raised global awareness about the problem, in addition to increasing awareness among civil society groups and the private sector. But they have been much less successful in getting governments to act on what needs to be done.

One reason for the limited success is the inability of the governments to agree on what would constitute a fair distribution of the burden of adjustment across countries. Developing countries have consistently argued that since the increase in the concentration of GHGs was almost entirely due to the industrialization of developed countries, the burden of reducing emissions should also rest with them. As latecomers to the development process, developing countries should not be burdened with having to reduce emissions. They are only just starting on growth and need a reasonable amount of carbon space, and they also lack the resources needed to undertake mitigation.

The Kyoto Protocol of 1997 was the first agreement negotiated under the UNFCCC and it fully reflected the position of the developing countries. It imposed emissions reduction obligations only on developed countries, exempting developing countries completely. However, the Protocol failed at an early stage, partly because the exclusion of developing countries proved unacceptable.[4]

This led to intensified efforts in successive COPs to persuade developing countries to take on some mitigation commitments. COP21, held in Paris in 2015, was a landmark in several respects. It produced the Paris Agreement in which the global community unanimously endorsed a target of containing global warming to 'well below 2°C and ideally 1.5°C above pre-industrial levels by 2100'. Until then, there was no explicitly agreed-upon target for global warming and there was no basis to judge whether the emissions reductions prescribed in the Kyoto Protocol were adequate. Developed countries agreed to reduce their emissions by 20–40 per cent from different baselines. Major developing countries did not undertake to reduce the absolute level of their emissions, but they undertook to reduce the 'emissions intensity of their Gross Domestic Product (GDP)'. The agreement also promised that developed countries would provide developing countries with additional financial assistance of $100 billion per year, to be reached by 2020 and continued up to 2025. The provision of financial assistance was an important element of climate justice.

The Paris Agreement quickly ran into two problems. The first arose when, shortly after the signing of the agreement, Donald Trump won the presidential election in the US and announced that the country would withdraw from the agreement. The withdrawal of the largest economy as well as the largest polluter in the world might have seemed reason enough to worry, but climate activists were not unduly anxious because there was strong support for decarbonization in Europe, and there was an expectation that despite the withdrawal of the US, individual states and the private sector would keep climate change on the public policy agenda.

The second and more serious problem was that technical analysis in the years following the signing of the agreement made it clear that the commitments made in Paris to contain emissions were insufficient to limit global warming to the targeted level. This led to renewed efforts to get all countries to accept stronger targets. As it happened, the US presidential election brought Joe Biden to the White House and he brought the US back into the Paris Agreement while also advocating taking stronger action. These efforts met with some success at COP26 held in Glasgow in 2021. Developed countries agreed to reduce emissions to reach net zero by 2050. Developing countries also agreed, for the first time ever, to reduce the absolute level of emissions to net zero, but at different dates.[5]

When these commitments were reviewed in COP28 in December 2023, the review showed that the actions promised were still not sufficient. Furthermore, the actions actually taken by many countries were not in line with what they had promised![6] The UNEP estimated that for the 1.5°C target to be achieved, global emissions had to be 42 per cent lower in 2030 than in 2019 but, in fact, they had increased by 3.3 per cent by 2023. The world was headed for global warming of about 2.5 to 2.9°C by 2100 unless much stronger action was taken. COP28 concluded with a strong call to all countries to come back before COP30 with a stronger set of commitments spanning the period from 2025 to 2035.

In other words, while the COP process generated some agreement to reduce emissions, it has not produced a set of country-wise commitments that would achieve the temperature target. This failure reflects a basic flaw in the way the negotiations have been conducted so far. The rational way would have been to agree on the 'remaining carbon budget' which would be consistent with global temperature targets, and then agree on a fair way of distributing this budget across countries. Admittedly, it would not have been easy to get all 198 parties to the UNFCCC to agree on what a fair distribution would be, but an effort to achieve this would at least have drawn attention to the critical issues that needed to be addressed. This issue was never addressed.[7] It was simply side-stepped in favour of a purely voluntary approach in which individual countries would be urged to take on purely voluntary commitments in the form of intended nationally determined contributions (INDCs).[8] This voluntary approach has clearly not succeeded.

The failure to build an adequate consensus on mitigation is paralleled by a similar failure in providing additional financial assistance to developing countries to help them undertake the energy transition. It was generally recognized in COP26 in Glasgow that the amount of $100 billion per year that had been pledged at the time of the Paris Agreement was grossly inadequate since it was fixed at a time when the obligations undertaken by developing countries were very weak. The much stronger obligations agreed upon in COP26 called for a much larger commitment. The task of coming up with a new collective quantified goal (NCQG) for the period between 2025 and 2035 to replace the earlier $100 billion was explicitly assigned to COP29.

COP29 met in Baku (Azerbaijan) in November 2024. The delegates had before them the report of the Independent High-Level Expert Group (IHLEG), co-chaired by Amar Bhattacharya, Vera Songwe and Nick Stern (by way of full disclosure, I should add that I am a member of this group). The IHLEG estimates of the investment requirements for developing countries other than China for 2030 and 2035 and the sources suggested for financing them are presented in Table 1.

Table 1: Total Investment Needed for Managing Climate Change

(US$ Billion in 2022 Prices)

	2022 (actual)	2030	2035
Total	590	2,440	3,260
-From domestic sources	400	1,440	1,960
-From external finance	190	1,000	1,300
... of which			
1. Private sources	40	500	650
2. MDBs	80	270	325
3. Bilateral sources	40	90	100
4. Other sources (carbon markets, philanthropy, etc.)	30	140	225

Source: Bhattacharya, et al., 2024. (The breakdown of external finance for 2035 [last column] is not in the report, but I based it on discussions with those involved in preparing the estimates.)

The total investment in different sectors for mitigation and adaptation was estimated to be $590 billion in 2022. It was projected that this would have to increase to $2.44 trillion by 2030 and $3.26 trillion by 2035. This is an increase from 2.4 per cent of the GDP of these countries in 2022 to 7.1 per cent in 2030 and 7.8 per cent in 2035. The investment needed would have to be financed by a combination of domestic and external sources of financing. The IHLEG estimated that about 60 per cent of the investment could be financed via domestic financing. This would come partly from (a) additional public and private savings—some of which would come from growth and some from an increased savings effort, and partly from (b) resources released from other areas as a result of the energy transition. For example, the redeployment of investment that would otherwise go towards setting up coal-based thermal plants or coal mining as well as petroleum exploration and refining would contribute to generating the resources for investment in renewable energy (RE).

As shown in Table 1, after taking credit for financing available from domestic sources, there would be a residual financing gap of $1 trillion by 2030 and $1.3 trillion by 2035. This would have to be met by external financing. The discussion in COP29 revealed sharp differences between developing and developed countries on the nature of this financing.

Many developing countries took the view that the entire amount of external financing should come in the form of public flows from developed countries. This was not what the IHLEG recommended. External financing was always meant to be a combination of public and private flows and the IHLEG envisaged about half the amount—$500 billion by 2030 and $650 billion by 2035—as coming from purely private flows, i.e. commercial debt and equity (see Table 1).

If the developing countries pitched for a much larger volume of public flows than the IHLEG recommended, the developed countries were willing to provide much less. As shown in Table 1, the IHLEG projected about $425 billion as coming from bilateral and multilateral public flows, with a further $175 billion from other sources such as carbon markets and philanthropies. Against this, the NCQG that emerged from COP29 for 2035 amounted to only $300 billion, which was significantly lower than what the IHLEG recommended. The representative of one developing country captured the mood of many when he criticized the outcome saying, '(I)t is not just a failure. It is a betrayal...'

The state of the global consensus before the US Presidential election in November 2024 can be summarized as follows:

(a) There was no agreement on a satisfactory set of mitigation actions to be taken by all countries. Recognizing this, COP28 called for all countries to come back with stronger commitments before COP30 in Belem (Brazil).
(b) The financial assistance package that emerged from COP29 was also much smaller than expected. It was certainly not consistent with what was expected given the principle of climate justice.

The return of Donald Trump to the White House has added new complications. He has once again taken the US out of the Paris Agreement. This time, however, there is more reason to be concerned. There is no evidence of a commitment on the part of individual states of the US or the private sector to pursue a serious mitigation agenda. Political developments in Europe also suggest some weakening in the commitment of some European countries. President Trump has also declared a preference for resolving issues through bilateral rather than multilateral discussions and this casts serious doubts on how much progress can be expected through COP and other multilateral meetings in future.

III. Towards a Credible Mitigation Plan for India

The inadequacy of the global consensus on climate change described above, and the uncertainty about how things will evolve, are bound to impact India's determination to pursue an ambitious decarbonization plan. However, since global warming remains a serious problem—one that will affect India adversely—we should not give up too quickly. A reasonable course of action to follow is to hope that global negotiations will ensure a better outcome in due course than seems likely right now and to push for this in ongoing negotiations. Meanwhile, we should work internally to develop an operational plan for the period from 2025 to 2035, which is consistent with the goal of reaching net zero emissions by 2070.

In practice, this means working to revise India's INDCs, the latest version of which (submitted after COP26) is given in Box 1. It is worth noting that India has not made any commitment thus far on the expected trajectory of our emissions. The present situation is that the emissions of developed countries have begun to fall, albeit very slowly, while India's emissions are continuing to rise. This is often subjected to international criticism. We can legitimately defend our position on the grounds that our per capita emissions are still very low—well below the average in developed countries and also lower than the average in other developing countries, excluding China.

Since our per capita GDP is also relatively low, it is a legitimate development objective to raise it. This involves aiming at rapid GDP growth, which implies that our total emissions will rise for some time before they begin to decline. However, for this argument to be credible, we need to indicate a peaking time followed by a subsequent decline in emissions, ultimately leading to net zero by 2070. China has said that their emissions will peak by 2030. We could legitimately seek a peaking point about 10 years later and build this into our 10-year plan.

Box 1: India's Current INDCs

The main elements of India's COP26 INDCs are the following:

» Reduce the emissions intensity of the GDP by more than 45 per cent by 2030 compared to the 2005 level. This is an improvement over the 33–35 per cent reduction committed in Paris in 2015.
» Increase the share of non-fossil-fuel-based electricity generation capacity to 50 per cent of the total capacity, or 500 GW by 2030, up from the previous target of 40 per cent. The new target includes 50 GW of large hydropower and nuclear energy and 450 GW of RE—consisting of 280 GW of solar and 140 GW of wind power capacity—by 2030, and 30 GW of other RE sources.
» The afforestation target announced in 2015—to create an additional 2.5–3 gigatonnes of carbon dioxide equivalent (Gt CO_2e) forest sink by 2030—remains in force, although it was not explicitly mentioned.

Reconciling Net Zero with Development

Accepting a trajectory which involves a decline to net zero by 2070 will be politically acceptable only if the public can be assured that it would not compromise our development objectives. This issue is best explored in aggregate terms by referring to the well-known Kaya identity which is reproduced below:

$$\frac{Em}{P} = \frac{GDP}{P} \times \frac{En}{GDP} \times \frac{Em}{En}$$

Em is GHG emissions, En is a composite measure of energy of different kinds, and P is population.[9]

The first term on the right-hand side (RHS) is GDP per capita. The Viksit Bharat objective of reaching 'developed country status' by 2047 implies a fivefold increase in the GDP over this period, and this will clearly raise emissions.[10] Whether we can still reduce emissions to net zero over time depends on what we can do to the other two terms in the RHS.

The second term measures the energy efficiency of the economy; it is, in fact, the weighted average of energy efficiency across different energy-using sectors. There are several ways of improving energy efficiency at the micro level, for instance by shifting to more energy-efficient appliances such as LED bulbs instead of fluorescent lamps or higher efficiency fans, refrigerators, air-conditioners or cars, or shifting to more energy-efficient industrial processes. Since energy-efficient appliances are usually more expensive, the adoption of these appliances would be aided by appropriate energy pricing. Consumers will be more willing to incur the additional capital expenditure of energy-saving appliances if energy is economically priced. Low energy prices make it uneconomic to incur the extra capital expenditure to gain efficiency.

Energy efficiency can also be forced by imposing statutory energy efficiency standards for a number of appliances and equipment. Since the whole world will be attempting to raise energy efficiency, we should ensure that our domestic producers are pushed to reach the efficiency levels being achieved in other countries.

Energy efficiency is not just a matter of choosing appropriate technologies, in particular applications. Switching to more 'energy-efficient systems' may be more important. Relying on public rather than private transport, or moving freight by rail rather than road, are examples of such shifts. This issue is examined in detail later in this chapter.

Finally, the demand for energy can also be reduced through a number of lifestyle changes. These include choosing rail rather than flying for short journeys, taking to hiking and walking or cycling as a leisure activity in preference to driving around in energy-guzzling cars, promoting the use of recycled products, and avoiding plastic packaging.[11]

Increasing energy efficiency will reduce the use of energy, which will, in turn, reduce emissions. However, it cannot eliminate the need for energy, and to that extent, we cannot expect to eliminate emissions by relying on energy efficiency alone.[12] This is where the third term on the RHS, which refers to the emissions intensity of energy, could be the real game-changer. Theoretically, if we could eliminate fossil fuels entirely by switching to non-fossil-fuel-based energy, the term would automatically go to zero, taking total emissions to zero as well. The main reason for being optimistic about the future is that technology is making the switch away from fossil fuels much more feasible than it seemed only two decades ago. However, the pace at which this is occurring is still slow, and the growing demand for energy for data centres associated with the rise of AI raises questions about how quickly developed countries will make the change. However, the change has to be achieved over a relatively long period during which technology will evolve rapidly, and this gives grounds for optimism.

The scope for reducing total emissions in India through a combination of interventions along the lines discussed above has been examined by several studies, and they have been reviewed in 'How India can reach net zero: a strategy for 2025–35' (2024) by Montek S. Ahluwalia and Utkarsh Patel.[13] The review suggests that India can reach net zero by 2070 if sufficiently strong action is taken in all GHG-emitting sectors such as the energy sector, transportation, industry, agriculture, buildings (for lighting, air-conditioning and cooking), and waste management.

It is not possible to identify all these interventions at this stage because in many cases the technology needed is still being developed. However, there are areas where it is sufficiently close to maturity, and these are the sectors we should focus on over the next 10 years. Three areas suggest themselves in this context:

(i) Electricity generation accounts for 36 per cent of India's total emissions and this should be a priority area. India is well endowed with solar insolation as well as wind power, and the technology for exploiting these sources has made remarkable progress over the past decade or so.

(ii) Transport accounts for nine per cent of total emissions, and the electrification of large parts of transport (though not all) is now feasible.

(iii) Industry is a large emitter, accounting for about 26 per cent of total emissions. This is a hard-to-abate area, so progress in the next 10 years may be limited but a start must be made.

Other areas which generate substantial emissions are agriculture, forestry and land-use (21 per cent of GHG emissions); buildings on account of lighting, heating and cooling (five per cent); and waste management (three per cent). However, while action in these areas should be explored, it may not be feasible to set specific targets at this stage.

Power Generation: Switching from Fossil Fuels to Renewable Energy

Switching from fossil fuels to RE for power generation is undoubtedly the most important area for action in the medium term. Our INDCs submitted after COP26 targeted an increase in RE capacity—from a base of only 36 GW in 2013 to 450 GW by 2030. There has been good progress with RE capacity increasing to 144 GW in 2023, but this fell short of the target of 175 GW that was set for 2022. Getting to 450 GW by 2030 will call for adding about 50 GW per year in the next six years compared with only 18.5 GW in 2023.

The RE capacity target will need to be scaled up to about 800 GW for 2035. This means we need to increase capacity by 50 GW per year between now and 2030, and then by 70 GW per year for the next five years. This will call for strong policy action in several areas, some of which are listed below.

Making RE Competitive vis-à-vis Coal

If electricity from solar and wind power was fully competitive with traditional coal-based power, market forces would ensure that all new capacity would be RE. In fact, although the cost of generating electricity from these sources has fallen drastically over the past several years, they are not fully competitive yet because the supply of electricity is not even, and it is necessary to invest in grid-scale storage so that some of the power generated during peak periods can be stored and made available during off-peak periods. When the cost of storage is added to the cost of supply, RE power becomes more expensive than coal-based power.

Since the costs of generation as well as batteries are expected to continue falling, the integration of renewable power will become easier in the future. However, until that happens, the government has sought to deal with the problem by imposing renewable purchase obligations (RPOs) on distribution companies (DISCOMs), with a progressive increase in these obligations over time. This raises the question whether the objective of pushing RE would be better served by administrative directions such as RPOs, or by imposing a price on carbon emissions via a carbon tax or some other equivalent intervention.

The Case for Carbon Taxes

Carbon taxation would raise the cost of coal-based electricity, making it more expensive than RE-based power, and market forces would then ensure that all future capacity expansion is RE-based. Such taxation is resisted because it will visibly raise the cost of electricity and, indeed, all other coal-using industries. This argument ignores the fact that the tax only brings the cost of coal-based electricity closer to its true social cost, including the cost on account of global warming as well as air pollution, which has become a major problem in urban India. It also has the advantage of raising the revenue which could be used to meet the additional expenditure needed to manage climate change.

It should be noted that pushing renewables through RPOs instead of carbon taxation also raises the cost of electricity to DISCOMs, but this cost is hidden. Nonetheless, it is real and is borne in the first instance by DISCOMs. But it has to be passed on to the consumers. Failing to do so will only worsen the financial condition of DISCOMs along with many other associated costs.

Although an explicit carbon tax is not under consideration, the finance minister has announced that India is preparing to introduce an emissions trading system (ETS) as the EU, the UK, South Korea, China, Indonesia and Mexico have done. There are many versions of the ETS but, in essence, it involves defining a sectoral area of coverage (which could include power generation, steel, fertilizers, cement, petrochemicals, and such others). Typically, coverage is limited to the large units in each sector. Each unit is given an emissions allowance (the basis of determining this allowance can differ); each unit must then limit its emissions to the amount allowed. Units which emit less than the permissible amount will be allowed to sell the unutilized entitlements to others that are emitting more. Allowing such trading is critical to ensure that the marginal cost of reducing emissions is equalized across industries.

At present, it looks as if power generation will not be included in the ETS. This means that the government will continue to rely upon RPOs to push for higher proportions of electricity being sourced from the RE sector. Even if this is the case, we should ideally plan to extend the coverage of the ETS to the power sector as well once the system has stabilized. This would equalize the cost of decarbonization across power and other sectors.

Implementing an ETS in the course of 2025 would greatly add to the credibility of our commitment to decarbonization. Before finalizing the design of the ETS, it would be useful if it is compared to the systems in use in other countries. We should also be willing to modify our ETS based on the experience of other countries.[14]

Other Supporting Actions

In addition to price-based interventions such as carbon taxes or ETS, a shift to RE on the required scale will need to be supported by other interventions along the lines outlined below.

Electricity markets are regulated around the world, but the regulatory system will need to be modernized to handle a rapidly increasing proportion of intermittent RE supply. Grid-scale batteries and pumped-hydro storage will help stabilize the supply, but they involve additional costs. It will be necessary to allow greater flexibility in pricing to balance the mismatch between supply and demand. At present, most electricity transactions are conducted through long-term power purchase agreements (PPAs), with only seven per cent of the total power traded on electricity exchanges at market-clearing prices. As the share of the RE increases, this will also have to increase.

Daily and seasonal variations in power generation should be reflected in wholesale prices and these variations, in turn, will have to be passed on to consumers through time-of-day (TOD) metering at the consumer end—with consumers paying higher prices in periods when the supply is low, and lower prices when supply is high. At present, the law allows variations in prices charged to industrial consumers and this is proposed to be extended to household consumers in 2025. However, this is only an enabling provision. Its implementation depends upon the state electricity regulation commissions and the DISCOMS.

The variation in prices facing the consumers is bound to be resisted. It is essential to educate politicians and the public that although prices will be higher in some periods, they will be correspondingly lower in periods of peak supply. In fact, over time, the extent of price variations allowed must also be widened greatly both at the wholesale and the consumer ends. At present, a variation of +/-20 per cent is allowed. This needs be increased. This will also incentivize the installation of grid-scale storage to even out the supply.[15]

Smart metering, which is essential to implement TOD at the consumer level, should be accelerated. It may also need to be calibrated to allow a minimum amount of electricity per day to be charged at a fixed low price, while consumption above this level would be charged on a TOD basis.

A positive feature of the Indian experience is that the domestic private sector has been very active in building and operating RE capacity thus far. This must continue since resource constraints will limit what the public sector can do. However, the ability to attract private investment on the required scale will depend critically on the financial strength of the DISCOMs. This is a weak spot at present, with most DISCOMs making losses. Unless this is remedied, they will be seen as posing a payment risk, which is bound to deter private investment.

The Central government has made several efforts to improve the performance of DISCOMs, but with limited success. An important reason is that electricity tariffs are held down by political pressure from State governments. The DISCOMs also suffer from managerial weaknesses typical of public sector organizations. Privatizing the DISCOMs would help but this remains a politically sensitive issue. However, there are States that have privatized some parts of the distribution system with great success, and more States should be encouraged to experiment with privatization, at least for parts of the distribution system.

The shift to RE will involve a change in the regional distribution of the generating capacity in favour of the south and the west, and it will be necessary to plan for HVDC transmission lines to carry surplus power from these regions to deficit regions. The public sector will have to take a leading role in developing this infrastructure since the private sector will find it difficult to invest in anticipation of demand, and will also find it difficult to deal with land acquisition and environmental clearances. The transmission infrastructure built by the public sector can be privatized once it is built and has become fully operational, and the sales proceeds can be used to build other infrastructure.

Nuclear power is another potential source of baseload power. At present the total nuclear capacity is only 8 GW, which provides only three per cent of the total electricity generated—much lower than in many other countries. A target for expanding this to 100 GW has been announced. The development of small modular reactors (SMRs) has also been endorsed with a clear indication of proceeding down this route with private sector participation. However, expanding the scale of nuclear generation will call for changes in existing policies.

India's nuclear power policy has already been relaxed to allow private sector entities in this sector, but at present, they are allowed to do so only as a minority partner with the Nuclear Power Corporation of India Limited (NPCIL) as the majority partner. There is also an additional restriction that the private partner will not be involved in operating the power plant. This is unduly restrictive. Private partners should be allowed to participate in these activities, subject to very strong independent regulation to ensure high standards of safety. The assumption that the public sector is somehow more concerned about safety is difficult to justify. Safety is best assured by a strong public regulator who should be independent of the nuclear operator, and the same safety standards set for the private sector should be applied to the public sector.

India's nuclear liability law is another constraint on private sector involvement because it is much more restrictive than current international norms. It will be necessary to bring the law into alignment with what is the practice elsewhere. The finance minister has indicated in the budget for 2025–26 that amendments are being considered. Early action to implement this announcement would give credibility to the government's declaration that it would welcome private participation.

It may not be possible to take decisions on all these issues quickly, but serious consideration should be given to the changes proposed above. Meanwhile, the following announcements can be made:

(i) We should quickly finalize the design of the proposed ETS, circulate it for comments, and set a date for when it would be made operational.

(ii) We could announce a date after which no new coal power plants will be approved. Reaching net zero by 2070 implies that all coal plants will have to be phased out before 2070. As these plants have an economic life of around +/-35 years, this means no new coal plant should come into operation after, say, 2035, which means that no new plant should be approved after, say, 2028.

(iii) China has announced that its emissions from coal-based power will peak within this decade. We would be entirely justified in setting a date for the end of the next decade. Such an announcement would make it clear to the world that while our emissions will continue to rise for some time, it is in a trajectory which envisages a decline over time.

(iv) The government has announced that it will review the restrictive conditions imposed on private partnership in the development of nuclear power as well as the nuclear liability law. The dates for submitting the amendments of the legislation to Parliament could be announced.

(v) A high-level independent review of the status of the electricity regulatory system to identify areas where change is needed to accommodate a rising share of RE should be initiated. This should not be a purely internal review by the Central Electricity Authority (CEA) or the Central Electricity Regulatory Commission (CERC). It should be done by an independent expert group set up by the CEA, which could include representatives of the private sector involved in both generation and distribution, as well as international experts familiar with the experience of other countries going through the same transition.

The Electrification of Transport

There are good prospects for shifting away from fossil fuels to electricity in both road transportation and the railways. The electrification of road transportation is as yet at a very early phase. The electrification of the track in Indian Railways is almost complete, but that of traction is lagging far behind.

The government of India has introduced a range of subsidies to encourage production of electric vehicles (EVs). However, progress has been uneven. The penetration of EVs in the new sales of three-wheel passenger vehicles and light commercial freight exceeds 50 per cent.[16] It is much lower (5.4 per cent) for two-wheelers and even lower (2.3 per cent) for cars.

The IEA (International Energy Agency) reports that China has reached 38 per cent penetration in terms of new sales for electric cars (2004). This reflects its early start combined with determined government support. The Chinese company BYD has become the largest EV car manufacturer in the world and offers EVs at a low cost. In sharp contrast to this, electric cars in India remain expensive although the availability of various models is expanding. Government spokespersons have talked of achieving 30 per cent EV penetration of sales in the passenger car segment by 2030, but industry representatives talk of reaching only 20 per cent by 2030. Even that may be difficult to achieve unless EVs become available at lower price points.

There are several ways in which the Central and State governments can accelerate the transition to EVs. These include:

(a) The Central government could announce a policy that all government vehicles (whether owned or hired) must be EVs. This could also be extended to Central public sector organizations. State governments could be encouraged to follow suit.

(b) State governments could mandate that all taxi licences be issued only to EVs from a predetermined date. Delhi, for example, has set 2030 as the date by which all cab aggregators must shift to all-EV fleets.

(c) The Central government, in consultation with the industry, could announce that all new sales in each vehicle category—two, three or four-wheelers—must be fully electric by a pre-specified date. This would provide a benchmark for assessing progress, with penalties imposed if the target for phasing out internal combustion engine (ICE) vehicles cannot be met, progress being slower than targeted. The best penalty would be to charge a higher rate of tax on the sale of ICE vehicles after the designated date.

(d) Establishing an efficient charging system, including fast charging possibilities, is perhaps the most important step that is needed to expand the adoption of EVs. The number of public charging stations across the country is just over 12,000, mainly in and around metropolitan areas.[17] This number needs to be increased by a factor of 10. Both the Central and State governments have a role to play in this process. Existing petrol and diesel refuelling stations, many of which are linked to public sector marketing companies, could collaborate with private sector players and State government DISCOMs to set up electric charging stations.

(e) Since public transport is much more fuel-efficient than private transport, a shift from private to public transport such as buses and metros would make a significant contribution towards reducing emissions. This would be so even if the public transport system remained dominated by ICE vehicles, though, of course, it would be better if the buses were also EVs. The bus transport fleet is being progressively electrified and several private sector firms have entered into the development of electric buses. However, the capital cost of EV buses is high though the operating cost is lower.

(f) The promotion of public transport requires supportive policies in many other areas, most of which are in the domain of State and local governments. These include:

(i) Seamless usability of bus and metro services in the city on the basis of the integrated planning of metro and bus services, with IT-enabled features like real-time information systems on service operations. Interoperable mobility passes (for example, the National Common Mobility Card) would make public transport much more convenient.

(ii) Shared mobility and active transport options (for example, bicycles) could be promoted to reduce the dependence on fossil fuels.

(iii) Finally, higher parking and/or congestion charges would help to discourage private car use and promote the use of public transport.

Indian Railways also have a major role to play in decarbonizing transport. The following initiatives could be considered for implementation in the period 2025–35:

(i) The electrification of the broad gauge network is now almost complete, but the Indian Railways still relies quite heavily on diesel traction. Phasing out diesel locomotives should be the next step. A target date should be specified by when new diesel locomotives will no longer be inducted. This could be 2030 since the locomotives have a lifespan of about 40 years, and the objective should be to phase them out almost entirely, well before 2070. Many of the existing diesel engines could be converted into electric engines as a matter of priority and this is being explored.

(ii) Since freight transport by railways is much more energy-efficient than transport by road, the railways should aim at reversing the trend decline in freight share which they have experienced and which has brought their share down to a low of 27 per cent in 2022. This will almost certainly require a rethinking of the age-old practice of overcharging for freight in order to subsidize passenger traffic. This has contributed to the shift of freight traffic to roads. Raising passenger fares will be politically difficult, but perhaps an expert committee can be set up to present an independent view—after extensive consultations with the objective of building public opinion in favour of rebalancing the fare structure. If this is done gradually over a 10-year period, it should be easy to absorb.

(iii) A growing proportion of freight transportation is now handled by private sector logistics firms that deal directly with businesses offering door-to-door delivery. These firms rely mainly on road transport, which they find more reliable than rail. Ideally, they should use the railways for long-distance movement, and road vehicles (which could soon be EVs) for pick-ups and last-mile deliveries. This calls for a much more reliable rail freight service, where movements of consignments can be tracked in real time. As private logistics companies will have to make investments to switch to intermodal transportation, they will need to be assured of a level-playing field with respect to public sector companies like the Container Corporation of India Limited (ConCor). In fact, there is a strong case for privatizing ConCor, or at least reducing the Ministry of Railways' shareholding in the company to a minority to ensure fair competition.

Hydrogen fuel cells are often mentioned as a viable means of transporting heavy freight by road and also for railway traction. The Indian Oil Corporation has gifted some H2-powered buses to Delhi, and the Railways have announced an H2-powered train. While these experiments may continue, the extent to which hydrogen fuel cells can be used will ultimately depend upon their commercial viability. Experiments elsewhere have not yet proved to be commercially successful, and several in Europe have been discontinued.

Decarbonizing Industries

Industries account for 26 per cent of total GHG emissions and decarbonizing this sector has to be an important part of any longer-term agenda, but as noted earlier, the progress we can expect in the next 10 years may be limited. A large part of industrial emissions comes from the use of coal to generate heat. It is technically possible to switch to electricity in many of these cases, and the electricity will hopefully become fully RE-based over time. However, this involves a high cost which small and medium units may not be able to bear.[18]

Fossil fuels are also used as feedstock—for example, in the steel industry—while reducing iron ore or the steam reforming of natural gas in fertilizer production. Several corporate managements have publicly announced plans for producing green hydrogen, targeting a sharp reduction in the costs of production. These are good developments, though the announcements may be driven by corporate PR since planning for such a shift looks good, especially in the context of raising capital internationally.

The critical factor that will determine the viability of using green hydrogen is the reduction in the cost of production of green H2 from between $5 and $6 per kg at present to $1 per kg. In case of steel, there is also the capital cost of reconfiguring factories to switch to green hydrogen. It is estimated that green steel—using green hydrogen as a substitute for coke—will be 40 per cent more expensive. We will have a better idea of how much can be achieved in a few years when the extent of technical advances becomes clearer, but on present prospects, unless steel producers are forced to change—for example, those wishing to export to Europe may have to because of CBAMs—the transition will be slow.

If carbon capture and its usage become economically viable over the next decade, it may be possible to use this method to offset the unavoidable GHG emissions from otherwise hard-to-abate areas. It makes sense, therefore, to make as much progress as we can in this area, but recognize that progress in the 2025–35 period will be limited.

IV. Balancing the Interests of Gainers and Losers

The previous section demonstrates that there are many steps that can be taken to reduce emissions over the next 10 years. However, implementing them poses formidable challenges because of conflicting interests. All policy initiatives involve gainers and losers; balancing the benefits to gainers against the cost to losers is part of the art of policymaking. This is especially difficult in the case of climate change because the gains will become evident only over a long term, whereas the costs have to be borne in the short run. In what follows, we present a few examples to illustrate the conflicts of interest that may arise in such cases.

Raising Electricity Prices to Reflect the Costs

Civil society groups are often highly environmentally conscious and, therefore, support the idea that energy must be obtained in a sustainable manner. However, they typically also emphasize that this must be at an 'affordable cost'. As pointed out earlier, technology has now made it possible to switch from coal-based electricity to RE, but the latter is not fully competitive yet and this means that the transition will raise the cost of the production of electricity, at least for some more time. This increase in cost either has to be passed on to the consumers of electricity or met by subsidies.

It is not easy to persuade the public to accept higher electricity prices as part of a package for slowing down global warming. Consumers belonging to higher income groups, who can afford to pay higher prices for electricity and are probably also more aware of the longer-term benefits thereof, may be willing to accept higher electricity prices. This is not the case with the much more numerous middle- and lower-income groups. These groups will also benefit from the shift to non-polluting electricity, but their awareness is not at the level where they would accept higher electricity costs.

Unfortunately, electricity pricing has become intensely political. Farmers have gotten used to free or highly subsidized electricity for agriculture. Urban consumers are increasingly being offered similar concessions for household consumption. It will be necessary to initiate a major programme to educate the public about the need to insulate electricity pricing from becoming a pawn in competitive politics. A small segment of the population could be insulated from the price increase, but the larger section should be persuaded that the higher costs of the energy transition will have to be reflected in higher electricity prices.

The Impact on Coal-Producing Areas

The phasing down of coal-based electricity will have an impact on coal demand. Initially, this may mean only a reduction in coal imports, but over time, a reduction in coal mining is unavoidable. This will affect over a million people currently engaged in coal mining and related activities in coal-producing States. There will be benefits in terms of the rapid expansion of the capacity of solar and wind power, which will generate increased employment of higher quality than what is offered by coal mining. However, this increase in employment will occur in other parts of the country. The transition will also involve a loss of coal royalty in States that are considered as low-income and backward at present.

It is relevant to note that if the transition were facilitated by carbon taxes in one form or another, the resulting gain in revenues would provide the government with resources to compensate the losers. In the absence of revenues from such taxes, there will be demands on the Centre to compensate the States in some way.

The Conflict between Consumers of Electricity and Domestic Producers of RE Equipment

Another type of conflict of interest will arise because the energy transition will create a demand for new products such as solar cells and panels, batteries, smart meters, hydrogen electrolysers, electric motors and turbines, among others. It is natural to want Indian industry to gear up to meet these domestic demands, and ideally also export these products to other countries going through the same transformation. However, domestic manufacturers worry that competition from China will make it difficult for them to do so.

China has invested massively in solar cell manufacturing—supported by direct and indirect subsidies from the government—and has built capacity that is more than twice the current global demand. As a result, the prices of solar cells worldwide have collapsed, making it difficult for the domestic industry to compete. There is obviously a conflict of interest between domestic producers wanting protection from what they call unfair competition, and the interests of the consumers of electricity—whether households or businesses—who want electricity at low prices.

There would be no conflict if the domestic manufacturers were supported through subsidies, as is the case in the US under IRA. But the US can afford huge subsidies, which we cannot match. If large subsidies are ruled out, we will be forced to rely on import duties or some form of import licensing. This is precisely what has happened. In April 2022, the basic customs duty (BCD) for solar cells and modules was raised from 15 per cent to 25 per cent for cells and 40 per cent for modules. However, the prices of Chinese solar cells have fallen so much in world markets that domestic manufacturers cannot compete with them despite the duty protection. As a result, RE developers selling solar power to state utilities are now required to source their solar modules from an approved list of domestic manufacturers. This is effectively a resort to licensing as a form of import protection.

This poses several problems. Domestically produced solar cells have a conversion efficiency of 19–20 per cent, but imported cells are available with higher efficiencies of up to 23 per cent. Scientists believe that technological advances that are underway will increase the efficiency substantially in the future. Forcing solar generators in India to purchase solar cells only from approved domestic manufacturers effectively denies them access to new technology cells that may become available in the world market. The problem will be compounded if it is decided, as advocated by some, to push indigenization further backwards and insist on solar cells produced in India using Indian wafers.

These are some of the problems which arise when we use 'industrial policy' which is gaining popularity around the world. The experience of East Asian countries is widely cited to defend this approach, but we should keep in mind that policy in East Asian countries was designed to measure success in terms of global competitiveness. Enterprises were given various types of support, but this was conditional on their success in export markets. We need to give much more thought to how policy design can be shaped to ensure international competitiveness in terms of both price and quality.

Conflicts Arising in Managing Water Scarcity

We have not dealt with adaptation in this essay for reasons of space, but it is worth noting that similar conflicts of interest arise in dealing with the growing water scarcity caused by climate change, which is a critical area in adaptation.

The availability of fresh water in 1950 was 5,000 cubic metres per person per year, which was well above the 1,700 cubic metres per capita that is regarded as water-stressed. Our rising population in the face of fixed availability has reduced the per capita availability of water to 1,500 cubic metres, which is below the water-stressed level. Global warming will worsen the situation, and this will happen in an environment where there is a rising demand from industries as well as a rapidly growing urban population. According to some estimates, the available supply will be able to meet only 50 per cent of the total water demand by 2050!

This is a crisis situation that could lead to potentially serious conflicts. Corrective steps are possible, but all of them present potential conflicts of interest as outlined below:

(i) The rapidly expanding demand for water in urban areas is leading to water for cities being drawn from distant reservoirs, creating a perception in rural areas that 'their' water is being diverted to meet the demands of pampered urban residents. Urban areas will have to do much more to limit their water consumption, which requires higher water prices and also for city-dwellers to reuse recycled water. The use of recycled water has been common in Singapore for many years and we need to introduce it in our major metropolitan cities as early as possible.

(ii) The practice of discharging industrial effluents without treating them is polluting freshwater sources and worsening water scarcity. India's environment policy clearly states that 'the polluter must pay', but State governments are reluctant to enforce these rules, especially where the polluting units are small and are often unable to bear the costs. In such cases, State governments should either assist them or close them down, allowing the stronger units that are able to comply to occupy their space. State governments are typically unable to provide financial assistance and they are unwilling to close the units. The resulting pollution imposes a heavy cost on those who are not stakeholders in this area.

(iii) The pricing of water supplied to households in cities is another problem. State governments feel politically obliged to keep the price of water low, which makes the water supply system financially unstable. Providing a minimum free 'lifeline' allowance for households can be defended on the grounds of equity, but it should not be excessively generous, and whatever the losses on account of the free lifeline supply, it should be recovered from other consumers.

(iv) The poor enforcement of land development policies in most States allows real estate developers to encroach on water bodies in urban areas with impunity. This interferes with the natural replenishment of groundwater and also leads to flooding even with moderate rains. State and local governments need to tighten enforcement in this area, but this is easier said than done as the issues are deeply enmeshed in local politics.

(v) The 'elephant in the room' as far as water scarcity is concerned is the agricultural sector which currently accounts for about 80 per cent of total water use in the country. As water scarcity increases, agriculture will have to become much more water-efficient. This is precisely what the slogan 'more crop per drop' means, but it will require a major restructuring of several aspects of the current policy. For example, the policy of giving farmers electricity for free or at very low prices only encourages the wasteful withdrawal of groundwater. But the idea of charging farmers more for electricity is viewed as politically impossible by most State governments.[19]

(vi) Finally, a massive afforestation programme is clearly necessary to increase water retention and reduce water runoff. Our existing INDCs promised the creation of an extra forest sink of 2.5 to 3 gigatonnes of CO2 equivalent. Since the base year to determine additionality was not specified, it is difficult to assess whether we are on track, but there is no doubt that we need to accelerate afforestation. This does not involve the same kind of conflict of interest as in the other cases, but it does involve substantial additional expenditure which has a fiscal cost. According to one estimate, it will require a fivefold increase in the annual allocations for afforestation and related activities in the Central and State budgets.[20] Since the benefits accrue to the whole country, it can be argued that the costs of this programme should be borne largely by the Centre, but given the fiscal strains on the Central government, it is clear that this will pose politically difficult choices: either Central government tax revenues will have to be raised or other expenditures have to be reduced.

V. Summing Up

Global negotiations on climate change were only able to make limited progress and this is now at risk because of the withdrawal of the US from the Paris Agreement. However, this should not lead us to abandon our declared intention to shift away from fossil fuels and towards RE. The transition towards renewable energy is necessary in our own interest. We should therefore remain engaged in global negotiations in the hope that the world will get around to recognizing the need for building a consensual approach. This should be combined with internal efforts to achieve our stated objectives.

The full transition—to reach net zero by 2070—will require action across all sectors of the economy. However, since the technology needed in many of these areas has yet to become commercially viable, the bulk of our efforts in the period 2025–35 should focus on areas where the technology is sufficiently advanced to justify concrete action.

The critical areas for the medium term are: (a) shifting away from coal-based electricity generation to renewables, (b) electrifying road and rail transport, and (c) electrifying heat generation in selected large industries to the extent possible. Several sector-specific targets have been suggested in **Section III**, which, together, would constitute a credible medium action plan for 2025–35 which has to be submitted by COP30.

The interventions listed in **Section III** include a large number of actions, some of which are in the jurisdiction of various ministries in the Central government, while others are in the jurisdiction of State governments and in some cases, even local bodies. A credible national plan coordinating these initiatives must consist of a Central plan for the 10-year period from 2025 to 2035, dealing with areas in the domain of the Centre, and separate but consistent State plans covering areas under the control of the States and lower levels of government. Consistency among these plans is perhaps best achieved by setting up a high-level commission on managing climate change, along the lines of what has been done in South Africa. It could be chaired by the prime minister and include key Central ministers and all the chief ministers of the States.

The NITI Aayog could serve as the secretariat of this body. It could be tasked with holding discussions with Central ministries, State governments as well as other stakeholders, including the private sector. It should be noted that while the private sector does interact with the ministries concerned, their relationship with the latter is one of dependence. The interaction would be much franker if it were with a third party such as the NITI Aayog. Based on these discussions, a national decarbonization plan could be outlined and submitted to the high-level commission for their final approval.

The task of devising State transition plans that are consistent with the national plan presents many technical challenges. The sectoral priorities may differ between States, reflecting each State's economic circumstances. The pace of transition may also vary: Kerala, for example, has already announced that being a more advanced State, it will aim for net zero by 2050—two full decades sooner than the national target of 2070. Tamil Nadu has announced a target date of 2060. Each State should undertake extensive consultations with the concerned stakeholders in the State and the private sector.

The biggest challenge is how to mobilize public support for actions that will combat climate change. Politicians facing elections typically hope to offer their electorate tangible benefits before the next elections. In the case of climate change, most of the benefits accrue over a long term, and that too, often in the form of avoiding future losses in output and income, whereas the costs have to be incurred upfront. As Jean-Claude Juncker, former president of the European Commission, famously said: 'We all know what needs to be done. We just don't know how to get re-elected after we've done it!' Only an enlightened public opinion, combined with a well-informed and energized civil society, could help politicians achieve both.

Emmanuel Jimenez

People Power: Human Capital Development in India and Other Asian Economies

In a highly regarded column, Shankar Acharya recently wrote that India's 'billion-strong population embodies an enormous potential for jobs and economic growth.'[1] He was referring to the 'demographic dividend'—the notion that the age structure of the population alone can affect economic growth. Such a dividend can be significant. The increase in the share of those working, relative to those who are not working (because they are children or are retired), has been estimated to explain about one-third of the growth of the countries that experienced the so-called 'East Asian Miracle' between 1965 and 1990.[2]

The dividend is not permanent. Because a population eventually ages, countries run the risk of having the window of demographic opportunity shut on them if they become old before they become rich. Some Latin American countries, such as Argentina, failed to take advantage of these opportunities while their demographic window was still open.[3] A recent article has argued that at least some Indian States have already fallen into the same trap.[4] Nor is the dividend automatic. Sound macroeconomic and open trade policies were also crucial for providing the job opportunities in high-performing East Asian countries. Equally important were policies to develop human capital through better education, and to safeguard this human capital through better healthcare.

Almost 20 years ago, Acharya had already warned us about the risk of India missing out on its demographic dividend because of poor policies.[5] His recent article—with its evocative subtitle, 'Cloudy, With High Chance of Thunder and Lightning'—sounds an even more urgent alarm. His message is stark: India must prioritize human development if it is to keep up with its Asian neighbours.

This essay first reviews recent evidence about where exactly India stands—relative to its Asian counterparts—on the development of its human capital. It uses the recently developed Human Capital Index (HCI) to show that India is not a star performer in this regard, and then asks what India can do about this. It then uses evidence from India and other Asian countries on what has worked to improve human development outcomes. If India's demographic dividend does close before it is able to take advantage of it, it will not be for lack of knowing what could be done.

▪

India's Human Capital Index Relative to Those of Its Comparators

By most measures, Asia's human development has improved substantially in the past 50 years. Primary school enrolment rates are now approaching 100 per cent in many countries. In East Asia and the Pacific, secondary school enrolment rates have risen from only 35 per cent (24 per cent in India) in 1970 to 88 per cent (74 per cent in India) in 2019.[6] The average life expectancy in Asia has risen from about 54 years in 1970 (below the world average) to almost 74 years (above the world average) in 2020.[7] But 258 million children are still out of school and 149 million children are stunted due to malnutrition. These statistics are unsettling, but they do not provide an overall picture of the various aspects of human capital. That requires an index.

Comparing human development across countries requires several dimensions to be combined. Doing so can be as much an art as it is a science, because neither theory nor practice provides much guidance, often resulting in what Martin Ravallion has referred to as 'mashup indices of development'.[8]

One index that tries to avoid this problem is the World Bank's Human Capital Index (HCI), a cross-country metric that uses available data to ask a simple but analytically clear question: what is the level of human capital a child born today can expect to attain by his or her eighteenth birthday, given the risks of poor health and poor education prevailing in his or her country of residence? The main components of the index are: (a) survival (under-five mortality), (b) education quantity (the number of years of schooling expected by age 18), quality-adjusted education (using harmonized learning outcomes[9]), and (c) health expressed as adult survival rate (the share of 15-year-olds surviving to age 60) and healthy growth under five (stunting rates).

The HCI summarizes how productive children born today will be as members of the future workforce, given the risks they face to their education and health. It follows the trajectory of the life of a child born today, from birth to adulthood. In the poorest countries or regions of the world, a child may not survive to his or her fifth birthday. Even upon reaching school age, the child may never enrol or may do so and then drop out before completing the full cycle of 14 years from preschool to grade 12, which is the norm in high-income countries. The time spent in school may not lead to the amount of learning expected, depending on the quality of teachers and schools (the relative quality of schools across countries can be assessed based on scores on comparable tests that measure learning outcomes). Finally, the productivity of an 18-year-old will be affected by poor health and nutrition in childhood that may limit his or her physical and cognitive abilities as an adult. The contribution of health to productivity is expressed relative to the benchmark of 'full' health, defined as the absence of stunting and a 100 per cent adult survival rate.

The HCI is measured in units of productivity relative to a benchmark corresponding to complete education and full health. A perfect score of 1.0 would be the score for a country with full survival, no stunting, 14 years of schooling, and a test score average of 625. However, a score of 1.0 would be impossible to achieve since not all children and adults survive to age 60.[10]

How do countries relate to one another when measured by this index? Table 1 shows the HCI calculations for selected East and South Asian countries as well as the Central African Republic and the United States for comparative purposes. The World Bank document does not rank countries because many countries achieve the same numerical score. Here, we report only the rankings with respect to the approximate decile of the HCI score distribution (because some countries at the decile cut-offs share the same score).

Table 1: Human Capital Index, Selected Economies, 2020

Decile Rank*	Economy	HCI Score
1	Singapore	0.88
1	Japan	0.82
1	Republic of Korea	0.80
1	Hong Kong, China	0.81
1	Macao SAR, China	0.80
2	USA	0.70
3	Vietnam	0.69
3	People's Republic of China	0.65
4	Thailand	0.61
4	Malaysia	0.61
4	Sri Lanka	0.60
5	Palau	0.59
6	Indonesia	0.54
6	Philippines	0.52
6	Fiji	0.51
7	Nepal	0.50
7	Cambodia	0.49
7	India	0.49
7	Myanmar	0.48
7	Bangladesh	0.46
7	Lao People's Democratic Republic	0.46
8	Papua New Guinea	0.43
8	Pakistan	0.41
9	Afghanistan	0.40
10	Central African Republic	0.29

Source: World Bank, 2022.

*Approximate to ensure countries with equal scores are in the same category.

Advanced East Asian economies achieve an HCI of 0.80 or more, and are all in the top decile of the 174 economies included in the World Bank report, with Singapore receiving the top score of 0.88, indicating close to full education and full health. In contrast, the country with the lowest score, the Central African Republic, achieved an index number of 0.29. European OECD countries and the US generally achieve rankings in the top two deciles. Upper-middle-income and middle-income East Asian countries are in the third to sixth deciles. South Asian economies generally rank in the bottom half of the table, with scores in the seventh to ninth deciles.

Among emerging Southeast Asian countries, Vietnam ranks best, with a score similar to that of the People's Republic of China (PRC) which is considerably richer. India leads all South Asian countries, but its score is lower than those of such middle-income Southeast Asian countries as Vietnam, Thailand, Indonesia and the Philippines. India's HCI score is comparable with those of the Lao People's Democratic Republic (Lao PDR) and Cambodia, which have considerably lower gross national product (GDP) per capita than India.

The components of the HCI also provide hints as to what could be targets for national development plans and public policies if economies are to improve on these scores. Table 2 breaks down the HCI scores into their main components for developing East Asia, South Asia and India. It shows that India lags behind its Southeast Asian counterparts in almost all of the components of the HCI. For example, by the time a child born in India today reaches his or her eighteenth birthday, he or she could expect to have completed 11.1 years of schooling, two years fewer than a child in the PRC or Vietnam. When adjusted for quality through harmonized test scores, the difference is even more striking; India's learning-adjusted years of schooling are about three years fewer than the PRC or Vietnam. With respect to other South Asian countries, India's education indicators lag behind those of Sri Lanka and Nepal, but exceed those of Bangladesh and Pakistan.

Children who do not survive cannot become productive adults. About 96 per cent of Indian children born today can expect to survive to age five, which is lower than the percentage in other East and Southeast Asian economies, except for Lao PDR and Pakistan.

It can also be anticipated that worker productivity in India will be reduced because of stunting and low rates of adult survival. For both of these components, India ranks second to last among the countries in Table 2.[11]

Addressing Basic Human Development Challenges

Many policies and programmes for ensuring that children live to become full and healthy adults, as well as for enrolling and keeping children in school and having them learn while there, have been proposed and tried, including many for India.[12] Which of them have worked and where? What is the evidence? India is fortunate because many of the studies that do exist have been conducted within the country.

The International Initiative for Impact Evaluation's Development Evidence Portal currently lists the records of over 13,000 impact evaluations.[13] These studies have been screened for their use of rigorous techniques to address causality. They employed a variety of techniques, including experimental methods (such as randomized control trials) and non-experimental methods (such as differences-in-differences, regression discontinuity and instrumental variables), which are considered robust ways of quantitatively ensuring cause and effect. Of these impact evaluations, 5,772 were in the health sector and 1,036 in the education sector. By region, 3,024 were from Asia, with 837 from India—more than any other country in the world.

What lessons do these studies offer for India if it is to make progress in tackling its human development challenges? The following five priorities may help India cash in on its demographic dividend.

Improve the Nutritional Status of Young Children

India is responsible for one-third of the global nutrition burden, with 149 million children deemed to be stunted. Nevertheless, childhood nutrition in India has improved significantly even though progress has been uneven. The percentage of children who are stunted fell from 43 per cent in 2005 to 35 per cent in 2019 according to the National Family Life Survey.[14]

Table 2: Human Capital Index Components for Selected Southeast and South Asian Countries

	HCI 2020	Probability of Survival to Age 5	Expected Years of School	Harmonized Test Scores	Learning-Adjusted Years of Schooling	Adult Survival Rate ASR	Fraction of Children Under 5 CU5 Not Stunted
Singapore	0.88	1.00	13.90	575.00	12.80	0.95	–
China	0.65	0.99	13.10	441.00	9.30	0.92	0.92
Vietnam	0.69	0.98	12.90	519.00	10.70	0.87	0.76
Malaysia	0.61	0.99	12.50	446.00	8.90	0.88	0.79
Sri Lanka	0.60	0.99	13.20	400.00	8.50	0.90	0.83
Indonesia	0.54	0.98	12.40	395.00	7.80	0.85	0.72
Philippines	0.52	0.97	12.90	362.00	7.50	0.82	0.70
Nepal	0.50	0.97	12.30	369.00	7.20	0.86	0.64
Cambodia	0.49	0.95	9.50	452.00	6.80	0.84	0.68
India	0.49	0.96	11.10	399.00	7.10	0.83	0.65
Bangladesh	0.46	0.97	10.20	368.00	6.00	0.87	0.69
Lao PDR	0.46	0.95	10.60	368.00	6.30	0.82	0.67
Pakistan	0.41	0.93	9.40	339.00	5.10	0.85	0.62

Case studies of four Indian States prepared by the International Food Policy Research Institute (IFPRI) concluded that improvements in the socioeconomic status of families and mothers were responsible for a significant portion of the improvement in nutritional status.[15] But they also pointed to several successful government programmes which had been scaled up. Helped by national programmes, several States also implemented specific initiatives between 2000 and 2016 to strengthen the reach and use of health services. In Gujarat and Tamil Nadu, the policy focus was on improving maternal and child health and nutrition, whereas in Chhattisgarh and Odisha, investments in nutrition and health programmes were driven by a focus on infant mortality. The IFPRI study also cited the need for these States to continue to build links between social protection, livelihoods, agriculture and poverty reduction programmes.

Several of these programmes identified vitamin supplementation and behavioural interventions to change feeding practices, along with early and exclusive breastfeeding, as among the most important post-natal interventions. Ensuring neo-natal survival through appropriate care is also key.[16]

Reduce the Number of Children Out of School

Despite the rise in enrolment rates, there are still 244 million children worldwide who are out of school; almost half are in Asia.[17] In India, about five per cent of all children of primary school age and 30 per cent of all children of upper secondary age are not in school. Most drop out after starting; some in remote areas never start. Since many of these children come from among the poorest and most disadvantaged groups in society, addressing their needs will contribute to reducing overall poverty and inequity.

However, the marginal cost of reaching these children may be high, since the disadvantaged may live in remote areas. Traditional supply-side interventions to enhance access—such as school-building—may not work; even if you build a school, pupils may not come. These interventions need to be supplemented by demand-side interventions targeting poor families, such as through conditional cash transfers.

There is now ample evidence that cash transfers that are conditional on school attendance have been successful in getting children to school and keeping them there.[18] Innovations for Poverty Action (IPA) has classified conditional cash transfers as a 'best bet' intervention.[19]

Improve the Quality of Basic Education

The quality of India's schooling refers to the idea that after adjusting for what children actually learn (as measured by harmonized test scores), the contribution of the expected years of schooling to productivity diminishes by the equivalent of four school years. This reduction is about double that of Vietnam. In rural India, nearly three-quarters of students in grade 3 could not solve a two-digit subtraction such as '46–17=29', and by grade 5, half of them could still not do so. Almost 40 per cent of grade 2 students in parts of Nepal could not read a single word of a short text; in rural India, the percentage was over 80 per cent.[20] Such children will not be able to acquire the skills that human capital theory argues are essential.

According to the World Bank's flagship *World Development Report 2018*, learners first need to be prepared and motivated, including through interventions in early ages via early childhood education and stimulating classroom interactions.[21] Nobel Laureate James Heckman explains this as follows:

> The highest rate of return in early childhood development comes from investing as early as possible, from birth through age five, in disadvantaged families [...] Efforts should focus on the first years for the greatest efficiency and effectiveness. The best investment is in quality early childhood development from birth to five for disadvantaged children and their families.[22]

In India, while there are clear and progressive policies to promote early childhood education, 'the learning outcomes of children continue to be suboptimal', according to a recent comprehensive review.[23] Opportunities are not offered universally and the system is fragmented. The report calls for the central Ministry of Education to coordinate and strengthen the learning content of the present pre-school programmes, which are currently health-focused.

Another focus of policy should be the performance of teachers across all levels of education. According to the World Bank's *World Development Report 2018*: 'equipped and motivated teachers are the most fundamental ingredient of learning,' and they also account for the largest budget item.[24] Yet, many education systems employ teachers who have little mastery of the subjects that they are supposed to teach. Teachers who are adequately trained and motivated, and who are provided with appropriate curricula and materials, are among the essential ingredients of human capital formation.[25]

Within schools, two sets of interventions have been successful in Indian settings. The first is 'structured pedagogy', which means:

> ...applying a combination of core supports to teaching and learning. These usually include teacher training, lesson plans, and teachers guides; materials for learners such as textbooks, worksheets, and storybooks; and ongoing support and monitoring of teachers through coaching, refresher trainings, and other system supports [...] These core elements are designed to be jointly integrated and mutually reinforcing, to promote evidence-based approaches to teaching literacy and numeracy.[26]

The second is Teaching at the Right Level (TaRL), an initiative that was piloted and scaled up by Pratham, an Indian NGO. TaRL recognizes that classrooms include children at different learning levels, yet teachers tend to focus on the highest end of the distribution. 'Fundamental principles of these interventions include focusing on foundational skills of literacy and numeracy, regularly assessing children on these skills, grouping children by their ability level rather than age or grade, and teaching key concepts such as phonics in active pedagogies, rather than simply focusing on completing curriculum.'[27]

Address the Health Transition by Improving Access to Health Services

Disability-adjusted life years (DALYs) are 'the sum of the years of life lost due to premature mortality and the years lived with a disability due to prevalent cases of the disease or health condition in a population, for every disease.'[28]

Using the DALY metric, it is clear that the nature of the global disease burden is changing, and India is no exception (Figures 1a and 1b). There is a marked shift from communicable, maternal and nutritional diseases to noncommunicable diseases, such as cardiovascular disease, cancers, and mental or substance use disorders. Such diseases are very costly, not only because they are debilitating, but also because they require expensive testing and treatment, including long and expensive stays in hospitals and other tertiary care facilities. A recent study showed that cancer had the highest likelihood of causing financial hardship for both inpatients and outpatients.[29]

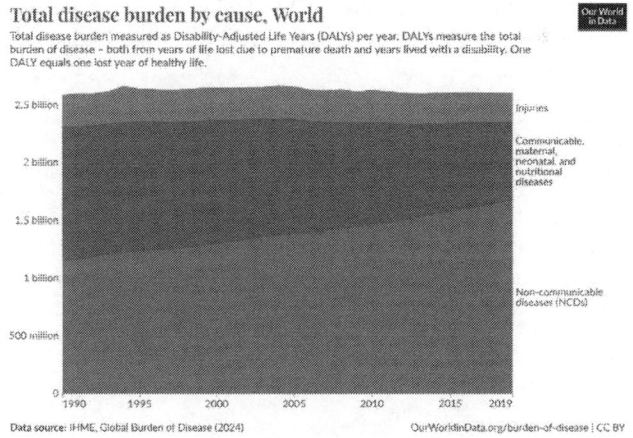

Figure 1a: Global Disease Burden

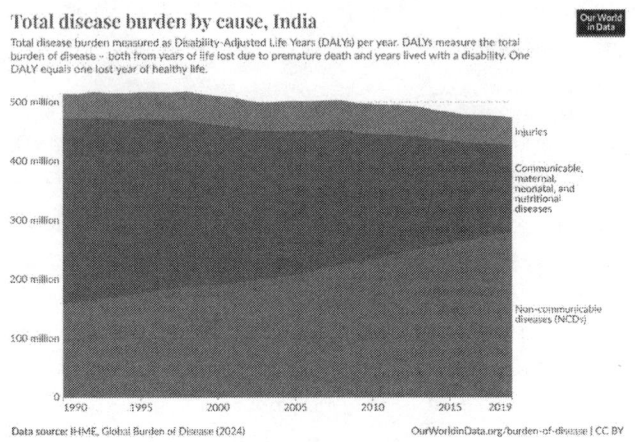

Figure 1b: India's Disease Burden

The policy challenge is to reduce this burden of noncommunicable diseases and its effects on the labour force. Evidence exists. As noted earlier, 5,772 of the impact evaluations in the International Initiative for Impact Evaluation's Development Evidence Portal were in the health sector.[30] Many of these evaluations were focused on which types of primary healthcare services work well. A recent systematic review pointed to key strategies such as:

> Community health programs or community-directed healthcare interventions, school-based healthcare services, student-led healthcare services, outreach services or mobile clinics, family health programmes, empanelment, community health funding schemes, telemedicine, promoting the role of traditional medicine, working with non-profit private sectors and non-governmental organizations (NGOs) including faith-based organizations...[31]

Many of these strategies involve effective prevention campaigns to reduce the incidence of disease. Behavioural change can be induced by disseminating information about health risks, for example on tobacco use or on poor diets. These efforts can only be mounted through collective action supported by governments.[32] Similarly, behavioural nudges which use mobile phone reminders or routine signalling through bracelets to promote childhood immunization are emerging innovations that can be scaled up.[33]

Another function of the government is to make it more affordable for people to seek and obtain the necessary care. This is an enormous challenge in developing countries. In low- and middle-income countries, 43–46 per cent of all health spending (including voluntary health insurance contributions) comes from households, compared with 21–26 per cent in high-income countries. These numbers reflect the budget constraints of governments, which are only partially offset by donor assistance (in low-income countries, 27 per cent of the health spending comes from external aid).[34]

Governments need to intervene because private markets for health insurance are inherently inefficient. Incomplete information leads to problems of moral hazard and adverse selection. Moral hazard occurs because if insurers pay, consumers may use more of the service or take less care of themselves, leading to higher costs for all. Adverse selection occurs because individuals face different risks; those who know themselves to be at higher risk are motivated to buy and use more insurance, leading to insurers trying to freeze them out or charge them higher prices. Some high-income countries mandate insurance through a single-payer (or national health) system. Others require private individuals to purchase health insurance, but subsidize the burden for the poor.

India has launched several schemes to tackle these well-known problems, including Ayushman Bharat, launched in 2018, which calls itself 'the largest health assurance scheme in the world'.[35] While Ayushman Bharat is promising, a recent review concluded that the scheme over-emphasized hospitalization, and that the level of financing of health by the government was low: 'Thus, the overall financial protection offered by the government schemes is limited, putting a lot of stress on the limited household finances.'[36]

Develop Skills for the Changing Nature of Work

A high HCI will not guarantee a demographic dividend if the human capital is not deployed appropriately. Macroeconomic and public finance policies must ensure economic growth that will provide income-earning opportunities for 18-year-olds. And of course, their contribution to productivity will be enhanced further if they continue developing human capital beyond that age.

This means countries need to put in place the right enabling environment for the youth to continue to acquire the skills that they need for the emerging and fast-changing labour market of a rapidly growing economy. At the highest levels, India seems to be doing well. According to a 2023 analysis, 56 of the Fortune 500 chief executive officers or CEOs (about 11 per cent) are immigrants in the United States.[37] They come from 28 different countries, but the study found that India, by far, has given America the most foreign-born chief executives—more than a third (10), followed some way behind by Italy (4), the UK (3) and Argentina (3). According to a recent article in *Forbes*, 'Companies currently led or owned by Indians have a market capitalization of more than $6 trillion, just over 10% of the total market cap of all companies listed on the NASDAQ.'[38] Many of these CEOs are the products of the top tertiary institutions in India, including the renowned Indian Institutes of Technology (IITs) and the Indian Institutes of Management (IIMs), as well as the top universities in India. But only a small proportion of Indians reach this level. Are young Indians across all socioeconomic levels ready for the job markets of the future?

The working environment is changing rapidly as technology is changing the skills needed for work:

The demand for less advanced skills that can be replaced by technology is declining. At the same time, the demand for advanced cognitive skills, socio-behavioral skills, and skill combinations associated with greater adaptability is rising.[39]

This means that the aspirations of young Indians to secure stable lifetime employment in an unskilled or semi-skilled job and earn a decent living in the formal sector may be difficult to achieve. What are the skills that will make India's human capital more adaptable? Skills that are in demand include problem-solving, rather than the rote memorization of facts. Young Indian workers will need 'noncognitive' characteristics to succeed in the new working world—including motivation, attitudes, self-belief, values and learning strategies—to enable them to apply their agency responsibly and effectively.[40] These noncognitive skills have been identified as drivers of cognitive performance in the Programme for International Student Assessment (PISA) tests,[41] although their impact on future earnings is more uncertain.[42]

India needs to improve the access to expensive upper technical and higher education needs. Budget constraints mean that this access generally cannot be granted through free places for all who apply. Such a policy would not only be unaffordable, but also inequitable because more of such subsidies would accrue to those who have finished secondary school and are from better-off families. Private returns from an investment in education remain very high,[43] although they are realized only after leaving school and starting a job. The priority should be to develop a market for student loans, combined with targeted scholarships for smart and promising students from poor backgrounds who would not be able to provide the collateral for such loans.[44]

The Way and the Will

While the emerging economies of Southeast and South Asia, including India, have improved some of their human development indicators dramatically over the past 50 years, there is a substantial unfinished agenda if they are to benefit fully from the demographic dividend that propelled the 'East Asian Miracle' in 1965–90. For India, the priorities include improving the nutritional status of young children, reducing the number of children and youth who are still out of school, improving the quality of basic education, addressing the health transition, and developing skills for the changing nature of work.

Robust studies of what works to improve human development

outcomes have been undertaken, many of them within India. More research is needed on those issues which are promising but not yet definitively shown to be effective. The evidence from these studies can show how India can benefit from its demographic dividend. But evidence will not be enough; for India to fully develop its human capital, it will also take a significant amount of will.

Roberto Zagha

Latin America's Failure to Catch Up: The Examples of Argentina and Brazil[1]

The focus of the World Bank's 1991 annual World Development Report was on 'The Challenge of Development'. In it, the chapter on the role of the state was controversial. The rise of Thatcherism in the UK and the Republican Revolution in the US, the collapse of communism, and developing country debt crises gave impetus to market fundamentalism and raised doubts that the state needed to play a leading role in development. This is the context of my first meeting with Shankar Acharya, who, as division chief for the public finance unit, gave comments on that controversial chapter. The wisdom, calm and lucidity—free of ideology—with which Shankar approached the chapter, and his clear guidance, were of invaluable help in my struggle to articulate a role for the state which was grounded in development economics and pragmatism. Shortly thereafter, Shankar left Washington to become chief economist of the government of India. The following 20 years of my working on India offered me many opportunities to benefit from his understanding and his insights. My wife Patricia and I also had the good fortune of meeting Shankar's wife Gayatri while living in India, and together we greatly enjoyed their immense knowledge and sure judgements on all manner of things, including literature. His columns in *Business Standard* were a particularly important source of analyses and insights. It is a pleasure and an honour to offer this tribute to all that Shankar has signified and brought me over the years.

■

With the collapse of European colonial empires after the Second World War came awareness that it was unacceptable for a large part of humanity to live in poverty and hunger in 'under-developed' Africa, Asia and Latin America. In what was to become the beginning of development economics, economists studied the problems of 'backwardness' and what would enable 'under-developed' countries to catch up with advanced economies.

Latin America stood apart. Contrary to peers in Asia and Africa, Latin American countries had long been free from their colonial masters. They had developed the modern nation state and some had already taken measures to industrialize, educate and accelerate their development. Most importantly, Latin America's per capita income in 1960 was three times that of Africa, four times that of South Asia, and five times that of China. Because of their vast natural resources, Latin America and Africa's development prospects were seen as promising, in contrast to those of overpopulated Asia—a view captured in Gunnar Myrdal's book *Asian Drama*.[2] In the 1960s, overpopulation and limited natural resources led many economists, including Nobel Prize winner James Meade,[3] to consider these countries as 'basket cases' which turned out to be development successes, for example Bangladesh, Indonesia, Korea, Singapore and Mauritius.

Some 60 years later, Latin America's per capita income continues to be three times that of Africa. However, whereas it was five times that of China in 1960, it is now 75 per cent as large. Whereas it was 400 per cent of South Asia's per capita income in 1960, it is now just 50 per cent higher. Clearly, natural resources have not powered superior growth, while high population-land ratios were not insurmountable liabilities. Except for Guyana which, thanks to oil discoveries, saw its annual per capita income grow at 3.2 per cent over 1960–2022, no Latin American country has been able to grow at rates significantly above two per cent a year, and most have grown at rates well below that. Often touted as a model, Chile's per capita annual income growth in the last sixty years has been 2.4 per cent—the highest in Latin America—compared with 6.4 per cent for China, 5.8 per cent for Korea, or 3.2 per cent for India and Indonesia.

What has held back Latin America's economic growth? While each Latin American country has its own story, in each case, a combination of four factors have been at play in different degrees.

First, the colonial period ended with highly unequal distributions of incomes and assets. In Bolivia, a few families owned the country's tin, silver, zinc and land. In other countries, it was the ownership of land and other assets which was highly concentrated. In Brazil, 60 per cent of the GDP went to 10 per cent of the richest households, whereas only 10 per cent went to the bottom 50 per cent. While Brazil has the reputation of being an extreme case, most Latin American countries have similar highly concentrated income distributions. In these countries, around 60 per cent of the GDP goes to the richest 10 per cent, and 10 per cent or less goes to the bottom 50 per cent. In East Asia, the corresponding figures are 40–45 per cent for the richest 10 per cent, and over 10 per cent for the bottom 50 per cent.[4]

The concentration of wealth and income in relatively few hands has created resistance to structural changes with long-term effects and broad-based impacts, such as education and labour-intensive industrial development. Redistributive industrialization and economic development programmes have tended to be resisted by the elites well served by the status quo.

Second, expanding on the 1823 Monroe Doctrine, the United States intervened in Latin American countries to counter domestic threats to elites aligned with the US. The case of Cuba is well known. Less known is the case of Guatemala where the US intervened in 1952–53 to protect the interests of the American-owned United Fruit Company—thwarting land reform and legislation discontinuing the landowners' forced use of unpaid labour. In Panama, El Salvador, Nicaragua and others, the US toppled governments to establish regimes sympathetic to the US. In Brazil in 1964, the US supported a military coup against a democratically elected government committed to land reform. In 1976, the US supported a military coup in Argentina against a Peronist government.

In Chile, in June 1970, months before Salvador Allende's electoral victory, Henry Kissinger, President Nixon's national security adviser, indicated, 'I don't see why we need to stand by and watch a country go communist due to the irresponsibility of its people. The issues are much too important for the Chilean voters to be left to decide for themselves.'[5] And once Allende was elected, Nixon told his National Security Council: 'Our main concern is [...] that [Allende] can consolidate himself, and the picture projected to the world will be his success [...] If we let the potential leaders in South America think they can move like Chile [...] we will be in trouble [...] No impression should be permitted in Latin America that they can get away with this.'⁶ These are a few examples of the US derailing governments committed to alternative development models.

Third, abundant natural resources bring with them the risk of Dutch disease, which puts pressure on the exchange rate to appreciate to levels that discourage industrialization. Furthermore, volatility in world commodity markets introduces short-term exchange rate fluctuations inimical to long-term investments and structural change. Most Latin American countries—with the exception of Chile—have done little to counter the Dutch disease effects.

Fourth, macroeconomic management has often performed very poorly. The popular narrative is that Latin American countries have suffered from excessive government intervention and fiscal excesses. Undoubtedly relevant, this assessment is, however, incomplete. This essay highlights the devastating consequences of macroeconomic programmes which were too often driven by orthodoxy rather than outcomes, were based on excessive external borrowings, and sacrificed long-term growth to stabilization. The cases of Argentina and Brazil— that have been examined in more detail—are illustrative of this. Equally important, Latin American countries have eschewed the East Asian growth strategy based on exports of manufactured goods and large investments in infrastructure.

The Growth Record

For low- and middle-income countries, the development challenge consists of catching up with advanced economies. At least until recently, the US per capita income, along with that of other advanced economies, has been growing at a secular rate of two per cent per year in real terms. Thus, developing countries need persistent growth at rates much higher than that to catch up within a reasonable time-horizon. Countries such as Korea, Singapore, Japan, and now China, India and Vietnam have been able to grow at such rates. Figure 1 shows that Argentina and Brazil have not been able to. Argentina has actually lost ground and fallen from its place among the world's richest countries at the beginning of the twentieth century; the gap between Argentina and the US has increased considerably. For Brazil, the evolution has been one of rapid growth followed by stagnation. Brazil doubled its per capita income between 1900 and 1940, and quintupled it between 1940 and 1980—the years of the 'Brazil miracle'.[7] Recent research has cast doubts on the magnitude of this growth and has suggested a correction of roughly 16 per cent to the compound annual growth rate.[8] Even with this correction, the performance was remarkable and only matched by East Asian countries after the Second World War. Brazil's per capita income thus increased from 10 per cent of that of the US in 1960 to 25 per cent in 1980. Since then, growth has been negligible and the ratio has declined to 20 per cent.

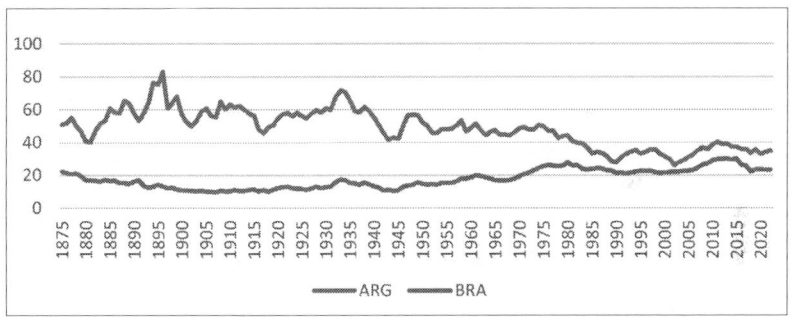

Figure 1: Per Capita Income in PPP Terms as a Percentage (%) of US Per Capita GDP, 1875–2022

Source: Maddison Project.

Argentina's Fall: Three Orthodox Shock Therapies[9]

At the end of the 1800s and the beginning of the 1900s, abundant foreign investment—mostly British—integrated Argentina's rich agriculture into the world economy. The First World War and the 1929 crisis brought those golden years to an end. Both caused price declines which disrupted agricultural exports—the heart of Argentina's economy. Foreign investment declined and the rich Western economies became protectionist and inward-oriented. The world changed, but Argentina didn't change its strategy. There was no consistent attempt to diversify the economy to render it less dependent on agriculture and external capital.

The Perón period brought change. During 1943–55, first as minister of labour, and then as the twice democratically elected president, Juan Perón introduced measures to industrialize Argentina and reduce dependency on foreign capital. Massive investments in infrastructure, reduction of external debt, social programmes and industrialization gave impetus to domestic demand and brought gains to low-income groups. Factory workers received paid vacations and unions gained unprecedented power. Women's suffrage was granted.

At the same time, however, high levels of industrial protection limited the industries' ability to compete internationally. The nationalization of the British-owned railroads and other properties antagonized business leaders and caused investment to dry up. State intervention in agriculture led to such disruption that one of the world's largest agricultural exporters had to briefly import cereals. Regulations inhibiting private sector activities and fiscal excesses also hindered growth. At the beginning of the 1950s, there were attempts to reduce government intervention and introduce better fiscal discipline, but it was too little and too late. Inflation soared to 40 per cent per year and real wages plunged. Labour strikes paralyzed the country; the military intervened in 1955 and sent Perón into exile. Mistakes notwithstanding, Argentina's per capita income grew at 1.6 per cent per year during 1943–55: a rate that was low in relation to the golden years, high in relation to what was to come.

Fiscal austerity, the weakening of labour protections, financial and market deregulation, openness to external capital, and import liberalization have since been seen as steps to resolve a crisis and put the country on the road to prosperity, as if undoing what had been done during 1943–55 was sufficient. Post 1955, Peronist and anti-Peronist governments, whether democratically elected or military dictatorships, supported by the IMF and external capital, often fell prey to the belief that extreme orthodoxy was a solution to Argentina's economic woes.

When these policies did not bring about the expected results, the conclusion was 'more needed': more fiscal austerity, tighter money, more labour market deregulation, more opening, more financial liberalization. In 2004, while Argentina had not yet emerged from the worst economic crisis in its history after a decade of orthodox reforms which were strongly supported by the IMF and external capital, the IMF deputy management director quoted Robert Louis Stevenson while commenting on the situation: 'Meant well, tried a little, failed much.'[10]

Following the first Peronist episode, this thinking inspired three orthodox shock therapies, the cumulative effect of which explains a great deal of Argentina's poor post-war growth performance. Each one of these episodes left unmanageable external debts. The first one (1976–83) followed a military coup led by General Jorge Rafael Videla. In a few weeks, Videla and Minister of Finance Martínez de Hoz introduced an economic programme to reduce import protection without giving the industry any time to adapt, froze wages, weakened trade unions, liberalized the financial system, cut public spending, increased interest rates, and appreciated the exchange rate to contain inflation—a measure which, coming on top of rapid reductions in import tariffs, led to an industrial crisis. When democracy returned in 1983, the per capita income was at the 1976 levels. The external debt had risen from $9 billion in 1976 to $46 billion in 1983. Industry—39 per cent of the GDP in 1976—had declined to 30 per cent (13 per cent at present).

The return to democracy was turbulent. 1983–89 were years of hyperinflation, agreements and disagreements with the IMF, an external debt crisis induced by the excessive borrowings of the previous periods, and more declines in the GDP—Argentina's per capita income in 1989 was 12 per cent below its 1983 levels.

The second shock (1989–2002) started in 1989 when the new, democratically elected Peronist government under President Carlos Menem with Minister of Finance Domingo Cavallo announced a radical conservative programme consisting of significant fiscal adjustments, import tariff reductions, large-scale privatization, labour reforms and an exchange rate set at parity with the US$ by law. Supported by the IMF and foreign investors, the programme initially had good results. Driven by consumption, large current account deficits accumulated— financed willingly by external lenders; the GDP per capita rose by 33 per cent in the first ten years of the programme.

However, the inability to depreciate the exchange rate to keep up with inflation, bulging current account deficits, a rising external debt, and the aftershocks of the East Asia and Russia external crises ended in a massive crisis in 2001–02 when inflation climbed to two digits. The fixed exchange rate regime was abandoned. A recession and the associated loss of tax revenue were aggravated by the cost of shifting the pension system from pay-as-you-go to a fully-funded one. Panic took hold and some decisions supported by the IMF compounded the problem. To contain fiscal deficits, a law was passed making them illegal, but had little effect. The government lost control of its public finances, was unable to honour its foreign debt ($65 billion in 1989, $153 billion in 2002), and lost access to external finance. Much of the per capita income gains obtained since 1989 were lost. In 2002, the per capita income was just five per cent above the 1989 levels.

Several Peronist governments followed and remained in power over a period of 14 years, during which a unilateral cancellation of a part of the external debt and a large devaluation in 2002 helped exports and growth recover: per capita income rose by two per cent per year during 2003–15. But bad economic habits came back—exchange appreciation and price controls to combat inflation, combined with fiscal excesses, brought growth to a halt and ended what might have been a sustainable recovery.

The third of Argentina's crises started in December 2015 when a democratically elected government brought 14 years of Peronism to an end and introduced a new shock therapy. Nine years later, in 2024, that crisis is ongoing and the prospects for its resolution are dim.

President Mauricio Macri was elected (four-year term) in December 2015 on the basis of popular and ambitious programmes. The electorate was tired of high inflation, unemployment and rising poverty. The Macri government promised growth (a target of cumulative 11 per cent during the four years of his mandate), reduction of unemployment, halving of poverty and lower inflation. The annual inflation rate in 2015 was 26 per cent, but would have been much higher were it not for freezes of utility prices and an exchange rate appreciation of more than 40 per cent.

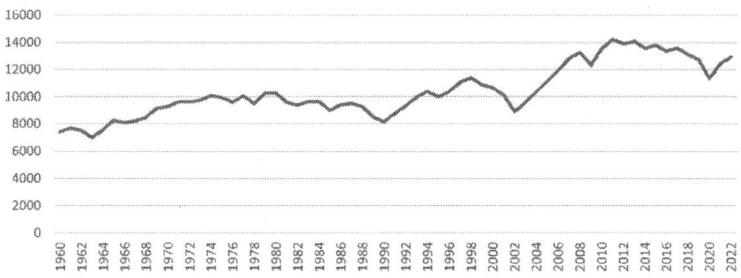

Figure 2: Argentina—GDP Per Capita (Constant 2015 US$), 1960-2022

Orthodoxy guided Macri's economic programme: fiscal austerity, independence of the Argentinian Central Bank (Banco Central de la República Argentina, BCRA), inflation targeting with a four to six per cent target to be reached by the last year of the Macri government in 2019, real interest rates as high as necessary, a floating exchange rate, and the elimination of all restrictions on the capital account. Macri's programme was strongly supported by foreign investors, the IMF, other international organizations (World Bank, OCDE), and the economic media. The IMF supported the programme with one of its largest loans in history without the foreign exchange controls which could have prevented the capital outflows that followed. In just four years, external debt rose from $177 billion in 2015 to $280 billion in 2019. Such was the external lenders' euphoria that, notwithstanding its history of defaults, Argentina was able to issue a $2.75 billion bond with the maturity of 100 years at 7.125 per cent in 2017. The bond attracted $9.75 billion in orders from investors.[11]

At the end of his term in December 2019, President Macri left Argentina in crisis. The results of the programme were worse than the most pessimistic forecasts. GDP growth was negative in three of the four years between 2016 and 2019, per capita GDP in 2019 was eight per cent below the 2015 levels, unemployment was over 10 per cent, and the poverty rate was the highest in history. The government's fiscal targets were not achieved; from 53 per cent of the GDP in 2015, public debt rose to 76 per cent in 2019. Inflation shot up with accumulated inflation at 340 per cent during 2015-19.

Accepting that orthodox policies had generated dismal results was difficult: 18 months before the unravelling of the economic programme, the IMF approved a $50 billion loan. A few weeks before Argentina made its difficulties servicing its external debt public, the IMF Deputy Director announced: 'The [...] authorities continue to show a strong commitment to their economic policy program, meeting all the applicable targets under the Fund-supported program [...] these [...] efforts are starting to bear fruit.'[12]

What Went Wrong?

In a Brookings Paper, the former Governor of the BCRA argues that the fiscal adjustment was too gradual and the BCRA was not granted enough independence,[13] a stance difficult to reconcile with what we know. In Macri's first months, the government ignored violent popular protests and increased public utility prices at once by 100–300 per cent—an adjustment equivalent to three per cent of the GDP over 2016–17, even though public debt was moderate at 53 per cent of the GDP. The BCRA freed the exchange rate and opened the capital account, leading to a 40 per cent devaluation in the first few weeks of Macri's term, and unbridled external borrowing thereafter. The BCRA also had sufficient autonomy to let real interest rates rise to 10–15 per cent in a world with real rates near zero. The interest cost of public debt rose from 1.6 per cent of the GDP in 2015 to four per cent of the GDP in 2019, creating further pressure on the fisc.

From the beginning, the Argentine Treasury and others[14] opposed the BCRA programme, arguing that the inflation targets were too ambitious and the required real interest rates excessive. Moreover, the economic logic of inflation targeting is to increase interest rates to contain demand, and thus not applicable to an economy plagued by recession and high unemployment. In fact, the problem with Macri's economic programme was not excessive gradualism or insufficient central bank independence, but faulty design in at least three respects. The contraction of the public sector, supply-side reforms, and liberalized capital flows were assumed to stimulate private investment and growth in an economy with high unemployment and excess capacity. It was naïve to expect entrepreneurs to invest in an economy with significant slack and so much relative price volatility.

Misdiagnosing the cause of inflation was also devastating to the plan. In a country as dollarized as Argentina, with a floating exchange rate and an open capital account, inflation is not driven by excess demand, but by expectations of exchange rate devaluation. As had been in the case of the hyperinflation in Brazil in the 1990s, the domestic currency continued to be used in transactions, but ceased to be the unit of account, which became the dollar. Inflation expectations reflect the expected evolution of the exchange rate.[15] Interest rates had to reach extraordinarily high levels to prevent a depreciation of the currency and contain inflation. High and unstable interest and exchange rates depressed, rather than increased, private domestic investment.

Finally, high real interest rates with an open capital account attracted foreign capital. Excessive borrowing meant that Argentina once again went through an over-borrowing spree. The 2017 100-year Argentina bond is now trading at half its value. IMF data suggests that the increase in external indebtedness financed capital outflows of residents protecting their assets from domestic uncertainty.[16]

The years since 2019 have been marked by a return to Peronism with the government under Alberto Fernández (2020–23) and Minister of Finance Martín Guzmán. Saddled with a large external debt, inflation, and the threat of a default, there was little that the Fernández government could do. The only solution would have been to repudiate the external debt, which he refused to do. Following a default in 2020, a debt restructuring gave the economy some respite, but not much, given the magnitude of the debt problem. The government implemented some fiscal adjustment measures which failed to stabilize the economy. Inflation continued, but the decline in the GDP was arrested. It even increased by a few percentage points.

After four years of inflation and unemployment, the electorate voted the Peronists out of office in December 2023 with the election of the anti-Peronist Javier Milei for the four-year period 2024–27. The new president was elected on a platform promising radical change for Argentina: dramatic cuts in government spending, the dismantling of important government agencies, shutting down the BCRA, large-scale privatization and labour market deregulation. Congress has resisted some of the most extreme measures and it is too early to assess the likelihood of the government's success. But past experience offers little ground for optimism.

Brazil's Decline

Since 1980, Argentina's per capita GDP has grown at an annual compound rate of 0.5 per cent and Brazil's at 0.7 per cent. This implies four decades of stagnation for the two countries once facing a bright economic future. Whereas Argentina's fall came from its faith in shock therapies and an open capital account, Brazil's decline followed a change in strategic priorities—stabilization became more important than economic growth. In a society traumatized by hyperinflation, it is natural for monetary stability to become an important social preference. But an exclusive concern with stabilization saps the foundations of growth and becomes a threat to stability itself: Brazil's stagnation resulted from economic asphyxiation.

Brazil's industrialization started in the nineteenth century when the 1844 Alves Branco Tariff raised tariffs on imported goods to a minimum of 30 per cent, and to 60 per cent for those with domestic equivalents. The opposition from traders and elites was strong. Persuaded that industrialization was needed for the country's future, Emperor Don Pedro II persisted; Brazil had its first surge of industrialization. Then in the 1880s, slavery was abolished, and in the 1890s, the empire became a republic.

There were other surges of industrialization, particularly during the First World War when import supply was constrained. Also, ironically, during the 1929 economic depression, large government purchases of coffee—to compensate politically powerful growers for the declines in international prices—amounted to unintended counter-cyclical fiscal policies which stimulated domestic demand and sustained industrialization and growth.

A more systematic approach to industrialization and growth took place in 1930–45—years during which an inspired politician Getúlio Vargas seized power in an army-supported coup and launched a number of initiatives: investments in state-owned enterprises, infrastructure, the modernization of labour laws and the establishment of the pillars of what later became Brazil's social security. Vargas was deposed in 1945, but returned to power in 1951 when he was democratically elected, remaining president until 1954. Vargas was one of the most influential figures in Brazil's history. His strategy was based on a feverish enthusiasm for growth and faith in economic progress and was shared by many. President Juscelino Kubitschek (1957–61) promised '50 years of progress in five', and launched one of the largest investment programmes in infrastructure in Brazil's history, including the construction of Brasilia in record time. The country's love affair with growth continued after a military coup in 1964. For the military, growth legitimized their hold on power. They took a keen interest in the modernization of institutions and the strengthening of the country's growth foundations. The Central Bank of Brazil (BCB) was established, the tax system reformed, and ambitious development plans were implemented with a strong emphasis on infrastructure. The net result was the per capita income doubling during 1900–40 and quintupling during 1940–80. What was puzzling was its sudden halt in 1980, after 80 years of exceptionally rapid growth.

There was vitality in the economy after 1980, showing what would have been possible. For example, established in the 1960s with significant government support, Embraer has become the world's third largest aeronautic company. Successive governments invested heavily in agricultural research which supported the development of local varieties of a wide range of agricultural products, challenging received wisdom regarding the suitability of the country's soil and climate. Brazil has since become one of the world's largest food exporters.[17] State-owned Petrobras, now one of the world's largest oil and gas companies, is a technological leader in deep-water drilling and has transformed Brazil from a net importer of oil to a net exporter. Companhia Vale do Rio Doce is the world's second largest mining company.

Also, large investments in health and education—particularly since the return to democracy in 1985—have led to improvements in virtually all social indicators, from literacy and high school enrolment to infant mortality and life expectancy. A universal health system has brought medical care to the entire population, not a mean achievement for a country with a surface area that is four times that of India, and 220 million inhabitants.

Brazil has also strengthened its political and economic institutions. Since the end of 21 years of military rule in 1985, a progressive Constitution has established robust voting systems and electoral tribunals, given voice to minorities, and shaped institutions which have held remarkably well against authoritarian threats such as that from President Jair Bolsonaro (2019–22). On the economic front, fiscal responsibility legislation, the rescheduling of the States' debt, and enhanced independence of the BCB have provided a solid foundation for macroeconomic stability.

These accomplishments notwithstanding, Brazil's aggregate economic performance has been dismal since 1980. Periods of growth alternated with periods of stagnation or decline during which the gains of one period were lost in the next. The end of the era of high growth took place over five periods.

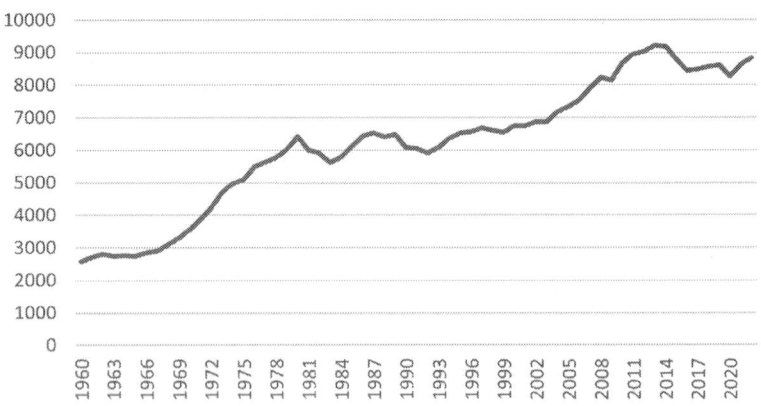

Figure 3: Brazil—Per Capita (Constant 20m US$), 1960–2022

Source: World Bank.

Unsustainable Growth (1973–80)

Brazil's economic decline started with the first oil shock. Even though during 1973–80 its per capita income rose at 4.5 per cent per year, that growth was achieved at the cost of weakening the economy's foundations. The first oil shock of 1973 hit a balance of payments that was overstretched by years of large private and public investments. As a reference, Korea's response to the same shock—being a country which was also carrying a large external debt and dependent on imports of oil, with a per capita income that was half of Brazil's (now twice Brazil's)—was to exit import-substitution, open the economy, and re-base growth on the export of manufactured goods. Brazil did the opposite. It exited a successful programme of manufacturing exports and increased tariffs to levels that exceeded 100 per cent, mostly on capital goods. The exchange rate lost touch with the real economy, was appreciated to contain inflation, and a long-abandoned regime of import licenses was reinstated. It was the start of a new phase of import-substitution—focused on substituting imports of capital goods. At the same time, a large expansion of public investment financed by external debt helped sustain growth. At the end of this period, Brazil was highly indebted and the economy had turned inwards.

Macro-Malaises (1980-94)

Inward-looking policies financed by external debt left Brazil ill-prepared for two severe external shocks: the second oil shock and the Volcker interest rate shock. From 1980 to 1994, the per capita income growth was nil, a novel reality for a country accustomed to eight decades of rapid growth.

The oil and interest rate shocks, difficulties servicing external debt, and turbulence associated with the return to democracy in 1985 derailed Brazil's macroeconomic policies for 14 years, with recurrent bouts of inflation and hyperinflation. Several stabilization packages failed. Inflation declined after each package, only to return a few months later.

Notwithstanding failures and shortcomings, one stabilization package left a strong imprint on the economy. It was introduced in March 1990, the day after the newly elected President Collor de Melo took over; inflation was then at 30 per cent per month. It was an orthodox conservative programme—ambitious and visionary—aimed at reshaping Brazil's economy and the role of the government. It combined a large privatization programme and the closing of government agencies, with a plan to reduce public sector employment by 300,000, liberalizing imports, cutting public spending, eliminating most fiscal incentives, raising public utility tariffs, freeing the exchange rate, and introducing a radical monetary freeze.

Two weaknesses of the programme were its speed, which left no time for economic actors to adjust or for the government to recalibrate the reforms as their impact became clearer, and the severity of the monetary programme. A monetary freeze aimed to stop inflation—80 per cent of all private financial assets were frozen for 18 months, remunerated at the inflation rate plus six per cent. The freeze did reduce inflation, but it also paralyzed the payments system and the economy. The GDP fell by four per cent in 1990, and would have fallen further were the economy not 're-monetized' chaotically, through a growing number of loopholes providing liquidity to selected sectors. With the 're-monetization', inflation climbed back to 20 per cent a month.

While the federal deficit could not be reduced for reasons ranging from an increased proportion of federal taxes to be shared with the states to a 'job-stability' clause for government employees in the 1988 Constitution, the privatization programme and the opening of the economy moved forward. Most importantly, the 1990 reforms sought to reduce the role of the government.

A costly legacy of this period has been the dismantling of the government planning and implementing capacities, a prowess of the high growth period. Notwithstanding the generous incentives for its participation in infrastructure building, the private sector has not been able to compensate for the public sector withdrawal. Public and private investments in infrastructure have been at barely one per cent of the GDP since then, below depreciation rates, whereas it is around six to seven per cent of the GDP in fast-growing emerging economies.

Under the threat of impeachment for alleged irregularities, President Collor resigned in September 1992 and was replaced by his vice president, but inflation continued to increase. It reached 40 per cent per month in February 1994 when the minister of finance, future president Fernando Henrique Cardoso, introduced the Plano Real.

The Third Period

The third period started with the 1994 Plano Real, a successful stabilization plan conceived by Brazilian economists.[18] The success gave Fernando Henrique Cardoso the popularity to be elected as president. In addition to a moderate fiscal correction, the plan was based on the insight that the price index itself could become the unit of account, and thus the basis for a stable new currency: the real. This unorthodox plan—which the IMF declined to support—brought inflation down to single-digit figures without the growth slowdown that typically accompanies stabilization. But it didn't reanimate growth. Per capita income rose by an annual rate of 0.6 per cent during these five years. One weakness of the plan was the exchange rate, which was maintained in a narrow band vis-à-vis the US dollar ($). This exchange rate policy helped control expectations, but it quickly became overvalued, even at the more modest rates of inflation that were prevailing then, and there was no correction until 1999. Another weakness was the absence of focus on the sources of long-term economic growth—infrastructure, manufacturing exports and industrial development were all neglected in favour of stabilization measures. Rising structural weaknesses—deindustrialization, increasing reliance on primary goods exports, rising informality in the labour market, plummeting investment levels, insufficient investment in infrastructure—did not attract much attention in the formulation of policies.

The Fourth Part of the Story (1999 to 2015)

This part is about the 'triad' which continues to guide Brazil's macroeconomic policies. The 1997 East Asia crisis triggered large capital outflows which put pressure on the already scarce foreign exchange reserves and threatened to re-ignite inflation. Ironically, the IMF recommendation at the time was to follow the example of the Argentina dollarization, just a few months before its collapse.[19] Fortunately in 1999, well advised by Brazilian economists, the government put in place a new and sophisticated macroeconomic policy, the triad, consisting of three pillars: a primary fiscal surplus (achieved with tax increases), a floating exchange rate (thus triggering a much-needed devaluation), and increased independence of a central bank mandated to achieve inflation targets.

The 'triad' was able to deal with the 1999 consequences of the East Asia crisis, capital flight, and the decline in reserves. Helped by a commodity boom, the annual per capita income grew at 2.5 per cent between 1999 and 2014. With the successful political and economic transition to a left-wing moderate President Luiz Inácio Lula da Silva (2002–11), the triad generated considerable optimism. In 2003, Goldman Sachs put forward the concept of BRICS,[20] a group of countries with strong growth potential. In 2012, Article IV of the IMF concluded: 'The past decade has seen a remarkable social transformation in Brazil, underpinned by macroeconomic stability and rising living standards,' and projected a GDP growth in the four to five per cent range from 2013 onwards. This optimism was shared by most international financial institutions and the economic press.

Conceived to deal with short-term stabilization, the triad was, however, maintained well beyond its useful life. Structural weaknesses that had developed since 1980—which the triad accentuated—were not addressed. The triad was based on the BCB's freedom to set interest rates as high as necessary to meet its mandate. The result was that in real terms, interest rates have been 'the highest on the planet' since 1999.[21] There was no concern with the impacts on the real economy, or exchange rate appreciation and exports. Growth was not part of this macroeconomic framework. The only concern was inflation.

High interest rates stimulated speculative financial inflows, kept the exchange rate overvalued, penalized investments and industrial production, undercut exports, and made interest payments on public debt (which would have otherwise been manageable) Brazil's largest fiscal expenditure item (six to eight per cent of the GDP since the Plano Real). Real interest rates exceeding real GDP growth for more than two decades made stabilizing the debt-to-GDP ratio unrealistic. Primary surpluses were achieved at the cost of reducing public investment to negligible levels for the last 25 years with serious consequences for infrastructure investment—now around one per cent of the GDP. Exchange rate appreciation penalized tradables. From over one-third of the GDP in 1980, manufacturing declined to 10 per cent of the GDP. Manufacturing exports became a negligible share of total exports. Total investment declined to less than one-fifth of the GDP. Once again, stability was achieved at the cost of weakening the economy's foundations.

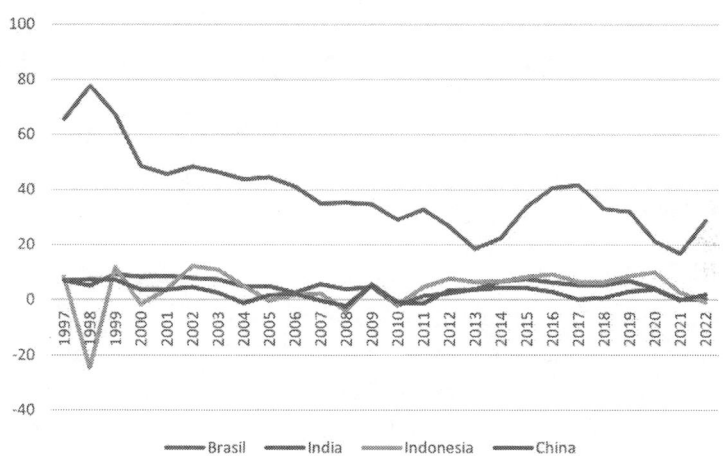

Figure 4: Real Lending Interest Rates, 1997–2022

Source: World Bank.

The Fifth Part of the Story (2015 to the Present)

The fifth part of the story is not a happy one. The GDP declined by five per cent in 2015 and a further four per cent in 2016, i.e. 10 per cent below its 2014 level. The economy has not fully recovered yet. Per capita income in 2023 is still slightly below 2014 levels.

What explains this collapse? The conventional answer is fiscal profligacy. Dilma Rousseff—first elected in 2011 after eight years of Lula as president—was seen to be spending her way to a second mandate in a close election in 2014. There were indeed fiscal and monetary excesses preceding the 2014 election: delays in adjusting utility tariffs, an artificially over-valued exchange rate, and politically motivated credit expansion through state-owned banks.

As her second mandate started, in January 2015, a number of economists persuaded President Roussef that an orthodox correction was needed. In retrospect, it is clear that it wasn't. Growth did not collapse because of President Dilma's excesses. It collapsed because of the way they were corrected. At around 70 per cent of the GDP, public debt was manageable and so was a 10 per cent inflation. Unemployment was in excess of 10 per cent. Yet President Dilma chose a path of rapid and severe fiscal contraction, large public utilities tariff adjustments, and increases in interest rates, which were at the heart of the 2015 GDP decline.

Applauded by the IMF, the World Bank, and the international and domestic financial press, notwithstanding the severe consequences for GDP, the authorities believed in the 'contractionary fiscal expansion'.[22] Even in the midst of a recession, the idea went: lower expected future taxation would lead entrepreneurs to expand their investments in the present. However improbable it would be for entrepreneurs with idle capacity to further expand their capacity, the belief persisted despite the insightful criticism from even the architect of the Plano Real, who called for a rethinking of fiscal and monetary policies.[23] In spite of this criticism, fiscal and monetary contraction measures multiplied. After President Dilma's impeachment in 2016, an unrealistic constitutional amendment fixed public spending at its 2015 level in real terms for a 20-year period. While GDP was collapsing, inflation targets were tightened from 4.5 per cent in 2017 to three per cent in 2021. These measures were strongly supported by the IMF, the World Bank and the international and domestic financial community. But growth has been anaemic since 2017, insufficient to compensate the dramatic decline resulting from the shock therapy of 2015–16.

As in Argentina, it was difficult to accept that the 'right' policies yielded the wrong results. Such was the enthusiasm generated by these measures that while the per capita GDP was 10 per cent below 2014 levels and investment was at its lowest in fifty years, in an interview with the *Financial Times* on 27 April 2016, the IMF Director for Latin America—surprised by high levels of FDI—declared: 'Brazil's "amazing" ability to attract foreign investment notwithstanding economic and political crises augurs a better future...' Statements by Brazilian authorities and articles in the Brazilian financial press[24] suggested: 'Direct Investment in the Country Ignores the Crisis', and even mentioned a director of the BCB celebrating the historic record of 4.4 per cent of the GDP in FDI in 2016: 'This indicates that FDI has specific characteristics linked to long-term decisions, and can grow even in years of weak economic activity'. As a percentage of the GDP, FDI in Brazil had far surpassed China and India—economies with growth rates above six to seven per cent per year.

Both the IMF and BCB directors ignored their own accounting rules. As a result of a change in an IMF accounting convention, inter-company loans could be counted as FDI.[25] As indicated in several IMF Article IV reports, there is ample evidence that much of what is recorded as FDI in Brazil is financial arbitrage responding to high interest rates, and does not represent increases in productive capacity.[26]

In January 2023, President Lula returned to power for a third mandate (2023–26). Even during his campaign, he questioned the policies of the preceding years, in particular the need for very high interest rates, inflation targets as low as three per cent when growth was anaemic, and for the continued low levels of infrastructure investment (typically less than depreciation). He even suggested that the government could take on debt to finance long-lived productive infrastructure. His questions have created turmoil among economists long accustomed to unquestioned orthodoxy. As of the time of writing this, President Lula has been successful in persuading the BCB to gradually reduce interest rates; even though at 10 per cent in real terms, they continue to be among the world's highest, but he has been less successful on the other two fronts. Time will tell whether in the remaining years of his presidency, he will be able to change the growth trajectory.

What Do Argentina and Brazil's Experiences Teach Us?

We draw nine lessons from Brazil and Argentina:

(1) Stabilization programmes without a growth strategy can plunge countries into stagnation. Concern with stabilization without bringing growth explicitly into the programme explains many of the policy choices made in Argentina and Brazil, and their poor growth performance over the last several decades. Contrast

this with India's 1991 reforms in which a growth strategy was part of the policies deployed to deal with severe stabilization challenges.

(2) Economists don't have a shelf dedicated to 'bad' economic policies, and a separate one for 'good' economic policies. Orthodoxy and heterodoxy are a false dichotomy. Most economic policies succeed or fail depending on the context, history, level of development, institutions, and the time of deployment. For example, inflation targeting regimes gave good results in many countries, but both in Argentina and Brazil, the targets were excessively ambitious without giving due consideration to their effects on growth. Likewise, fluctuating exchange rates which proved destructive in Argentina are in place in a large number of countries and have borne good results. With respect to public spending, there are cases where it is necessary to reduce it, but in others, increases are needed. In short, policies that are needed in one period may become counterproductive in the next.

(3) Gradualism permits avoiding errors. Protectionism is illustrative of this. The Argentinian economy continues to be one of the least open amidst the emerging economies. Argentina exhausted the potential gains of import-substitution a long time ago. Opening the economy is important in any programme of reforms. But rushing it was counterproductive. In the three Argentina episodes, and in the Collar Plan in Brazil discussed in this essay, there were no preparations, discussions, consultations, transition periods or well-defined tariff objectives. Nor was there any concern with the appreciation of the exchange rate which penalized both exports and production for the domestic market, contributing to further deindustrialization. The same applies to most other policy areas, such as the pace of inflation reduction, especially in the case of Argentina.

(4) Both Argentina and Brazil have suffered from the lack of emphasis on exports of manufacturing products. Contrary to Asian countries, both countries have tended to think that the domestic market was sufficient to propel manufacturing growth. They ignored the fact that the size of their domestic market was a very small portion

of the global economy. Brazil's GDP is just half of California's, for example.

(5) A 'strong currency' has costs. One of the major policy errors of successive governments has been to succumb to the temptation of a strong currency to reduce the price of tradables and combat inflation. In addition to penalizing the real economy, a strong currency stimulates speculative financial capital, subsidizes imports and capital flight, and is often the preamble to a serious external crisis. Over the course of development, productivity increases lead to a natural appreciation of the exchange rate. This has been the experience of Japan, many countries in Europe and other nations which developed successfully. However, in many Latin American countries, in particular in Argentina and Brazil, the process went backwards with the currency appreciating ahead of productivity gains, facilitated—if not encouraged—by an open capital account. The importance of the exchange rate for both the macroeconomy and the microeconomy was not sufficiently appreciated.

(6) The costs and risks of an open capital account are high. Economic theory teaches us that financial liberalization brings benefits. It increases available savings, diversifies risks, accelerates financial sector development and reduces the cost of capital. Experience tells another story regarding when and where these effects dominate. Whereas foreign direct investment has positive effects on the economy—assuming the economy is not highly protected—this does not necessarily apply to financial investment. The evidence is so strong[27] that after the East Asia 1997 financial crisis, the IMF no longer pressures countries to open their capital accounts.

In the 1997 East Asia financial crisis, except for Thailand, all other countries had solid macro-foundations: low fiscal deficits, high saving rates, growth, low inflation, modest current account deficits and low external debt. But these solid foundations were unable to resist speculative flows of international capital.

One lesson from history is that the opening of the financial account of the balance of payments should take place in an advanced phase of development.[28] Restrictions on movements of capital were eliminated in Europe only in the 1980s. Switzerland did not hesitate to reintroduce restrictions to capital inflows following the 2008 crisis when the volume of foreign capital seeking a safe haven appreciated the Swiss franc and threatened the economy's competitiveness. Poor regulations are another reason for avoiding a premature opening of the capital account.

(7) There are advantages to maintaining a slightly undervalued exchange rate. In addition to the benefits an undervalued exchange rate brings to the real economy, it also limits the impact of depreciation expectations on inflation.

(8) External debt can be disruptive. Economic analysts in the media, the financial sector, the IMF, the World Bank, and the OECD largely blame public sector debt for Argentina's failures, ignoring the role of foreign debt. The omission is important.

In an economy less dependent on foreign finance, for example where the government does not borrow in foreign currency and restricts the external indebtedness of the private sector, excess domestic or public spending translates into currency depreciation and inflation, indicating excess public or private demand. This inflation tends to emerge gradually, giving fiscal and monetary authorities the time and space to take the necessary steps to reduce it to politically and socially acceptable levels. An external crisis is unlikely in an economy that is not dependent on external finance capital.

On the other hand, in an economy with liberalized access to external borrowing, there is little warning of imminent imbalances. Both in the Menem-Cavallo experience and in the more recent case of the Macri government, the IMF declared a few weeks before the crisis that the Argentine economy was on its way to macroeconomic equilibrium. The distance between a semblance of normalcy and a crisis can be very short.

With an open capital account, excesses of public or private spending are reflected in deficits in the balance of payments that, in the initial phases, can easily be financed with increases in external debt—public or private—which, in turn, put moderate pressure on the exchange rate. This results in a rise in foreign debt and the illusion of prosperity, with the economy living beyond its means.

But there is a limit even for deep-pocketed foreign investors. At some point, for rational or non-rational reasons, due to concerns with country risk or developments elsewhere, capital flows reverse and financial panic spreads quickly, and the mistrust is hard to dispel. The exchange rate depreciates abruptly and the domestic currency is dislodged as the unit of account. Cuts in public or private spending have little effect and the government loses control of external accounts and inflation. Given this dynamic, it is surprising that IMF programmes are so severe on domestic debt and yet so lenient on external debt.

(9) Central bank independence—with a unique mandate to contain inflation—has its merits, but is not a panacea. Argentina and Brazil's experiences have shown that the discipline this offers can stifle growth and doesn't necessarily avoid crises. Xhou Xiachouan, governor of the Chinese Central Bank between 2002 and 2018, used to say that a central bank needs, at times, to be independent from the treasury, while at other times, it should follow the treasury's guidance. There are many central banks in highly successful economies—the US, China and India, to name a few—who achieve a great deal with a mandate that includes growth and employment.

Shyam Saran

Moving China from the Margins to the Centre of Global Finance

I consider it a privilege to offer this contribution to the Festschrift in honour of Dr Shankar Acharya, who enjoys high respect and admiration as one of India's finest economists and public intellectuals. While serving in Prime Minister Narasimha Rao's office as joint secretary, I witnessed the stellar contribution he made as economic adviser to the pioneering economic reforms and liberalization measures adopted in 1991–92. I have followed his work and later his writings, in and out of public office over the years. It has been my good fortune to engage in the most stimulating conversations with him and not just on economic matters, particularly as members of the editorial advisory committee of *Business Standard*, one of India's finest business newspapers.

■

It should come as no surprise that China's spectacular economic trajectory, its rising influence both in Asia and the world, and how India has so far, and must, in the future, deal with the challenge this poses to its own aspirations and prospects as an emerging great power, have been a constant preoccupation in our interactions. This essay seeks to address some of the key issues that we have often grappled with, and which have both economic and geopolitical dimensions. Hopefully, it will provide the trigger for a more animated but better informed debate.

■

China is the second largest economy in the world; its GDP of $18 trillion is second only to the US with a GDP of $27 trillion. It is the world's largest trading nation with a total trade volume of $6 trillion. And yet, it has a financial industry which is still at the margins of global finance and its currency—the renminbi (RMB)—plays a marginal role in trade and investment financing, and in serving as a reserve currency. For the past several years, China has pursued a policy of raising the international profile of its currency, leveraging the expanding scale of its equity and bond markets to integrate more deeply with international financial markets and set up institutions and arrangements to emerge as a key player.

It has also been a pioneer in pursuing a digital central bank currency and digital cross-border payments, which could offer credible, more efficient financial channels, less vulnerable to geopolitical risks. Some analysts see a future where there will be three parallel and overlapping currency zones—an Asian zone dominated by the Chinese RMB, a European zone dominated by the euro, and the rest by the US dollar ($). How likely is this scenario? And where do India's interests lie?

China likes to talk about its pursuit of comprehensive national power which comprises economic, technological and military dimensions. More recently, its leaders have spoken about the need to develop 'discourse power' or the ability to craft the 'right' narrative about China, aligned with its aspirations as a great power. In terms of hard metrics, China is already a great power.

Rapid Economic Growth

Four decades of unprecedentedly rapid economic growth has built an economy in China which is the second largest in the world, just behind the US. Its current GDP, in nominal terms, is worth $18.3 trillion, compared to the US figure of $34 trillion. China's GDP was 16.9 per cent of the global GDP in 2023 and is still rising, though slower than before. Even though the Chinese economy appears to have entered a phase of slower secular growth, it is reducing the gap with the US, and may overtake the latter eventually.

China's current per capita income is $13,140, which puts it in the category of a high middle-income country. Its population of 1.4 billion has begun to decline and this will rob its economy of one key source of dynamism. But this also means that a smaller increase in GDP will spread over fewer people and enhance its per capita income. India's current GDP is $3.9 trillion, with a per capita income of $2,391. Even with a relatively high rate of growth at seven per cent per annum, its GDP will be around $7 trillion in 2030. There are various estimates of Chinese GDP growth over 2021–30, but an analysis by the economist Alicia García-Herrero in a Bruegel brief[1] appears to be the most credible. She prepares her estimates by comparing the records of other Asian economies after they achieved a per capita income of $10,000; Japan and South Korea, for example, grew roughly at around four to five per cent per annum thereafter for a decade. China achieved a per capita income of $10,000 in 2021. García-Herrero projects China growing at 4.9 per cent per annum between 2021 and 2025, and at 3.6 per cent between 2026 and 2030 to reach a per capita income of $20,000 in 2030, yielding a GDP of about $28 trillion—four times India's projected GDP in that year. The Bruegel brief also projects China's GDP drawing level with the US in 2035 and then pulling ahead thereafter, but at a slower rate.

For the foreseeable future, therefore, the key metric of economic power puts China way ahead of India and level with the US. China will also have broken out of the dreaded middle-income trap. India's prospects for doing so are ambiguous at best.

China is the world's largest trading nation, with $6 trillion in exports and imports, constituting around 15 per cent of global trade, and this gives it significant commercial clout. Given its dominance of global supply chains, it is unlikely that China will lose its front-ranking position in the foreseeable future. The re-ordering of these supply chains away from China has not been successful so far, except in high-tech areas such as semiconductors. China is a major producer of various commodities and the largest consumer in some categories as well. Its demand and supply patterns in respect of this wide range of commodities exercise significant influence on the international markets for these commodities. China's participation in the Regional

Comprehensive Economic Partnership (RCEP)—the largest regional trade grouping in the world—will also enhance its economic profile in Asia.

Growing Outward Investment

China has also emerged as the second largest contributor to global outward investment. As per figures released by the Chinese Ministry of Commerce, by the end of 2022, it had reached $163 billion and the cumulative outward direct investment (ODI) stock was worth $2.7 trillion. At the same time, Chinese investors established a significant global presence with 47,000 offshore enterprises in 190 countries. About 60 per cent were located in Asia, 13 per cent in North America and 10.2 per cent in Europe. In all, 16,000 or 34 per cent were set up as part of the Belt and Road Initiative (BRI). Chinese financial institutions such as its large policy banks, and China-led financial institutions such as the Asian Infrastructure Investment Bank (AIIB) and the BRICS Development Bank have emerged as increasingly prominent sources of development finance, rivalling established multilateral institutions such as the World Bank and the Asian Development Bank.

But though China is undoubtedly an economic giant, it is still a virtual pygmy in the global financial markets. Its currency, the renminbi (RMB)—popularly known as the yuan (the two terms are used interchangeably)—is only partially convertible. The US dollar ($) is still the currency of choice for foreign exchange transactions across the world, and for foreign exchange reserves maintained by central banks (60 per cent). About half of global trade is settled in US dollars ($), while the US accounts for only 10 per cent of global trade. According to estimates of the Bank for International Settlements (BIS), the US dollar ($) is used in about 90 per cent of foreign exchange transactions globally and accounts for 85 per cent of transactions in spot, forward and swap markets. It is this domination of the global financial markets by the US which is seen as a geopolitical threat by China. This threat perception has been heightened by the wide-ranging economic and financial sanctions imposed on Russia by the US and the Western countries in the aftermath of Russia's invasion of Ukraine.

China has had a long-standing policy of making the RMB an international currency, thereby diminishing the role of the US dollar ($). China first announced its aim to 'gradually make the RMB a convertible currency' at the Third Plenum of the 14th Central Committee of the Communist Party of China (CPC) in 1993. Current account convertibility was basically achieved by 1996. In 2003, it was announced that China's aim was now to 'gradually achieve capital account convertibility'.

Managed Convertibility

However, in the wake of the global financial and economic crisis of 2007–08, China began to talk about 'managed convertibility', retaining state control to manage risks from cross-border capital flows and maintaining the stable value of its currency. It is within this framework that China has gone about promoting the internationalization of its currency, initially through encouraging its use for trade settlement, launching yuan-denominated financial instruments such as the well-known 'panda bonds', setting up alternative arrangements for cross-border payments, and promoting digital central bank currency domestically while exploring cross-border digital payments using such digital currencies. Project mBridge,[2] involving the central banks of China, Thailand and the United Arab Republic, alongside the Hong Kong Monetary Authority, is one such initiative.

The setting up of futures markets providing trading and clearing services for financial futures, options and other derivatives denominated in RMB has been another initiative in the direction of making China an important and influential actor in the world's financial markets. The futures markets started being established in China in 1998 and were then gradually expanded and made more sophisticated. Initially, they were only open to domestic clients, but since 2018, they are gradually and incrementally being opened to foreign clients. These futures exchanges leverage China's role as both a significant producer and consumer of a whole range of commodities, but whose international price determination lies in the hands of established futures exchanges, such as the London Metal Exchange and the Chicago Mercantile Exchange.

Planning Rival Exchanges

The London-based Brent and the US-based West Texas Intermediate (WTI) are primary crude oil benchmarks. All the futures, options and derivatives traded in these markets are designated in US dollars and contracts are also settled in that currency. China is determined to change this situation by setting up its own rival exchanges offering RMB-denominated products. This effort has gained urgency following US sanctions imposed on Russia in 2022 over the latter's invasion of Ukraine. The heightened concern in this respect was reflected in Chinese President Xi Jinping's speech at the financial work conference convened in October 2023. Xi observed that 'a small number of countries treat finance as tools for geopolitical games. They repeatedly played with currency hegemony and frequently wielded the big stick of financial sanctions [...] All these have presented new challenges to maintaining financial security under the new situation.'

China's approach in establishing and developing these financial markets has followed the one adopted in respect of its equity and bond markets. It first developed and scaled up its own domestic financial platforms and institutions before incrementally opening them up to foreign participation. It also diversified its external exposure. For example, China held $1.3 trillion in US treasury bonds in 2013. In February 2024, these holdings were down to $775 billion and steadily decreasing, being substituted by other convertible currencies such as the euro and more lately, by large purchases of gold.

This essay will examine in greater detail the various dimensions of China's strategy to translate its economic power into significant finance power in international markets, and what its geopolitical implications may be.

The Internationalization of the RMB

It has already been pointed out that China does not intend to make its currency convertible to the same extent as the US dollar or other fully convertible currencies, such as the euro or the Japanese yen. It has achieved current account convertibility and has allowed capital account convertibility subject to certain prudential limitations. It has introduced the market determination of the exchange value of the RMB against a basket of currencies by limiting the variation in the rate of exchange to +/-2 per cent over the previous day's rate. There has been greater effort to promote the use of the RMB in the settlement of trade, and some success has been achieved in this. According to estimates of the Bank for International Settlements (BIS), the RMB is used in the settlement of six per cent of global trade and transactions, overtaking the 5.8 per cent figure for the euro.

Despite not meeting all the criteria set by the IMF for the inclusion of convertible currencies in the basket of currencies which constitutes its special drawing rights (SDRs), the Chinese currency was accepted as such in 2015 with a weight of 10 per cent. But currently, only 2.45 per cent of global foreign exchange reserves are held in RMB. In terms of international payments, the RMB accounted for 5.8 per cent of the total transactions in September 2023, as per the data maintained by the Society for Worldwide Interbank Financial Telecommunications (SWIFT). This makes it the fourth most used currency for international payments. It may be noted that the spike in RMB usage is mainly due to Russia, Iran and Venezuela—being under US sanctions and being denied access to US dollar payments and trade settlement—using it.

China has also promoted the use of local currencies in its trade with several countries. This has been facilitated by a number of swap lines that the People's Bank of China (PBOC) opened, mainly with developing countries but also a few advanced economies. According to IMF data, as of April 2022, there were 38 operational bilateral swap lines amounting to 4 trillion yuans. The swap lines provide yuan liquidity to a trading partner for both trade and financial transactions. When such need for yuans arises, the foreign central bank can activate the swap and request the Chinese central bank to deposit yuans in its account, which may then be loaned to foreign financial institutions to provide yuan-related payments. The foreign central bank deposits the equivalent amount in its own currency with the Chinese central bank as collateral. At the end of the swap, the foreign central bank is expected to return the yuans to its Chinese counterpart. Swap lines normally operate for three years but may be extended by mutual consent. The record so far has registered minimal activation of these swap lines. They have served mainly as a risk mitigation instrument.

In contrast to swap lines, the Chinese central bank has been more successful in promoting the use of yuans through the operation of its offshore clearing banks. According to IMF data, there are currently 27 offshore clearing banks in 25 economies to facilitate yuan payments. The first such offshore bank was established in Hong Kong in 2003, but there was a rapid and significant increase in their numbers in the aftermath of the global financial and economic crisis of 2007–08. In the initial phase, these offshore RMB processing centres were mainly offshore branches of Chinese banks. However, since 2018, the PBOC has also licensed a number of foreign banks to conduct such business. For example, in the US, J.P. Morgan is the designated offshore clearing bank. Reliable figures on the volume of trade and other transactions processed through these regional banks are not available, but are likely to be modest as of now.

One may now consider the other important Chinese initiative to promote cross-border payments in its currency without the intermediation of other reserve currencies, particularly the US dollar. China was one of the first major economies to explore a central bank digital currency (CBDC). The project was first revealed in 2014 when PBOC established a research group to explore the feasibility of a state digital currency. The Digital Currency Research Institute (DCRI) was established by PBOC in 2018 to carry the project forward, including the development of related technologies, standards, laws and regulations to make the CBDC a reality.

The Digital Currency Project

In 2019, PBOC began pilot projects around the CBDC and an electronic currency to be called e-CNY. Twenty-six cities served as a test bed and 5.6 million merchants were registered to use the electronic currency as of 2023. An estimated 260 million wallets were issued across these 26 cities. The use of the digital currency has rapidly expanded, and by the end of 2023, the volume of transactions reached 950 million, with a cumulative value of 1.8 trillion yuans ($250 billion).

At the end of the previous year, it was $100 billion. The stage has been set to explore its use in cross-border transactions. From September 2023, foreigners in China can acquire an e-CNY wallet using their international mobile telephone numbers, and top up with overseas Visa or Mastercard credit cards. The wallet balance may be transferred back to their offshore accounts whenever required. The e-CNY was launched at the Beijing Winter Olympics in February 2022, but since then, the publicity on the project has been somewhat muted. However, there is no doubt that China intends to press ahead with the e-CNY as an instrument of cross-border payment, bypassing the US dollar. This is where Project mBridge becomes relevant.

Project mBridge is an experiment to validate a multi-CBDC platform for digital wholesale cross-border payments. It is a collaborative initiative among the BIS Innovation Hub and four founding central banks, which are the DCRI of the PBOC, the Hong Kong Monetary Authority, the Central Bank of the United Arab Emirates and the Bank of Thailand. In addition, there are 25 observer members, but India is not represented among them. Interestingly, the Federal Reserve Bank of New York in the US is among the observers, as are the European Central Bank, the IMF, the World Bank, the central banks of France, Italy, South Korea and Norway, and even Nepal Rastra Bank next door.

A 31 October 2023 update from the BIS spells out the mandate of the project, detailing the progress achieved so far and the next steps. The update says:

> Project mBridge experiments with a multi-CBDC common platform for wholesale cross-border payments focusing on the use case of international trade, which has the potential to connect central banks and commercial banks around the world as a public good. The platform developed for Project mBridge is underpinned by custom-built distributed ledger technology (DLT), a set of comprehensive legal rulebook documents and a fit-for-purpose governance structure.

That China is the leading actor in this initiative is obvious from the fact that the mBridge platform uses the so-called Dashing Protocol developed by the DCRI and China's Tsinghua University, which received funding from the Chinese Ministry of Education.

The update claims that in 2022, 'a pilot involving real corporate transactions was conducted on the platform among participating central banks, selected commercial banks and their corporate customers in 4 jurisdictions.'

Based on the experience gained there, the next step is to 'see if the platform tested can evolve to become a minimum viable product.'

The project appears to have made remarkable progress in a fairly short period of time, and the association with the BIS gives it both credibility and legitimacy. The possibility of this becoming an alternative cross-border payments channel bypassing the US-dollar-dominated system is now real. This requires serious study by our own central bank and financial experts.

Project mBridge may be linked with the alternative payments system that China established, and which is already being used by at least its trading partners—like Russia and Iran—who have been barred from SWIFT. SWIFT was founded in 1973 by 293 banks from 15 countries, and is headquartered in Brussels. It enables speedy transmission of payment instructions among participating and correspondent banks. In a sense, it serves as the financial plumbing of the international financial market.

As of April 2022, the US dollar accounted for 41.8 per cent, the euro 34.7 per cent, the pound 6.3 per cent, the Japanese yen 3.1 per cent, and the Chinese RMB 2.1 per cent of the total value of transactions handled by SWIFT. China set up its own China International Payment System (CIPS) in 2015. It has 140 direct participants—mainly overseas branches of Chinese banks—and 1,371 indirect participants or correspondent entities. CIPS may be compared with the US-based Clearing House Interbank Payments System (CHIPS), which is a private sector entity. It has 10 times as many participants as CIPS, and in March 2022, the daily volume of transactions that it handled was worth $1.8 trillion as against $45.8 billion under CIPS. It is interesting to note that even while setting itself up as a rival to SWIFT, CIPS nevertheless signed an MOU with it in 2016, which has introduced a high degree of interoperability between the two systems and enabled CIPS to adopt international standards for its messaging service. CIPS may currently be lagging behind CHIPS and SWIFT, but it has put in place the building blocks of an alternate payment and messaging system which challenges the Western, in particular the US, stranglehold on international finance. The arbitrary use of sanctions by the US encourages targeted countries to use the Chinese alternative. Even other countries may welcome the availability of another viable option.

China's Securities and Bond Market

As in the case of the planned internationalization of the RMB, China has also leveraged the size and steady growth of its domestic securities and bond market to enable foreign participation in graduated and incremental steps. The country has the largest banking system in the world with $53.1 trillion in assets. Its banks hold a massive $40 trillion in deposits as of February 2024. Its stock market capitalization today stands at $11.5 trillion, second only to the US figure of $52 trillion.

Its bond market has been growing at the rate of seven per cent per annum in recent years, and is already over $20 trillion. There has been a consistent policy of progressively easing the entry and participation of foreign entities to both the securities and bond markets. In 2002, the Qualified Foreign Institutional Investor (QFII) Scheme was introduced to license a limited number of foreign institutional entities to buy and sell shares within a numerical and financial quota. Investment was limited to 'A' shares listed on the Shanghai and Shenzhen stock exchanges. This was later expanded to include investment through offshore RMB holdings, and also to permit qualified domestic institutional investors (QDIIs) to use these holdings to trade in shares of Chinese companies listed in Hong Kong and other exchanges, including depositary receipts representing shares of Chinese companies listed on foreign exchanges. The quotas have been progressively expanded and investment limits raised.

The share markets are broader, constituting over 4,000 stocks of the current value of $8.5 trillion. The Chinese equities traded in Hong Kong are of a smaller value, around $3.4 trillion. However, foreigners own only about five per cent of Chinese stocks. The QFII scheme and the Renminbi Qualified Foreign Institutional Investor (RQFII) scheme have, in 2020, merged into a single qualified investor scheme with simpler qualifying rules and a wider set of investment products available in addition to shares, such as bonds and derivatives on commodity markets.

China has two bond markets. One is the China Interbank Bond Market regulated by the PBOC, and the other is the exchange bond market regulated by the China Securities Regulatory Commission. In 2016, qualified foreign institutional investors were, for the first time, allowed to invest in the China Interbank Bond Market without quota limits. In 2022, they were permitted to trade in bonds listed on the Shanghai and Shenzhen exchanges. By the end of 2023, overseas investors held $523 billion in Chinese bonds. These are mainly Chinese government or treasury bonds and bonds issued by China's policy banks—the Agricultural Development Bank of China, the Export-Import Bank of China, China Development Bank, and the Bank of Communications.

It may be noted that in addition to participation through the qualified investor schemes, foreigners can also invest in Chinese securities and bonds through the unique mechanisms of the Shanghai-Hong Kong and the Shenzhen-Hong Kong Stock Connect and Bond Connect. The Hong Kong-Shanghai Stock Connect was established in 2014 and was extended to Shenzhen in 2016. The Shanghai-London Stock Connect was established in 2019. These also permitted qualified Chinese domestic investors to invest in designated securities listed on the Hong Kong and London exchanges. This came to be known as the Southbound Stock Connect, just as the former came to be known as the Northbound Stock Connect. Through these 'connects', Chinese investors and foreign investors could invest in designated equities listed on their respective exchanges, subject to financial limits which have been progressively liberalized.

In 2017 the Bond Connect Scheme was introduced, offering foreign investors and Chinese domestic investors similar mutual opportunities to invest in bonds listed on each other's markets. Northbound trading in bonds commenced on 3 July 2017, offering foreigners access to the

Chinese Interbank Bond Market (CIBM). The Southbound Connect started operating on 24 September 2021, providing Chinese institutional investors the opportunity to trade in offshore bonds listed on the Hong Kong exchange. It has been difficult to collate overall trading volumes under the various connect schemes, but these are reported to be sizeable. It was reported in *The Nikkei* that net purchases of yuan-denominated government bonds by foreign entities had reached $28.2 billion in January 2024.

Despite the liberalization of the Chinese bond market, foreign holdings of Chinese bonds are less than three per cent at present. The inclusion of Chinese government bonds in key international indices will help in expanding the foreign ownership of Chinese bonds. These are now included in the FT Russel Bond Index, J.P. Morgan Government Bond Index and the Bloomberg Barclays Global Aggregate Index. This follows the inclusion of China A-shares in global securities indices, such as the Morgan Stanley Capital International (MSCI) Emerging Markets Index. These are important steps in China's measured integration into global financial markets.

China's Participation in Regional Groupings

China is an active member of the Bretton Woods institutions—the World Bank and the IMF. It is also a member of regional multilateral development banks, including the Asian Development Bank, the African Development Bank, the Inter-American Development Bank, and the European Bank for Reconstruction and Development. It participates in several key economic organizations and groupings in Asia, such as the ASEAN Plus Three Cooperation which brings together the 10 ASEAN states (Brunei, Cambodia, Indonesia, Laos, Malaysia, Myanmar, Philippines, Singapore, Thailand and Vietnam), China, Japan and South Korea. It is represented at the South East Asian Central Banks Research and Training Centre, and it is, of course, a leading member of the Shanghai Cooperation Organisation (SCO) and BRICS (Brazil, Russia, India, China, South Africa). BRICS has now been expanded to include Egypt, Ethiopia, Saudi Arabia, the UAE and Venezuela. China took the initiative to establish the Asian

Infrastructure Investment Bank (AIIB) in 2016 and the BRICS New Development Bank (NDB) in 2014. China is the largest shareholder in both banks. The AIIB is capitalized at $100 billion, and has 109 members. The NDB is capitalized at $50 billion, and has, in addition to the BRICS founding members, Bangladesh, the UAE and Uruguay as members. With the expansion of BRICS, the bank may admit newer members and raise its registered capital. India is the second largest shareholder in both the banks.

The growing role of the AIIB has been acknowledged by the World Bank which concluded an MOU with it in April 2024 to strengthen their cooperation on infrastructure development and the implementation of Sustainable Development Goals (SDGs). The two institutions had already concluded an initial MOU back in 2017 to cooperate on financing projects in developing countries. As in the case of mBridge where it is collaborating with BIS, and CIPS where it is collaborating with SWIFT, China seems to be following an approach of both competing with and working together with institutions it seeks to rival, if not replace entirely. Such collaboration also enables a learning process through exposure to the more advanced and exacting standards followed by these institutions.

Recently, the revival of interest in an Asian Monetary Fund, first mooted in 1997 in the aftermath of the Asian financial crisis, has also witnessed an active Chinese role. The idea of an Asian Monetary Fund was originally proposed by Japan. It was welcomed by the ASEAN countries which were resentful of the harsh conditionalities imposed upon them for receiving IMF support to deal with the balance of payments crises several of them were facing. However, the proposal did not take off due to US opposition. Instead, ASEAN Plus Three settled for a modest safety mechanism—known as the Chiang Mai Initiative Multilateralisation (CMIM)—in May 2000, to provide short-term liquidity in times of economic distress faced by any of its members. This was the first regional currency swap agreed upon as an incremental step. Under CMIM, China concluded six bilateral currency swap agreements with Japan, South Korea, Thailand, the Philippines, Malaysia and Indonesia. It committed $16.5 billion to a common pool created by the participants, which eventually totalled

$120 billion, and was raised to $240 billion in 2012. However, this safety pool has never had to be used. In February 2023, the Malaysian prime minister Anwar Ibrahim revived the idea of an Asian Monetary Fund. While China has not commented on the idea so far, it has been active in promoting regional financial arrangements using its own currency. These could serve as a launch pad for a future Asian Monetary Fund with China as a key player.

In June 2022, the PBOC and the BIS jointly launched a Renminbi Liquidity Arrangement (RMBLA), with the participation of Bank Indonesia, the Hong Kong Monetary Authority, the Monetary Authority of Singapore and the Central Bank of Chile. The goal was to provide liquidity to participating central banks from the Asia-Pacific region (which explains the participation of the Chilean central bank) through a reserve pooling scheme. The BIS specified that 'each participating central bank contributes a minimum of RMB 15 billion [$2.2 billion] or US dollar equivalent, in RMB or USD, placed with the BIS, creating a reserve pool.' This initiative has become part of China's strategy of using regional currency cooperation as a way of promoting a diversification of the global reserve currency system. China has similarly promoted the use of local currencies within both the SCO and the BRICS groupings.

As pointed out earlier in this essay, China has been hesitant to fully liberalize its capital account. Nevertheless, it is promoting the use of its government bonds as collateral for derivative trade. The Hong Kong Stock Exchange and the London Stock Exchange are working towards including Chinese government bonds as eligible collateral. Once this is implemented, the functionality of Chinese government bonds will increase, create more demand for them, and help build liquidity in Chinese government bond markets. This would be another step towards promoting the status of Chinese currency as a global reserve currency.

Financial Futures and Commodity Exchanges

China has established a number of commodity exchanges which could serve to expand the use of its currency in commodity trading, along with giving it a degree of influence over commodity price determination. Initially, these exchanges served domestic clients, but more recently, these have begun to allow foreign participation. There are five important exchanges at the national level, but there are also regional exchanges with more limited mandates. The five key exchanges are:

(1) The China Financial Futures Exchange (CFFEX): Set up in 2006 by the Shanghai Futures Exchange, the Zhengzhou Commodity Exchange, the Dalian Commodity Exchange, the Shanghai Stock Exchange and the Shenzhen Stock Exchange, the CFFEX is dedicated to trading in financial derivatives and trade settlement. It is a platform for dealing in treasury bond futures.

(2) The Dalian Commodity Exchange: Established in 1993, it is the world's largest futures trading market for agricultural products, plastics, coal and iron ore, and different categories of soybeans, palm oil and corn starch.

(3) Shanghai Futures Exchange: It lists 16 futures products on its platform. These include copper, zinc, aluminium, lead, nickel, tin, gold and silver, steel products, crude oil, fuel oil, bitumen, natural rubber, and paper pulp.

(4) Zhengzhou Commodity Exchange: First established in October 1990, it is one of the earliest commodity exchanges in China. It is a platform for futures trading in grain, cotton, edible oils, sugar, fruits, energy, chemicals, textiles, metallurgy and construction materials.

(5) Shanghai International Energy Exchange: Set up in 2018 as a subsidiary of the Shanghai Futures Exchange and the only one open to global futures investors in crude oil, natural gas and petrochemicals, it seeks to leverage China's position as the largest crude oil consumer and a prominent importer of both natural gas and LNG so as to promote RMB-denominated trade in these commodities—both spot trade and term contracts. It aims to rival the London-based Brent and the US-based West Texas Intermediary (WTI), which currently dominate global oil and gas trade. Since its launch in 2018, the Shanghai Exchange provides its own benchmark for oil and gas contracts denominated in Chinese

currency. It has already emerged as the third largest oil futures market behind Brent and WTI.

China's National Offshore Oil Corporation (CNOOC) and France's TotalEnergies contracted their first RMB-denominated LNG trade through the Shanghai International Energy Exchange. China has also been urging Saudi Arabia to accept at least part of its oil sales to China in RMB. Saudi oil sales to China in 2022 amounted to 176 million barrels per day, and even if a part of this was routed through the Shanghai Exchange, it would be a major boost to the internationalization of the Chinese currency.

Following the setting up of the Shanghai International Energy Exchange specifically targeting foreign derivative traders, China has also opened up the other exchanges to qualified foreign institutional investors (QFIs). QFIs will now be able to trade in 27 commodity futures contracts and 18 commodity options across various exchanges that are otherwise not open to foreigners.

In recent years, China has taken particular interest in strategic minerals and metals, and set up commodity exchanges to regulate derivative trade involving them. The Baotou Rare Earth Products Exchange was set up in 2016. The Ganzhou Rare Metal Exchange was launched in 2019. The aim was to establish its own trading hubs and benchmarks priced in RMB, as part of its effort to lessen the dominance of the US dollar on commodities trade. This has, of course, intensified in the wake of US sanctions imposed on Russia since 2022. For example, in July 2023, the Guangzhou Futures Exchange launched contracts tracking the price of lithium carbonate which is used in electric vehicles. China is also a large producer of lithium and controls mining assets abroad. It is reported that within three weeks after trading opened on the Guangzhou Exchange, 20,000 lots were traded, far outstripping trading activity on the Singapore Exchange and on the Chicago Mercantile Exchange in the US.

The Chinese Strategy

This essay has sought to map the evolution of China's financial industry and its gradual integration in international financial markets.

The country initially focused on building up and upgrading its own domestic financial industry in its various dimensions, leveraging the enormous size and scale of its economy. It is only after achieving a fair degree of consolidation that it incrementally and gradually allowed foreign participation in its financial markets. The very scale of its financial industry—whether in the size of its securities market or its bond market—created opportunities for profit which few foreign traders would want to miss. This provided it with international leverage which might yield geopolitical advantage. China tried to reduce its vulnerability in a global financial industry dominated by the US and the West in general. This included the internationalization of its own currency, achieving current account convertibility, but only limited capital account convertibility. It sought to overcome the disadvantage inherent in limited capital account convertibility by promoting a digital central bank currency which could enable cross-border payments without requiring full convertibility. Project mBridge was an effort in this direction. The association with the Bank of International Settlements (BIS) lent it credibility.

China promoted the use of the RMB in trade settlement. A progressively larger proportion of China's own exports and imports are being settled in its own currency. It actively promoted the use of regional currencies and set up RMB clearing banks in several countries to facilitate this.

Over the years, China has developed a fairly comprehensive derivatives and futures market through a number of commodity and financial futures exchanges. These enhanced its ability to influence the pricing of commodities of which it is a large producer and consumer. They are being gradually opened to foreign investors. The Shanghai International Energy Exchange is already a major player in the oil and gas trade, and its oil benchmark is just behind the more established Brent and WTI indices in terms of importance.

The China International Payment System (CIPS) was an effort to set up a banking transactions messaging network that was not dominated by the US, like SWIFT is—the latter has become an instrument through which the US imposed economic sanctions against countries like Iran, and more recently Russia. The role of CIPS is still very limited, but is likely to grow as concerns grow—even among countries friendly with the US—that they are vulnerable to US unilateralism in the matter of economic sanctions.

It is striking that China is collaborating with institutions that it seeks to provide an alternative to, such as SWIFT or the World Bank. CIPS has an MOU with SWIFT and the AIIB has one with the World Bank. It is also noteworthy that the BIS, which is an institution of the world's central banks, has been collaborating with China's central bank on the creation of both a digital cross-border payment system and a reserve liquidity arrangement for participating countries in the Asia-Pacific region. Chinese strategy may be described as 'engage, integrate and if possible, dominate'. Its collaboration with possible rivals also enables a learning process through which advanced practices and norms may be inculcated.

While China is still some distance away from becoming a major player in global finance, it has already achieved substantial progress. Its aim does not seem to be to create, as one analyst fears, 'a parallel financial universe', but it is certainly geared towards a diversification of this universe away from its current domination by the US and the West in general.

There does not appear to be much awareness in India about the evolution of China's financial industry. There is a real possibility that a Chinese currency zone in Asia may become a reality, perhaps sooner rather than later. This will pose both an economic and a geopolitical challenge to India. Should India participate, for example, in Project mBridge? Should it join the RMB Liquidity Arrangement promoted by the PBOC and BIS, but in which there are several other Asian participants? Should Indian banks join CIPS as participating institutions? These are complicated issues but they need to be addressed. The default outcome could be both the economic and geopolitical marginalization of the country, even within its Asian homeland.

Ajay Chhibber

Reforming the Bretton Woods Institutions for the Twenty-First Century[1]

Shankar Acharya is someone I have admired for a long time—even before we ever met. When I joined the World Bank in 1983, I was asked to work on its flagship document, the World Development Report, in 1985, and discovered Shankar had led the team that produced the first one. I later went on to lead the 1997 World Development Report on the role of the state and felt very proud to have worked on something Shankar started. Over the years, we became friends and I admired his rigour, his even-handedness, and his amazing ability to present his views without offending even those he might not agree with. Lately, he and I worked together on India's G20 external advisory body for the Finance Track, which he chaired—where a key issue was reforms of multilateral institutions. This is a revised version of my paper prepared for the Bretton Woods 2.0 project of the Atlantic Council and my contribution to this well-deserved Festschrift in his honour.

■

Why Is Reform Needed Now?

In July 1944, during the Second World War, the United Nations Monetary and Financial Conference—known more popularly as the Bretton Woods (BW) Conference—reached agreements on an international financial architecture which, with some modifications and additions, has existed until today. This agreement was designed to create a rules-based international financial architecture and open trading system that would reduce protectionism, rampant nationalism, growing inequalities and beggar-thy-neighbour policies that had led to the financial crash of 1929, the Great Depression, and eventually the Second World War. For the next 70 years or so, despite hiccups, the project succeeded. The world has seen not only reconstruction and recovery from the Second World War, but also rising incomes and lowered poverty in large parts of it—especially where they have been drawn into the global economy.[2]

The 2008 global financial crisis (GFC) marked a turning point in many ways. While there was a brief period of heightened global coordination to deal with the crisis, that coordination and cooperation have since been badly frayed. Rising protectionism and a lack of global coordination on the Covid-19 pandemic[3] have exposed huge differences and disparities in the world. Conflicts and wars have erupted in several parts of the world. However, even more dangerous challenges have emerged that threaten the globe. The most serious of these is the threat of climate change, along with rising temperatures,[4] leading to a greater frequency of natural disasters.

The institutions that were created at the BW Conference, and subsequently the IMF and the World Bank Group, managed to adapt to a changing world to try and remain relevant. They were broadly successful in contributing to reduced poverty and faster growth in large parts of the developing world. They helped many low- and middle-income countries deal with global shocks through finance and improved domestic policies. Many emerging economies that liberalized and participated in the global trading system converged towards the advanced economies, especially after 1990 and in the years before the GFC.[5] But while the BW institutions tried to adapt their workings to a changing world, they are no longer fit to meet today's global challenges. This is because (a) their governance structures have more or less remained the same as what was created at the end of the Second World War, and (b) their size and mandate make them less able to address today's challenges. This essay will focus on (b) their size and mandate, but without fixing (a) their governance structure,[6] no new set of institutional arrangements will have legitimacy and therefore acceptability.

What Ails the Bretton Woods System?

The problems with these institutions can be put into two broad categories: (a) their size and leverage, and (b) their mandate and effectiveness.

(a) Size and Leverage

With the re-emergence of global crisis with the GFC in 2008–09, and now with the pandemic in 2020, it has become clear that the IMF remains too small and its resources too constrained to help the world address these challenges.[7] Bilateral swap lines[8] and regional safety nets[9] are today twice as large as the resources of the IMF. Along with unused SDR issues, IMF resources now amount to about $1 trillion—only about 1.1 per cent of global GDP,[10] barely enough to deal with crises in a few countries, but certainly not enough to manage a global crisis. Of these, about half are from quota resources and the remaining are from borrowing arrangements available on a discretionary basis. The size of IMF programmes that were needed in recent years has reached as much as 32 times its quota for Greece and 25 times its quota for Portugal.[11]

The same problem of size applies to the World Bank and the multilateral development banks (MDBs) as well, whose combined lending is now smaller than that of bilateral development finance institutions (DFIs) and sovereign wealth funds (SWFs), and form a small share of the resources flowing to the developing world.[12] [13] While each of the 27 MDBs or so has introduced some variations in its working, they all follow the same financial intermediary model as the World Bank.[14] In 2019, just before the pandemic, they provided less than 10 per cent of all financial flows to the public finances of the developing world, according to World Bank and OECD data. In 2019 and 2020, they provided only about $40 billion in climate finance—a small share of what is actually needed.[15] The World Bank provided less support to offset the effects of Covid-19 ($13 billion) than what was granted during the 2008–09 global financial crisis ($28 billion). Remittances at $630 billion now form the largest flow of funds to developing economies, with official development assistance (ODA) at about $200 billion in 2022, according to the World Bank.[16] When the Addis Ababa Action Agenda—the financing plan for the SDGs—was announced in 2015, the MDBs had promised to turn the billions they provided into trillions by leveraging in private finance—but that promise remains unfulfilled.[17]

More broadly, there is considerable underfinancing of global public goods (GPGs) as it is difficult to get countries to pay for activities outside their borders. ODA has fallen well short of the agreed target of 0.7 per cent of the GDP—and, in fact, is closer to just 0.2 per cent.[18] GPG funding from ODA is only about 10 per cent of the total. Global thematic funds to support specific development challenges—the Global Alliance for Vaccination (GAVI), the Global Fund to Fight AIDS, Tuberculosis and Malaria (GFATM), the Global Environmental Fund (GEF) and older funds like the Consultative Group for International Agricultural Research (CGIAR)—have been successful in addressing specific development challenges through projects in specific countries, especially for agriculture, the environment, and health. But the Green Climate Fund which devotes a 50:50 share of funding for adaptation and mitigation has received extremely limited funding so far—despite the commitment to provide $100 billion a year over and above ODA.

Let us now turn to the question of how effective these institutions have been, and what role they have played in the progress made so far.

(b) Mandate and Effectiveness

The IMF

The IMF is accused of having missed one of its major functions— to warn the world of impending global crises and conduct adequate surveillance of the global monetary and financial system.[19] It has spent much of its energy not only trying to develop new instruments to help emerging market economies deal with crises and low-income countries reduce poverty, but has now also turned its programmes to issues such as climate finance, gender and human development—issues which many other agencies are better suited for tackling.[20] But the IMF is also criticized for other aspects of its programmes.

Premature Capital Account Liberalization: Unlike the effects of trade openness, the effects of financial openness are more dependent on the nature of the flows. FDI tends to reduce inequality in the recipient country—but will increase it in the country where the flows originate. Foreign portfolio investment (FPI) flows tend to widen inequality unless they help deepen financial markets, and short-term flows have increased volatility and crisis; they also end up creating greater economic pain for the poorer sections of society.[21] A major criticism of the IMF is that until recently, it prematurely pushed for capital account liberalization—despite its own articles which would allow countries to constrain capital flows.[22] But the strong criticism of its policies, especially after the Asian financial crisis and other crises, has forced it to temper its advice on this issue.[23]

Excessive Austerity and Pro-Cyclical Programmes: A second critique of the IMF is that its standard advice to emerging economies is pro-cyclical, which ends up increasing the depth of the crisis. But when it comes to advanced economies, a completely different recipe is used to lower their immediate pain, as argued by Reinhart and Rogoff.[24] This double standard in the method of dealing with debt and financial crisis has left IMF programmes in emerging markets with a huge—political or market—stigma.[25] Those capable of it have also built up large reserves (excess and costly reserves as an insurance), and are often against having to go to the IMF.[26]

Weak Surveillance in Advanced Economies: The IMF's key role in advanced economies remains surveillance—but its analysis and advice are not taken seriously in these countries.[27] [28] Its analysis of the spillover effects of the policies of advanced countries, which have global implications and make macroeconomic management and financial stability more difficult for the less advanced economies, is also ignored. This may also have added to its inability to predict global financial crises as its warnings are muted and ignored.

Arbitrary Programme Size: This bias is also found in the size of its programmes where arbitrary allocations are sometimes as high as over 30 times the quota, as in the case of Greece. Larger programmes in comparison to the quota for Portugal and Ireland, two other EU countries, have also reduced its credibility for even-handedness. These were partly driven by the nature of the euro arrangements,[29] but leave an impression among borrowers of uneven treatment and policies driven by political expediency and the exposure of major shareholder banks to the programme country.[30] Many of the politically less important countries or those without some political support from key G-7 countries struggle with much smaller programmes, which then also often result in much greater austerity and a much smaller ability to permanently come out of the crisis, leading to repeat programmes—a problem seen again in recent programmes like those in Sri Lanka, Zambia and Pakistan.

Serial Lending: Another major critique of the IMF is that once it lifted its restriction against lending into arrears, it has become a serial lender and lends not only for illiquidity, but also into insolvency. Its programmes also often bail out private creditors whose commercial and sovereign debt is turned into public debt and becomes the responsibility of taxpayers. As many as 48 (over 25 per cent) of its member countries have been under IMF programmes for more than half of their membership years—in a state of perpetual IMF tutelage. Half of them have been under IMF programmes for more than 30 per cent of the duration of their IMF membership.[31] This has given IMF programmes a stigma as they signal insolvency, and in many cases[32] new lending helps evergreen official and private credit. Reinhart and Trebisch (2016) show that in the 1990s and 2000s, about 40 per cent of all IMF lending programmes involved some sort of default, restructuring, or arrears on official debt.

Mission Creep: A final critique of the IMF is 'mission creep'—that it is getting itself involved in sectoral and social issues which are best left to the MDBs and other bilateral and specialized UN organizations. While gender and social issues are important for inclusive growth and the IMF must have the analytical capacity to understand the effects of climate change, it is not clear if the IMF is best suited to address these issues. In the case of climate change, where it can be shown that macro-effects are large, the IMF may have a role, but it is unlikely that it would be the prime financier of a global clean energy transition that the world needs. By using its new instrument, the Resilience and Sustainability Trust facility, set up with borrowed funds with a lending of 20-year maturity, it is beginning to look like an aid agency.

The World Bank

The World Bank has also been criticized for its effectiveness, mission creep and orientation. What the world needs today is a global institution tasked with guiding a global transformation towards a sustainable planet for shared prosperity—where the WBG is missing in action, according to former Vice President Al Gore. Other critiques of the World Bank are:

Failed Structural Adjustment Programmes and Ease of Doing Business Index: The World Bank has also been criticized for the support it gave to structural adjustment programmes (SAPs) focused on trade liberalization and privatization. There were two problems. First, trade liberalization increased trade deficits as imports surged, but exports did not increase as much because the underlying infrastructure needed for exports did not exist. Second, privatization also meant that sometimes public monopolies became private monopolies as there was inadequate competition, or private players to supply services did not exist. Lately, the WBG has been pushing a flawed ease of doing business (EODB) index which was easily gamed, and it always pushed for less regulation without including environmental and labour standards.[33]

Lending vs. Non-Lending Services: The World Bank has been accused of focusing too much on lending targets and not on the quality of their advice or analytical support. Surveys of recipient countries show that they consistently find the policy advice and analytical work to be far more useful than is acknowledged.[34] More funding should be provided for such activities in these institutions.

Insufficient Focus on Catalyzing Private Flows: The World Bank Group has the International Finance Corporation (IFC), the private sector arm, and Multilateral Investment Guarantee Agency (MIGA) to provide political risk guarantee.[35] Today, the world has large financial savings looking for returns, and many low- and middle-income countries starved of capital—especially for infrastructure.[36] But this could change. WB's own instruments allow it to provide not only loans but also guarantees—both project and policy—to leverage in private capital. But this International Bank for Reconstruction and Development (IBRD) instrument and MIGA's political risk guarantee have seen surprisingly limited use.[37] Part of the problem lies with credit rating agencies with guarantees at face value, which makes leverage much smaller.[38] It has financed a few insurance backstops, but could do a lot more. Its private sector arm has also been accused of not doing enough to help move private capital to underserved sectors and SMEs, but going for less risky projects with larger corporates and in safer investments.

Too Slow and Bureaucratic: In addition to these, bureaucratic procedures and excessively cumbersome safeguards have made the World Bank and many of the MDBs terribly slow and costly. This is also one of the reasons cited as to why private sector entities are reluctant to partner with the World Bank Group. Also, too much time is spent on project preparation and board approvals and not enough on project implementation.[39] And the overall success rate of country programmes is much less than successful ratings on individual projects, suggesting that the MDBs choose easier projects to finance, while overall country progress remains underwhelming.[40]

Country Focus Neglects Global and Regional Financing Needs: Finally, the World Bank, and more broadly the MDB system, is very country-focused, which has improved its in-country programmes but at a cost. It means that regional and global programmes which are needed to address global public goods are given a short shrift.[41]

What Should the Reformed IMF and World Bank Group Look Like?

A more flexible international financial architecture with strengthened Bretton Woods institutions, but woven together with regional and issue-specific institutions and non-state actors, may be the right way forward. It will help build a more resilient and responsive system of cascading and interconnected institutional structure that can adapt to future uncertainties.[42] As we foresee a multipolar world, the G20 (modified) can become the forum for providing overall guidance in setting priorities to the new Bretton Woods institutions, along with their existing governance structure—the International Monetary and Finance Committee (IMFC), the World Bank Group and the Development Committee (DC) (see Figure 1).

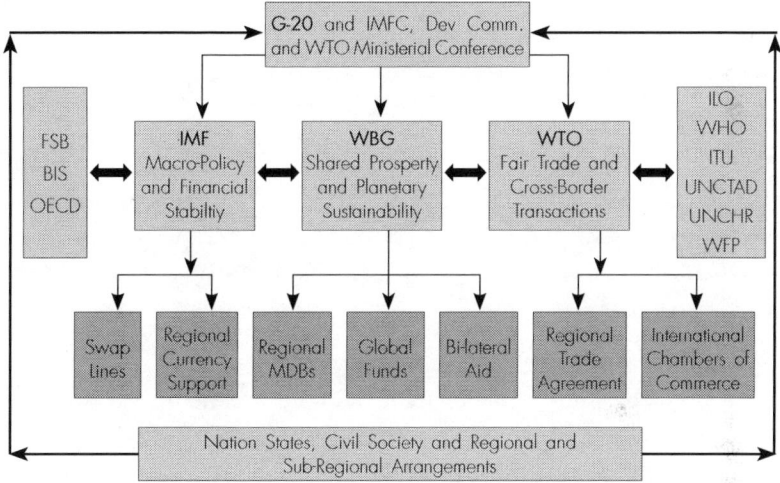

Figure 1: The Proposed New Bretton Woods System

The proposals for a new system can be put into two buckets: (a) remit and (b) resources.

(a) Remit

The remit of the new BW institutions must be global in specified areas—the IMF for macroeconomic policy and financial stability, the WBG for a livable planet and shared prosperity.

IMF

A strengthened IMF must be a core pillar of the system, but it should see its primary role as a monitor and arbiter of the rules. Its success should not be judged by the size of its programmes or how much it has lent. Instead, it should see its success by how little it must lend to keep the global financial system more stable. It should be seen as the lender of last resort, and it should not try to invent new facilities to keep itself relevant and keep lending. A good firefighter should judge their success by how well they prevented fires rather than by how many fires they respond to. In this regard, it should be working to encourage central bank swap arrangements and regional support mechanisms, and not resisting them as it has often done in the past. It should be working towards helping to create a stronger, multi-instrument financial resilience compact rather than being the sole provider of support to countries in balance of payments and financial distress. Other issues at the IMF that need addressing are:

Have a Stricter Rules-Based System to Programme Size and Frequency: IMF programme sizes varied hugely. This arbitrariness led to the loss of the IMF's credibility and legitimacy as a rules-based international organization. IMF resources must be increased, but they should be used in a less arbitrary manner to help restore its credibility.[43]

Focus on Debt and Help Prepare a Debt-Restructuring Framework: Given the likelihood that many countries are likely to enter debt crises in the coming years, the IMF—working closely with the World Bank and the FSB—should be tasked with establishing a debt-restructuring framework that can be acceptable to DAC and non-DAC countries.[44] The existing framework which uses a case-by-case approach is too slow and insufficient.

Reduce Mission Creep: Of course the IMF should work on social, gender and climate change issues to better understand their macroeconomic and financial impacts, but it should avoid any programmes and lending on these issues, and leave that function to other aid agencies within the international financial system.

World Bank Group

The World Bank Group must become the apex global institution for the greening of the world economy. Just as we needed a Marshall Plan to help the world recover from the ravages of the Second World War, we now need actions on a similar scale internationally to engineer energy and ecological transformation for a more sustainable planet. Its name could be changed from the International Bank for Reconstruction and Development (IBRD) to the International Bank for Sustainability and Development (IBSD).[45] Its success must be judged not just by how much it lends, but by the volume of resources it can catalyze to address global climate change challenges. In addition, it must help build the institutions for well-functioning market economies and human capital advancement to draw in more FDI. It must be able to help both in country and on global challenges.[46]

Shift the Focus from Lending to Catalyzing Resource Flows: The World Bank Group should focus not just on financing infrastructure but also on helping build the institutions and regulatory systems to crowd in private capital. Financing yet another school, health centre, road, dam, irrigation system, power plant or rail line is not what it should use its limited capital for. Instead, it should help build the road, rail and airport authorities, the energy and telecom regulators, and the judicial and governance systems that will help the country attract private capital.[47] More innovative financing of the MDBs is needed and this should include ways in which guarantees and loans are treated on the books of the World Bank and other MDBs. A guarantee or an insurance back-stop facility has only a small probability of being called and must be booked differently from a loan, as otherwise it creates a huge disincentive to its use.[48]

(b) Resources

The size of the BW institutions—relative to global needs—remains exceedingly small, and if these institutions are to play a central global role, their resource base must be enhanced. The IMF has the capacity to lend up to $1 trillion (about one per cent of the global GDP), of which less than half (about $450 billion) is from quotas (callable capital).[49] The rest comes from borrowings—which are discretionary.[50] Its quota size must be at least doubled[51] and adjusted more automatically as the global GDP rises, especially as the world enters a phase when widespread debt crises are likely. In turn, the IMF must help encourage swap arrangements and regional liquidity arrangements to help make the system more secure. The total stock of SDRs amounting to $660.7 billion is equivalent to around $950 billion, which is just over one per cent of the global GDP.

The World Bank Group's capital base must also be increased, but at the same time, there must also be changes to the way they use their funds. The World Bank and MDBs now provide an exceedingly small share of net flows to emerging markets, and they together cater to only about a third of the financing needs of even low-income IDA-eligible countries.[52] Doubling their capital base—to start with—and then having a formula to increase their capital base every five years, linked to a share of the global GDP, would make their financing less political and arbitrary.[53] They have been overly conservative in their equity-to-loan ratios, despite having preferred creditor treatment and AAA ratings based on their shareholder ratings. According to Humphrey (2020),[54] their equity-to-loan ratios have been between 30 and 35 per cent—compared to 10 to 15 per cent for commercial banks. They could also be allowed more leeway in their use of capital by changing their capital adequacy ratios and allowing them to use a share of callable capital, and not just their paid-in capital.[55] The objective is to find ways to raise resources in an expeditious, prudent manner without becoming excessively conservative.[56]

The underfunding by the WBG and the MDB system with respect to global challenges must be addressed, as their current funding use is very country-focused. With the Addis Ababa Action Agenda (AAAA), the financing plan for the SDGs agreed upon in 2015 pushed for new modes of financing. In that context, it is surprising that more global sources of finance were not considered for GPG financing. At least three such options exist and they could go a long way towards financing GPGs.

The first is a carbon tax or the auctioning of carbon emissions permits. This is an idea with huge appeal as it will also help discourage the use of fossil fuels and could lower emissions globally, but is unfortunately and unsurprisingly opposed by all the major emitters. Carbon taxes have been introduced in a few countries to reduce fossil fuel use without any damage to long-term growth.[57] The EU has a proposal to link carbon taxes to trade and it would end up increasing their use, but may also drive the world to greater protectionism.[58] Emission permits have also been tried in some countries to reduce emissions of some harmful chemicals. But they have not been used internationally.

The second is to add a pollution user fee on the use of the global commons—the oceans, the atmosphere and such others. This could be done by charging this fee on obvious emitters like shipping and air travel—whose pollution costs are not fully captured and would be easy to collect. But their CO_2 emissions of around 2 billion tons per year are less than five per cent of total CO_2 emissions and would require a heavy fee of around $100 per ton to collect $200 billion per year. A fairer and more universal idea would be to charge a fee on accumulated CO_2 emissions by each country instead of targeting a particular sector—like a rent on the parking space provided by the atmosphere for CO_2. A fee of $1 per ton of CO_2 per year would raise close to $800 billion per year. Much of this money could be used in the country that pays the fee for addressing climate change, and a fixed share could be passed on to a strengthened WBG to finance global actions needed to address climate change.

The third option is to allow the issuance of SDRs and use part of it to finance GPGs. The US has proposed to increase quotas proportionately without a change in voting shares, but it will be difficult to get consensus on it by the 16th Review of IMF quotas, along with approval from the US Congress.

The Way Forward

A return to a pre-Second World War world with beggar-thy-neighbour policies and rising nationalism haunts the world. If such a fate must be avoided, a strong multilateral system is the only answer, with a G20-type arrangement to guide it.[59] Some argue that we need to start from scratch and think of completely new institutions. But such a grand restructuring will be exceedingly difficult and it may be much easier to start with what we have today. As some have said, if the

BW institutions did not exist, we would have to invent them—so it's better to revitalize those that exist and make them fit for purpose.[60] At the same time, a reform of their governance structure is also needed, with a re-ordering of their voting shares to better reflect the twenty-first century.

During India's G20 chairmanship, a high-powered expert group for the MDBs concluded that an additional $3 trillion per year until 2030 is needed to attain the SDG goals, of which $1.8 trillion would be dedicated to climate change every year. $1.2 trillion per year is needed to attain other SDGs—mostly health and education—where the world is falling woefully short. Of this $3 trillion per year, the expert group proposed that external sources will provide only $1 trillion per year; the additional $2 trillion per year was conveniently assigned to domestic resources. Of the external $1 trillion per year, $500 billion must come from increased official assistance (one-third concessional and two-thirds non-concessional), and $500 billion from leveraging in external private finance. Of the $500 billion in official assistance, $260 billion per year would come from MDBs, of which $200 billion is non-concessional, and they must also leverage in most of the private finance.

It's Easy to Come Up with Neat Numbers but How Do You Make It Happen?

First, with so many countries in debt and under fiscal distress, how are they expected to raise an additional $2 trillion per year that the expert group calls for, when they will struggle to maintain even what they have? This cannot be done unless there is comprehensive debt restructuring and more innovative debt-for-climate swaps. Secondly, the MDBs must not only raise their support by an additional $200 billion in non-concessional finance but also use it to leverage in $500 billion per year from the private sector—a 2.5:1 leverage, where they have only raised 60 cents to every dollar so far—implying a four-fold increase in their ability to leverage. Of this, $240 billion per year will come in co-financing with the MDBs and $260 billion in additional FDIs induced by reforms supported by the MDBs—a huge stretch in many countries with governance challenges and regulatory weaknesses. Natarajan and Nageswaran,[61] while acknowledging the need to bring in private capital, point to the challenges involved in generating such leverage. ODA requires an additional $90 billion per year in concessional assistance, lower than the $100 billion promised earlier and about $133 billion per year in non-concessional assistance. Additional concessional ODA of that magnitude remains a pipedream, and non-concessional assistance of $133 billion would largely have to go to only a handful of countries as most developing countries are already mired in huge and unsustainable debt.

An earlier G20 capital adequacy framework (CAF) report suggested ways to squeeze additional lending from the MDBs through the better use of their capital, without hurting their creditor status, by relaxing statutory lending limits, better accounting of callable capital, and preferred creditor treatment, which was estimated to add an additional $80 billion per year in MDB lending.[62] But some argue that the use of callable capital—instead of just paid-in capital—is risky, as it could affect their credit ratings which would increase the cost of borrowing for developing countries. A third window in the report is the creation of a Global Challenges Funding Mechanism (GCFM) to increase lending by an additional $20 billion per year in non-concessional finance to address global problems. But given the externalities of common goods, global problems need concessional finance. Unfortunately, concessional global funds like the US's $100 billion Green Climate Fund remain grossly underfunded. Unless the G20 is willing to engage in other forms of more automatic funding for global challenges, as suggested earlier in the essay, the means for tackling global challenges will remain grossly underfunded.

The World Bank—under new president Ajay Banga—has produced its own initial reform plan called the Evolution Roadmap, which has clearly signalled that it will add climate change to its goal of eradicating poverty under a catchy new objective: eradicating poverty and shared prosperity on a livable planet. It has also incorporated some ideas from the CAF report, such as changing its equity-to-loan ratio to 19 per cent from the earlier 20 per cent, and a promise to use more guarantees to draw in private capital. Based on this, it expects to increase lending by only $5 billion to $6 billion per year, and will need more innovative solutions to raise its capacity to lend and lever in private capital. It has considerably improved its ability to leverage private capital by creating a broader guarantee platform at MIGA which includes in one place IBRD and IFC guarantees together with MIGA's political risk guarantee.

The G20 expert group also suggests a general capital increase for the MDBs to enhance their lending capacity. That is badly needed but is unlikely to happen anytime soon; not until the MDBs can demonstrate a better use of their existing capital base. The US Treasury has sent a request for an additional $25 billion for the World Bank to the US Congress, which could allow it to lend perhaps $200 billion more; but given the fractured politics, it's doubtful if it will get approved even though it would be very helpful. The report by the G20 expert group provides a framework for thinking about the financing needs and correctly notes the need for the MDB reform to work faster and better to leverage in private capital, but it lacks clear and automatic funding mechanisms, and expects two-thirds of the financing to come from additional domestic financing—not a fair burden, given the principle of 'common but differentiated responsibility' which no longer gets even a mention.

The time to act on it has come. The global pandemic, the Russia-Ukraine war, the Israel-Hamas war (which risks becoming a larger conflict) and the looming threat of climate change, where tipping points are being breached, and increasing natural disasters require a much enhanced system of organized global cooperation and reformed Bretton Woods institutions fit for the twenty-first century. Archimedes said it best: 'Give me a strong base and a lever long enough and I can change the world.' But if the base is weak and the lever is too long and not strong enough, it can break. That is the challenge ahead.

Section II

India: The Domestic Economy

Sajjid Z. Chinoy

Getting Rich before Getting Old: India's Macroeconomic Imperatives in a Post-Pandemic World

I had the good fortune of meeting Dr Shankar Acharya relatively early in life while I was still a student. I was finishing up my doctorate at Stanford and met Dr Acharya on campus, at a conference on Indian economic policy reforms. Two things become immediately obvious: first, he was a fountainhead of economic wisdom and policymaking; second, he was genuinely interested in mentoring the next generation. Those two qualities have typified my interactions with him over the last 25 years. He is one of the finest thinkers and practitioners on the Indian economy and I learn from him on every occasion we interact. Separately, he has been a wonderful mentor and was instrumental in facilitating my return to economics after a family setback.

Over the decades, Dr Acharya has cared deeply, and written frequently, about the key challenges that India must overcome, from jobs and exports to deficits. I hope this chapter goes some way in doing justice to these issues that are close to his heart, and will shape and drive the macro outlook over the next decade.

■

The urgency of achieving strong and sustained growth in India has only increased in the post-pandemic period. This is because (a) five years after the pandemic, output still remains discernibly below the levels implied by the pre-pandemic path, suggestive of some pandemic-induced scarring, (b) public debt levels have gapped up in India (as around the world), and strong growth is crucial to safeguarding debt-sustainability, and (c) the economy needs to dramatically ramp up job creation, both to cope with a rapidly-evolving demographic transition and make up for the pandemic's impact.

Where will the growth come from? Post-pandemic growth has been underpinned by new drivers: clean bank balance sheets, a resurgent real estate cycle and service exports. That said, a determined public investment push has been crucial to India's investment and growth outcomes in recent years. Yet, for public investment to continue doing the heavy-lifting will be challenging for both fiscal sustainability and state capacity constraints. The investment baton will therefore have to pass to the corporate sector for growth to sustain. Given this imperative, why has corporate investment not lifted more convincingly, given the healthy balance sheets? This is because demand visibility is currently the binding constraint on corporate capex. As the fisc consolidates, demand will need to be generated both by private consumption and broad-based export growth. Only then can the corporate capex cycle be expected to rise sustainably.

For all this to happen, however, three macroeconomic imperatives need to be fulfilled. First, both the quality and quantum of employment will need to be significantly boosted in the coming years to generate adequate domestic demand. This will not just entail higher levels of growth but also make growth more labour-intensive. Second, defying the current global export pessimism, exports will need to be at the heart of any growth strategy, because no economy has experienced strong and sustained growth without it being underpinned by strong exports. Third, public sector revenues (taxes and asset sales) will need to be boosted so that authorities can fund the crucial investments (education, health, infrastructure, and such others) needed to fulfil the aforementioned imperatives, while simultaneously bringing down fiscal deficits, and protecting and preserving macroeconomic stability.

What's Driving Post-Pandemic Growth in India?

The imperative for strong growth in India has only increased following the pandemic. But before we assess the need for a new-found growth urgency, it's important to understand what has been driving growth in recent years to understand their sustainability. Four new drivers of growth have emerged in the post-pandemic period and we start by analyzing each of them.[1]

1. **Public Infrastructure Push:** The Central government made a strategic decision during the pandemic to boost infrastructure spending as a counter-cyclical response, and the Centre has thus far delivered on that commitment. The Centre's capex spend, as a share of GDP, has doubled between FY20 and FY24 before witnessing some signs of flattening in FY25. On their part, States were slow to get off the block but have delivered a sharp capex increase in 2023–24[2]. However, once again, its momentum appears to have stalled in 2024–25. To be sure, some of the Centre's capex increase reflects PSU (public sector undertaking) capex moving onto the Centre's balance sheet. Furthermore, PSU capex has independently slowed down. But even after accounting for all this, total public capex (Centre + States + PSU) increased between 2017–18 and 2023–24, before softening in 2024–25.

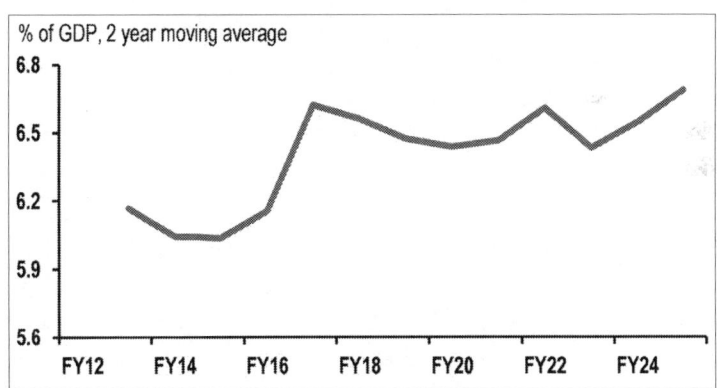

Figure 1: Consolidated Public Sector Capex

Source: Budget documents, State Budgets, RBI, J.P. Morgan.

2. **Residential Housing Cycle Inflects:** After languishing for a decade, India's housing cycle has taken hold. A combination of rising affordability over the last decade, deeply negative real interest rates during the pandemic, and increased housing demand on account of work-from-home during and after the pandemic,

has contributed to the uptick in the cycle. Inventories which had peaked at 33 months of demand in 2017 were down to just 12 months in 2023, which has triggered new launches. Residential construction and an infrastructure push have, in turn, combined to drive a construction cycle.

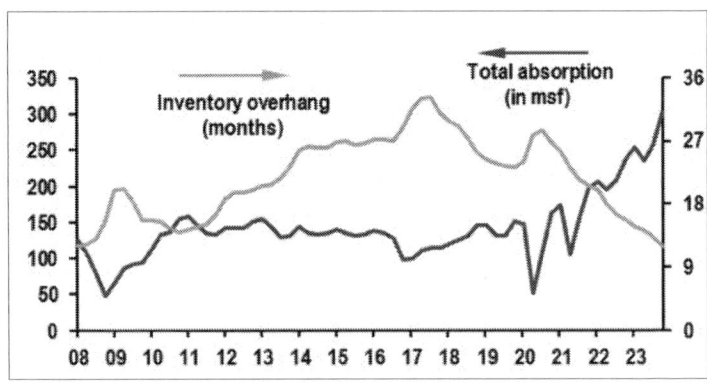

Figure 2: Total Absorption vs. Months of Inventory

Source: J.P. Morgan India Real Estate team.

3. **Healthier Bank Balance Sheets:** As banks have progressively worked through their elevated NPAs in recent years, bank balance sheets are the healthiest they have been in a decade, with net NPAs at their lowest in 12 years. This has eased lending standards and—in conjunction with the economic recovery—spawned a credit cycle. Credit growth averaged 16 per cent in 2023–24, 1.3 times the nominal GDP growth. To be sure, a large fraction of credit has gone towards unsecured lending, which has understandably made regulators cautious and invoke macroprudential measures as a means to throw sand in the gears. Tighter macroprudential norms, in conjunction with a cyclical slowing in growth, slowed credit meaningfully in 2024–25. But balance sheets remain healthy and are unlikely to become a binding constraint on growth anytime soon.

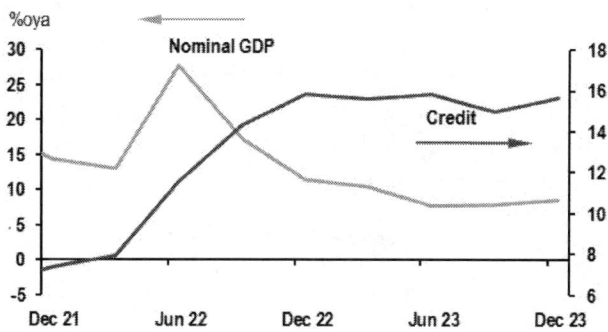

Figure 3: Bank Credit vs. Nominal GDP

Source: RBI, MoSPI, J.P. Morgan.

4. **Surging Service Exports:** Even as there has been much anticipation about the extent to which India would benefit from the 'China-Plus-One' opportunity on merchandise exports, the real revelation during the pandemic was the surge in service exports, which increased by 60 per cent in just the last three years and have now almost overtaken goods exports! This is not just India's growing IT exports but a richer suite of services (research, legal, accounting) that multinational companies are undertaking to service global operations from their captive 'Global Capability Centres' in India. Growth on this front has remained consistently strong in recent years.

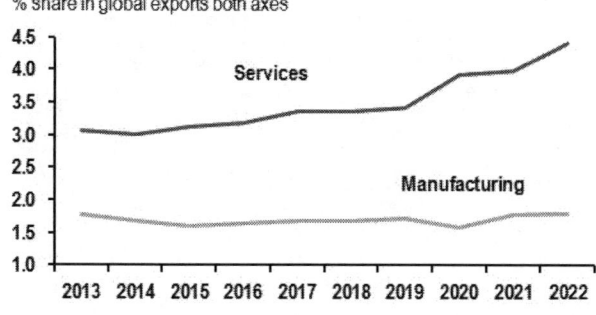

Figure 4: India's Share of Global Exports

Source: ITC Trademap, J.P. Morgan.

The Urgency for Strong and Sustained Growth

The emergence of new growth drivers in recent years is encouraging because the urgency for strong and sustained growth has only increased in the post-pandemic period. We lay out at least three reasons why achieving and sustaining high growth is so crucial in the coming years.

1. Alleviating Hysteresis from the Pandemic

The slowing economic growth of 2024–25 comes on the back of three years of strong growth, during which it averaged 8.8 per cent. But that, in turn, came on the back of a contraction (-5.8 per cent) in the pandemic year (2020–21), and very soft growth (3.9 per cent oya) in the year before the pandemic.

Given these gyrations, it's important to assess the cumulative performance in recent years. We do so in two ways—by looking at (a) the compound annual growth rate (CAGR) of GDP over the last six years, and (b) the distance of India's GDP from its pre-pandemic path. What do we find in our assessments?

- The six-year CAGR of India's GDP growth (2019–25) is more modest at close to five per cent.
- A related method to judge how economies have emerged from the pandemic is to assess what the level of output is vis-à-vis the counterfactual. Where would output have been absent the pandemic, and how does that compare to the realized output? To make this judgement, however, one has to make assumptions around what the economy's potential growth rate was in the pre-pandemic period. In India's case, we remain agnostic and take the average GDP growth rate in the five years leading up to the pandemic (6.7 per cent).

Using this approach, we find that the level of output by the end of 2024–25—five years after the pandemic—is still about 4 per cent below the counterfactual (Figure 5). To be sure, barring the United States, almost all economies are below their pre-pandemic paths to different degrees. But the extent and duration for which output remains below the pre-pandemic counterfactual suggests a hysteresis from the pandemic that will need to be combatted. For example, India's growth will have to be 7.5 to 8 per cent over the next five years just to get back on the pre-pandemic path and avoid permanent scarring. This must drive an urgency for sustained high growth.

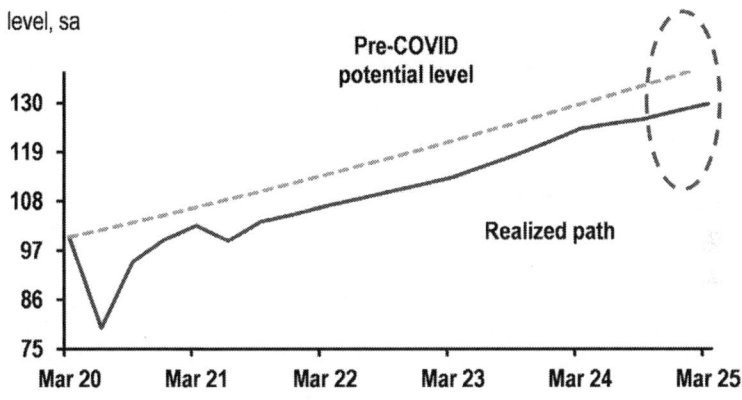

Figure 5: GDP Levels

Source: J.P. Morgan.

2. Stabilizing and Reducing Debt: The Role of Growth

Quite apart from the need to mitigate the scarring from the pandemic, sustained high growth is also necessary to stabilize fiscal metrics in a post-pandemic world laden with public debt. Like most economies, India's public debt as a percentage of the GDP ballooned in the pandemic from 71 per cent in 2018–19 to 89 per cent by 2020–21. The high inflation that followed in the next two years had a salutary impact on public debt, bringing it down to 83 per cent in FY24. But with inflation softening to more sustainable levels, strong real growth will be a critical prerequisite to ensure that public debt remains sustainable and does not force excessive fiscal austerity.

More generally, the evolution of public debt is the interaction between the starting stock of public debt, the primary deficit and borrowing costs, and can be expressed as:

$$D_T + 1 = Dt \times (1+r) + PD_{t+1}$$

Where, D_t is the absolute debt stock at time t, r is the average interest rate on debt, and PD_t is the primary deficit at time t.

While there are no sacrosanct *levels* of public debt in a post-pandemic world, a sufficient condition for debt unsustainability is a monotonic increase in public debt in the post-pandemic steady state. At a minimum, therefore, emerging markets will have to stabilize public debt and then aim to gradually bring it down to create fiscal space for future shocks. Doing so would require that there be a balance between credible fiscal consolidation and strong growth to stabilize debt.

Debt Dynamics under Different Growth Scenarios

To see the importance of growth in the evolution of India's debt dynamics, consider this. The Central government has budgeted a fiscal deficit of 4.4 per cent of the GDP for 2025–26. State deficits are expected to print upwards of three per cent of the GDP this year. Let's assume that they eventually stabilize at three per cent of the GDP, which is the threshold up to which States are allowed to borrow. That would imply a combined fiscal deficit of about 7.1 per cent of the GDP.[3]

Under these fiscal assumptions, the trajectory of growth over the next decade will have a crucial bearing on future debt dynamics.

- For example, nominal GDP growth will have to average 10 per cent over the next decade—corresponding to 6.5 to 7 per cent real growth—just to stabilize public debt dynamics.
- If public debt is to be brought down—as the policy objective must be, to make space for the next shock—then the nominal GDP will need to be about 11 per cent—corresponding to the real GDP growth of 7.5 to 8 per cent on a sustained basis (Figure 6).
- Conversely, if real GDP growth disappoints and averages 5.5 to 6 per cent over the next decade (such that nominal GDP growth is around nine per cent), India's public debt will keep inching up towards 85 per cent over the next decade.

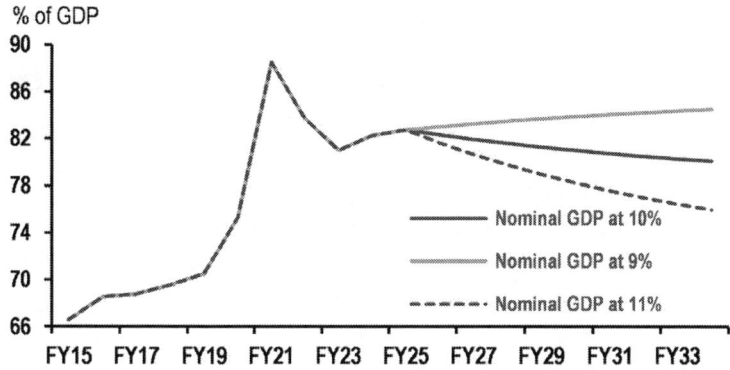

Figure 6: Debt Dynamics with Combined Deficit at 7.1 per cent of GDP

Source: RBI, J.P. Morgan.

In other words, not only is sustained high growth crucial for job creation and livelihoods, it is also a prerequisite for keeping public debt sustainable over the next decade.

To be sure, there is a bidirectional causality between growth and fiscal deficits. For starters, strong growth impacts debt through multiple channels. Apart from the direct influence that growth exerts on the debt-to-GDP ratio, it has a catalytic effect through its impact on fiscal deficits. Stronger growth typically boosts tax buoyancy and revenue generation which, ceteris paribus, can enable further fiscal consolidation—a phenomenon visible in India in the first decade of this millennium. On the other hand, the absence of strong growth will force policymakers to achieve debt sustainability through more aggressive fiscal consolidation, which itself can further impinge on future growth prospects, creating a vicious cycle.

In sum, boosting potential growth will be crucial to debt sustainability and avoiding difficult fiscal choices.

3. Harnessing the Rapidly Evolving Demographic Transition

A third imperative for strong, labour-intensive growth is to help encash the rapid demographic transition that India is currently undergoing. In contrast to ageing populations across many parts of the world, India has a very young population with a median age of 28. As a consequence, India is experiencing a rapid rise in the ratio of working age to the total population.

Prima facie, a bulge in the working age population creates the opportunity to significantly boost output and per capita incomes because a larger share of the population is eligible to work, supporting fewer dependents. This also boosts savings rates, creating the conditions to support higher investment, all of which together are typically dubbed as the 'demographic dividend'. Several economies—East Asia in the 1970s and the 1980s, China in the 1990s and 2000s, among others— have been able to harness this dividend to boost income levels. Some estimates suggest that as much as one-third of East Asia's growth can be attributed to a demographic dividend.[4] Others go even further. Kelley and Schmidt (2005)[5] suggest that the demographic transition accounted for 44 per cent of the per capita income growth between 1960 and 1990. In the case of China, estimates suggest that a quarter of the economic growth between 1978 and 2017 was on account of the demographic dividend.[6]

But no demographic dividend is automatic. It only fructifies if there are sufficient job opportunities to accommodate the increased working-age population and potential workers are endowed with sufficient human capital to become employable and productive.

The implication is that harnessing the demographic dividend needs (a) strong sources of demand growth, either external or domestic, (b) growth to be more labour-intensive and create the requisite job opportunities, and (c) the state to undertake significant investments in human capital (education, health, skilling). As David Bloom notes, 'the demographic dividend only translates into sustained periods of economic growth under a policy environment that emphasizes public health, education and policies that promote labour-market flexibility, openness to trade, and savings.'[7]

India's demographic transition, therefore, creates an urgency for demand and job creation to accommodate the increased share of the working-age population. If India can achieve this, per capita incomes can expect to benefit meaningfully. Conversely, if an increased working-age population does not translate into higher employment rates, social, economic, fiscal and political risks can be expected to rise.

Did You Know? The Demographic Transition Peaks in a Decade

What's less appreciated is that India's demographic transition has been in the works for the last two decades, and peaks in less than a decade. The ratio of working-age population to total population bottomed at 55 per cent in 1965, and has been rising since. However, the increases over the following three decades were relatively modest, with the ratio rising to 60 per cent at the turn of the millennium.

Since then, the increase has been much more pronounced, with the working-age-population ratio increasing to 67 per cent by 2020, i.e. rising by 3.5 per cent a decade—twice the pace of the previous two decades. The ratio is expected to continue increasing, though much more modestly, from here on end. The United Nations (UN) estimates an increase to 69 per cent by 2032 (i.e. 1.3 per cent this decade, slower than the last two decades), staying around that level between 2032 and 2037 before beginning to decline.

In other words, the peak of India's demographic transition is just a decade away, after which dependency rates will start to increase. One can also appreciate this in the growth rates of the working-age population which, as Figure 7 reveals, have been slowing and will continue to slow. The growth rate of the working-age population has slowed to 1.1 per cent in the current decade and is expected to slow to half that level a decade from now. To the extent that the growth of the working-age population is slowing, an economy's potential growth rate also slows, ceteris paribus. Of course, in an economy where employment ratios are well below working-age population ratios, growth can rise from just an increase in employment rates and the working-age population is not a binding constraint.

But what all this shows is that India's demographic transition is rapidly playing out: the ratio of the working-age population peaks in a decade, after which dependency ratios will start to rise and the growth rate of the working-age population will continue to slow, which will have implications for potential growth. So the time span for harnessing the dividend is much shorter than commonly presumed.

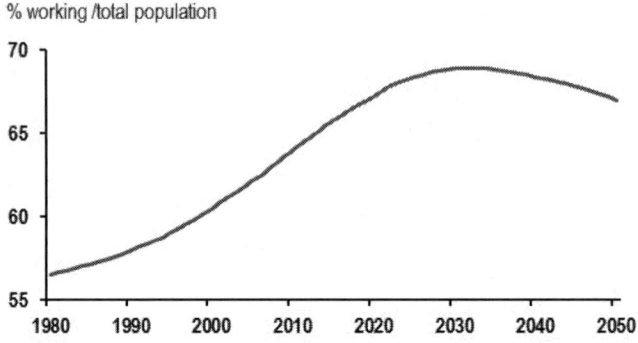

Figure 7: Working-Age/Total Population

Source: UN.

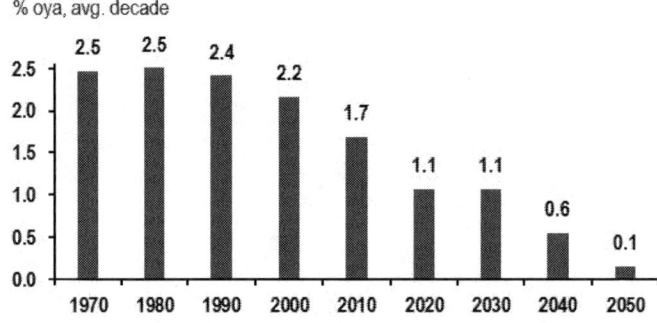

Figure 8: Growth of Working-Age Population

Source: UN.

Where Will Growth Come from? Looking Back to Look Ahead

The urgency for high growth over the next decade should be clear. But where will this growth come from? Recall, GDP on the expenditure side can be represented as private consumption (C) + investment (I) + government spending (G) + net exports (X-M).

$$GDP = C + I + G + (X\text{-}M)$$

As Figure 9 reveals, much of the growth since the pandemic has been driven by exports and investment. Exports have grown at almost eight per cent over the last five years, in part because of the strength of service exports as discussed above. Investment has supported this, growing at a CAGR of above seven per cent over the last five years. Meanwhile, private consumption growth has lagged, growing at 5.2 per cent. Imports, on the other hand, subtracted from GDP growth, have grown at 5.5 per cent.

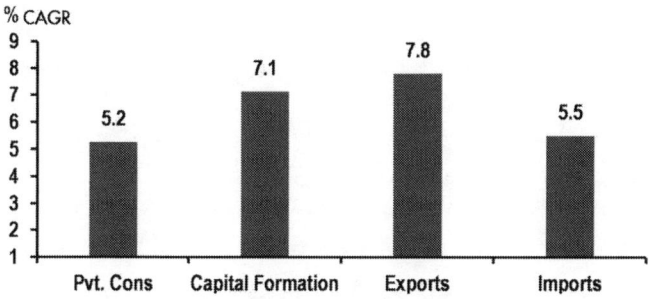

Figure 9: Real GDP Growth FY25 over FY20

Source: MoSPI, J.P. Morgan.

So what do these dynamics suggest for the future? What is driving investment, and can it sustain? Can export growth hold up at this pace? And what will it take for private consumption to lift? We will examine these questions in turn.

Public Investment Will Face Fiscal Constraints

Over the last two years, India's investment rate has finally risen such that the gross fixed capital formation as a share of the GDP has increased to 33.5 per cent in 2023–24 from 31.6 per cent in 2019–20, just before the onset of the pandemic. Importantly, more than half of this increase can be explained by the recent pickup in public capex, which has increased from 7.1 per cent of the GDP in FY20 to 8.4 per cent of the GDP in FY24.

The question is whether the upturn in public capex can increase further or even sustain at its current levels, given both absorptive capacity issues and the need to reduce fiscal deficits in the coming years. While the total public sector borrowing requirement (PSBR) reverted to pre-pandemic levels at 8.0 per cent of GDP in 2024–25, similar to 8.2 per cent of GDP in 2018–19 (Figure 10), public debt levels have gapped up. This rise in public debt would necessitate more fiscal consolidation in the coming years to stabilize it without putting excessive pressure on growth. Towards that end, the Central government is committed to reducing its deficit to 4.4 per cent of the GDP by 2025–26 (i.e. a consolidation of 1.1 per cent of the GDP across two years). That said, even greater consolidation may be needed to stabilize public debt and then bring it down if growth disappoints, as we will discuss later, as part of the third macroeconomic imperative.

So, it will be challenging to maintain or increase capex as a share of GDP in the years ahead when deficits will need to be brought down further if revenue is not boosted. Some of this is already visible. There is a risk that State and Central capex could dip (as a share of the GDP) in 2024–25 compared to the previous year.

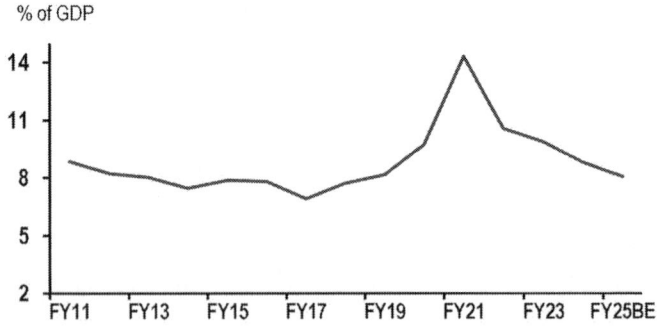

Figure 10: Public Sector Borrowing Requirements (PSBR)
Source: Budget documents, J.P. Morgan.

The Need for Private Investment

All this suggests that private investment will have to pick up the baton sooner rather than later. To be sure, household residential investment has picked up smartly, as discussed earlier, rising to above 9% of GDP in recent years from below 8 per cent in the years before the pandemic. Outside of housing, however, private investment looks much more worrying. Corporate investment—which had remained sluggish at almost 12 per cent of the GDP in the five years before the pandemic and constitutes close to 40 per cent of all gross fixed capital formation—has declined to 11.5% of GDP in FY24.

The good news is that the binding constraints on private capex for much of the last decade—high leverage—have been alleviated. Corporate debt to GDP had surged in 2011, forcing a deleveraging over the last decade. That process is now complete with corporate debt/GDP at much lower levels, alongside strong corporate balance sheets. Instead, the constraints to private corporate investment have likely moved from the supply side (balance sheets) to demand visibility. This is because capacity utilization in manufacturing, for example, continues to remain close to 75 per cent—where it has been for the last 12 years, barring the pandemic. With capacity still to be utilized, imports from China continuing at a strong pace (the bilateral trade deficit with China is close to decadal highs), and fears that a US-China trade war 2.0 will cause more of China's excess capacity to be redirected to other markets, including India, it's understandable that corporates are reluctant to invest just yet. For example, CMIE data reveals that private project announcements have declined so far in 2024–25, and the pace of private capex projects under implementation has slowed in the same period.

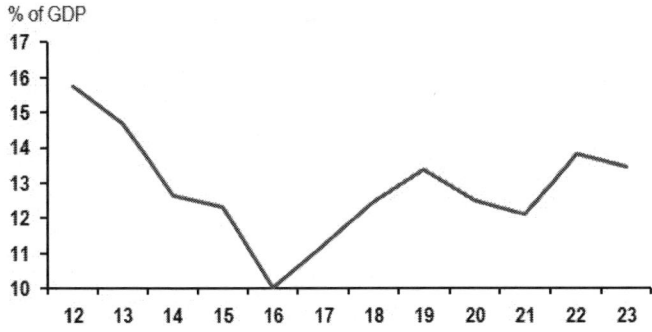

Figure 11: Household Investment

Source: MoSPI.

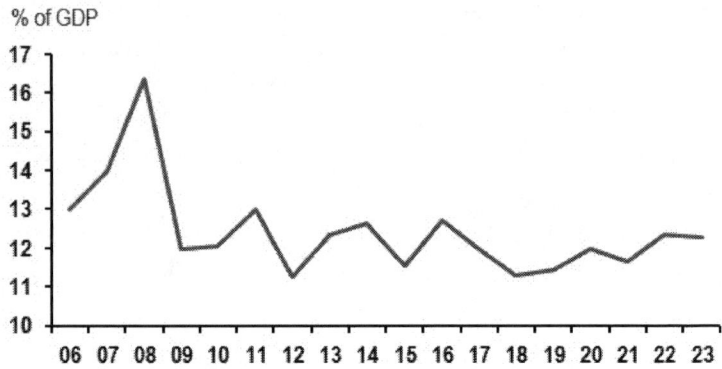

Figure 12: Private Corporate Investment
Source: MoSPI.

The key to a private investment cycle, therefore, is greater demand visibility. Thus far, aggregate demand has been driven largely by the public sector through higher deficits and increased capex spending. But with the public sector being forced to eventually retrench, demand will have to come from some combination of private consumption and exports—topics to which we turn next.

Post-Pandemic Consumption Has Been Tepid...

On its part, private consumption has been tepid since the pandemic. This can be seen in several different ways. First, as Figure 9 reveals, the compound annual growth rate of private consumption has been just 5.2 per cent between 2019 and 2024—well below investment and exports. Second, the growth undershoot in recent years has meant that the *level* of private consumption is well below its pre-pandemic path (Figure 13).

A key reason for the consumption undershoot is the duality that has characterized consumption in the first few years after the pandemic, marked by strong upper-end consumption but soft mass consumption.[8] This can be seen across a cross-section of sectors. For example, jewellery demand was very robust, yet the volume growth of the largest mass-consumption goods remained in the low-to-mid single digits. In the auto sector, four-wheeler vehicle sales significantly outstripped two-wheeler sales in the post-pandemic period. In 2023–24, four-wheeler sales were 24 per cent above the corresponding period in 2019, while two-wheeler sales were still 10 per cent below it (Figure 14). Even within categories, there is increasing evidence of 'premiumization'. For example, between 2019–20 and 2023–24, the share of mid-sized SUVs doubled from 11 per cent to 23 per cent, while that of entry-level cars declined from 20 per cent to 14 per cent (Figure 15).

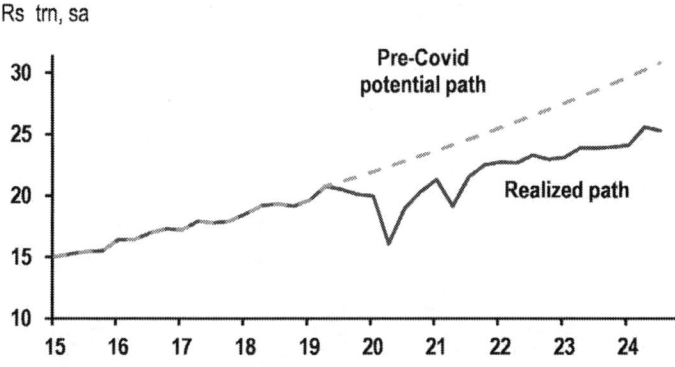

Figure 13: Private Consumption: Realized vs. Pre-Pandemic Trend

Source: MoSPI.

This duality is also visible in the real estate sector. New residential real estate launches, reflecting demand patterns, reveal that the share of affordable (lower-end) housing dropped from 44 per cent to 18 per cent between 2019–20 and 2023–24. Meanwhile, the share of upper-end and luxury or super-luxury launches surged from 23 to 55 per cent.

The aggregate consumption undershoot is therefore a function of the fact that it is not broad-based but more narrowly driven by the top.

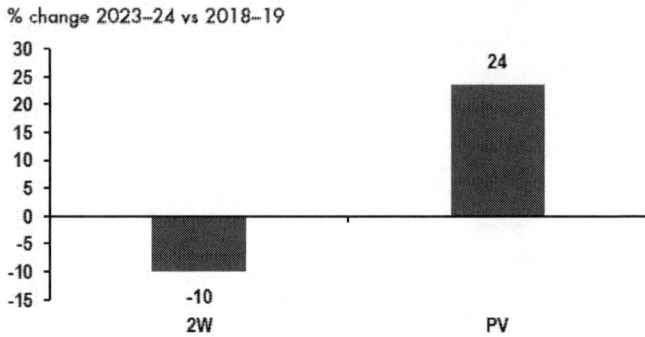

Figure 14: Two-Wheeler and Passenger Vehicles

Source: VAHAN.

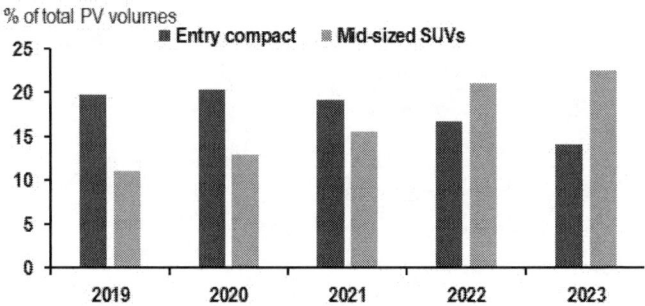

Figure 15: PV Volumes by Category

Source: J.P. Morgan India Autos team.

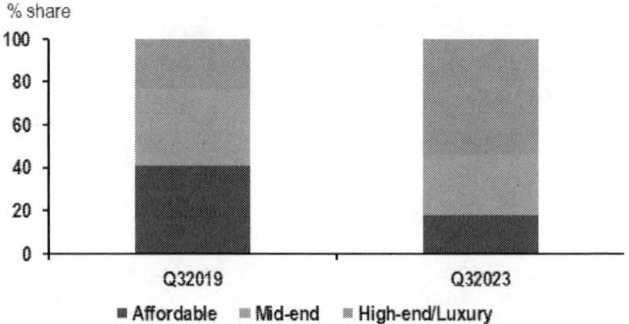

Figure 16: New Houses Launched

Source: Anarock, Represents top seven cities in India.

...Likely Mimicking Labour Market Dynamics

So what was driving the consumption duality? While some of the premiumization is a natural upgradation of quality as people move up the income ladder (the shift from 'inferior' to 'superior' goods), the stark divergences in consumption patterns are likely mimicking dichotomous labour market dynamics. Upper-end consumption appears to be driven both by excess savings and wealth effects at the top of the income pyramid, but also by the strong performance of white-collar or organized-sector jobs over the last two years. This can be proxied by the staff costs of 2,800 listed companies, which have grown at 16 per cent (in nominal terms) between 2021–22 and 2023–24, reflecting a combination of new employees and strong real wage growth. Furthermore, service export jobs of multinational companies not listed in India (Global Capability Centres) would be above and beyond this. Cumulatively, these jobs likely reflect the increased formalization of the economy, the surge of white-collar service exports in 2021 and 2022, and a healthy financial sector that is growing again.

That said, these jobs account for a very small share of the labour market. In contrast, the informal job market—which accounts for the vast majority of jobs—appears to be characterized by much more slack. This can be seen in different ways.

- Nominal rural wages have grown at just six per cent over the last four years—negative on average in real terms—in sharp contrast to formal sector wages (Figure 17), suggestive of a slack in the rural labour market.
- To be sure, the Periodic Labour Force Survey (PLFS) shows that the workers participation ratio (another name for employment as a percent of the population) has risen sharply from 34.7 per cent in 2018 to 43.7 per cent in 2024. But what jobs were created? The PLFS reveals that 85 per cent of the new jobs created were in the rural economy and more than 50 per cent in the agricultural sector. Even between 2023 and 2024, the PLFS reveals that 50 per cent of the jobs created were in agriculture. The latter is already overpopulated, raising questions about disguised unemployment.

All told, it's the dichotomous nature of the labour market—strong formal sector employment but weak informal sector employment—that likely explains the stark difference in consumption patterns in recent years.

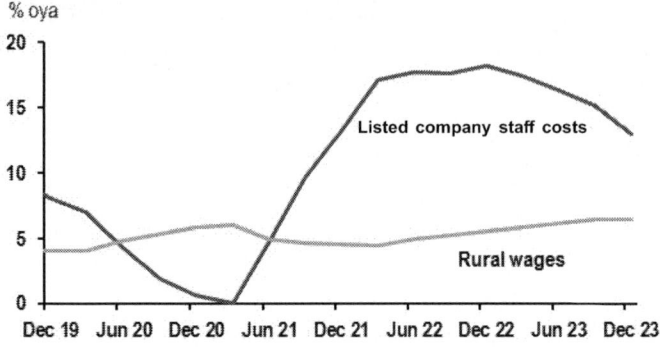

Figure 17: Staff Costs of Pvt Listed Companies vs. Rural Wages
Source: RBI, Labour Bureau.

The First Signs of a Consumption Convergence

While the consumption duality characterized consumption patterns in the first three years after the pandemic, there are some signs of convergence across urban and rural consumption in 2024–25. After a strong run in recent years, urban consumption has begun to slow because (a) the stock of excess financial savings built up in the pandemic has been largely exhausted, (b) urban wage growth has slowed in recent quarters, and (c) regulatory tightening has meant that unsecured lending—which was partially supporting consumption—has slowed sharply (this was, however, much needed because lending had become very imprudent and would have resulted in asset quality issues down the line). To be sure, rural consumption is picking up, but off a low-base—two-wheeler sales growth has been strong this year but the number of two-wheelers sold in calendar year 2024 is still below the levels seen in 2018. The expectation is that rural consumption, after a prolonged soft patch, will pick up, but it remains to be seen how strong the recovery is.

The Consumption Slowdown Pre-Dated the Pandemic

While there has been a lot of analysis on consumption patterns in the post-pandemic period, it's important to recognize that private consumption had likely slowed even before the pandemic, per the Household Consumption Expenditure Survey (HCES). As the figure given below suggests, the growth of real per capita private consumption expenditure fell discernibly between 2011 and 2023 compared to the 2005–12 period (Figure 18).[9]

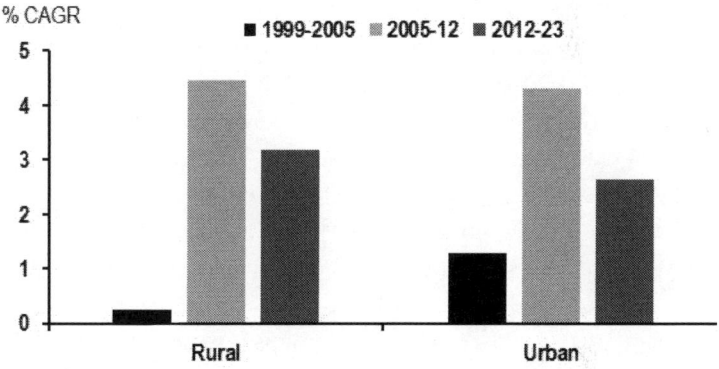

Figure 18: Real Consumption Per Capita

Source: HCES.

In sum, consumption has slowed over the last decade, and pressures have accentuated since the onset of the pandemic. There will always be proximate explanations that aim to explain soft consumption at any point in time (financial sector tightening in 2019, lack of income support in 2020 and 2021). However, in our view, the more secular slowing in consumption over the last decade is on account of a more fundamental pressure: employment. This is reflected in both the quantity and quality of the jobs being created over the last two decades. We, therefore, identify employment as the key macroeconomic imperative for India over the next decade and will discuss it in more detail later, as the first imperative.

The Importance of Exports

Before we turn to employment and its impact on consumption, however, it is important to recognize that exports need to be an important source of demand in the coming years. Recall, no economy without a significant commodity endowment has grown at a sustained strong pace for years on end, like India must, without strong export growth. Indeed, India's own experience reinforces this fact. The growth surge in the early 2000s—where GDP growth clocked an eight per cent average between 2003 and 2007—was driven largely by an exports surge. Exports grew at 18 per cent a year on average in those years as India made a foray into IT services, alongside goods exports such as pharmaceuticals and automobiles. Strong and consistent end-demand, in turn, induced a private investment cycle that decade.

Exports will, therefore, have to be key to any growth strategy going forward. As discussed above, service exports have surged since the pandemic. Between 2005 and 2021, services exports grew at 8.5 per cent a year. Over the last three years, however, that growth rate has almost doubled to 17 per cent as a growing suite of value-added services are now undertaken in the Global Capability services (Figure 19). But all this creates white-collar jobs, which accentuates the consumption duality. In contrast, blue-collar jobs have faced more headwinds. This is in part because goods exports have slowed sharply over the last decade. Between 2005 and 2012, goods exports grew 14.4 per cent. Since 2012, however, they have grown at just 3.5 per cent a year. Therefore, their share in the GDP has been consistently falling.

For exports to be seen as a more reliable driver of demand, both services and goods will need to flourish in tandem. This will necessitate creating an ecosystem that incentivizes trade and an outward orientation—an issue that will be further explored in the second macroeconomic imperative.

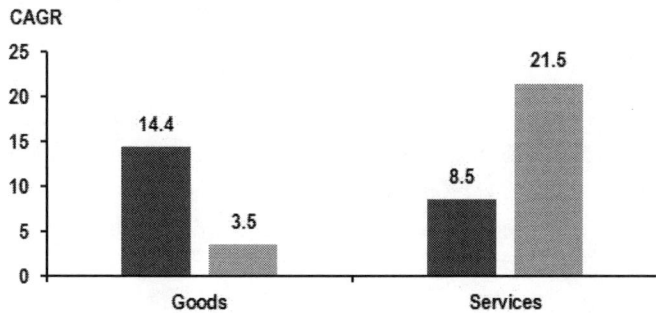

Figure 19: Goods and Services Exports (Goods Exports Shown for the Periods 2005–2012 and 2012–23; Services Shown for the Periods 2005–21 and 2021–23)

Source: Ministry of Trade & Commerce, J.P. Morgan.

Three Medium-Term Economic Imperatives

As the previous section highlighted, strong and sustained GDP growth will necessitate private investment picking up the mantle from public investment. But a private investment cycle, in turn, will require visibility which will need to emanate from private consumption and exports.

So what macroeconomic imperatives are needed to achieve these outcomes? That is the focus of this section.

Imperative #1: Job Creation by Making Labour a More Attractive Factor of Production

As alluded to in the previous sections, given the demographic transition that India is undergoing and the need to create commensurate good-quality jobs, employment creation will need to be India's foremost macroeconomic imperative over the next decade. It is needed not just to ensure more balanced growth, given that the binding constraint to growth has moved to demand visibility, but job creation is also key to domestic consumption and investment prospects.

To quantify the nature of the challenge before policymakers, we use a more composite growth-accounting approach. Recall, GDP growth can be decomposed into contributions from capital, labour, human capital and total factor productivity (the efficiency with which inputs are used in the production process). We combine physical labour and human capital into a combined 'labour variable' for ease of exposition. We use data both from the Penn World Tables (PWT)[10] and the KLEMS database.[11]

What does the data reveal? It shows that despite India undergoing a demographic transition, the contribution of labour (including human capital) to growth has been low and falling. As the IMF notes,[12] 'Emerging market economies tend to have labor as an important driver of growth [...] India's growth recently has however been more capital-driven [...] Like many other emerging markets, India has a large population of low-skilled workers. Unlike other emerging markets, however, growth in India is driven in large part by capital and TFP, making it more comparable to advanced economies.'

To be sure, the percentage point contribution of physical labour can be expected to fall because the growth rate of the working-age population is also falling over time. But there are at least two caveats. First, improvements in human capital can often partially offset the fall in the growth rate of workers. Second, it's important that labour's contribution to growth is not falling disproportionately in relation to the slowing of the growth of the working-age population, which would be symptomatic of inadequate labour force participation and/ or job creation.

To assess this, we look at how India's working-age population and their growth contribution have evolved vis-à-vis the other economies that also experienced a large demographic transition—China and South Korea. As Figures 22 and 23 reveal, both variables move closely in tandem in China and Korea. In fact, there are decades when labour's contribution to growth exceeds the growth rate of the working-age population, suggesting large improvements in human capital. In India's case, however, both variables moved in tandem in the 1970s, 1980s and 1990s. However, over the last two decades, the contribution of labour (both increases in employment and human capital) has fallen well short of the growth rate of the working-age population.[13] This is an ominous sign for the challenges associated with both the quantum and quality of jobs—topics to which we turn next.

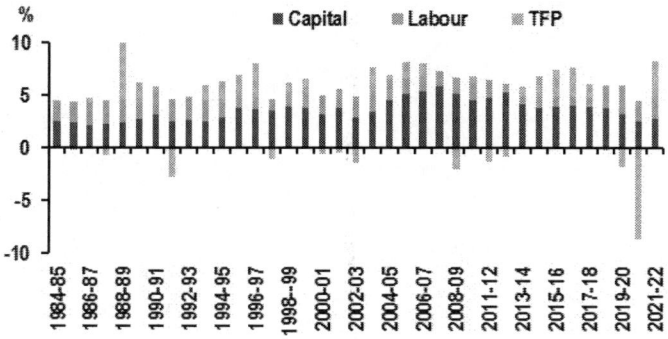

Figure 20: India Growth Accounting

Source: KLEMS.

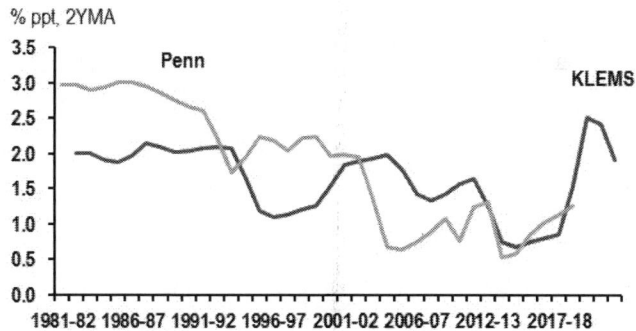

Figure 21: Labour Contribution to Growth

Source: Penn World Table, KLEMS.

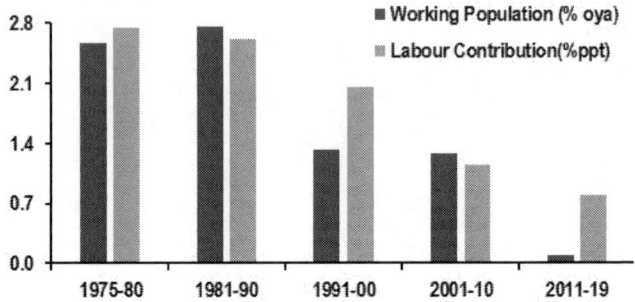

Figure 22: China's Working-Age Population vs. Labour Contribution

Source: Penn World Table.

Figure 23: Korea's Working-Age Population vs. Labour Contribution

Source: Penn World Table.

Figure 24: India's Working-Age Population vs. Labour Contribution

Source: Penn World Table.

The Quantum of Jobs

As previously discussed, India's demographic dividend—already in the works for the last 25 years—has meant that India's share of working-age population, as a function of total population, has been increasing at a rapid clip over the last two decades. In contrast, however, the employment-to-total-population ratio has increased much more modestly over the last two decades (Figure 25). Unsurprisingly, therefore, the ratio of employment/working-age population has seen a sharp decline since the early 2000s.[14] To be sure, after bottoming in 2018, it has increased over the last five years, which is encouraging (Figure 26). It remains to be seen, however, whether (a) this can sustain, and (b) where these jobs are being created—topics to which we turn next.

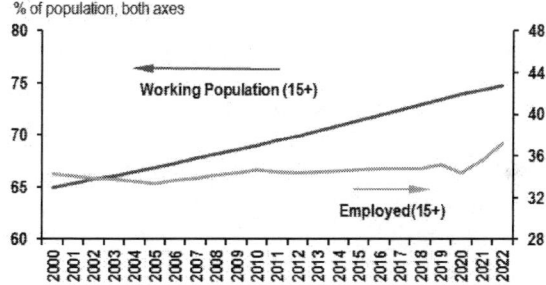

Figure 25: Labour Market

Source: ILO, UN.

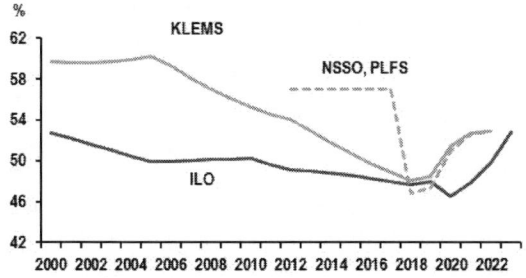

Figure 26: Employment/Working-Age Population

Source: ILO, NSSO, PLFS, KLEMPS, UN.

The Quality of Jobs

The quantum of jobs apart, their quality also matters crucially. Higher-productivity jobs and commensurately higher wages and incomes are crucial to sustainable livelihoods. The quintessential 'structural transformation' typically entails moving workers from lower-productivity agriculture into higher-productivity manufacturing and services. So how is India doing on that front? The increase in the ratio of employment to working-age population in recent years is very encouraging. But what kinds of jobs are being created?

One can cut the data in different ways. As it turns out, between 2018 and 2024, more than 50 per cent of the jobs created were in agriculture which was already over-populated, and therefore created concerns about disguised unemployment. Excess labour in agriculture also explains why the demand for MGNREGA was elevated in the post-pandemic period, though, encouragingly, demand has abated in recent months. Agriculture apart, about 18 per cent of the new jobs were created in the construction sector, reflecting the government's infrastructure push. About 20 per cent of the new jobs were in services, and less than 10 per cent in manufacturing.

Looking through the prism of gender, men moved out of agriculture and into construction jobs (Figure 29). On the other hand, the vast majority of new jobs created in agriculture were for women.

Finally, the share of regular and casual jobs fell, replaced by a sharp increase in the 'self-employed' segment. Interestingly, the fastest growing segment within this group is 'unpaid family labour'. All this suggests that even though jobs have been created, labour productivity—and thus wages and incomes—remains a challenge.

All this should underscore the jobs challenge in India and the need to create higher-quality jobs in scale.

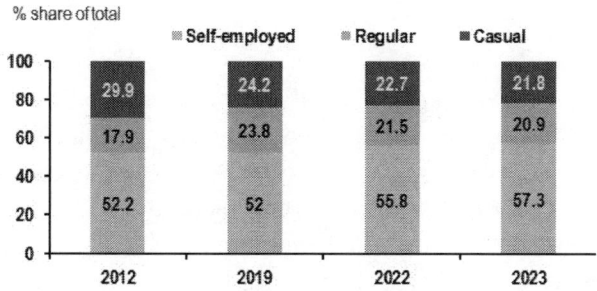

Figure 27: Share of Employment

Source: ILO.

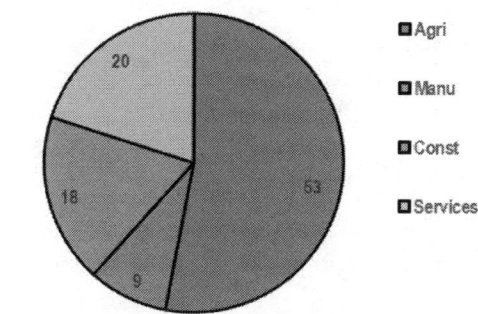

Figure 28: Sector-wise Job Creation in Last Five Years

Source: PLFS.

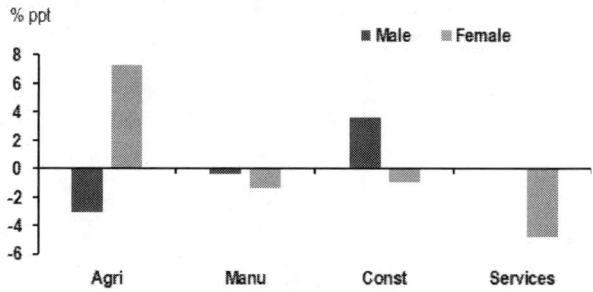

Figure 29: Change in Employment Share (2018 to 2023)

Source: PLFS.

Endowment-Defying Increase in Capital Intensity

The fact that labour's contribution to growth has been underwhelming over the last two decades is likely an upshot of the fact that manufacturing in India has become increasingly (and worryingly) capital-intensive since about 2008 (Figure 30), despite India's natural endowment of vast pools of cheap, unskilled labour, and the economy being in the midst of a demographic transition.

Increased capital intensity can also be seen across India's export basket, wherein the share of labour-intensive exports (textiles, leather, gems and jewellery) has declined even as capital-intensive exports have actually increased. In other words, there is a growing proclivity of entrepreneurs to choose capital-intensive industries and capital-intensive techniques in production.

What all this suggests is that labour is progressively seen as a less and less attractive factor of production.

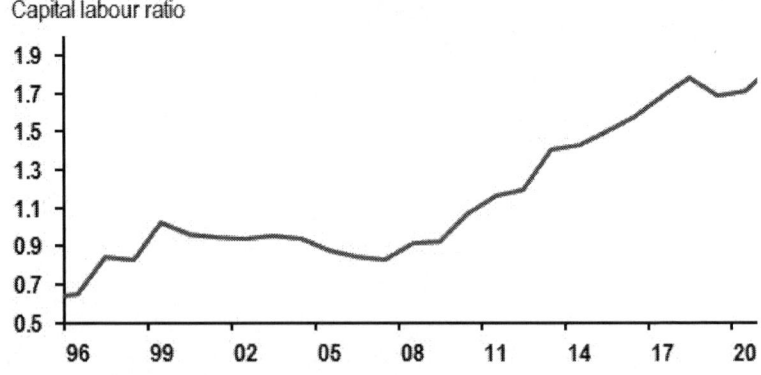

Figure 30: Capital Intensity
(Defined as a Ratio of Real Fixed Capital and Total Persons Engaged)

Source: ASI, J.P. Morgan.

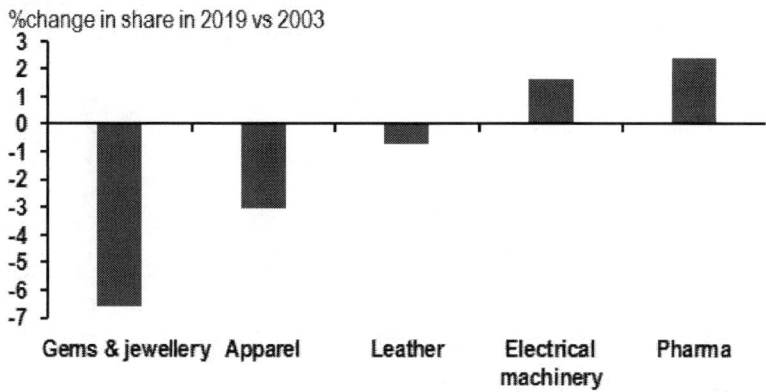

%change in share in 2019 vs 2003

Gems & jewellery Apparel   Leather   Electrical   Pharma
                                           machinery

Figure 31: Goods Export Basket

Source: Ministry of Commerce and Industry.

What Can Be Done?

It is beyond the scope of this essay to attempt a deep dive into India's employment travails. But suffice to say, the key is a combination of policies—both on the supply and the demand sides—to increase the attractiveness of labour as a factor of production. The supply side will require large investments in human capital (education, health, skilling) to improve the employability of labour. Indeed, as the Wheebox's *India Skills Report 2023* notes, overall employability among the youth is still at only 50 per cent. Currently, India's spending in health and education lags behind that of many of its peers (Figures 32 and 33). Given the positive externalities associated with health and education, the private sector will necessarily under-provide in these areas. Therefore, boosting public spending in health and education—alongside a policy framework that catalyzes private investments in these sectors—is crucial.

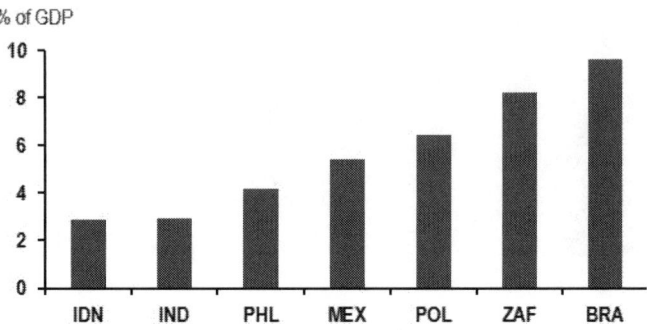

Figure 32: Health Expenditure

Source: World Bank.

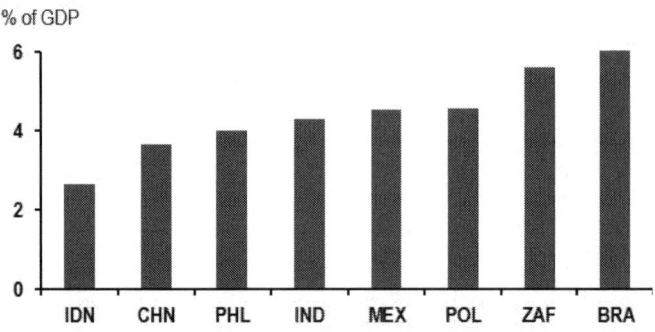

Figure 33: Government Expenditure on Education (ref. year 2017)

Source: World Bank.

Additionally, efforts to boost female labour force participation rates (FLFPR) are much needed. At 27.8 per cent, India's female labour force participation is below historical levels and significantly lags behind that of its economic peers. Similarly, the LFPR for women with advanced education in India is well below most other countries, which is not the case for men with advanced education.[15] Prima facie, several factors are likely driving these outcomes (the time spent in domestic care-giving, education and skill deficits, social norms, safety and transportation). Understanding the social, cultural or economic causes behind this and crafting an appropriate policy response is key to boosting the employment ratio, harnessing the power of half of India's population and thereby boosting India's potential growth.

Equally, however, a set of demand-side measures will be needed to incentivize firms to hire. First, labour laws will need to be rationalized to reduce frictions associated with hiring or firing—frictions that de facto increase the perceived cost of labour, and end up making labour a 'fixed cost' rather than a variable cost. Second, labour-intensive manufacturing or exports vis-à-vis capital-intensive sectors will need to be incentivized. Third, tax wedges associated with formal employment—which increases the cost of labour for employers, thereby disincentivizing labour over capital—will need to be rationalized.

Stronger growth in manufacturing and services is the de facto prescription to pull labour out of agriculture and into higher-productivity manufacturing and services. But that won't necessarily create enough jobs if the capital intensity of non-agricultural sectors remains high. The key, therefore, is a policy ecosystem on the demand and supply sides that seeks to make labour a more attractive input into the production process, and thereby generates more labour-intensive growth.

Imperative #2: Exports As a Source of Demand

As alluded to above, if India seeks strong and sustained growth, exports will have to be a key part of the strategy. The growing 'export-pessimism' is understandable, given concerns about de-globalization, economic balkanization, and the aggressive use of industrial policy in advanced economies to reshore manufacturing.

Looking through the fog, however, several export opportunities are emerging and will emerge, some of which the economy has begun to leverage:

1. **China's focus on new-age manufacturing and technology production is vacating crucial space in the traditional low-skill, labour-intensive manufacturing that India should, in theory, have a natural comparative advantage in.** Chatterjee and Subramanian[16] have quantified this impact (see Figure 34).

This creates a real opportunity for India to create labour-intensive manufacturing jobs. That said, India has been losing its share in the labour-intensive clothing and apparel sectors thus far, thereby defying its natural comparative advantage—suggesting that for India to harness this opportunity, several measures will need to be taken, a few of which are briefly enumerated below.

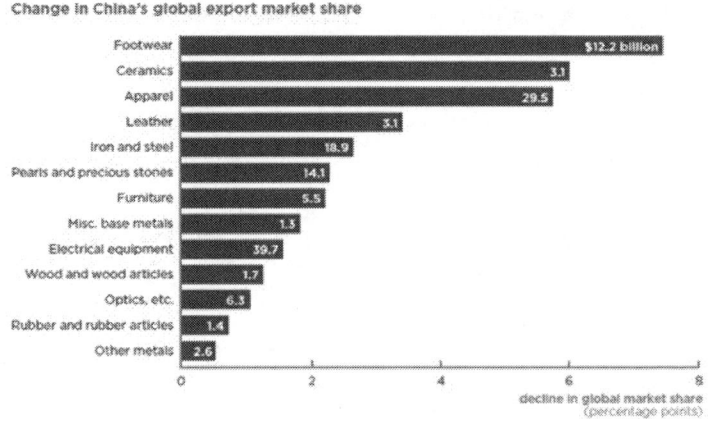

Figure 34: Change in China's Global Export Market Share

Source: Chatterjee and Subramanian (2023).

2. **A protracted US-China trade war 2.0 should accentuate the China-Plus-One dynamics and throw up opportunities for India as multinational firms seek to diversify away from China.** Exploiting this opportunity will be the most seamless way for India to progressively integrate into global value chains (GVCs). How has India done on this front thus far? While there have been some notable majors entering India (for example Apple), a more holistic assessment suggests this is very much work in progress. One way to assess who is gaining from the firms diversifying out of China is to look at how export shares from Asia to the United States have evolved. This is, of course, just illustrative because countries outside Asia (such as Mexico) have also gained, and the recalibration of supply chains is not limited to just the US market. Notwithstanding those caveats, what is apparent is that

while India is gaining a share of what China has given up in the US market, it is still behind a few others (Vietnam, Taiwan and Korea) for now. For example, between 2018 and 2023, China's share of Asian exports to the United States fell by eight percentage points. Of that, India gained about 1.2 percentage points. Similarly, while FDI into all the emerging markets (EM) has slowed over the last two years, India's share of EM-FDI has declined, suggesting that much more needs to be done to harness the China-Plus-One opportunity. But the opportunity exists, is unique, and may not arise again for decades.

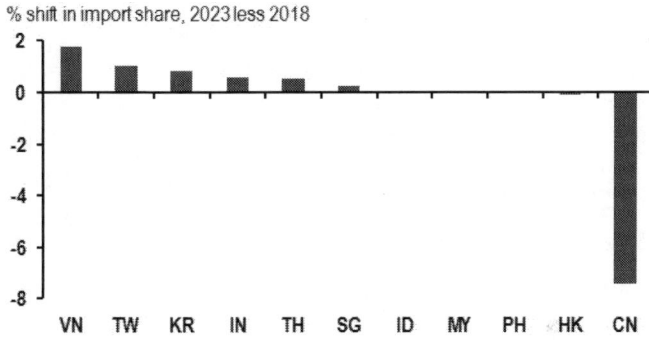

Figure 35: Shift in US Import Share

Source: US Census Bureau.

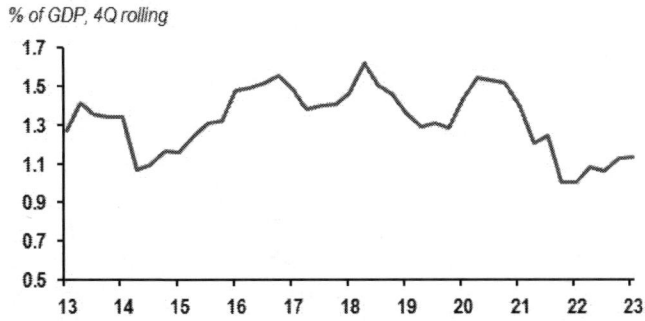

Figure 36: EM ex. China Net FDI

Source: Haver, J.P. Morgan.

3. **Service exports is an opportunity which India has already begun to seize.** With populations of advanced economies ageing and their workforces contracting, or their growth rates slowing sharply, their search for workers in other countries is only going to grow. Furthermore, with immigration becoming increasingly politically sensitive, one can envisage that the attractiveness of offshoring goods and services will only increase. Rapid technological progress during the pandemic has meant that many services previously deemed non-tradable have become tradable. All these factors suggest that the runway of service export demand from advanced economies is long. Instead, the constraint that India is likely to eventually face is supply, not demand. Can India produce the skilled labour that service exports will require year after year? In the case of the information technology sector, for example, a NASSCOM report estimated[17] that India had a tech talent demand-supply gap of 21 per cent in 2022. The report also noted that the tech sector demand-supply mismatch would rise from 0.6 million in 2021 to 1.4–1.9 million by 2026. The gap would be most acute in digital tech talent, where it is expected to increase 3.5 times.

An Ecosystem of Exports

So what will be required to make exports a key part of any growth strategy? It is beyond the scope of this essay to lay out a comprehensive game plan to boost exports—especially as other chapters in this volume conduct a much deeper dive into export challenges and opportunities. Suffice to say, however, that it will take a series of complementary and mutually reinforcing policy actions.

- On the goods front, for example, policy actions that make labour a more attractive factor of production (as discussed above) will allow India to harness its comparative advantage and become more competitive on labour-intensive exports.
- Furthermore, a policy where exports are concentrated into 'coasting economic zones' proposed by Arvind Panagariya (2016)[18]—wherein factor market reforms are concentrated

(land, labour and power) and manufacturing becomes globally competitive—should be seriously considered.

- Integrating into global value chains—a prerequisite to boost goods exports—will also entail greater integration with the world, necessitating tariff rationalization (as the Lerner symmetry theorem points out, an import tariff is equivalent to imposing an export tax) and participation in mega-regional trade deals.
- This will need to be complemented by deft exchange rate management that keeps India's exports competitive.[19]

In other words, an entire ecosystem geared to an export-promotion strategy on the goods side will need to be prioritized. None of this is new or surprising, but needs to be reiterated.

On the services side, demand is unlikely to be a constraint, but supply is likely to be an issue. Therefore, investments in health, education and skilling will need to be undertaken in scale to ensure enough skilled white-collar workers are available as demand continues to ramp up.

Imperative #3: Fiscal Consolidation without Expenditure Compression

A running theme in this essay has been the need to undertake a big push on health and education. To be sure, while resources remain a constraint, they are not the only one. Instead, how those resources are deployed is crucial. This necessitates improvement in processes, greater decentralization, and improved incentive-compatibility. Even within the resource envelope, much will eventually have to be undertaken by the private sector. Even after accounting for all this, however, it's clear that increased public investments in health and education is a necessary—if not sufficient—condition to dramatically boost human capital accumulation in the country.

These investments apart, the public sector will have to continue with its infrastructure push, given that (a) the infrastructure deficit is still large, and (b) private corporate investment still remains tepid. A public sector investment push will therefore have to stoke demand for the foreseeable future.

Finally, engineering the green transition is likely to have a fiscal cost. In other words, the expenditure needs of the public sector will only have to grow in the coming years. At the same time, fiscal deficits will have to come down to ensure that the post-pandemic public debt stabilizes. From a debt-sustainability perspective, the combined fiscal deficit will need to be reduced by one to two per cent of the GDP in the coming years.

Squaring the Circle: Increasing Tax-to-GDP Ratio

So how does the public sector simultaneously reduce the combined deficit by this quantum in the coming years while increasing the expenditure on health, education, infrastructure and other public goods? The only way to square the circle is to work on the revenue side by boosting tax/GDP and asset sales.

The news on the former front is very encouraging. Combined Central and State tax/GDP is on course to surpass 18 per cent of GDP for the first time in 2023–24. Much of this has been on account of personal income taxes. But more efforts are needed to fundamentally overhaul direct taxes—broaden the base, lower the rates, reduce the exemptions—to boost tax/GDP.

The temptation to meaningfully rely on indirect taxes should be resisted. This is because indirect taxes are regressive and will simply accentuate the dualistic nature of the income and consumption recovery in the post-pandemic period. Furthermore, the ratio of indirect taxes to total taxes in India has remained higher than desired, and has been sticky at 60 per cent over the last decade, higher than the emerging market economy (EME) average of 40–50 per cent (Figure 38). So finding ways to increase direct taxes will be key to both generating revenues and doing so in a progressive manner.

This is not to suggest that the current GST structure should not be further simplified, rationalized and broadened to improve the ease of compliance, reduce complexities, and eke out more efficiency. But the overarching focus must be on reforming direct taxes and personal taxes in particular.

Finally, the new administration must double down on asset sales (PSU disinvestments and strategic sales, as well as infrastructure asset recycling) as a means of raising resources to fund critical investments in human and physical capital. This should be thought of as a 'productivity-enhancing' asset swap on the public sector's balance sheet. Furthermore, to the extent that raising revenues through asset sales vis-à-vis taxes is non-contractionary, it allows the public sector to reduce deficits and thereby stabilize debt in the least growth-impinging manner.

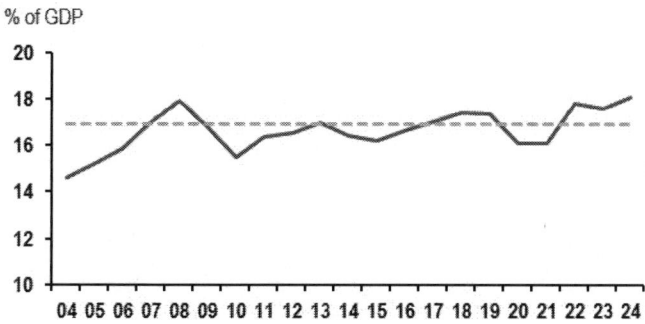

Figure 37: Combined Gross Tax/GDP (Centre + States)

Source: RBI, J.P. Morgan.

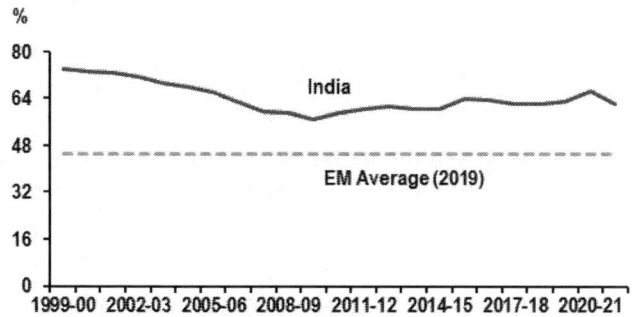

Figure 38: Percent Contribution of Indirect Taxes to All Taxes

Source: Progress of the Personal Income Tax in EM and Developing Countries (IMF, 2022).

Michael Debabrata Patra

Monetary Policy Challenges and Choices in Heightened Uncertainty

As a professional economist and a policymaker, Dr Shankar Acharya is among the finest in his generation and those that follow. Working with him, or to put it more accurately, watching him at work from the time he took over as chief economic adviser to the government of India (GoI) in the Ministry of Finance, I have been struck by the remarkable incisiveness in his thinking, and the astuteness with which he crested challenges and shepherded the economy through one of the most tumultuous periods in India's economic history. Drawing on a vast repository of hands-on experience in India and abroad, he oversaw macroeconomic adjustment and structural reforms, including the liberalization of the economy and the shaping of an outward orientation in a break from an inward-looking past. An abiding interest in monetary policy has been a key element in his macroeconomic policy orientation. Among his many contributions to the design and implementation of monetary policy in India, the absorbing discussions on the overheating of the economy due to surges in capital flows in the 1990s and the disinflation that followed shall always remain imprinted in memory. From the time he returned to his roots in academia in 2001, his sage counsel during policy consultations with the Reserve Bank of India has been a beacon of light shining on the path along which monetary policy has been fashioned. This essay is a small tribute to a journey of exceptional achievements.

■

With the turn of the 2020s, the conduct of monetary policy worldwide encountered uncharted terrain. Buffeted first by a once-in-a-century pandemic and then by the outbreak of geopolitical conflicts in Ukraine and Gaza, monetary policy has been tested on both sides. The pandemic inflicted the most precipitous crisis of growth, while the wars fuelled an inflation surge that is arguably unprecedented in its height and persistence. The monetary policy response has also been extraordinary. During the pandemic, interest rates were taken down to unusual lows, including into negative territory. Enormous amounts of liquidity were funnelled in by expanding the central banks' balance sheets to put a floor under the severe contraction of economic activity, to the point that the systemically important ones among these institutions are staring at large losses and negative equity.

In response to the inflation unleashed by geopolitical strife, central banks engaged in the most synchronized and aggressive monetary policy tightening in recent history that has heightened financial stability risks, including commercial bank failures in some jurisdictions. The efficacy of these actions is the subject of animated debate even today, especially in the context of the stubbornness of inflation in aligning with targets.

In India too, a similar *danse macabre* has been playing out. At the height of the pandemic's first wave, India's gross domestic product (GDP) plunged 23.1 per cent in April–June 2020—among the most pronounced contractions in the cross-country experience at that time. In the year 2020–21 (April–March), the GDP declined by 5.8 per cent, the first drop in 40 years, and it was not until 2021–22 that pre-pandemic levels of GDP were sighted.

In the aftermath of the Ukraine war in February 2022, inflation levitated to a peak of 7.8 per cent in April 2022 and breached the upper tolerance level (six per cent) of India's inflation targeting framework in 2022–23. What started from the war-driven escalation of international commodity prices was exacerbated by frequent extreme weather-induced food price shocks in India. Beginning in May 2022 and up to December 2024, a combination of monetary policy actions—including a cumulative increase in the policy rate of 250 basis points—and supply management measures has resulted in core inflation easing to an all-time low in the current 2012-based consumer price index (CPI) series (3.1 per cent in May 2024) with deflation in fuel prices (since September 2023).

Recurring supply shocks have, however, kept food inflation high and volatile. Consequently, although headline inflation has softened from 6.7 per cent in 2022–23 into the inflation tolerance band at 5.4 per cent in 2023–24 and 4.9 per cent in 2024–25 (April–December), the disinflation has been halting and uneven. The Reserve Bank of India (RBI) projected that inflation may ease further to 4.4 per cent in Q4: 2024–25, but it will not be until 2025–26 that a convergence with the target of four per cent can be envisaged.

While India's experience has broad similarities with the global growth-inflation flux during 2020–24, there are nuanced differences— some stark and others more subtle. The country-specific distinctiveness of the challenges faced by India has, in turn, conditioned its monetary policy response. These differentials assume significance from empirical and practitioner perspectives. They provide valuable inputs for guiding monetary policy in the navigation of heightened uncertainty by drawing from the recent experience of 'crossing the river by touching the stones', as the traditional Chinese folk saying goes. This is the motivation driving this essay, as it teases out specific facets of the design and implementation of monetary policy during this period vis-à-vis the peer experience. They relate to the measurement of uncertainty, monetary policy and supply shocks, monetary-fiscal coordination, managing regime shifts, modelling monetary policy processes, and the role of communication in monetary policy implementation. The chapter concludes on the note that policy choices can be country-specific even when uncertainty is globally pervasive and overwhelming.

Measuring Uncertainty

Uncertainty pervades human behaviour; it is a fact of life. Uncertainty is the only certainty there is, and knowing how to live with it is the only security.[1] In the context of monetary policy, uncertainty reflects opaqueness in the minds of economic agents about the state of the economy, its structure, and the inferences that can be drawn from policy actions and about potential outcomes. As it renders policymaking vulnerable to costly errors, this amorphous concept needs to be factored into analytical frameworks underlying decision-making.

Hence, measuring uncertainty is the pragmatic approach. By doing so, the more lucid communication of policy challenges and the associated trade-offs can be developed; this can anchor a common set of expectations among policymakers and the public that eventually minimizes policy errors.

Uncertainty encompasses both its 'Knightian' connotation in which the probability distribution of outcomes is unknown, and 'risk', for which the uncertainty of outcomes is characterized by a known probability distribution.[2] Different methods for its quantification have been employed: (a) movements in financial market indicators at high frequency; (b) surveys of professional forecasters (SPF); (c) news articles; and (d) internet-based searches of economic and financial events. It is observed that using SPF data to measure uncertainty is superior to the other measures as it incorporates information on both common uncertainty—variations in uncertainty across different forecasters that are common to all—and idiosyncratic uncertainty—disagreements between professional forecasters.[3]

A real-time index of macroeconomic uncertainty in India— which is constructed as an unweighted sum of forecast errors and disagreements in the forecasts in the RBI's SPF and aggregated by using a dynamic factor model to extract latent common elements—provides some interesting insights.[4] First, common temporal uncertainty is much more pronounced than disagreements, pointing to the role of unanticipated shocks in purveying generalized uncertainty. Second, growth-related uncertainty—which remained moderate during the pre-Covid period—became accentuated after the outbreak of the pandemic. Third, credit-growth-related uncertainty emerged from 2022. Fourth, growth uncertainty is highly correlated with fiscal uncertainty; inflation uncertainty is highly correlated with monetary policy uncertainty; and uncertainty related to the current account deficit (CAD) is correlated with that of output growth, inflation, the fiscal deficit and the 91-day treasury bill rate. Uncertainty related to monetary and fiscal policy is found to be correlated, indicating the role of common shocks and their spillovers.

High uncertainty leads to dampening of demand and a rise in inflation, posing a policy dilemma: boost output by easing monetary policy but risk aggravating inflation, or contain inflation by conducting a restrictive monetary policy, but at the cost of depressing already weak demand?[5] This trade-off is timeless, but in the absence of a measure of uncertainty that is explicitly incorporated into analytical frameworks, policy actions and stances can turn out to be inefficient and oscillating in space and time. Non-linear and time-varying effects of uncertainty on macroeconomic variables should be accounted for in the most pragmatic way so as to imbue precision into policymaking.

Monetary Policy and Supply Shocks

Monetary policy's response to supply shocks in the context of the goal of price stability has been the subject of considerable discussion. The received wisdom is that these shocks are transitory and hence, monetary policy can and should ignore their initial impact as they lie outside its realm and remit. If, however, these shocks generate spillovers as they do when they are persistent or repetitive, then it is essential for monetary policy to respond to prevent second-round effects that cause the generalization of inflation. The dilemma for monetary policy sharpens when the economy is going through a contractionary phase— the central bank can ill afford to weaken demand conditions further by responding to the inflationary impact of the supply shock.

Hence, the conduct of monetary policy emphasizes the role of inflation expectations. If agents in the economy believe in monetary policy's steadfast commitment to inflation, policy rate increases can be of small magnitudes, or even avoided. If, on the other hand, credibility is low, inflation expectations will become adaptive and this can lead to the broad-basing of inflationary pressures. Hence, a higher policy rate than otherwise will be required to quell the second-round effects of repeated supply shocks. Another dimension of monetary policy credibility is the timing of its response. With imperfect credibility, a delay in the monetary policy response to repeated unfavourable supply shocks leads to a further loss of credibility, the unhinging of inflation expectations, and eventually, higher inflation outcomes with a greater sacrifice of growth. On the other hand, by frontloading monetary policy actions, the credibility in their commitment to the inflation target is enhanced. This will anchor inflation expectations, necessitating less aggressive policy rate increases and, therefore, a lower growth sacrifice.

In the period since 2020, monetary policy in India has been confronted with multiple overlapping food price shocks that produced an overbearing influence on headline inflation, imparting volatility and persistence. Food has a weight of 45.9 per cent in the CPI, but its contribution to overall inflation increased from 48 per cent in April 2022 to 75 per cent in April 2024 and hovered around 70 per cent during the rest of the year. Two features stand out in this experience. First, the rising vulnerability of food prices to climate change—the heat wave during March–May 2022; crop production shortfalls due to uneven southwest monsoons; La Niña conditions for the third year in a row, impacting rainfall patterns in the post-monsoon season; unseasonal rainfall and hailstorms in March 2023; temporal monsoon variability in 2023 (which included its delayed onset, torrential rainfall in July, and historically severe dry conditions in August); and strengthening El Nino conditions until the first half of 2024—suggests that food inflation in India may be acquiring a structural character. Second, the weaponization of food—as a consequence of geopolitical conflict and restrictive trade practices embedded in geoeconomic fragmentation—is resulting in large spillovers propagating into non-food inflation across geographies. These forces are causing headline inflation in India to diverge—often persistently—from its target of four per cent.[6]

Traditionally, monetary policy should be concerned with changes in the absolute level of prices as reflected in headline inflation; relative prices do not matter as they should be counterbalancing within the budget constraint. The appropriate monetary policy response should, however, be conditioned by the question: will relative prices adjust without any spillovers so that the monetary policy reaction can be to look through food price movements on the grounds that they are supply-driven and transitory in nature? Or do food prices exhibit some core-like properties which are relevant for monetary policy, and cannot be ignored? Large relative price changes triggered by adverse supply-side factors have been identified as cost-push shocks that shift the Phillips curve upwards and to the right.[7]

The stylized facts on food inflation formation in India reveal that: (a) certain subgroups like oils and fats, spices, and meat and fish have exhibited higher average inflation during 2020–24; (b) food inflation volatility, measured by its intertemporal standard deviation (SD), has been markedly higher than the volatility of headline and core inflation; (c) the cross-correlation between the moments of food and headline inflation suggests that the skewness in food inflation is positively correlated with the mean and SD of headline inflation, implying that large relative price changes in food inflation impacts the headline inflation path; and (d) the persistence in food inflation is non-trivial in certain food subgroups; this increases the risk of spillovers to non-food inflation through inflation expectations and cost-push pressures.[8]

An analysis of spillovers of food prices to non-food prices in an autoregressive distributed lag (ARDL) cointegration framework[9] suggests a long-run cointegration between prices of food and non-food items. The error correction term is negative and statistically significant for food inflation, but it is not significant for non-food inflation. This indicates that food prices undergo deviations from the equilibrium after a shock, but they converge with non-food prices within a year. The low magnitude of this coefficient indicates that only large and persistent food price shocks affect non-food prices.[10]

Estimates from a time-varying regression framework reveal that on an average, 10 per cent of food inflation is driven by demand factors, warranting monetary policy vigil on the sources and nature of shocks to food prices.[11] Simulations in a quarterly projection model show that in the case of a transitory food price shock, the initial price spike reverses, inflation falls, and monetary policy sees through the shock by not changing the policy rate. On the other hand, if monetary policy chooses to react to the transitory shock by increasing the policy rate, this will induce volatility in the output gap without having a discernible impact on the inflation path. A persistent food price shock warrants monetary policy action to prevent un-anchoring of inflation expectations and spillover effects. If monetary policy decides to see through this shock, inflation expectations become unsettled, leading to a persistent upward drift in inflation from its pre-shock level, even after the initial shock has completely dissipated.[12] The objective of monetary policy should, therefore, be to prevent inflation expectations developing inertia around high levels. This underscores the complementarity between aggregate demand and supply management policies.

Reading all this together, it seems that there are times when food inflation mimics core inflation. With its large share in the consumption basket, food inflation has the potential to affect headline inflation, and it can also affect non-food inflation in the event of large and repeated food price shocks. The wielders of monetary policy need to be conscious of the dangers of overkill in reactions to a transitory food price shock and also of the pitfalls of the benign neglect of looking through persistent food price shocks.[13]

Monetary-Fiscal Coordination

When food price spikes impact headline inflation disproportionately, inducing fatter right tails and high positive skews in the inflation distribution, the effective coordination between monetary and fiscal policy becomes necessary for managing inflation without undermining growth prospects. Accordingly, in response to the war-induced inflation experience of 2022–24, monetary measures focused on raising the policy rate as stated earlier, normalizing the pandemic-era excess liquidity and anchoring inflation expectations, while fiscal policy addressed idiosyncratic price pressures through proactive supply management measures.

Supply management measures included allowing free imports or reductions in import duties, restricting exports, increasing export duties, applying minimum export prices, prescribing stockholding limits on traders, wholesalers and retailers, and building buffer stocks with open market sales in a timely manner to augment domestic availability and stabilize the prices of key inflation-sensitive food items. At the same time, the government also cut excise duties on petrol and diesel prices in phases during 2021 and 2022 to contain the pass-through of rising international crude prices to domestic inflation.[14]

A nominal index of supply management measures (G_t) is constructed by collating all these actions and aggregating them by using the weights of corresponding items in the CPI basket. Regressing the change in inflation on changes in its second moment (SD) and its third moment (skewness) after adjusting for inflation persistence over the period from January 2012 to December 2023, and augmenting the equation with ΔGt for a shorter period from January 2020 to December 2023, reveals that the coefficient of skewness is positive and statistically significant for the full sample, while SD turns out to be insignificant. In the shorter period from January 2020 to December 2023, Gt does not have a significant direct impact on headline inflation, but there is a statistically significant and negative impact of the interaction term between skewness and Gt on headline inflation. This indicates that with aggressive supply management interventions (higher value of Gt), the positive impact of high relative price changes on headline inflation declines.[15] Thus, large relative price changes do have a significant and positive impact on the inflation trajectory, but this can be moderated by supply management measures.

The combination of flexibility built into the monetary policy framework and supply management measures has helped in diminishing the adverse impact of large relative price changes on headline inflation. It is important to guide this coordination by an assignment rule under which well-communicated and transparently conducted monetary policy prevents inflation spirals, while fiscal policy focuses on containing specific price pressures. Both complement and reinforce each other without undermining the quality of either policy. This produces the best growth outcomes. In the context of the global inflation surge of 2020–23 and the lessons drawn from it, India's experience with disinflation through monetary-fiscal coordination can serve as a good practice template for countries vulnerable to inflationary pressures emanating from the incidence of supply shocks.[16] The influential view that 'inflation is always and everywhere a monetary phenomenon'[17] has, in fact, been nuanced—supply shocks can impact the price level in the short run.[18]

Regime Shifts and Monetary Policy

Why was monetary policy ambushed by the regime shifts in inflation caused by the pandemic and the war in Ukraine? Following influential work on the subject,[19] it is important to statistically identify these regimes and transitions, the behaviour of trend inflation, and its persistence and stochastic volatility in order to examine the state of inflation expectations. Externalities associated with these regime changes are also important to determine generalization tendencies.

The Markov switching model[20] is among the most popular non-linear time series regime switching models in the literature. This model examines multiple structures that can depict inflation behaviour in different regimes, characterizing the switches in complex dynamic patterns between these structures. A Markov switching model applied on year-on-year (y-o-y) inflation rates in India from January 2012 to March 2023 reveals that with the de facto introduction of flexible inflation targeting (FIT) in India in 2014, inflation shifted from a high regime, in which it averaged over eight per cent in 2012–14, to a lower regime averaging 4.4 per cent. With the outbreak of the pandemic in early 2020, inflation moved back to a high regime for a brief period. As the pandemic abated, inflation reverted to a low regime by early 2021, and remained there till the Ukraine war in early 2022 caused it to move back to a high regime in the first half of 2022–23. Since the second half of 2022–23, there has been a rising probability that inflation is transiting away from the high regime.[21]

These results indicate that it was the succession of supply shocks during 2020–22 that transited the Indian economy to a high inflation regime. Cyclically sensitive inflation remained persistently lower than acyclical inflation even after the incidence of the shocks, indicating the absence of demand-pull in the transition to the new regime.[22] In the transition, inflation exhibited persistence and an upshift in its trend. Alongside this, the volatility of both trend and cyclical components surged. Taken together, these results point to inflation expectations breaking loose from the anchoring that had occurred during 2016–19. The clear vision of hindsight shows that monetary policy action was warranted to restore credibility and re-anchor expectations. This highlights the importance of monetary policy being pre-emptive when the risk of a transition to a high inflation regime increases. Delaying the response will warrant more forceful actions inevitably, with implications for the sacrifice of growth.

The supply shocks of 2020–22 also increased the total variance of headline CPI inflation as well as covariance among inflation in its subgroups. This translates to evidence that in the high inflation regime, there was a generalization of price pressures—they have spread across many subgroups which are experiencing more co-movement of high inflation than normally seen. This is a clearer call for monetary policy action to quell inflationary pressures and contain their broad-basing. The monetary policy actions and stance of the Reserve Bank through 2022–23 are hence validated.

In terms of the regime shift exercise, there is a rising probability that since the second half of 2022–23, in the absence of unfavourable idiosyncratic shocks, conditions are right for early signs of a grudging disinflation to firm up into a central tendency. Also, inflation persistence and trend are on the decline, suggesting that inflation expectations are slowly getting re-anchored as policy actions and stance are gaining traction.

For the future conduct of monetary policy, the recommendation would be: wait and watch while guiding inflation towards the imminent onset of a low inflation regime. Localized price movements that are influencing headline inflation month to month call for fine-tuning measures to align the demand and supply of specific goods and services, rather than orthodox monetary policy responses. Additional evidence that inflationary pressures in India are easing is found in the decline in the month-on-month momentum of core inflation, reinforcing the proposition that headline inflation will inevitably converge with its core. A dissonant note is that cyclically sensitive inflation is increasing. This indicates that demand-pull is increasingly gaining traction. For monetary policy, therefore, there can be no letting down of the guard. The readiness to act pre-emptively to ensure that the disinflation is not interrupted by demand pressures is the policy recommendation for the way forward.

Modelling Monetary Processes and Outcomes

The core of the monetary policy framework in India is inflation forecast targeting. Consistent and reliable forecasts are prerequisites for the conduct of forward-looking monetary policy under which the forecasts act as the intermediate target for monetary policy. Hence, a theoretically consistent and empirically founded model—taking into account the specific characteristics of the Indian economy—is needed. Section 45ZM of the RBI Act mandates the RBI to publish a half-yearly Monetary Policy Report (MPR), including inflation forecasts for 6–18 months. In pursuance of this requirement, the RBI developed a macroeconomic model—the quarterly projection model (QPM)—for generating medium-term projections and policy analysis.[23]

Fundamentally, the QPM is a framework designed to answer one question: what is the path of the policy rate, given the macroeconomic and financial conditions? The policy interest rate is endogenous and consistent with the inflation target. For any deviation of inflation from its target, however, there are many alternate interest rate paths that would bring inflation back to the target over the medium term. For example, large early policy rate changes may get inflation to the target quickly, but with a substantial adverse impact on output. More gradual policy actions will achieve the target slowly, but with less loss of output. Thus, this model can be calibrated to generate alternate interest rate paths, taking into consideration the policymakers' assessments of evolving macroeconomic conditions. The QPM is specifically designed to be representative of India's macroeconomic dynamics, and helps to generate internally consistent forecasts and policy scenarios. This provides policymakers with relevant information and scenarios for a more informed judgement.[24] In this context, the period from the summer of 2020 was characterized by massive and frequent supply shocks, providing a 'laboratory' setting for modelling the resilience of India's inflation targeting framework under 'bad luck'.

The QPM is a forward-looking open-economy-calibrated gap model, broadly following a theoretical framework founded on New Keynesian principles.[25] [26] It consists of (a) an aggregate demand block, (b) an aggregate supply block, (c) a monetary policy rule, and (d) an uncovered interest rate parity condition. The aggregate demand block relates the output gap and bank lending conditions. The aggregate supply block models the components of inflation separately, considering India-specific characteristics like the dominance of food and the role of food and fuel price spillovers in a conventional expectations-augmented Phillips curve framework. The policy reaction function is a Taylor-type rule, and the transmission to long-term interest rate is modelled through the term structure of interest rates. The exchange rate is determined by using an uncovered interest rate parity condition modified to incorporate the effects of capital flows and the role of forex interventions to capture characteristics specific to the Indian context. In addition, the QPM also has a fiscal block which takes into account monetary-fiscal coordination, debt dynamics and their impact on aggregate demand, the exchange rate and inflation. Being an open economy model, it incorporates an external sector block representing the dynamics of the rest of the world.

Several India-specific characteristics are included in QPM Version 2.0: (a) the interlinkages of inflation components, (b) the sluggishness in interest rate transmission, (c) the preponderance of the credit channel, (d) central bank credibility and its linkage to inflation expectations formation, (e) monetary and fiscal coordination, (f) the intricacies of fuel pricing, and (g) capital flow management and forex interventions.[27]

The determinants of inflation post-2020 can be identified by using a historical decomposition (HD) generated from the QPM. The contraction of the economy during the pandemic contributed -1.0 percentage points to average inflation. Food price shocks contributed 1.2 percentage points in 2020–21 owing to supply disruptions, which emerged again in 2022–23 and 2023–24 on account of inclement and irregular weather conditions. The favourable effects of the initial decline in crude oil prices in 2020–21 (-0.5 percentage points) were offset by the subsequent increase in taxes on petroleum products, but its positive impact on inflation was tempered by the reduction in taxes in 2021–22. The war-induced supply disruptions led to crude oil price shocks contributing positively to headline inflation in 2022–23 (0.9 percentage points) and 2023–24 (0.8 percentage points). Furthermore, global and domestic supply disruptions triggered a series of cost-push shocks to core inflation that contributed positively (1.7 percentage points) to inflation since 2020, although these effects waned considerably by 2023–24. Both fiscal and monetary policy turned accommodative in response to output conditions in 2020–21, which contributed to inflationary pressures (1.0 percentage points) in 2021–23. With policy normalization, however, their inflationary impact slowly waned by 2023–24. The depreciation of the INR (₹) also non-trivially contributed to inflation (0.5 percentage points) during 2020–23. Most importantly, the contribution of the inflation target remained significantly negative during 2020–23 (-2.2 percentage points). This underscores the resilience of the FIT framework which could withstand a host of 'bad luck' factors. A significant contribution to this outcome came from the fiscal measures targeted at supply management, especially of food items.[28] The validation of the accuracy of the QPM's forecasts can be done by using pseudo-out-of-sample forecasts. The root mean square errors (RMSEs) of the headline inflation forecasts five to eight quarters ahead are significantly lower than for a competing class of time series model forecasts. Similar results are also obtained in the case of core inflation forecasts.[29]

Communicating Monetary Policy

Over the last few decades, central bank communication has undergone a revolution—from being cryptic and obfuscating prior to the 1990s to being eloquent and prescient in recent times. In the first half of the last century, the Bank of England was the epitome of reticence vis-à-vis the public, and was subject to increasing criticism.[30] From then and till the advent of inflation targeting in the early 1990s, central banks were shrouded in mystery with books like *Secrets of the Temple*,[31] and expressions like 'monetary mystique',[32] bearing ample testimony to this phenomenon. It was, in fact, widely believed that communication from the central bank needed to be couched in 'constructive ambiguity', a term coined by Gerald Corrigan, former president of the New York Fed.[33]

To paraphrase a Latin proverb, times changed and central banks changed with the times. Reflecting this sentiment, central bank communication in recent years has become more precise, succinct and transparent—in which active communication has become a potent tool. It has been observed that 'monetary policy is 98 percent talk and two percent action, and communication is a big part.'[34] Thus, the view that monetary policy is largely about managing expectations is conventional wisdom by now both in academia and in central banking circles. Therefore, it is no exaggeration to call this a revolution in thinking.

The potency of communication is reflected in the statement of the former president of the ECB: 'Within our mandate, the ECB is ready to do whatever it takes to preserve the euro…'[35] The global financial crisis (GFC) was a watershed moment for central bank communication as it led to resorting to unconventional tools such as asset purchases and forward guidance on interest rate paths to further stimulate the economy. By its very nature, the Covid-19 pandemic brought about further challenges for central bank communication. At a time when the evolution of the pandemic and its likely impact on the economy was unknown, central banks had to perform the role of an anchor to allay any fears of collapse of the financial system by providing support to their economies to prevent the loss of livelihood and restore financial stability.

Sometimes, however, communication can have its pitfalls. While Draghi's 'whatever it takes' declaration boosted market sentiments amidst the eurozone debt crisis, the press conference held by the US Fed in May 2013 on its future monetary policy path triggered the taper tantrum episode of heightened global financial market volatility. Therefore, communication needs to be balanced and well telegraphed to avoid unintended consequences. Recent empirical evidence suggests that after controlling for policy actions and the sentiment in policy texts, a positive tone in the voices of central banks has a significant impact on financial markets.[36]

Against this backdrop, it is useful to see how the RBI's communication policy has evolved over time. Historically, the RBI has been releasing information on the economy, banking and financial sector as well as its market operations at various frequencies. The RBI's approach is to provide all the relevant information and analysis to the general public with a view to enabling them to make informed judgements and decisions. Since the adoption of flexible inflation targeting (FIT) in 2016, the RBI's monetary policy communication practices have encompassed the publication of analyses on evolving economic conditions, outlooks for growth and inflation, the associated balance of risks, and the rationale for policy decisions in policy statements and through press conferences. This is completed by the release of the MPC minutes two weeks after the policy. The RBI has generally refrained from providing explicit forward guidance, although there has been experimentation with both time- and state-contingent guidance during the Covid-19 period. Amidst heightened global uncertainty and overlapping shocks, it has been the considered view of the RBI that forward guidance itself could be a source of policy uncertainty, undermining credibility. Accordingly, a balance has been sought to be maintained between both high-frequency and low-frequency communication of monetary policy.

In recent years, significant emphasis has also been placed on the complementary role of explanation, engagement and education (the three E's of public interface) in furthering central bank communication.[37] Learning from the Covid-19 experience, the RBI has increased its pre-policy consultations with various stakeholders—analysts, economists, academics, banks, industry bodies and domain experts—and it has also enhanced its post-policy interactions with the media to reach out to the general public. Speeches and interviews in various fora are intended to sensitize, engage and educate the public about policy decisions and challenges. At the same time, central banking research has increasingly focused on contemporary macroeconomic and policy issues. For instance, the theme-based Report on Currency and Finance (RCF) 2020–21—which dealt with 'Reviewing the Monetary Policy Framework'—was released before the renewal of the inflation target for the second five-year term. The 2021–22 Report adopted 'Revive and Reconstruct' as its theme in view of the devastating impact of the Covid-19 pandemic on the economy. The 2022–23 report dealt with climate change issues to enrich public policy.

The RBI's communication strategy has been appreciated in policy circles in recent years. For example, it has been noted that 'the Reserve Bank of India issues short and simplified press releases for an audience with limited financial literacy. Establishing links with the media, such as through background briefings, is another common tool.'[38] Moreover, empirical evidence suggests that forward guidance played a key role in moderating uncertainty and supporting asset prices during the initial waves of the Covid-19 pandemic.[39]

There are, however, times when central bank communication needs to be circumspect. Hawkish forward guidance in response to high inflation unleashed bouts of high turbulence in global financial markets, amplified the tightening of financial conditions, and triggered an exodus of capital from the emerging world. With banking collapses in some jurisdictions, the view gaining ascendency is that financial stability considerations should be incorporated into formulating monetary policy and in communicating it. Implicit in this view is the idea that a shrill pitch in forward guidance can be deeply destabilizing in a tightening phase of monetary policy.[40]

While the utility of forward guidance at very low policy rates is unambiguously proven, its efficacy at higher rates is questionable. This is consistent with the asymmetric nature of the monetary policy cycle—the way down has a lower bound at zero, but the way up is technically unbridled by any upper bound. Under heightened uncertainty, discretion in forward guidance is increasingly under the active consideration of major central banks: 'Recognising that explicit guidance in a rate tightening cycle is inherently fraught with risks, the MPC has also eschewed from providing any future guidance on the timing and level of the terminal rate.'[41]

Empirical research indicates that forward guidance through the policy stance is a useful instrument of monetary policy in extraordinary times that warrant ultra-accommodation. In these periods, the policy stance becomes valuable because of its influence on longer-term interest rate expectations—the central bank leapfrogs the structure of interest rates in transmission, and nudges long-term rates towards the level of ultra-low short-term rates. It loses steam, however, as the policy rate increases. The separate articulation of a policy stance loses its relevance when monetary policy is in a tightening mode and the economy is returning to normalcy. The results of an autoregressive conditional heteroskedastic (ARCH) model on overnight indexed swap rates indicate that forward guidance has a statistically significant impact on long-term interest rate expectations, but it progressively loses potency as the policy rate rises from highly accommodative levels.[42]

Some Policy Perspectives

What are the main lessons of India's experience with the great inflation of 2020–24? First, inflation in India did not rise to the levels seen in many advanced and emerging economies, and it peaked earlier than the cross-country experience. While goods inflation reflected the pass-through of input costs, services inflation remained subdued, especially due to housing. Second, the pandemic response of liquidity support was time-bound and targeted; consequently, the unwinding was smoother. Third, the policy rate was not lowered to the zero lower bound, as in several advanced economies. Instead, it was lowered to the level of the inflation target. Fourth, the inflation targeting regime has in-built framework flexibility that stood India in good stead: a dual mandate that accords primacy to price stability while being cognizant of growth; an inflation target defined as an average rather than as a point; a tolerance band around the target rather than a point target; and the achievement of the target over a period of time rather than continuously, with failure defined as three consecutive quarters of inflation lying outside the tolerance band, rather than every instance of such deviation. Fifth, inflation management in India is a shared responsibility under which the government sets the target, and the central bank achieves it. This allows monetary-fiscal coordination without posing risks to financial stability, fiscal consolidation, or growth. In fact, the balance-sheet size of the RBI was brought down to its pre-pandemic level by 2022–23. Sixth, forward guidance is extremely useful and, in fact, a tool of monetary policy when interest rates are being lowered. On the other hand, when monetary policy is being tightened and interest rates are being raised, the role of forward guidance is not intuitively useful and may even contribute more noise than signal. Overall, in the context of the post-pandemic global inflation surge and lessons drawn from it, India's experience with disinflation can serve as a 'good practice' template for countries vulnerable to inflationary pressures emanating from the incidence of supply shocks.

Sudipto Mundle and Manish Gupta

Fiscal Performance in a Soft State: A Review of Central and State Government Finances in India

Shankar Acharya had a very distinguished career as an economist, first for several years with the World Bank, and later as the longest-serving chief economic adviser at the Ministry of Finance in India. He has left his mark in many areas of macroeconomic policy and structural reforms. In this tribute, we focus on fiscal policy—which has been one of his main fields of interest.

The concept of the 'soft state' was first defined by Gunnar Myrdal in his celebrated volume *Asian Drama*.[1] Though the volume purported to be about Asia, it was really mostly about India. The Indian state is a classic case of what he described as a soft state, one which is buffeted by many competing special interests. Decision-making and implementation get gridlocked in the attempt to accommodate all these interests, despite the limited capacity and resources of a weak state. These challenges are made more complex by India's federal structure, where the State governments are competing for resources with the Central government and with one another.

The state is unable to adequately deliver pure public goods such as defence or law and order, or merit goods such as basic education or public health, yet it is driven by political compulsions to deliver many private goods at subsidized rates.[2] Large fiscal deficits, high debt and chronic fiscal stress are typical features of the soft Indian state. This essay assesses the fiscal performance of the Central government and the States of India under these complex conditions.

The first section of the essay reviews recent fiscal performance of the Central government and the combined performance of all the State governments. In particular, this section asks whether the Central and the State governments have fully recovered from the 2020–22 pandemic shock. It compares the fiscal performance of the governments today (2023–24, 2024–25) with a baseline of their performance prior to the pandemic (2019–20). The next three sections deal with the fiscal performance of the States, which account for about two-thirds of public spending and a third of total revenue. The States' performance has always been an important component of India's overall fiscal performance. It is all the more important now, with the shift in political power in favour of the States following the recent national elections.[3]

The second section proposes a developmental taxonomy of the States as a lens through which to assess their fiscal performance. This lens is used in the third section to compare the intra-group and inter-group fiscal performance of the States, to assess whether their fiscal performance is related to their development orientation. The fourth section presents a longitudinal analysis of how the fiscal behaviour of individual States in different developmental groups has evolved over time. The fifth and final section concludes the essay.

Fiscal Performance since the Pandemic Shock

Three features stand out as the defining features of the Central government's fiscal performance during the period since the pandemic: fiscal consolidation, a commitment to high capital expenditure (capex) and buoyant revenues, especially tax revenues.

Following convention, we use the fiscal-deficit-to-GDP ratio (henceforth FD or the 'deficit') and debt-to-GDP ratio as the principal indicators of fiscal consolidation. Much of the action on the ground in coping with the pandemic was undertaken in the States—public and private hospitals, healthcare workers, and such others—but the fiscal burden was mainly borne by the Central government. There was much criticism at the time that the government was doing little to address the pandemic shock, which led to a 6.6 per cent contraction of the GDP. Indeed, much of the ₹20 trillion stimulus package announced at the time was in the form of various schemes for subsidized credit in the financial sector, with little impact on the budget. The government's own stimulus package and its deficit spending were not comparable at all to the stimulus provided by the governments of some of the advanced countries.

Nevertheless, the deficit of the Central government did nearly double from 4.7 per cent in 2019–20 to 9.2 per cent in 2020–21. Social safety net spending jumped from nine per cent of total expenditure to nearly 22 per cent in 2020–21, and this was largely financed by increased deficit spending. The Central government also managed to compress its 'committed expenditure' (wages and salaries, pensions, interest payments, and such others) that year, presumably through reduced hiring. There was only a mild compression of under half per cent each in the shares of capital expenditure (capex) and social expenditure during that year (Table 1).

Subsequently, the Central government very quickly reined in deficit spending, reducing it in one shot from 9.2 per cent in 2020–21 to 6.7 per cent in 2021–22. Thereafter, it has continued to reduce the deficit at an average rate of 0.5 per cent of the GDP per year to get to a target rate of 4.5 per cent of the GDP by 2025–26. There is a view that this is a very timid pace of fiscal consolidation. But there are others— including one of us—who felt that the initial sharp contraction by 250 basis points in the very first year after the pandemic was premature. A more gradual fiscal consolidation would have led to a faster recovery from the contraction of 2020–21. But that is history. What matters is that the economy has grown at a sustained pace of seven to eight per cent since the contraction of 2020–21—much higher than the average growth of 6.6 per cent during the period of eight years leading up to the pandemic, not to mention the 3.7 per cent growth recorded in 2019–20 just prior to the pandemic.[4]

Such robust growth—the highest among all major economies—is probably attributable in large measure to a sustained thrust to public sector capex by the Central government. As noted above, the share of capex was only marginally reduced from 12.5 per cent in 2019–20 to 12.1 per cent in the pandemic year 2020–21. Since then, the capex share of total Central government expenditure has risen monotonically each year to a peak of 23 per cent in the budget for 2024–25 (Table 1).

There is a striking contrast between the Central government's focus on capex, and its spending on social services and the social safety net. There was a sharp spike in the social services share of total expenditure in 2021–22, following a mild compression during the pandemic in 2020–21. But since then, it has remained stationary at around 5–5.5 per cent. The same is true of the share of social safety net spending, mainly consisting of the food subsidy, income support and the MGNREGA relief employment scheme. After the spike to nearly 22 per cent in 2020–21, it has tapered down to less than eight per cent in the 2024–25 budget. Clearly, growth-promoting capex is prioritized over social spending by the NDA government.[5]

However, restrained social spending alone would not have enabled the massive push to capex while reining in the deficit at the same time. This combination of fiscal consolidation along with the push to capex was possible primarily thanks to buoyant revenues, especially tax revenues. Gross tax revenue as a percentage of the GDP increased from 10 per cent in the pre-pandemic year 2019–20 to 11.7 per cent in 2023–24, and is budgeted to increase further in 2024–25 (Table 1). Barring revenues from excise duties, which declined relative to the GDP due to a reduction in rates, all the other direct and indirect taxes have either had a buoyancy of one or more. Customs duties have remained at around 0.8 per cent of the GDP between 2021–22 and 2023–24 due to the slow growth of imports. Revenues from corporation tax have remained stable at around 3–3.1 per cent of the GDP during 2021–22 and 2023–24, while a robust growth in personal income tax has raised it from 2.5 per cent of the GDP in 2019–20 to 3.5 per cent in 2023–24. CGST revenues have also been buoyant, rising from 2.5 per cent of the GDP to 2.8 per cent during this period (Table 1). How these dynamics of revenue and expenditure might change with a new coalition government in power at the Centre remains to be seen.

Turning to the States, we discuss in this section the combined finances of all the States in vertical comparison with the finances of the Central government from the year of the pandemic (2020–21) and onwards, setting aside the horizontal comparison of fiscal performance across individual States for subsequent sections. This vertical comparison of the combined finances of all States with the Central government reveals some similarities but more contrasts. One important similarity is the buoyancy of revenues, especially tax revenue. There also seems to be a strong commitment to capex, though nowhere near comparable to the commitment of the Central government and this too with some qualifications which are discussed below. A striking contrast is the relatively muted impact of the pandemic on State finances as compared to the finances of the Central government discussed earlier. A second important difference is the much larger share of expenditure on social services (on this, see Note No. 5). A third difference, which is particularly concerning, is the recent apparent weakening of the commitment to fiscal consolidation.

For all the States combined, their own revenue receipts (ORR) declined mildly to 6.5 per cent of the GDP during the pandemic, compared to 7.1 per cent during the pre-pandemic baseline in 2019–20. It has since exceeded the baseline at 7.8 per cent in 2023–24 and is budgeted to rise further in 2024–25 (Table 2). The increase in the States' ORR was largely driven by the increase in their own tax revenue (OTR) which, on an average, account for about 86 per cent of the ORR. The OTR of all the States as a percentage of the GDP declined marginally from the pre-pandemic baseline of 5.8 per cent to 5.7 per cent in 2020–21, but then it increased to 6.7 per cent in 2023–24 and is budgeted to increase further to 6.9 per cent in 2024–25—implying a buoyancy of well over one. Central transfers—consisting of devolution and grants—are the other component of the States' revenues. It increased by 0.3 percentage points of the GDP from 2019–29 to 2020–21, mainly on account of the increase in grants. Devolution fell during this period as the economy contracted due to the pandemic (Table 2). After the pandemic, with the revival of economic growth, devolution went up to 3.6 per cent of the GDP by 2023–24, while grants declined to 2.3 per cent during the same period. The combined budgets of all the States project a further fall in grants in 2024–25. One important reason underlying the decline in the share of grants to the States is that the period of GST compensation grants to States ended in 2022–23.

A second feature of combined State finances in recent years is their continuing strong focus on the provision of social services. The share of social spending in total expenditure rose to 37.8 per cent in the pandemic year 2020–21, up from 37.1 per cent in 2019–20, presumably due to the additional public health spending that year to cope with the pandemic. But this share has continued to rise even after the pandemic, going up to 39.3 per cent in 2023–24. The provision for social services in 2024–25 is even higher at 39.5 per cent in the combined budget of all the States (Table 2). The other large item of expenditure is committed expenditure, for example, interest payments, wages and salaries, pensions, and such others. It was somewhat lower at 37 per cent, compared to 42 per cent for the corresponding component of Central government expenditure (Tables 1 and 2). Unfortunately, data on this major component of public spending is not available in the public domain for the period after 2022–23.

The spending pattern of State governments also reveals a commitment to capex, though this is not nearly as pronounced as in the case of the Central government. The share of combined capital expenditure of all the States in total expenditure was stationary at around 13–14 per cent until 2022–23, then it jumped to over 16 per cent in 2023–24—a level increase of over 45 per cent in a single year (Table 2). However, there was no commensurate jump in revenues or cuts in spending elsewhere. The sharp increase in capex was largely financed through additional borrowing. In particular, it was financed by the Union government scheme for Special Assistance to States for Capital Investment wherein it provided 50-year interest-free capital expenditure loans to States. The provision for loans under this scheme was ₹1 trillion in 2022–23, and it increased to ₹1.3 trillion in 2023–24. For 2024–25, the allocation under this scheme has been further raised to ₹1.5 trillion. Despite this, the combined capex of all the States is budgeted to increase by only six per cent in 2024–25, with an actual decline in capex in several States. Evidently, the States are now mostly using their revenues to meet revenue expenditure, and largely relying on loans to finance their capital expenditure.[6] In several States, there are also revenue deficits, implying that loans are even being used to finance revenue expenditure.

The very generous terms of the new capex assistance scheme notwithstanding, it is important to note that it is a loan, not a grant. It adds to the annual fiscal deficit of the States and further increases their indebtedness. After peaking at four per cent during the pandemic year 2020–21, the combined fiscal deficit of all the States came down during the next two years. Although it rose to 3.4 per cent in 2023–24, it is budgeted to decline to 3.1 per cent in 2024–25 (Table 2). The States' fiscal consolidation seems to be on track after the 2020–21 pandemic shock.

The outstanding liabilities relative to the GDP, aggregated across States at just over 27 per cent, is well below the indebtedness target set by the 15th Finance Commission.[7] However, when added to Central government debt, the level of total debt (net of Central loans to the States) remains very high. From a base level of 75.1 per cent of GDP in 2019–20, debt spiked to 89 per cent in the pandemic year 2020–21. It has gradually come down since then, but still remains elevated at over 80 per cent as budgeted for 2024–25 (Table 1). More importantly, the interest on this high level of debt is the single largest item of expenditure in the Central government budget and in most State government budgets. It is a committed expenditure amounting to about a quarter of total government expenditure on an average, which crowds out other more productive and socially desirable spending on education, health and infrastructure.

A Development Taxonomy of States

In the previous section, we discussed the fiscal performance of the Central government and that of all the States combined. However, there are vast differences across States—both in terms of their level of economic and social development as well as their fiscal performance. These differences in performance are important not only because of their impact on overall development and fiscal performance, among other things, but also because of their political-economic implications.[8] These political-economic differences have become all the more important following the recent national elections, which marks a distinct shift in the balance of political power in favour of the States vis-à-vis the Central government. The next two sections analyze these inter-state variations in fiscal performance. This is done through the lens of development distances among States to assess if there is any distinct relationship between fiscal performance and development outcomes. In this section, we develop that lens: a development taxonomy of States.

Per capita income is a standard measure of economic performance. But it does not measure social development, which is an equally important attribute of development if by development we mean, following Amartya Sen,[9] 'the capability and freedom to live fulfilling lives.' Other attributes of a jurisdiction, such as the level of education attained by its constituents, their health, longevity, have to be included in our measure of development. The Human Development Index (HDI) is clearly a candidate for such a measure, but it is a complex index, sensitive to the weights of its constituent indicators which are themselves evolving over time. Instead of squeezing all the attributes of development into a single complex index, we have adopted a bivariate lens. We have taken per capita income as an indicator of economic development, and longevity as an indicator of social development. A principal architect of the HDI concept in 1990, Sen argued later that if any single indicator is chosen to measure social well-being, then life expectancy is the best candidate for that.[10] Though per capita income has an important impact on longevity, the latter also reflects the impact of a whole host of other dimensions of social development.[11]

Using this bivariate classification of per capita income (GSDP) and life expectancy, we have classified the 20 States for which the required data was available into four different groups:

Balanced Development States: States with higher-than-median per capita income as well as higher-than-median life expectancy—Andhra Pradesh, Kerala, Tamil Nadu, Gujarat, Himachal Pradesh, Maharashtra, Uttarakhand.

High Economic Development States: States with higher-than-median per capita income but below-median life expectancy—Haryana, Telangana, Karnataka.

High Social Development States: States with below-median per capita income but higher-than-median life expectancy—Punjab, West Bengal, Odisha.

Lagged Development States: States with below-median per capita income and also below-median life expectancy—Rajasthan, Madhya Pradesh, Assam, Chhattisgarh, Jharkhand, Uttar Pradesh, Bihar.

The distribution of the States in this bivariate classification is presented in Figure 1.

Geographically, all the States of southern or Peninsular India have higher-than-median income, and four of them belong to the balanced development group: Kerala, Tamil Nadu, Andhra Pradesh and Maharashtra. In contrast, all the lagged development States, some of them described as the BIMARU States, belong to a central belt between the States of Peninsular India, Gujarat in the west and the States of northern India.

Development Outcomes in States Appear Unrelated to Their Fiscal Performance

We now examine the relationship between development outcomes in the States and their fiscal performance. The fiscal indicators being used for this assessment include the ratio of own revenue receipts to total revenue receipts (ORR/TRR), the share of capital expenditure in total government expenditure (capex/totex), the share of social service expenditure in total government expenditure (social service expenditure/totex), and, most importantly, the fiscal deficit (FD/GSDP) and public debt ratio (debt/GSDP). High values of the first three indicators and low values of the last two would be indicative of sound fiscal performance. The data pertaining to 2022–23—the most recent year for which all the relevant data is available for 20 States—is presented in Table 3. These 20 States together account for 98.5 per cent of the total population and 98.6 per cent of total GSDP. A measure of the huge fiscal distance between the States of India is the difference in their per capita public expenditure. It varies from only ₹17,104 for Bihar to as much as ₹67,696 in the case of Himachal Pradesh. Had some small States with high economic development like Goa or Delhi been included in the database, the distance may have been even greater.

On the receipts side of the budget, there is a distinct variation across groups in their capacity for own revenue mobilization to finance public spending. The high economic development group of States, essentially States with high per capita income, raise about 75 per cent of their revenues from their own sources, going up to 80 per cent in the case of States like Haryana. States in the balanced development group, which also have above-median per capita incomes, also raise two-thirds of their revenues from their own sources, whereas the high social development States with below-median per capita income are able to raise only half their revenues from their own sources. The lagging States with the lowest per capita incomes manage to raise only 44 per cent of their total revenue from their own sources.

The picture is less clear when we turn to expenditure. The share of capex in total State government expenditure (capex/totex) varies very widely across individual States, from a low of 3.5 per cent (Andhra Pradesh) to a high of 21 per cent (Karnataka). But there seems to be no discernable relationship between the capex ratio and the development status of a State. The average capex ratio is 11.7 per cent for the balanced development States and the high social development States. It is higher at 15.5 per cent for high economic development States, but even higher at 15.7 per cent for the lagged development States which have the lowest per capita incomes. There are also significant intra-group variations in the capex share of individual States within the groups.

There is a similar ambiguity in the social expenditure pattern of the States. The average share of social expenditure in the high economic development group of States is 35.8 per cent. It rises to 37.1 per cent for the balanced development group, further to 39.8 per cent for the lagged development States, and finally 41.4 per cent for the high social development group of States. But curiously, the State with the lowest share of social expenditure, Punjab (27.3 per cent), and the State with the highest share of social expenditure, West Bengal (51.3 per cent), both belong to the high social development group of States. The very low share of social expenditure in Punjab is more than offset by the very high share in West Bengal in this group. Barring such outliers, the share of social expenditure in most States lies in a narrow range of around 35–40 per cent, hence it is difficult to draw any clear relationship between the social expenditure share in government spending and the development orientation of a State.

Finally, we look at the two most important indicators of fiscal performance, namely, the fiscal deficit and the level of public debt in a State. The level of fiscal deficit ranges from a low of 0.8 per cent (Gujarat) to a high of 6.5 per cent (Himachal Pradesh). However, high and low fiscal deficit States co-exist in the same development group. In fact, Gujarat and Himachal Pradesh both belong to the balanced development group. Gujarat is also the least indebted State (18.5 per cent), while Punjab is the most indebted (46.5 per cent). In terms of group averages, the level of indebtedness rises from 24.9 per cent for the balanced development group to 26.1 per cent for the high economic development group of States, 31 per cent for the lagged development group, and 34.2 per cent for the high social development group of States. Thus, the balanced development group of States are also fiscally the most prudent, followed by the high economic development group, and then the lagged development group. The high social development group of States appear to be the most fiscally lax. However, this is at best a weak inference. As has been pointed out, States with high and low levels of deficit and indebtedness co-exist within the same development groups.[12]

The lack of a clear relationship between development outcomes and fiscal performance—except in the case of revenue receipts—is perhaps surprising. It leads us to draw an important conclusion, that a State's fiscal performance has not been an important driver of its development outcomes. Other factors have determined those outcomes, which lie beyond the scope of this essay. However, this is the past. Going forward, it is arguable that capex and social expenditure need to have a much larger share of public spending to have an impact on development outcomes. Also, the fiscal performance of a State is intrinsically important, since sound fiscal discipline is a part of good governance. As explained in the first section, the interest burden of public debt is now the single largest item of expenditure in most States as well as the Centre, pre-empting a quarter or more of total expenditure. It is crowding out other items of priority spending.

Fiscal Performance of States: A Longitudinal View

We have seen that there is no clear relationship between the fiscal performance of States and their development outcomes in the recent period. But are there any distinguishing features of the different development groups of States in longitudinal trends of fiscal performance? In this section, the longitudinal trends in the fiscal performance of the States in the different developmental groups are tracked from 1991–92 onwards. This dynamic picture has been summarized in a single but complex table (Table 4). The detailed supporting data is presented in Appendix Tables A2.1 to A2.3. The period since 1991–92 has been divided into three subperiods: 1991–92 to 2001–02, 2001–02 to 2011–12, and 2011–12 to 2022–23. For each indicator of each subperiod, data in the Appendix Tables shows whether it improved, deteriorated or stayed the same during the subperiod. Each indicator in Table 4 has a column of three letters for each State, corresponding to the three subperiods. The letter I indicates improvement during the subperiod, D indicates deterioration, and S indicates no significant change. Thus DIS, for instance, would indicate deterioration during the period from 1991–92 to 2001–02, improvement during the period 2001–02 to 2011–12, and no change during the period from 2011–12 to 2022–23.

On the resource mobilization side, recent performance is disappointing in the balanced development group of States. The share of own revenue receipts in total revenue (ORR/TRR) has been deteriorating during the recent period (2011–12 to 2022–23) in all these States, though it had been improving during the first period (1991–92 to 2001–02) and continued to improve during the second period in some States (Andhra Pradesh, Himachal Pradesh, Kerala and Uttarakhand). The own resource mobilization share has also been declining during the recent period in the high economic development States, Haryana and Karnataka. There is no longitudinal track record for Telangana, which was created only recently. Among the high social development group of States, Odisha has consistently improved its own share of total revenue throughout the reference period, while there is a sustained decline of that share in Punjab and West Bengal. The picture is mixed for the lagged development States. The own revenue share has been rising in Bihar and Jharkhand in the recent period. It has been falling in all the other States in the group, though it had been rising earlier in Assam, Rajasthan and Uttar Pradesh.

Turning to capex on the expenditure side, there are intra-state variations in trends even within the individual group of States, but the aggregate group-wise picture is more coherent. For the group of balanced development States, the capex share of total expenditure was stable during the first period, then improved during the second period, but it has unfortunately declined during the third period. The same pattern is seen for the high economic development States—a stable ratio in the first period followed by improvement in the second period and deterioration in the third period. For the high social development group as well as the lagged development group, the trend is more encouraging. The capex share declined during the first period, but has been improving since then.

The share of social expenditure in total spending in the balanced development group, ignoring intra-group differences, was stable during the first period, improved during the second period, and deteriorated in the third period. In the high economic development group of States, it was deteriorating in the first period, then improved in the second period, and remained stable during the third period. For the high social development group as well as the lagged development States, the intertemporal pattern is encouraging. It deteriorated in the initial period, then improved during the second phase, and continued to improve in the third subperiod.

We turn finally to our two key indicators of fiscal performance, namely, fiscal deficit and public debt. Setting aside intra-group differences, for the high economic development group, a deterioration in the initial period was followed by improvement in the second period and a fairly stable FD in the third period. All the other three groups of States reveal a very similar intertemporal pattern of initial deterioration, followed by strong improvement in the second period, and once again deterioration in the third period. Though the levels of indebtedness vary, the intertemporal pattern is similar once again for all the four groups of States: deterioration in the first period, followed by improvement in the second period, and deterioration again—sometimes quite sharp—in the third period.

To summarize, the intermediate period (2001–02 to 2011–12) seems to have been the best period when most of the indicators of fiscal performance in all the groups of States were improving. In the earlier period (1991–92 to 2000–2001), most indicators in all the groups were either deteriorating or did not change. In the more recent period (2011–12 to 2022–23) as well, most indicators in most groups have either deteriorated or remained the same, which is more concerning. The exceptions are the shares of capex and social expenditure in the high social development States and lagged development States. These have continued to improve in both groups through the second and third periods, which should be welcome. Unfortunately, in the recent period, these improvements have come at the cost of rising deficits and debt, which these States can ill afford as they are also the poorer States.

Observed Patterns and Concerns Going Forward

The dominant feature of the fiscal performance of the Central government has been its sustained commitment to high capex combined with a commitment to fiscal consolidation. Its fiscal deficit level remains above the path recommended by the 15th Finance Commission. However, following the sharp spike in the deficit during the pandemic, the Central government has made a concerted effort to cut down the deficit every year to reach a target deficit level of 4.5 per cent by 2025–26. This combination of high capex with deficit reduction has been made possible by very buoyant tax revenues, along with restraint in revenue expenditure. The main concern in the Central government's finances today is the high level of public debt. The consolidated public debt of the Centre plus States is around 80 per cent—well above the target level recommended by the 15th Finance Commission—and most of it is Central government debt.

There are very large variations in the fiscal performance of the State governments. To make an analysis of these variations tractable, we have grouped these States according to their levels of economic and social development, represented respectively by per capita income and longevity: balanced development States with both per capita income and longevity above the median; high economic development States with per capita income above the median but longevity below the median; high social development States with per capita income below the median but longevity above the median; and lagged development States with per capita income and longevity both below the median. The fiscal performance of the States has been analyzed through this bivariate lens of socioeconomic development.

One important conclusion is that in the past, the shares of capex and social spending have had no statistically significant impact on development outcomes. It is arguable that the shares of capex and social spending need to be much higher going forward to significantly impact development outcomes. The relatively modest allocation for capex in the States is in sharp contrast to the very high allocation by the Central government. Indeed, there was a boost to capex allocation by the States, incentivized by the 50-year interest-free loan from the Central government. But these loans are now being used to substitute the States' own revenues, which are being entirely diverted to revenue expenditure. In fact, even a part of the loans raised by many States is being used to finance revenue expenditure such that total capex allocation in the States remains modest.

On the receipts side of State finances, there is a strong, statistically significant correlation between the level of economic development (per capita income) and the share of own revenues in total revenues. States with higher-than-median per capita income have a much higher share of own revenue in total receipts compared to States with lower-than-median per capita income. As a consequence, the former are less dependent on borrowed resources. The level of indebtedness is higher and rising for the States with below-median per capita income.

Thus the Central government's main focus going forward should be on reducing its level of debt, while the economically more developed States (above-median per capita income) need to focus on raising the allocation of expenditure on capex and social spending. The economically less developed States (below-median per capita income) have been raising the share of capex and social services in their total expenditures, but they also need to focus on reversing the declining share of their own revenues in total receipts and their rising levels of public debt.

Table 1: Key Fiscal Indicators—Central Government (per cent)

		2019–20	2020–21	2021–22	2022–23	2023–24PA	2024–25BE
01	NRR/GDP	8.4	8.2	9.2	8.8	9.2	9.6
02	GTR/GDP	10.0	10.2	11.5	11.3	11.7	11.8
03	Corporation Tax/GDP	2.8	2.3	3.0	3.1	3.1	3.1
04	Income Tax/GDP	2.5	2.5	3.0	3.1	3.5	3.6
05	Union Excise Duties/GDP	1.2	2.0	1.7	1.2	1.0	1.0
06	CGST/GDP	2.5	2.3	2.5	2.7	2.8	2.8
07	Customs Duty/GDP	0.5	0.7	0.8	0.8	0.8	0.7
08	NTR/GDP	6.8	7.2	7.6	7.8	7.9	7.9
09	ONTR/GDP	1.6	1.0	1.5	1.1	1.4	1.7
10	Capex/Totex	12.5	12.1	15.6	17.6	21.4	23.0
11	Social Services Expenditure/Totex	5.3	4.9	7.1	5.3	5.6	5.2
12	Committed Expenditure/Totex	45.8	39.8	42.1	NA	NA	NA
13	Social Safety Net Expenditure/Totex	8.9	21.5	12.2	10.3	8.2	7.5
14	FD/GDP	-4.7	-9.2	-6.7	-6.4	-5.6	-4.9
	Outstanding Liabilities (% of GDP)						
15	Centre	50.8	60.8	57.4	56.5	57.1	55.7

	2019–20	2020–21	2021–22	2022–23	2023–24PA	2024–25BE
16	States	25.2	29.6	27.7	26.8	27.3	27.4
17	General Government (Centre and States)	75.1	88.9	83.1	81.2	82.0	80.2

Notes: 1) Data for fiscal indicators social services expenditure/totex, committed expenditure/totex, social safety net expenditure/totex and outstanding liabilities/GDP for Central, State and general government (i.e. Centre and States) for 2023–24 pertains to revised estimates (RE).

2) NRR (net revenue receipt) of the Centre is defined as total revenue receipt net of devolution; NTR (net tax revenue) of the Centre is defined as gross tax revenue net of devolution.

3) PA: Provisional Actuals; BE: Budget Estimate; GTR: Gross Tax Revenue; Capex: Capital Expenditure; Totex: Total Expenditure; GDP: Gross Domestic Product; FD: Fiscal Deficit; ORR: Own Revenue Receipts; CGST: Central Goods and Services Tax; ONTR: Own Non-Tax Revenue; NA: Not Available.

4) Social safety net expenditure includes expenditure on food subsidy, Mahatma Gandhi National Rural Employment Guarantee Scheme (MGNREGS), National Social Assistance Programme (NSAP) and Pradhan Mantri Kisan Samman Nidhi (PM-Kisan).

5) Committed expenditure comprises expenditure on salaries and wages, pension payments and interest payments.

6) Net liabilities of the Centre and States is the sum of outstanding liabilities of the Centre and all States (here, 26 States) net of Central loans to the States.

Source: Finance accounts and budget documents of the States; budget documents of the Union government; salaries data of the Central government from Lok Sabha Unstarred Question No. 4269 (27 March 2023); GDP from Ministry of Statistics and Programme Implementation (MoSPI).

Table 2: Key Fiscal Indicators—State Governments (per cent)

		2019-20	2020-21	2021-22	2022-23	2023-24RE	2024-25BE
01	TRR/GDP	12.7	12.4	13.0	12.9	13.7	13.7
02	ORR/GDP	7.1	6.5	6.9	7.3	7.8	8.0
03	OTR/GDP	5.8	5.7	5.9	6.3	6.7	6.9
04	ONTR/GDP	1.3	0.8	1.0	1.0	1.1	1.2
05	CT/GDP	5.6	5.9	6.2	5.6	5.9	5.6
06	Devolution/GDP	3.2	2.9	3.8	3.4	3.6	3.7
07	Grants/GDP	2.4	2.9	2.4	2.2	2.3	1.9
08	Capex/Totex	13.0	12.1	13.7	13.7	16.5	16.2
09	Social Services Expenditure/Totex	37.1	37.8	38.2	38.4	39.3	39.5
10	Committed Expenditure/Totex	39.4	39.5	38.5	37.3	NA	NA
11	FD/GDP	-2.6	-4.0	-2.7	-2.7	-3.4	-3.1
12	Outstanding Liabilities/GDP	25.2	29.6	27.7	26.8	27.3	27.4

Notes: 1) The States' data is for 26 States and does not include data for Sikkim and Arunachal Pradesh.
2) RE: Revised Estimate; BE: Budget Estimate; TRR: Total Revenue Receipts; ORR: Own Revenue Receipt; OTR: Own Tax Revenue; ONTR: Own Non-Tax Revenue; Capex: Capital Expenditure; Totex: Total Expenditure; GDP: Gross Domestic Product; FD: Fiscal Deficit; NA: Not available.
3) Committed expenditure comprises expenditure on salaries and wages, pension payments and interest payments.

Source: Finance accounts and budget documents of States; GDP from Ministry of Statistics and Programme Implementation (MoSPI).

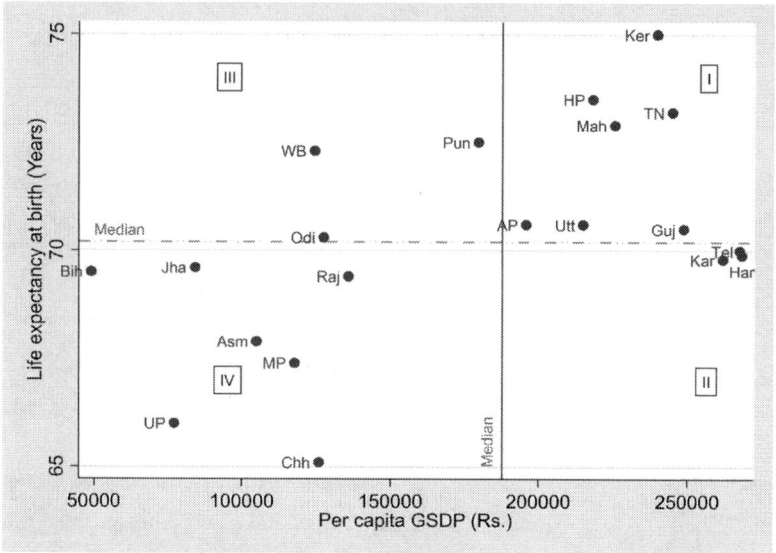

Figure 1: Classification of States Based on Socio-Economic Development

Notes: 1) For economic development, we have considered three-year average per capita GSDP (PCGSDP) (average of the years 2019–20, 2020–21 and 2021–22). The vertical line represents the median average PCGSDP. States on the right and left of it are States with higher and lower than median income, respectively.

2) For social development, we have considered life expectancy at birth for 2016–20. The horizontal line represents the median life expectancy at birth. States above and below the horizontal line are States with higher and lower than median life expectancy respectively.

3) These two median lines divide the graph into four quadrants. Balanced development States are in quadrant I; high economic development States are in quadrant II; quadrant III includes high social development States; and quadrant IV has the lagged development States.

Source: PCGSDP from the Ministry of Statistics and Programme Implementation (MoSPI); life expectancy from SRS-based abridged life tables 2016–20, Office of the Registrar General and Census Commissioner, Ministry of Home Affairs, Government of India.

Table 3: Fiscal Performance Indicators of States (2022–23) (per cent)

		Per capita Totex	ORR/ TRR	Capex/ Totex	Social Service expd./ Totex	FD/ GSDP	Debt/ GSDP
A	**Balanced Development States**						
1	Andhra Pradesh	39,281	52.9	3.5	42.6	-4.0	32.0
2	Gujarat	30,224	71.8	16.5	40.9	-0.8	18.5
3	Himachal Pradesh	67,696	35.4	11.9	38.4	-6.5	45.2
4	Kerala	44,091	65.6	9.0	34.2	-2.4	36.8
5	Maharashtra	37,165	72.5	13.1	36.8	-1.9	18.7
6	Tamil Nadu	41,620	68.6	12.4	32.3	-3.5	29.2
7	Uttarakhand	44,850	43.7	15.8	38.8	-1.0	25.8
	Total (7 States)	38,533	66.1	11.7	37.1	-2.4	24.9
B	**High Economic Development States**						
8	Haryana	39,568	80.4	9.9	40.2	-3.2	31.0
9	Karnataka	40,425	68.8	21.0	34.3	-2.1	23.5
10	Telangana	45,077	79.4	10.4	35.2	-2.5	26.9
	Total (3 States)	41,542	74.5	15.5	35.8	-2.4	26.1

		Per capita Totex	ORR/ TRR	Capex/ Totex	Social Service expd./ Totex	FD/ GSDP	Debt/ GSDP
C	**High Social Development States**						
11	Odisha	35,609	59.3	20.3	37.2	-2.0	14.9
12	Punjab	37,304	55.3	5.5	27.3	-5.0	46.5
13	West Bengal	24,761	43.9	9.0	51.3	-3.3	38.2
	Total (3 States)	29,867	51.6	11.7	41.4	-3.3	34.2
D	**Lagged Development States**						
14	Assam	33,118	33.7	13.6	46.3	-5.8	25.3
15	Bihar	17,104	27.9	14.6	43.8	-6.0	39.0
16	Chhattisgarh	32,828	51.5	13.5	37.3	-1.0	21.9
17	Jharkhand	20,555	47.3	17.4	40.7	-1.2	30.1
18	Madhya Pradesh	28,362	45.4	18.2	39.6	-3.3	29.2
19	Rajasthan	30,532	55.3	8.0	40.2	-3.7	37.0
20	Uttar Pradesh	20,154	45.0	19.7	36.8	-2.9	28.9
	Total (7 States)	23,345	44.1	15.7	39.8	-3.4	31.0

Notes: Totex: Total Expenditure; ORR: Own Revenue Receipt; TRR: Total Revenue Receipt; GSDP: Gross State Domestic Product; Capex: Capital Expenditure; FD: Fiscal Deficit Debt means outstanding liabilities.

Source: Budget documents of States; GSDP from Ministry of Statistics and Programme Implementation (MoSPI).

Table 4: Changes in States' Fiscal Performance over Three Periods: 1991–92 to 2001–02, 2001–02 to 2011–12 and 2011–12 to 2022–23

		ORR/TRR	Capex/Totex	Soc. Ser./Totex	FD/GSDP	Debt/GSDP
A	**Balanced Development States**					
1	Andhra Pradesh	IID	IID	DII	DID	DID
2	Gujarat	IDD	DID	III	DII	DII
3	Himachal Pradesh	IID	DDS	DII	DID	DID
4	Kerala	IID	DII	DSI	III	DID
5	Maharashtra	IDD	DII	IID	DID	DII
6	Tamil Nadu	IDD	IID	IID	IID	DID
7	Uttarakhand	ID	II	ID	II	ID
	7 States	IDD	SID	SID	DID	DID
B	**High Economic Development States**					
8	Haryana	IDD	ISD	DII	DID	DID
9	Karnataka	DID	DII	DIS	DIS	DID
10	Telangana	-	-	-	-	-
	3 States	IDD	SID	DIS	DIS	DID
C	**High Social Development States**					
11	Odisha	III	DII	DID	DID	DII
12	Punjab	IDD	IDI	DIS	DID	DID
13	West Bengal	DDD	DDI	DII	DIS	DII
	3 States	DDD	DDI	DII	DID	DID

D	Lagged Development States	ORR/TRR	Capex/Totex	Soc. Ser./Totex	FD/GSDP	Debt/GSDP
14	Assam	IID	DII	DII	DID	IID
15	Bihar	DSI	DID	DII	DID	DID
16	Chhattisgarh	DD	ID	ID	ID	ID
17	Jharkhand	DI	SI	DI	IS	ID
18	Madhya Pradesh	DDD	DII	DII	DID	DID
19	Rajasthan	IID	DID	ISI	DID	DID
20	Uttar Pradesh	SID	III	DII	DID	DII
	7 States	IDD	DII	DII	DID	DID

Notes: 1) Totex: Total Expenditure; ORR: Own Revenue Receipt; TRR: Total Revenue Receipt; GSDP: Gross State Domestic Product; Capex: Capital Expenditure; FD: Fiscal Deficit; Debt means outstanding liabilities.

2) The table summarizes changes in the States' fiscal performance over three periods: 1991–92 to 2001–02, 2001–02 to 2011–12, and 2011–12 to 2022–23. In each column, the three letters refer to changes in the first period, the second period and the third period, respectively. However, for the three States, Uttarakhand, Chhattisgarh and Jharkhand, there are only two letters in each column, referring to the second and third periods respectively, since these States were created only in 2000–01. Consequently, the geographical coverage of Uttar Pradesh, Madhya Pradesh and Bihar in the second and third periods are different from that in the first period. The detailed data underlying the letter grading in these columns is provided in the Appendix tables A2.1–A2.3.

3) The letters indicate improvement in performance (I), deterioration (D) or similarity (S). In case of FD/GSDP, and Debt/GSDP, the letter I would imply improvement or a reduction in the ratio, the letter D would indicate a deterioration or a rise in the ratio, and the letter S would indicate similarity or no significant change during the relevant period. For all the other fiscal performance indicators, I indicates a rise in the ratio while D indicates a fall in the ratio.

Source: Summary of appendix table, which is based on finance accounts, budget documents of States and GSDP data from Ministry of Statistics and Programme Implementation (MoSPI).

Appendix Tables

Table A1: Regression Results

	PCGSDP	PCGSDP	Life Expectancy	Life Expectancy	Per Capita ORR	Fiscal Deficit
	(1)	(2)	(3)	(4)	(5)	(6)
Capex/Totex	-4,027.95					
Per Capita Capex		16.63				
Soc. Ser. Expd./Totex			-0.106			
Per Capita Soc. Ser. Expd.				0.0003*		
PCGSDP					0.073***	-1.522
Constant	271,184.4***	142,727.6***	74.41***	66.77***	787.66	-3,210,282***
Adj. R-square	0.048	0.136	0.048	0.182	0.82	0.004
No. of Observations	20	20	20	20	20	20

Notes: 1) T-statistics in parentheses; ***, **, and * denote significance at one per cent, five per cent, and 10 per cent levels, respectively.
2) Totex: Total Expenditure; ORR: Own Revenue Receipt; GSDP: Gross State Domestic Product; Capex: Capital Expenditure; FD: Fiscal Deficit; Soc. Ser. Expd.: Social Services Expenditure.

Table A2.1: States' Fiscal Performance: 1991–91 to 2022–23 (per cent)

		ORR/GSDP				ORR/TRR			
		1991–92	2001–02	2011–12	2022–23	1991–92	2001–02	2011–12	2022–23
A	**Balanced Development States**								
1	Andhra Pradesh	9.9	9.2	8.8	6.4	64.2	66.2	69.5	52.9
2	Gujarat	13.1	10.5	8.0	6.4	80.3	81.3	78.7	71.8
3	Himachal Pradesh	8.1	6.5	8.3	7.0	26.9	30.0	41.4	35.4
4	Kerala	10.9	8.3	7.8	8.3	66.9	71.4	74.5	65.6
5	Maharashtra	10.5	9.5	7.5	8.3	79.2	86.2	79.0	72.5
6	Tamil Nadu	13.1	9.8	8.7	7.1	71.6	77.4	76.5	68.6
7	Uttarakhand	NA	7.2	5.9	7.1	NA	43.4	49.3	43.7
	7 States	11.3	9.4	8.0	7.4	72.0	75.1	73.8	66.1
B	**High Economic Development States**								
8	Haryana	11.3	10.1	8.4	7.3	82.4	87.3	82.2	80.4
9	Karnataka	11.7	9.7	8.3	6.9	73.7	71.4	72.4	68.8
10	Telangana	NA	NA	NA	9.7	NA	NA	NA	79.4
	3 States	11.6	9.9	8.4	7.8	76.5	76.7	75.4	74.5

C	High Social Development States							
11	Odisha	6.7	6.8	8.6	11.9	38.1	44.8	49.4	59.3
12	Punjab	14.0	9.8	7.6	7.2	85.8	87.1	77.1	55.3
13	West Bengal	6.7	4.7	5.0	5.6	57.6	50.3	44.7	43.9
	3 States	8.8	6.4	6.5	7.5	62.9	59.8	53.0	51.6
D	Lagged Development States							
14	Assam	6.5	5.5	7.3	6.1	32.0	35.0	38.3	33.7
15	Bihar	5.7	4.5	5.5	6.4	36.2	26.5	26.3	27.9
16	Chhattisgarh	NA	9.2	9.3	10.4	NA	62.1	57.1	51.5
17	Jharkhand	NA	7.0	6.6	9.6	NA	54.2	44.6	47.3
18	Madhya Pradesh	9.7	7.2	10.9	7.4	58.7	56.0	55.0	45.4
19	Rajasthan	9.9	7.8	7.9	7.9	55.2	59.1	60.6	55.3
20	Uttar Pradesh	7.1	6.4	8.7	8.3	47.3	47.3	48.0	45.0
	7 States	7.7	6.7	8.3	7.9	47.5	48.1	47.8	44.1

Note: ORR: Own Revenue Receipt; TRR: Total Revenue Receipt; GSDP: Gross State Domestic Product; NA: Not Available.

Source: Finance accounts and budget documents of States; GSDP from Ministry of Statistics and Programme Implementation (MoSPI).

Table A2.2: States' Fiscal Performance: 1991–91 to 2022–23 (per cent)

		Soc. Ser./Totex				Capex/Totex			
		1991–92	2001–02	2011–12	2022–23	1991–92	2001–02	2011–12	2022–23
A	**Balanced Development States**								
1	Andhra Pradesh	35.2	31.3	37.3	42.6	6.1	11.1	13.2	3.5
2	Gujarat	32.2	35.1	37.9	40.9	15.2	7.2	18.8	16.5
3	Himachal Pradesh	38.4	34.7	35.1	38.4	16.1	12.4	11.5	11.9
4	Kerala	39.5	33.8	33.7	34.2	8.2	4.6	7.7	9.0
5	Maharashtra	32.5	34.6	40.2	36.8	8.8	7.1	12.6	13.1
6	Tamil Nadu	33.1	35.8	38.0	32.3	3.1	7.6	16.3	12.4
7	Uttarakhand	NA	36.5	41.8	38.8	NA	6.6	15.2	15.8
	7 States	33.9	34.2	38.1	37.1	8.2	8.0	13.9	11.7
B	**High Economic Development States**								
8	Haryana	30.6	28.8	37.5	40.2	6.0	14.5	14.4	9.9
9	Karnataka	33.5	32.1	34.6	34.3	13.7	10.2	19.2	21.0
10	Telangana	NA	NA	NA	35.2	NA	NA	NA	10.4
	3 States	32.7	31.0	35.5	35.8	11.4	11.6	17.7	15.5

C									
	High Social Development States								
11	Odisha	33.2	31.6	38.3	37.2	19.9	8.2	11.5	20.3
12	Punjab	23.6	23.1	27.8	27.3	6.5	7.2	4.6	5.5
13	West Bengal	40.7	34.3	42.5	51.3	5.6	5.1	3.6	9.0
	3 States	33.1	30.6	38.0	41.4	9.4	6.4	5.9	11.7
D	**Lagged Development States**								
14	Assam	40.1	37.2	40.0	46.3	11.7	7.0	8.6	13.6
15	Bihar	35.8	30.0	35.3	43.8	7.1	6.2	16.0	14.6
16	Chhattisgarh	NA	37.3	43.0	37.3	NA	8.8	15.2	13.5
17	Jharkhand	NA	36.5	33.8	40.7	NA	13.2	13.1	17.4
18	Madhya Pradesh	35.4	30.0	35.5	39.6	12.4	9.3	14.7	18.2
19	Rajasthan	34.2	39.8	39.4	40.2	22.9	10.2	11.7	8.0
20	Uttar Pradesh	32.4	27.0	36.1	36.8	6.4	10.1	14.8	19.7
	7 States	34.6	32.0	37.0	39.8	11.0	9.4	14.0	15.7

Note: Capex: Capital Expenditure; Totex: Total Expenditure; Soc. Ser.: Social Services Expenditure; NA: Not Available.

Source: Finance accounts and budget documents of the States.

Table A2.3: States' Fiscal Performance: 1991–91 to 2022–23 (per cent)

		FD/GSDP				Debt/GSDP			
		1991–92	2001–02	2011–12	2022–23	1991–92	2001–02	2011–12	2022–23
A	**Balanced Development States**								
1	Andhra Pradesh	-2.8	-4.3	-2.1	-4.0	23.1	30.3	20.4	32.0
2	Gujarat	-4.7	-5.3	-1.8	-0.8	30.4	36.7	24.5	18.5
3	Himachal Pradesh	-6.7	-8.8	-2.2	-6.5	45.0	59.6	38.8	45.2
4	Kerala	-4.6	-4.2	-3.5	-2.4	33.0	37.2	25.6	36.8
5	Maharashtra	-2.3	-4.0	-1.6	-1.9	20.0	27.0	19.2	18.7
6	Tamil Nadu	-3.5	-3.2	-2.3	-3.5	22.1	25.5	16.9	29.2
7	Uttarakhand	NA	-3.9	-1.5	-1.0	NA	29.3	20.5	25.8
	7 States	-3.2	-4.2	-2.0	-2.4	24.1	30.5	20.8	24.9
B	**High Economic Development States**								
8	Haryana	-2.3	-4.2	-2.4	-3.2	21.0	26.0	18.3	31.0
9	Karnataka	-3.0	-5.2	-2.0	-2.1	21.8	28.9	17.0	23.5
10	Telangana	NA	NA	NA	-2.5	NA	NA	NA	26.9
	3 States	-2.8	-4.8	-2.2	-2.4	21.5	27.8	17.4	26.1

C	High Social Development States								
11	Odisha	-6.5	-8.5	0.3	-2.0	42.4	59.6	18.4	14.9
12	Punjab	-5.0	-6.2	-3.2	-5.0	35.6	42.6	31.2	46.5
13	West Bengal	-2.8	-7.5	-3.4	-3.3	25.3	41.8	39.9	38.2
	3 States	-4.2	-7.3	-2.5	-3.3	31.4	44.9	32.7	34.2
D	Lagged Development States								
14	Assam	-2.1	-3.8	-1.1	-5.8	41.0	32.8	22.0	25.3
15	Bihar	-3.9	-4.5	-2.4	-6.0	41.5	55.3	27.4	39.0
16	Chhattisgarh	NA	-3.7	-0.5	-1.0	NA	25.1	10.8	21.9
17	Jharkhand	NA	-3.9	-1.3	-1.2	NA	22.3	20.3	30.1
18	Madhya Pradesh	-3.0	-4.2	-1.8	-3.3	27.0	28.3	25.9	29.2
19	Rajasthan	-3.4	-6.3	-0.8	-3.7	33.1	43.6	24.5	37.0
20	Uttar Pradesh	-4.4	-5.2	-2.1	-2.9	35.1	39.6	31.7	28.9
	7 States	-3.7	-4.9	-1.6	-3.4	34.8	37.7	26.0	31.0

Note: GSDP: Gross State Domestic Product; FD: Fiscal Deficit; NA: Not available. Debt means outstanding liabilities.

Source: Finance accounts and budget documents of States; GSDP from Ministry of Statistics and Programme Implementation (MoSPI).

Radhicka Kapoor[*]

India's Quest for Productive Employment and the Role of MSMEs

The post-Covid-19 period in India witnessed a notable shift in employment towards the agricultural sector, with its share rising from 42.4 per cent to 45.7 per cent between 2019–20 and 2022–23.[1] In absolute terms, approximately 61.2 million people were added to this sector. Even prior to the pandemic, India's structural transformation had been sluggish, characterized by the inability of its manufacturing sector to emerge as an engine of productive job creation.[2] Historic evidence of successful structural transformation points to the pivotal role of the manufacturing sector in absorbing the less educated workers into relatively high productivity occupations. Accelerating the growth of the manufacturing sector, particularly labour-intensive manufacturing, is imperative for India's growth and employment strategy.[3]

Policy recommendations must acknowledge the dominance of micro, small and medium enterprises (MSMEs) in labour-intensive industries, and strive to enhance the productivity and competitiveness of the sector. This chapter proposes a new policy narrative focusing on dynamic growth-oriented MSMEs, advocating for a shift away from indefinitely subsidizing subsistence entrepreneurs. Central to this framework is the establishment of a 'productivity ecosystem approach' which addresses the main drivers of productivity in the MSME sector at the macro, meso and micro levels.[4] Beyond improving the business environment and workforce skills, and supporting the adoption of digital technologies, a sectoral and local perspective is crucial for dealing with the varied productivity challenges across regions and industries.

---

[*] *Views shared are personal and do not necessarily reflect those of the organization.*

Encouraging the entry of young educated entrepreneurs in the MSME landscape is vital for fostering growth-oriented enterprises. Importantly, any support provided to MSMEs should not inadvertently incentivize remaining small. The chapter proceeds to present key stylized facts on the MSME sector's growth, followed by an outline of the productivity ecosystem approach and concluding remarks.

Stylized Facts

Before examining the stylized facts on the evolution of enterprise size distribution, it is important to define MSMEs for the purpose of this analysis. In India, the Micro, Small and Medium Enterprises Development (MSMED) Act (2006) provided the legal framework for categorizing manufacturing and services enterprises into micro, small and medium categories. The definitions according to the MSMED Act—based on investment limits in plant and machinery/equipment (which are relevant for the time period of our analysis)—are reported in Table 1.[5]

Table 1: Definition of MSME (as per the MSMED Act, 2006)

Classification	Manufacturing Enterprise (Investment in Plant and Machinery)	Service Enterprise (Investment in Equipment)
Micro	Upto ₹25 lakh	Upto ₹10 lakh
Small	Above ₹25 lakh to ₹5 crore	Above ₹10 lakh to ₹2 crore
Medium	Above ₹5 crore to ₹10 crore	Above ₹2 crore to ₹5 crore

Source: Micro, Small and Medium Enterprises Development (MSMED) Act, 2006.

Ideally, to obtain the relevant stylized facts on the employment distribution across MSMEs, we need to apply the definitions reported in Table 1 to these two surveys, the Annual Survey of Industries (ASI) for formal enterprises, and the NSSO's Key Indicators of Unincorporated Non-Agricultural Enterprises (Excluding Construction) in India survey for informal enterprises, and then classify the enterprises into micro, small and medium categories. However, significant challenges arise in creating this categorization using the two enterprise databases as the surveys do not provide disaggregated information on investment in plant and machinery to the extent required by the above definitions.[6] Given the difficulties in matching the industrial statistics as reported in the enterprise surveys, which are mostly classified in terms of employment with the promotional policies for MSMEs carried out in terms of capital investment limits, we choose to use an employment-based definition of MSMEs instead of an investment-based one. Data on employment breakdown is most easily available—for both formal and informal enterprises—from the ASI and NSS enterprise surveys respectively. Applying the definition used by the Organisation for Economic Co-operation and Development (OECD) to the two enterprise surveys in India, we classify enterprises into the following five categories:[7]

- Self-Employment/Own Account Enterprises: No hired workers
- Microenterprises: One to nine workers
- Small Enterprises: 10 to 49 workers
- Medium-Sized Enterprises: 50 to 249 workers
- Large Enterprises: 250 or more workers

Stylized Fact 1: India's firm landscape is dominated by informal microenterprises.

Combining establishment-level data from the ASI and NSS enterprise surveys, it is observed that the enterprise landscape in India has been dominated by enterprises hiring less than five workers. Table 2 shows that approximately 95 per cent of all enterprises have less than five workers for all time periods under study. The four time periods correspond to the years in which the NSSO's Unincorporated Non-Agricultural Enterprises survey was conducted: 1999–2000, 2005–06, 2010–11, and 2015–16.

Table 2: Distribution of All Enterprises across NSSO and ASI Databases by Size

Size Bin	2000–01	2005–06	2010–11	2015–16
Less than 5	95.29	94.69	95.07	96.19
6 to 9	3.09	3.17	3.03	2.41
10 to 19	1.17	1.39	1.47	1.05
20 to 49	0.35	0.39	0.44	0.35
50 to 99	0.09	0.11	0.15	0.13
100 to 199	0.05	0.05	0.08	0.07
200 to 249	0.01	0.01	0.01	0.02
250 to 299	0.01	0.01	0.01	0.01
300+	0.02	0.03	0.04	0.04

Source: Kapoor, Radhicka, 'Stylized Facts on the Evolution of the Enterprise Size Distribution in India's Manufacturing Sector'.

Importantly, the statistics reported in Table 2 include own account enterprises (OAEs) which operate without any hired labour. Although OAEs account for roughly 85 per cent of all enterprises in the manufacturing landscape, we choose not to include them in the analysis that follows because operating without any hired labour, OAEs are unlikely to become engines of productive job creation. It has been noted that such enterprises are often simply eking out a subsistence living using primitive, unchanging technology and employing family labour to the fullest extent as their opportunity cost is zero.[8] This is evident from their very low gross value-added (GVA) per worker (Table 3), compared to those enterprises which operate with hired labour (both in the informal and formal sectors). In 2010–11, the GVA per worker in enterprises which operated without hired labour in the informal sector was 2.6 times higher than in the OAEs, while the ratio of GVA per worker in formal enterprises was over 30 times higher than in the OAEs. In 2015–16, the corresponding ratios were 2.6 and 24.2, respectively. At such low levels of GVA per worker, it may well be argued that OAEs are nothing more than survival efforts of underemployed labour.[9]

Table 3: Annual GVA per Worker by Enterprise Type in the Manufacturing Sector (Nominal in ₹)

	Unincorporated Enterprises				Formal Enterprises	
	OAEs	Establishments	All	Ratio of GVA per Worker in Establishments to OAEs	ASI	Ratio of GVA per Worker in Formal Enterprises to OAEs
2010–11	26,844	70,000	44,314	2.61	813,027	30.29
2015–16	46,088	122,344	74,379	2.65	1,117,114	24.24

Note: An enterprise which is operating with at least one hired worker on a fairly regular basis is termed as an establishment in the NSSO Unincorporated Enterprise Surveys.

Source: Kapoor, Radhicka, 'Stylized Facts on the Evolution of the Enterprise Size Distribution in India's Manufacturing Sector'.

Dropping OAEs from the analysis, Table 4 presents the distribution of firms. Microenterprises, i.e. those with one to nine workers, account for 90 per cent of total enterprises for the entire time period under study. The next highest share is that of small enterprises at about 10 per cent, followed by medium-sized enterprises, which account for one to two per cent of total enterprises over all four time periods. Large enterprises (i.e. those with 250 or more workers) account for less than 0.5 per cent of total enterprises. Therefore, as noted in Hseih and Olken's analysis (2014), the enterprise size distribution is dominated by a large number of very small enterprises and both medium-sized and large enterprises are few and far between.[10]

Table 4: Distribution of Enterprises in the Manufacturing Sector (Excluding OAEs) by Size

Size Bin	2000–01	2005–06	2010–11	2015–16
1 to 5	69.30	68.24	70.23	74.03
6 to 9	19.06	18.64	16.82	15.10
10 to 19	7.98	9.11	8.58	6.77
20 to 49	2.43	2.58	2.59	2.33
50 to 99	0.63	0.75	0.88	0.84
100 to 199	0.33	0.36	0.50	0.48
200 to 249	0.06	0.07	0.09	0.10
250 to 299	0.04	0.05	0.06	0.06
300+	0.17	0.20	0.25	0.29

Source: Kapoor, Radhicka, 'Stylized Facts on the Evolution of the Enterprise Size Distribution in India's Manufacturing Sector'.

It needs to be pointed out here that the MSME sector in India is marked by a segmented and dualistic structure wherein a large number of informal micro and small enterprises coexist with a few formal medium and large enterprises. Table 5 presents the distribution of MSMEs in the formal and informal sectors. Almost all microenterprises are informal in nature. In the small category, the share of informal enterprises has remained over 70 per cent, although it has declined over time. The medium category largely comprises formal enterprises, and the share of informal enterprises in this category is below 20 per cent for the time period under study. In the large category, the share of informal enterprises is miniscule. Understanding and recognizing the dualistic structure of the enterprise distribution in the MSME category is important from a policy perspective, especially when we are trying to design instruments to support these enterprises. Their institutional and legal characteristics need to be borne in mind while conceptualizing the nature of support they should be provided.

Table 5: Share of Informal Enterprises (i.e. Those in NSSO Unincorporated Enterprise Survey) in Each Size Bin

	2000–01	2005–06	2010–11	2015–16
Micro	98.71	98.79	98.66	98.43
Small	75.47	77.87	75.15	71.95
Medium	17.44	18.67	20.92	19.47
Large	0.66	2.25	1.18	0.80

Source: Kapoor, Radhicka, 'Stylized Facts on the Evolution of the Enterprise Size Distribution in India's Manufacturing Sector'.

Stylized Fact 2: The distribution of employment has been dominated by microenterprises. However, over time, the share of medium and large enterprises has risen, while that of micro and small enterprises has declined.

Table 6 reports the distribution of employment over time across the ASI and the NSSO Enterprise Surveys. Microenterprises (i.e. those with one to nine workers) accounted for the largest share of total employment. Over time, their share in total employment declined from 44.8 per cent (2000–01) to 36.3 per cent (2015–16). The next highest share of employment is reported in large enterprises (i.e. those with 250 or more workers). Significantly, the share of employment in this category increased from 20.5 per cent in 2000–01 to 30.3 per cent in 2015–16. Small enterprises (i.e. those with 10–49 workers) saw a decline in employment share from 21.6 per cent to 17.2 per cent over the 15-year period, while medium-sized enterprises (50–249 workers) witnessed an increase from 12.7 per cent to 16 per cent.

Table 6: Distribution of Employment by Enterprise Size
(without OAEs)

Size Bin	2000–01	2005–06	2010–11	2015–16
1 to 5	27.87	25.93	23.65	24.51
6 to 9	16.94	15.88	13.13	11.81
10 to 19	12.77	13.70	12.29	9.70
20 to 49	8.89	8.92	8.35	7.53
50 to 99	5.49	6.25	6.74	6.40
100 to 199	5.67	5.91	7.43	7.17
200 to 249	1.61	1.86	2.16	2.52
250 to 299	1.22	1.53	1.73	1.72
300+	19.28	20.23	24.30	28.57

Source: Kapoor, Radhicka, 'Stylized Facts on the Evolution of the Enterprise Size Distribution in India's Manufacturing Sector'.

The shift in the employment distribution towards large enterprises is driven by changes in the distribution in the formal sector. Table 7 shows the employment distribution for the formal manufacturing sector using data from the Annual Survey of Industries (ASI) since 2000–01. Here, it is noted that while the share of employment in small enterprises fell from 18.4 per cent to 12.8 per cent, that of large enterprises increased from 51.1 per cent in 2000–01 to 58.5 per cent in 2016. It is the latter which explains the substantial shift in the overall distribution towards large enterprises observed in Table 6 (covering both the ASI and NSS Unincorporated Enterprise Survey).

Table 7: Distribution of Employment in the Formal Sector by Size Bin

Size Bin	2000–01	2001–02	2002–03	2003–04	2004–05	2005–06	2006–07	2007–08	2008–09	2010–11	2011–12	2012–13	2013–14	2014–15	2015–16
Micro (1–9)	2.21	2.26	2.24	2.19	2.01	1.84	1.56	1.53	1.53	1.67	1.63	1.78	1.8	1.8	1.68
Small (10–49)	18.4	18.58	18.33	18.13	18.4	17.41	16.09	16.44	15.7	15.2	14.52	14.02	13.95	13.42	12.89
Medium (50–249)	28.26	28.55	28.58	29.07	29.54	29.87	29.36	28.03	29.27	29.19	28.33	27.98	27.32	26.66	26.88
Large (250+)	51.14	50.61	50.85	50.61	50.05	50.88	52.99	54	53.5	53.94	55.51	56.21	56.93	58.12	58.55

Source: Kapoor and Krishnapriya (forthcoming).[11]

Stylized Fact 3: The shift in the distribution of employment towards larger plants in the formal sector appears to be driven by two factors—one, the expansion of previously smaller plants and their transition to larger size bins, and two, the entry of new mid-sized plants.

Identifying and understanding the drivers of the change in the employment distribution is important from a policy perspective. In particular, the question of whether it is the expansion of previously small plants or the entry of new plants that is causing an increase in the share of large plants in total employment merits attention. Answering these questions requires tracking the growth and life cycle dynamics of firms. However, the nature of enterprise datasets in India makes it difficult to undertake such an exercise. While the NSSO Enterprise dataset does not provide panel data, the ASI dataset does. But the sample design of the ASI does not permit us to track the growth and life-cycle dynamics of all factories over time. The sampling strategy is such that only the larger factories (i.e. those factories which are in the 'census scheme' of the sample and typically have 100 or more workers) are surveyed each year. The remaining smaller units which are in the sample scheme cannot be tracked every year.

Given the data difficulties in tracking factories in all size bins in the ASI, Kapoor and Krishnapriya (in a forthcoming publication) use an alternative approach to understand the factors driving changes in the employment distribution. First, they examine approximately 3,000 plants that are captured in the ASI surveys in all 16 years to assess if there is any evidence of transition among these plants from lower- to higher-size bins. Since these plants are drawn from the census scheme of the ASI sample, they have 100 or more employees. The analysis suggests that a quarter of the plants that were reported to be in the large-size bin (i.e. had 250 or more employees) in 2015–16 had been surveyed as a smaller plant in at least one earlier year.[12] Importantly, the estimate that a quarter of large plants in 2015–16 transitioned from being smaller plants in the earlier years is a conservative one, as some of the large plants that were surveyed in all 16 years could have started out as smaller plants in the years prior to the time period of our analysis (i.e. before 2000–01). This analysis points to evidence of plants moving up the size distribution and becoming large over time. Therefore, there is a case for supporting small and medium plants that have the potential to grow, expand and transition to larger-size bins through schemes and programmes that improve their access to credit, markets, skilled workers and infrastructure, among other factors.

However, only looking at the factories in the census scheme of the ASI sample—which appear in all 16 years of the panel—is not enough, as these factories typically have 100 or more employees. And the stylized facts above suggest that a vast majority of factories have fewer than 100 workers. To understand what is driving the change in the distribution, we need to examine these remaining firms as well. To draw inferences about the dynamics of such plants, Kapoor and Krishnapriya (forthcoming) construct a panel dataset at the 'size-bin level' by aggregating the plant-level data provided in the ASI surveys for each year across the following size bins: one to nine employees, 10 to 19 employees, 20 to 49 employees, 50 to 99 employees, 100 to 249 employees, 250 to 300 employees, and 300+ employees, within each of the available three-digit National Industrial Classification (2004) in each State. This new panel helps to consistently track the set of plants in specific size bins across 16 years. The age of the firm emerges as a noteworthy characteristic in this analysis. More specifically, in the cohort analysis, the findings vis-à-vis the share of young firms (i.e. those which are between zero and four years) in a given size bin are of particular interest. It is observed that the higher the share of young plants, the lower the growth of employment in a size bin. However, in the size bin of 100–249 employees, the reverse is found to be true. This result suggests that in the medium size bin (100–249 employees), young plants are driving employment growth.

The two findings given above indicate that in addition to creating an enabling environment for the growth and expansion of incumbent small and medium-sized firms, it is important to encourage and facilitate the entry of new medium-sized firms.

Stylized Fact 4: Large firms are on average more productive than MSMEs and offer higher wages.

A vast body of literature highlights that significant productivity differentials exist between MSMEs and large firms. This is found to be the case not just in India but other developed and developing countries as well.[13] The lower productivity of SMEs is partly attributed to external factors (such as their overrepresentation in sectors with lower-than-average labour productivity levels), and partly to internal factors, in particular their inability to take advantage of economies of scale. SMEs tend to face significant difficulties in getting access to credit, markets, skilled labour, information and technology, and often function through informal contracts with clients and suppliers. On the other hand, large firms are more efficient in production because they can use more specialized inputs (including through outsourcing), coordinate their resources better, invest more in machinery and skilled workers, and enjoy the advantages of economies of scale. Given their higher productivity, it is easier for larger firms to access foreign markets and grow even more by exporting.

Apart from productivity differentials, it is also observed that on average, larger plants offer higher wages than smaller plants. Computing wages of production workers across plants of different sizes in the ASI database for the formal sector, Kapoor and Krishnapriya estimate wage differentials for the registered manufacturing sector in India in a forthcoming publication. Figure 2 shows the ratio of wages in each size bin to the wages in the size bin of 10–19 employees using data from the ASI. As expected, the ratio of wages in the largest bin (300+ employees) is approximately double the wages in the 10–19 size bin for the entire period from 2000–01 to 2015–16. However, it is worth noting that this ratio has declined over time. While in 2000–01, the ratio stood at 2.4, by 2015–16, it had fallen to 1.7. The question of what is driving the decline in the wage differential is not the focus of this chapter. However, one factor to which this trend can be attributed is the contractualization of labour in larger plants during this time period.[14]

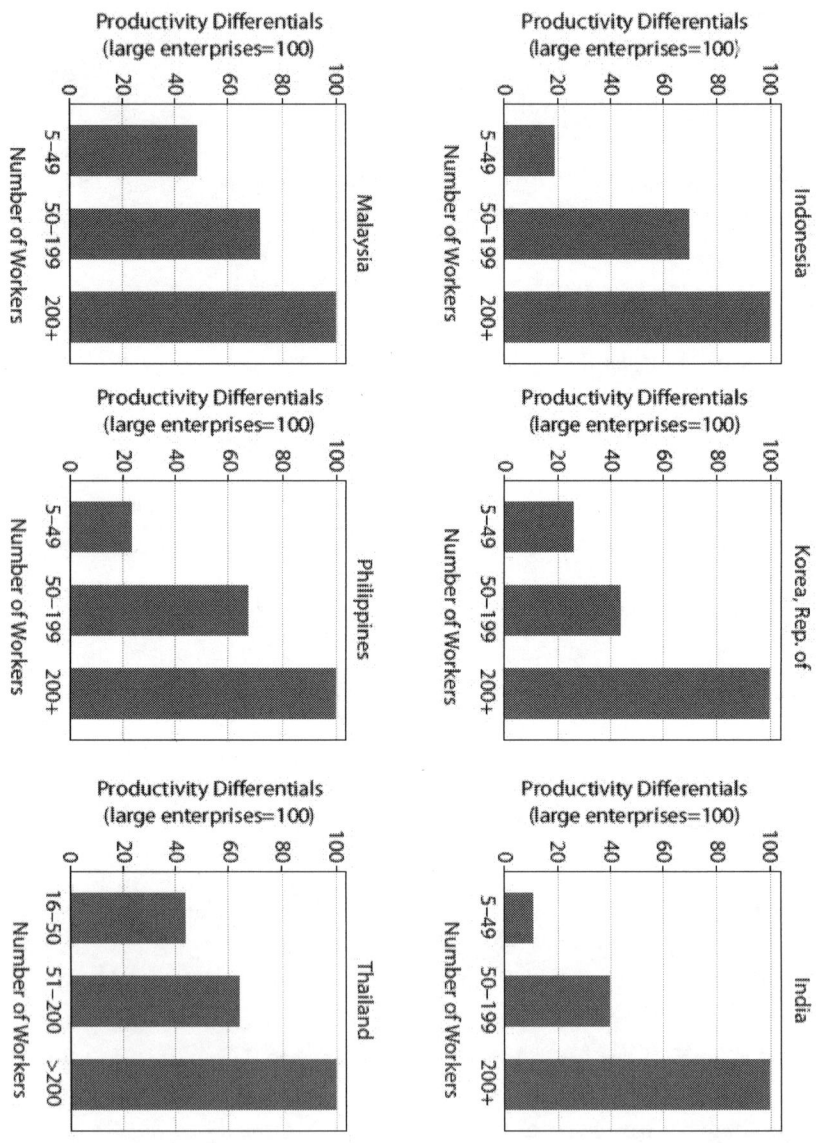

Figure 1: Productivity Differentials across Firm Size Distribution

Source: Hasan, Rana, and Karl Robert L. Jandoc, 'The Distribution of Firm Size in India: What Can Survey Data Tell Us?', Asian Development Bank, August 2010.

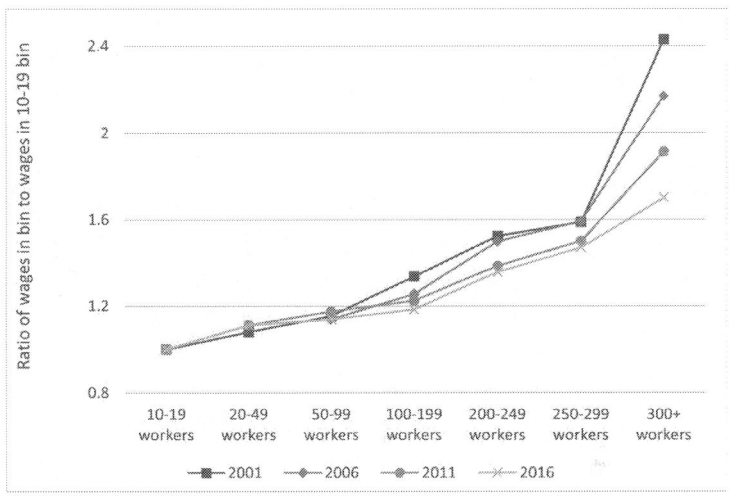

Figure 2: Wage Differentials across Different Size Bins in the Formal Sector

Source: ASI Plant-level data.

A New Policy Narrative for the MSME Sector

Fostering robust enterprise growth is essential for generating well-paying and productive jobs to accommodate a burgeoning working-age population. In India, where labour-intensive industries are predominantly comprised of smaller enterprises compared to capital-intensive ones,[15] the empowerment of MSMEs assumes paramount significance. This section delves into the key factors driving their growth. Before delineating these factors, it is crucial to underscore why the policy emphasis on fostering growth-oriented MSMEs holds exceptional importance within the Indian context.

In the literature, there are broadly two kinds of entrepreneurs— subsistence and transformational.[16] The former category comprises those who become entrepreneurs to earn a subsistence income, while the latter category consists of those who aspire to create larger businesses that grow to provide jobs and income for others and not just meet their own subsistence needs. Subsistence entrepreneurs are dominant in developing countries such as India, where, in the absence of unemployment insurance and other social protection programmes, the poor cannot afford to remain unemployed or exit the labour force when they are unable to find a job. So they are compelled to resort to self-employment or own account employment as a survival mechanism. The statistics in Section 2 highlights the very low gross value-added (GVA) per worker in OAEs compared to enterprises which operate with hired labour (both in the informal and formal sectors). Further, the persistence of a very large share of OAEs in the distribution over time (Table 2) suggests that subsistence enterprises are not expanding the size of their businesses, and that there is not much transition happening from the subsistence to the transformative category. Herrera and Lora (2005) and Schoar (2010) argue that the absence of a more continuous enterprise size distribution in developing countries compared to developed countries suggests a strong discontinuity between subsistence and transformational entrepreneurship, with only minimal transition between the two groups.[17] In fact, Schoar (2010) argues that the notion that subsistence entrepreneurship is the first step towards transformational entrepreneurship does not appear to be true. Against this backdrop, support provided for these subsistence enterprises should be categorized under poverty-alleviation measures, and not policies fostering MSME growth or productive job-creating measures.[18]

The policy focus for the MSME sector in India, therefore, must turn to dynamic growth-oriented enterprises that can create productive employment opportunities. As the stylized facts in the preceding section show, there are dynamic incumbent MSMEs which are growing and moving up the firm size distribution. Additionally, there are new or young medium-sized plants driving employment growth. Designing policy interventions that encourage the entry of new plants and facilitate the growth of dynamic small and medium-sized firms by alleviating their constraints are critical to the agenda of productive job-creation. Equally important is ensuring that policy instruments do not incentivize firms to remain small by restricting support to enterprises that are below a certain threshold of investment, employment, or turnover, as defined in the current architecture of MSME programmes.

Central to the framework of unshackling dynamic growth-oriented enterprises is enhancing MSME productivity. Business scaling is closely tied to enhancing firm productivity, which demands a comprehensive, integrated approach across macro, meso (sectoral) and micro (firm) levels, rather than focusing on interventions at just a single level.[19] The low productivity levels of MSMEs are not solely due to factors such as limited technical knowledge or poor managerial skills at the firm level. Structural barriers at the macro and meso levels—including limited access to capital and markets, a difficult business environment, and insufficient policy support for the industries or sectors in which these firms operate—also play a significant role. These challenges must be addressed comprehensively to foster sustainable growth and competitiveness within the MSME sector. Importantly, such bottlenecks cannot be addressed by the Labour or the MSME ministries alone, but require an integrated approach involving institutional and private stakeholders in the MSME ecosystem. The key drivers of MSME productivity growth which form the pillars of the productivity ecosystem approach are outlined below.[20]

At the macro level, the main challenge pertains to creating an enabling business environment that supports the productivity growth of MSMEs. Compared to large enterprises, MSMEs find it more challenging to navigate a difficult business environment as they lack the necessary resources to do so. Burdensome tax procedures and business regulations create particularly high costs for the MSMEs as they don't have skilled staff to deal with complex business procedures. Apart from facing a higher cost of credit compared to the larger enterprises, MSMEs experience significant difficulties in accessing finance due to their inability to provide collateral and establish their credit worthiness. Further, their inability to access information about markets compared to large firms constrains them from identifying potential markets. A poor business environment negatively impacts enterprise productivity by distorting decision-making, lowering capital accumulation, creating uncertainty, and constraining opportunities for scale-up. Tackling this issue requires maintaining a sustained process of simplifying regulations and reducing bureaucratic bottlenecks for MSMEs. This can be achieved by streamlining business registrations, reducing compliance requirements, and improving the transparency of regulatory and administrative decisions for firms. The first step in this direction requires undertaking a comprehensive review of all the regulatory requirements and statutory compliances for MSMEs.

At the meso level, adopting a sectoral approach to bolster MSME productivity growth is pivotal. Industries within the MSME sector exhibit significant productivity differentials, warranting an industry-based analysis to identify sectors offering higher productivity and better paying jobs. Alongside a sectoral perspective, a focus on the local business environment is paramount. The quality of the local business environment greatly impacts MSMEs, which rely more on external knowledge and support. For instance, the Morbi ceramic cluster's success underscores how local State promotional agencies providing amenities like a natural gas pipeline and improved infrastructure facilitated competitiveness against Chinese imports.[21] This underscores the vital role of State and local governments in attracting and supporting industries.[22]

At the micro (firm) level, supporting the upgrading of managerial skills is crucial. Managerial skills are an important determinant of productivity growth and are found to partly explain the income gap between high-income and middle-income economies, as the latter have a much larger share of ill-managed companies.[23] Managerial skills are also a good predictor of the use of formal management practices at the firm level, which, in turn, have a positive impact on productivity.[24] Building the capacity of MSME business owners through training, mentoring and coaching services, including the establishment of a national network of recognized business development service providers, is crucial for enhancing MSME productivity growth.[25] Importantly, the digital transformation is now offering new instruments to deliver business advice to MSMEs through online diagnostic tools and training platforms.[26] Online training holds the potential of reaching out to many MSMEs that were previously unattended by training services. Online diagnostic tools can also enable MSME owners to benchmark their business operations against similar firms from the same sector and/or region.

The adoption of digital technologies by MSMEs also offers a range of opportunities to enhance productivity levels through lower operation and transaction costs, reduced information asymmetries, greater capacity for product differentiation and dissemination, and greater possibilities for accessing finance, training, skilling, networks and markets (both global and domestic). Survey evidence from India suggests that the increasing integration of MSMEs with e-commerce platforms has not only enabled enterprises to enhance market access, but also improved their sales and profit margins.[27] Similarly, India's digital public infrastructure is being leveraged to improve access to finance for MSMEs through the Account Aggregator (AA) network—a financial data-sharing system that aims to empower MSMEs to digitally access and share their financial data across financial institutions in a secure and efficient manner. Finally, an important but oft-ignored aspect at the micro level is the need to encourage social dialogue at the firm level to ensure that workers understand and implement new productivity-enhancing practices introduced by managers, and adequately benefit from productivity gains through higher wages.[28]

Before concluding the discussion on the policy narrative, it is important to reiterate that apart from creating an enabling environment for dynamic growth-oriented MSMEs to enhance productivity, it is also important to encourage the entry of new dynamic growth-oriented entrepreneurs by making it easier for them to start a business. Here, the policy focus needs to turn to more educated entrepreneurs as they are found to run more efficient and productive firms compared to uneducated entrepreneurs. The firm landscape in India is dominated by informal subsistence enterprises run by less educated or uneducated entrepreneurs. It may be useful to direct entrepreneurship support to the educated unemployed (who are often unable to find the jobs they aspire for) as these individuals are more likely to operate growth-oriented enterprises.[29]

In Lieu of a Conclusion

The discussion in this chapter has focused on supporting dynamic growth-oriented enterprises and alleviating the constraints faced by them. However, the subject of identifying growth-oriented firms which are held back by policy-fixable constraints warrants further research and analysis in India. To push the debate forward, it is worth drawing attention to an innovative empirical strategy applied by Grimm and others to a sample of entrepreneurs in seven capital cities in Francophone West Africa.[30] They identified three groups of entrepreneurs: (a) the well-known success stories or top performers, (b) a group of 'constrained gazelles' who shared some characteristics with these top performers, such as education, language skills, sector choice and some basic management abilities, but who were not (yet) successful (the term 'gazelle' originates from the United States literature on high performance small firms),[31] and (c) a group of survival entrepreneurs. While constrained gazelles and top performers have some similarities, the former possess very low levels of capital. The empirical strategy used by Grimm and others enabled them to arrive at a clear criterion for identifying constrained gazelles which could benefit from targeted interventions to unlock their potential. Developing such an approach using Indian enterprise data could also help identify constrained gazelles and improve the efficacy of policy interventions designed to support MSMEs.

Another issue that merits attention in the design of MSME policy support is that of formalization. The stylized facts in this chapter suggest that the share of micro and small enterprises which are informal in nature is disproportionally high, and has diminished significantly over time. While the issue of whether interventions providing assistance with the formalization process unleash MSME growth remains ambiguous in the literature, it is important to highlight that formalization processes are not restricted to legal considerations vis-à-vis registrations. They are also about increasing the productivity of informal enterprises by providing them with technical and business skills, infrastructure services, financial services, enterprise support and training to better compete in the markets. Many people working in the informal economy have real business acumen and dynamism, and could flourish if obstacles in the path to entrepreneurship were removed. This would enable an organic process of transition to the formal sector. At its core, boosting enterprise productivity should be central to any policy initiative aimed at unshackling India's MSME sector.

Rakesh Mohan

Indian Urbanization Is Slowing Down: What Can Be Done about It?[1]

I have had the privilege of knowing Shankar Acharya since the mid-1970s when we both found ourselves in the research complex of the World Bank. At the time, it was the place to be for any aspiring economist interested in economic development, from both developed and developing countries. Those were heady days full of hope, excitement, optimism, and unlimited possibilities for constructive work. We lived, breathed and discussed global development issues on a 24/7 basis, whether at work, lunch, coffee, tea or dinner, weekdays as well as weekends.

Shankar was among the few—along with Montek Ahluwalia and D.C. Rao—who were the real high-flyers in this extended group. Montek had become the first division chief of the newly minted income distribution division in the World Bank, and probably the youngest division chief ever in that institution. As a member of the first World Development Report (WDR) team in 1978, Shankar has the distinction of being a pioneer in the world of global development thinking. While D.C. Rao was the lead author of this first report, Shankar followed him for the second report. In World Bank president Robert McNamara's words, 'This year's report emphasizes issues of employment, industrialization and urbanization in developing countries and discusses the policies necessary to pursue the twin objectives of growth and poverty alleviation.' This was the tall order that Shankar delivered on at the tender age of 33–34. Soon after completing this task, he decided to give up this charmed life as a member of the global elite and returned to India in 1981.

I had also returned to India in December 1980 on a temporary basis to work on urban development for three years in the contemporary Planning Commission. He followed soon after, and joined the National Institute for Public Finance and Policy, which had been founded and led by the redoubtable Raja Chelliah. As one might expect from Shankar, he landed on his feet very quickly and authored his very well-known report on black money in India, a pioneering effort which is still the only well-researched document on this slippery subject. He has always been known for the clarity of his thought, careful research and elegant writing. Luckily, the mandarins of the North Block figured this out very quickly and inducted him into those hallowed corridors as an economic adviser in the Ministry of Finance within two years of his arrival in India.

Being among the few escapees from the World Bank in Delhi at that time, we developed a great personal and professional friendship ever since. This also gave me my first opportunity to work with him, before he joined the government. As an input to a task force on 'Financing of Urban Development', I worked with Shankar to make an estimate of the financing needed for urban infrastructure development.[2] I learnt a great deal on the art of analytical writing from him in the process.

The second time I worked with Shankar was more than two decades later, when we co-edited a Festschrift[3] in honour of Montek Singh Ahluwalia. Since I was in a state of flux at that time as I had left the Reserve Bank of India and had gone to Stanford University, Shankar was extremely generous in incurring much of the load in compiling that book. In this activity as well, Shankar displayed his skill in choosing leading authors in each field, deploying his meticulous diligence in editing the chapters that he worked on.

We have one other thing in common: both of us served as chief economic advisers (CEA) in the Ministry of Finance. But he has the distinction of having been the longest serving CEA (1993–2001), and I of being the shortest-serving one (2001–02)!

Why have I chosen the issue of urban development as my contribution to this Festschrift? Mainly because this was the theme of the only article that we ever co-authored. Furthermore, for about 14 years from around 1974 to 1988, I worked almost exclusively on urban development, but have moved on to other issues ever since.

This gives me an opportunity to come back to my original professional interest and re-examine the process of Indian urban development as it has evolved over the past few decades, along with some speculation about its future.

A Brief History of Urbanization in India: Steady but Slow

The world became more than 50 per cent urban around 2007. So the existence of cities and continuing urbanization are seen as normal. In a historical framework, however, the experience of living in towns and cities is relatively new: it is mainly a twentieth-century phenomenon which will continue into the twenty-first century, for the foreseeable future.

In 1900, the global level of urbanization was only about 15 per cent, which was a significant rise from the two per cent level a hundred years earlier. There were only about 250 million urban residents in the world then—just over half of India's urban population today. By the turn of the millennium in 2000, global urban population had shot up to about 2.9 billion, an increase of 2.1 billion in the previous 50 years. So, there was a remarkable acceleration in urban population and in the number of towns and cities during the second half of the twentieth century. The estimate of the current global urban population is just over 4.5 billion, which is expected to reach about five billion by 2030. The accretion to urban population of about 2.1 billion in the 30 years between 2000 and 2030 would be about the same as it was in the second half of the twentieth century—another significant acceleration. About 55 per cent of this increase is happening in Asia, with India contributing 300 million—only about 25 per cent of the accretion in Asia.[4]

What I find remarkable is that despite this unprecedented phenomenon, there is no exceptional attention being devoted to urbanization that one might have expected at the present time, in academic or policy circles. Equally remarkable is the fact that the world has been able to cope with this unprecedented accretion to urban population over the last 30 years, and so have we, without any especially focused policy effort. Despite all the problems that we observe in large cities, in emerging markets and developing economies, the fact is that most urban residents in most developing countries do have access to key public services which are usually better than those available in rural areas and in urban areas in the past.

Where Is India in This Context?

Although the world crossed the 50 per cent level of urbanization around 2006–07, the level of urbanization in India is only about 35–36 per cent now. We cannot be sure of what the current level is, since the 2021 census has not even begun yet—a break from the regular decennial census that has been conducted in India since 1872.

Indian urbanization went up from 11 per cent in 1900 to only about 28 per cent at the end of the century (Charts 1 and 2), while global urbanization expanded from 15 per cent in 1900 to almost 50 per cent by 2000. So India was not a major participant in the new phenomenon of urbanization in the twentieth century. Indian urbanization was slow and steady, adding about 260 million to its urban population over the twentieth century. Although the rate of growth is still slow, the accretion to Indian urban population in the first 30 years of this century—about 300 million—will surpass the total accretion of the previous 100 years as a whole. This illustrates the magnitude of the problems that we need to face in terms of our policies related to urban development.

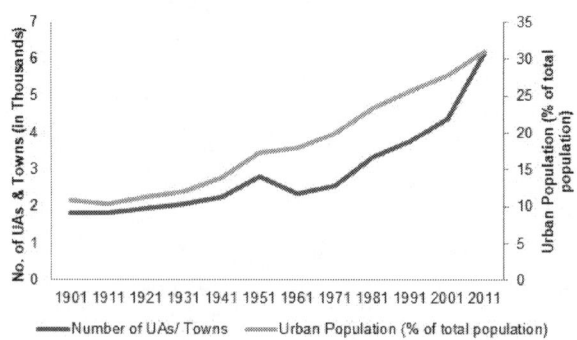

Chart 1: Urbanization in India

Note: Urban Agglomerations (UAs), which constitute a number of towns and their outgrowths, have been treated as one unit.

Source: Census of India, 2011.

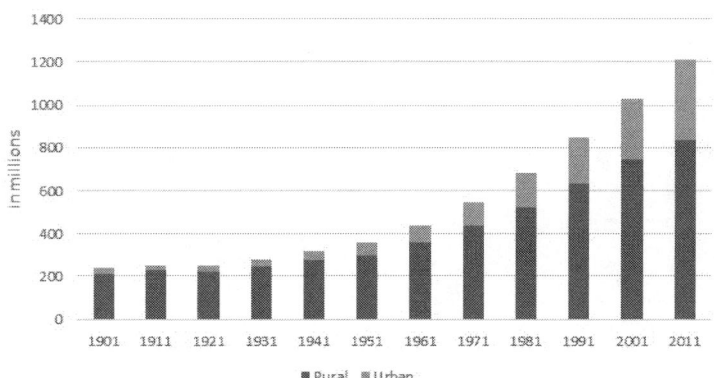

Chart 2: Population in India

Note: The urban and total population of India for the years 1981, 1991 and 2001 include the estimated population of areas where the census could not be conducted.

Source: Census of India, 2011.

The Indian census definition of an urban settlement posits three conditions:

- The settlement population must be greater than 5,000.
- 75 per cent of male employment should be non-agricultural.
- Minimum population density of 400 per square kilometre.

It also includes those towns that have been administratively classified as statutory towns.

It is often argued that the level of India's urbanization is actually much higher than what is estimated by the census.[5] Some even place it around 50 per cent. There are two possible bases for these assertions. The first is that India has many villages that have populations greater than 5,000. As Om Mathur[6] notes, if we merely take the population size of settlements as the sole criterion for classification as urban, a cut-off point of 5,000, including large villages, would yield an urbanization level of over 47 per cent, and a cut-off point of 2,500 would yield 65 per cent as India's urbanization level. The second reason is that satellite maps have begun to be used to demonstrate the density of lighting in settlements, which is often taken as an indicator of urban settlements.

I believe that the definition given in the Indian census is an appropriate one, and merely using settlement size would not be correct since an urban settlement should exhibit 'urban' characteristics. On the issue of lighting density, the progress in rural electrification could mean dense lighting in large villages now. But this is a new methodology that needs to be understood and investigated further for these purposes.

It is pertinent to note that the average level of urbanization in low-middle-income countries is now above 40 per cent, and that in low-income countries is about 34 per cent,[7] which corresponds to the Indian level, even though India is at the low-middle-income level.[8] So Indian urbanization has clearly slowed and is lower than expected.

There has been a popular view in India that larger cities of the country have grown faster than small and medium ones. This is simply not true, as I had demonstrated back in 1982.[9] Om Mathur has corroborated this more recently.[10] Despite our low level of urbanization, India has some of the largest cities in the world. There are already three cities in India with populations over 15 million, with three more likely to join this club over the next 10 years or so (Table 1). By 2030, India is likely to have six of the 30 largest cities in the world, and coincidentally, so will China.

Table 1: Projected Population of Megacities (millions)

Megacities	2000	2005	2010	2015	2020	2025	2030	2035
Mumbai	16.1	17.3	18.3	19.3	20.4	22.1	24.6	27.3
Delhi	15.7	18.7	22.0	25.9	30.3	34.7	38.9	43.3
Kolkata	13.1	13.6	14.0	14.4	14.9	15.8	17.6	19.6
Chennai	6.6	7.5	8.5	9.7	11.0	12.3	13.8	15.4
Bengaluru	5.6	6.8	8.3	10.1	12.3	14.4	16.2	18.1
Hyderabad	5.7	6.5	7.5	8.7	10.0	11.3	12.7	14.2

Source: World Urbanization Prospects 2018, UN.

There is great variation within the country in terms of the level of urbanization. On the one hand, as of 2011, there were three major

States exhibiting less than 20 per cent urbanization levels: Bihar[11] (11.3 per cent), Assam (14.1 per cent), and Odisha (16.7 per cent); at the other end of the scale were Kerala (47.7 per cent) and the more industrialized States of Gujarat (42.6 per cent), Maharashtra (45.2 per cent), and Tamil Nadu (48.4 per cent). So, only in one part of the country is the level of urbanization like what it was on a countrywide level at the turn of the last century.

This also illustrates the complexity that urban development policy will need to deal with in India: the management of some of the least urbanized regions in the world, along with that of some of the world's largest cities, and at relatively low income levels.

To put matters in context, the level of Chinese urbanization in 1980 was around 20 per cent, comparable with 23 per cent in India. It reached almost 50 per cent by 2010, when India's level had reached only about 31 per cent. The Chinese urbanization level is estimated to have reached about 65 per cent now, compared with the estimated level of about 35–36 per cent in India. This very rapid urbanization has been accompanied by its unmatched pace of industrial growth, fuelled by the rapid increase in manufactured exports leading to high overall economic growth, along with the almost universal delivery of urban public services to those residents who possess the *hukou* status. A high proportion of rural-urban migrants—perhaps as many as about a quarter of the total urban residents who do not have the *hukou* status in their places of residence in the cities—may not have proper access to these services.[12] The current expectation is that India's urbanization level will not cross 50 per cent until around 2050. The Chinese experience tells us that rapid urban growth can indeed be managed.

Our rate of urban growth has been slower than what might have been expected. On the one hand, many people celebrate the fact that we have been urbanizing slowly: how would we have coped if our towns and cities had grown even faster? On the other hand, is our slow urbanization a cause for worry in terms of the quality and speed of our development process? The biggest cause of concern is our relative lack of industrial development in terms of both value-added and employment. There has been a marked slowdown in organized-sector industrial employment in urban areas, which should clearly be a cause for worry.

Why Is Indian Urbanization Slow?

The title of my 1977 PhD dissertation was 'Development, Structural Change and Urbanization: Explorations with a Dynamic Three Sector General Equilibrium Model Applied to India 1951–1984'. I had developed a dynamic three-sector model, encompassing agriculture, manufacturing and services, enabling the simultaneous transfer of labour to both manufacturing and services in urban areas—in contrast to the more prevalent two-sector models of growth and development.[13] They focused exclusively on the transfer of labour from agriculture to manufacturing. This dominated much of the thinking concerned with industrialization, development and urbanization until very recently.

Structural change in the development process was traditionally associated with the transfer of people from agriculture to manufacturing, and from rural to urban areas, leading to an acceleration in economic growth since productivity in manufacturing is a multiple of that in agriculture. But the share of services is now greater than that of manufacturing in both value-added and employment in almost all countries, and is particularly striking in India. As labour moves from agricultural pursuits to various kinds of urban pursuits, including both manufacturing and services, underemployment in rural areas eventually goes down and the average productivity in agriculture in rural areas goes up, thereby adding to economic growth. The process of urbanization is, therefore, associated with higher economic growth.

However, faster urbanization has typically been associated with high growth in manufacturing and manufactured exports, as exhibited by countries in Southeast and East Asia. The remarkable economic growth of Japan, South Korea and, later, China has been associated with corresponding faster urbanization. The dramatic growth of Chinese manufacturing and exports—along with urbanization from about 20 per cent in 1982 to almost 65 per cent now—bears witness to this phenomenon.

The slow growth of manufacturing value-added, manufactured goods exports and manufacturing employment shares in India is consistent with the corresponding slow rate of urbanization in the country (Tables 3 and 4). The share of manufacturing value-added has fallen from 17–18 per cent in the early 1990s to less than 15 per cent now. Ironically, the share of manufacturing and industry in the GDP has remained stagnant since the onset of economic reforms in the early 1990s.

Much of the manufacturing activity in East and Southeast Asia, including China and Japan, has been located in those countries' coastal regions. These regions have excellent connectivity with the rest of Asia and the rest of the world through prime shipping routes. Manufacturing in China's hinterland started much after the success of its original manufacturing exports from its coastal regions, which was a result of explicit policy. This has not been the case in India, which could be among the reasons for lower manufacturing competitiveness, growth and exports, also associated with slower urban growth. It is possible that, with the improvements taking place in Indian infrastructure and logistics, manufacturing could start becoming more competitive over time. This is corroborated by the fact that Indian economic competitiveness has exhibited itself in the IT services sector, which can just as happily be located in the hinterland as it is in the hubs of Hyderabad, Bengaluru and Pune, among others, and it is these cities which have exhibited the most dynamism and growth since the turn of the millennium.[14]

While India's urbanization trend has followed the standard script of continuously increasing over time, there seems to be a break in the trend as far as urban share of income is concerned. According to official estimates, whereas the share of urban GDP within the total grew constantly until the turn of the century, it stagnated at about 52 per cent from 1999 to 2012 (Table 4).[15] My colleagues Shishir Gupta and Ashley Jose estimate that this proportion is around 55 per cent now.[16] Moreover, as reported by some researchers,[17] the share of rural areas in manufacturing has been increasing in recent decades. Whereas it went down consistently from about 56 per cent in 1950–51 to 32 per cent in 1980–81, it has reversed course since—rising to 42 per cent in 1993–94 and 51 per cent in 2011 (Chart 3). It is difficult to update this measure without the 2021 census.

Table 2: Change in Sectoral Share in Real GDP (2011–12 prices) (per cent)

	1950–51	1960–61	1970–71	1980–81	1990–91	2000–01	2010–11	2020–21	2022–23
Agriculture and Allied Activities	59.5	54.1	46.0	39.7	32.3	24.6	17.0	14.4	14.1
Industry	11.7	14.0	15.3	17.2	19.2	19.1	20.3	19.1	17.5
Manufacturing	8.8	10.7	12.1	13.3	14.2	14.7	16.5	17.0	15.6
Services	32.0	33.0	35.8	39.5	44.0	50.7	55.5	58.8	60.4

Note: Industry includes manufacturing, mining and quarrying. Services include electricity, gas, water supply and other utility services, construction, trade, repair, hotels and restaurants, transport, storage, communication, and services related to broadcasting, finances, real estate, ownership of dwellings and professional services, public administration and defence, and such others.

Source: Central Statistical Organisation, National Accounts Statistics.

Table 3: Sectoral Employment Share in Rural and Urban Areas

NSSO Rounds	Survey Period	Rural (% Share of Rural)			Urban (% Share of Urban)		
		Primary Sector	Secondary Sector	Tertiary Sector	Primary Sector	Secondary Sector	Tertiary Sector
38	January–December 1983	83	9	9	21	33	47
45	July 1989–June 1990	77	12	11	17	31	52
55	July 1999–June 2000	78	11	11	12	31	57
61	July 2004–June 2005	75	13	12	12	33	55
66	July 2009–June 2010	71	16	13	10	34	56
68	July 2011–June 2012	67	19	14	8	35	57
PLFS 1	July 2017–June 2018	64	18	18	7	33	60
PLFS 2	July 2018–June 2019	62	19	18	6	32	61
PLFS 3	July 2019–June 2020	66	18	16	7	31	62
PLFS 4	July 2020–June 2021	65	19	17	8	31	61
PLFS 5	July 2021–June 2022	63	19	17	8	33	59

Note: Employment is for all (principal + subsidiary status) persons usually employed

Primary sector: agriculture and allied activities

Secondary sector: mining, manufacturing, electricity, gas, water, etc., and construction

Tertiary sector: trade, hotel and restaurants, transport, storage, communication and other services

Source: Multiple NSS and PLFS rounds, RBI, Ministry of Statistics and Programme Implementation (MOSPI).

Table 4: Net Domestic Product (NDP) and
Population in Rural and Urban Areas

Year		Net Domestic Product (₹ billion)	Population (million)	Per Capita NDP (₹)	Percentage Share of Urban Areas in GDP
1	2	3	4	5	6
1970–71	Total	368	541	680	
	Rural	229	434	529	
	Urban	139	107	1,294	38
	Urban as a % of Rural	60		2.45	
	Urban as a % of Total		19.80		
1980–81	Total	1,103	679	1,625	
	Rural	650	522	1,245	
	Urban	453	157	2,888	41
	Urban as a % of Rural	70		2.32	
	Urban as a % of Total		23.10		
1993–94	Total	7,161	891	8,037	
	Rural	3,849	655	5,876	
	Urban	3,312	236	14,035	46
	Urban as a % of Rural	86		2.39	
	Urban as a % of Total		26.50		
2004–05	Total	26,516	1,089	24,349	
	Rural	12,765	778	16,407	
	Urban	13,751	311	44,215	52
	Urban as a % of Rural	108		2.69	
	Urban as a % of Total		28.60		

2011-12	Total	71,895	1,220	58,930	
	Rural	34,089	838	40,678	
	Urban	37,806	382	98,996	**52**
	Urban as a % of Rural	111		2.43	
	Urban as a % of Total		31.30		

Note: NDP and per capita NDP are at current prices.

Source: Central Statistical Organisation, National Accounts Statistics, Various Issues.

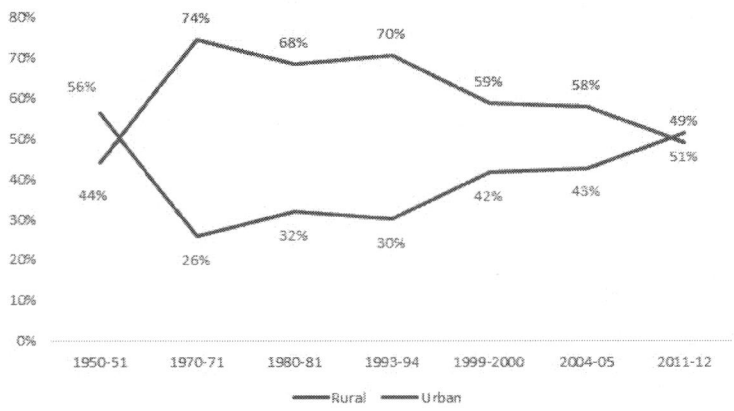

Chart 3: Share of Rural/Urban in Manufacturing GVA

Source: MoSPI.

This anomalous development would explain the slowing of urban growth in India over the last three or more decades. It is quite inconsistent with the experience elsewhere, in both advanced and developing economies, historically and in contemporary experience. Typically, as manufacturing moves from cottage and village industries to more organized formats needing larger factories, it must urbanize to have access to a larger pool of labour and benefit from other agglomeration economies related to business services.

The Indian experience over the last three decades or so has been the opposite. Moreover, Indian industrialization has been relatively more capital-intensive and not labour-using, leading to a relative stagnation in the share of urban employment in organized manufacturing (Table 5). This is also anomalous given the high labour endowment of the country relative to capital. At the same time, manufacturing in urban areas is getting more informalized, and is hence exhibiting slowing productivity growth, leading to slow income growth in urban areas and slow urbanization. It is possible that with Indian organized sector manufacturing being more capital-intensive, it locates itself in areas which are some distance from towns and cities to get access to land at lower costs. With low labour intensity, it also does not need the kind of large labour pool that urban areas would provide. This observation necessitates a more detailed analysis of the available data.

Table 5: Workers in Organized-Sector Manufacturing (millions)

Year	Rural	Urban	Total	Share of Urban in Total (per cent)
2000–01	2.34	3.80	**6.14**	61.9
2010–11	4.25	5.66	**9.90**	57.1
2020–21	5.78	6.81	**12.59**	54.1
2021–22	6.12	7.49	**13.61**	55.0

Source: ASI.

Why this reluctance on the part of Indian industry to be in labour-intensive sectors? First, many of the leading labour-intensive industries like clothing, shoes, furniture, toys and many other such consumer goods were reserved for the small-scale sector beginning in 1967, when just 47 items were reserved. At its peak, this number went up to 836 items by 1991. The logic was that employment would expand faster since small-scale industries were more labour-intensive. Second, industrial policies discouraged the situating of manufacturing in urban areas.[18] At its most stringent, by the 1980s, no manufacturing unit could be located within 50 kilometres of the largest cities, and not within cities of any size. These provisions were diluted in 1991, but the thinking that led to these regulations may have continued to permeate the permitting process. Third, labour regulations—lacking adequate flexibility—have also discouraged investment in labour-intensive industries. Fourth, given the regulations governing urban land and the difficulties encountered in terms of its availability, land price is also found to be too high for industries that need extensive land. In any case, the Urban Land (Ceiling and Regulation) Act introduced in 1976 made the assembly of large parts of land in cities very difficult until it was repealed in 1999. Fifth, it is also possible that managers of manufacturing firms find it difficult to manage large pools of labour and, hence, prefer more capital-intensive modes of production. Sixth, in view of all these issues regarding industrial location, labour laws and the like, industries could have been pushed to go into more capital-intensive sectors which could then be located in non-urban areas.

What is interesting is that the pace of industrialization has consistently lagged behind the expectations of the government, as exhibited by the projections provided by the Planning Commission in successive plan documents (Table 6). As early as the formulation of the fourth Five-Year-Plan in 1969, the expectation was that the manufacturing share in GDP would reach 25.8 per cent by 1981. That level has not been reached till date. Each successive plan had to lower its starting point and yet, the projection was almost always higher than what was achieved. This is in spite of the fact that most of the Five-Year Plans succeeded in achieving their overall growth objectives within a 10 per cent range (Chart 4). The share of manufacturing has remained between 14 and 16 per cent since the mid-1980s until now, and that of industry between 18 and 20 per cent over the same period. While the share of industry (manufacturing) has broadly remained constant in recent decades as shown earlier, the urban share of manufacturing GDP has fallen (Chart 3). Similar is the record of projections of urbanization in plan documents, though these projections are not as systematic as the industry ones (Table 7). The broad observation is that urban growth has been lower than expected.

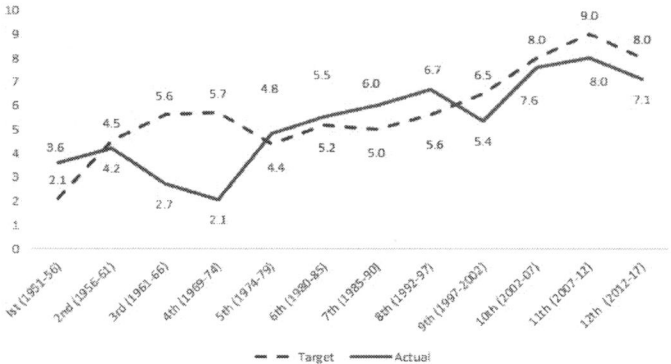

Chart 4: GDP Growth Performance in Five-Year Plans: Target vs. Actual

Source: Five-Year Plan Reports, MoSPI.

Urbanization started to slow down in the 1980s. I had made projections of urbanization from 1981 to 2001 then on the basis of the 1981 census results. According to the two variants that I had projected, the level of urbanization in India should have reached 31 to 31.5 per cent by 2001. I had also projected total population growth over that period, which turned out to be relatively accurate (Table 8). In the event, the 1991 level of urbanization reached 25.7 per cent and the 2001 level only 27.8 per cent. The 31 per cent level was reached 10 years later in 2011. This is another illustration of how Indian urban growth has been slower than expected. That Indian urban areas are not generating enough new employment opportunities is illustrated by the low share of net rural-urban migration between censuses. It is remarkable that the share of net migration in total urban population growth over 50 years has been steady at about 20 per cent (Table 9). The rest is accounted for by natural growth, the addition of new towns, and the reclassification of existing towns and cities. Contrary to popular impression, rural-urban migration has not been high and has not been increasing in proportionate terms. This feature of Indian urbanization is also at variance from the experience of other developing countries.

Table 6: Industry (Manufacturing) Share of GDP—Projections and Actuals

FYPs		1974	1979	1981	1984	1985	1986	1989	1990	1991	1992	1995	1997	2000	2002	2007
Fourth*	1969–74	21.0														
Fifth	1974–79		24.4	25.8												
Sixth**	1980–85				21.2 (19.2)											
Seventh**	1985–90					18.1 (14.6)		20.3 (18.6)	19.8 (15.0)							
Eighth	1992–97										23.5 (21.5)		25.6 (23.3)			
Ninth	1997–2002												21.2 (19.4)	23.6 (19.8)	22.0 (20.2)	
Tenth	2002–07														17.6 (15.3)	18.6 (16.7)
Actuals		16.4 (13.0)	17.4 (13.9)	17.2 (13.3)	18.3 (13.9)	18.2 (14.0)	17.9 (13.7)	18.7 (13.9)	19.1 (14.3)	19.3 (14.3)	18.9 (13.7)	19.3 (14.4)	20.3 (15.7)	18.7 (14.2)	18.6 (14.3)	20.0 (16.0)

Note (Sixth** 1984 value: 19.0 (17.4)).

Note: The data for all FYPs are projections. *Data for the Fourth FYP is as a share of National Domestic Product; **Data as a share of Gross Value-Added. Actuals are the sectoral share of GDP.

Source: Five-Year Plan Reports, MoSPI.

Table 7: Urban Population (Percentage of Total Population)—Projections and Actuals

FYPs	1980	1985	1986	1989	1990	1991	1996	1997	2001	2006	2011
4th*				24.86							
5th	21.81	22.93			24.09		25.4				
6th**			25.23			27.48	30.01		33.06		
7th**							27.82	28.32	30.5	33.48	36.57
8th							27.23		28.77	30.35	31.99
9th											
10th											
Actuals	23.34*	23.9**				25.7	26.3#		27.8	28.6##	31.1

Note: The data for all FYPs are projections. Actuals Data for the years: *1981; **1983; #1994 ##2005. The FYPs correspond to the years: 4th (1969–74), 5th (1974–79), 6th (1980–85), 7th (1985–90), 8th (1992–97), 9th (1997–2002), 10th (2002–07).

Source: Multiple Five-Year Plan Reports; Census.

Table 8: Projections of Urbanization in India, 1980–2001

	Level of Urbanization (per cent)				
	1981	1986	1991	1996	2001
Urban Variant I	23.53	25.57	27.52	29.35	31.04
Urban Variant II	23.53	25.38	27.32	29.35	31.47

	Urban and Rural Population Projections (millions)									
	1981		1986		1991		1996		2001	
	Urban	Rural	Urban	Rural	Urban	Rural	Urban	Rural	Urban	Rural
Urban Variant I	164	533	198	578	236	620	275	661	315	701
Urban Variant II	164	533	197	579	234	622	275	661	320	696

	Implied Rates of Population Growth (per cent per year)			
	1981–86	1986–91	1991–96	1996–2001
Urban Variant I	Urban	3.84	3.49	3.1	2.75
	Rural	1.63	1.44	1.29	1.18
Urban Variant II	Urban	3.73	3.5	3.28	3.08
	Rural	1.67	1.44	1.22	1.03

Source: Mohan, Rakesh, 'Urbanization in India's Future', *Population And Development Review*, Vol. 11, No. 4, 1985, pp. 619–45.

Table 9: Estimates of the Relative Share of Natural Increase, Net Migration and Reclassification in Decadal Urban Growth—1961-2011*

	1961-71	1971-81	1981-91	1991-2001	2001-11
Urban Population Increase (million)	30	50	58	68	91
Percentage Share (%)					
Natural Increase	65.2	51.7	62.7	60.9	43.3
Net Migration	19.6	19.9	22.6	21.2	22.7
Reclassification#	15.2	28.5	14.7	18.1	34.0

*Excludes Assam and Jammu and Kashmir for the decades 1971-81 and 1981-91
#Includes new towns and reclassification of existing cities and towns.
Source: Census of India 1991, 2001, 2011.

Overall, there is no doubt that Indian urbanization has been slow over the last half century or so and slower than what was expected by the government of India and other observers. Its level is lower than the average in other low-middle-income countries. The Indian urbanization experience has been rather anomalous: the share of manufacturing in the GDP has been stagnating, contrary to expectations of an increasing share; there is a similar stagnation in the share of urban manufacturing employment; the share of net rural-urban migration in urban population growth has been a constant low 20 per cent, contrary to the experience in other emerging market countries; manufacturing seems to be ruralizing rather than urbanizing; the urban-rural income differences are narrowing rather than increasing, implying an inadequate increase in urban productivity; although this atypical experience may be welcome to many, it indicates inadequate structural change in Indian growth and development. This slow urbanization indicates inadequate structural transformation of the economy in terms of the transfer of people from low-productivity rural activities to urban ones comprising both manufacturing and services, thereby slowing economic growth to the detriment of both rural and urban areas.

It is important for the health of our cities and for the Indian economy in general that more research is done to understand this strange phenomenon of industrialization and urbanization in India, which is quite inconsistent with the historical experience of other fast-growing countries. Casual empiricism suggests that the lack of growth in quality employment could be leading to higher rates of unemployment, particularly among the educated young whose numbers have grown exponentially since the turn of the millennium. The increasing occurrence of social tensions and the resulting violence may also be a consequence of inadequate manufacturing output and employment growth in our cities.

Large Cities

Despite slow urbanization, India is emerging with some of the largest cities in the world (Table 1). It is inevitable that as some of these largest cities reach sizes of about 20 million, there is a reasonable probability that their growth will slow down. The next level of cities will then start growing faster, as is happening in China. This needs to be facilitated and provided for in terms of adequate urban infrastructure investment and the universal provision of essential public services.

There were 52 million-plus cities in India according to the 2011 census. Without the 2021 census, one can only guess how many there are now. Most projections seem to suggest that there are probably around 65 million-plus cities in India at present. China already has about 115 or so. According to current expectations, India will reach such a number by around 2050—when it will also be at the 50 per cent urbanization level (Chart 5).

With the existence of 65 million-plus cities now, it is imperative that more policy attention be given to the emergence of such cities and to their continued healthy expansion. Are they good for us? Should we encourage them? How do we make them more productive? How do we manage them? How do we make them more liveable?

In general, large cities increase overall economic productivity, which leads to higher incomes and potentially greater social welfare, along with a higher quality of life. A great deal of research across the world

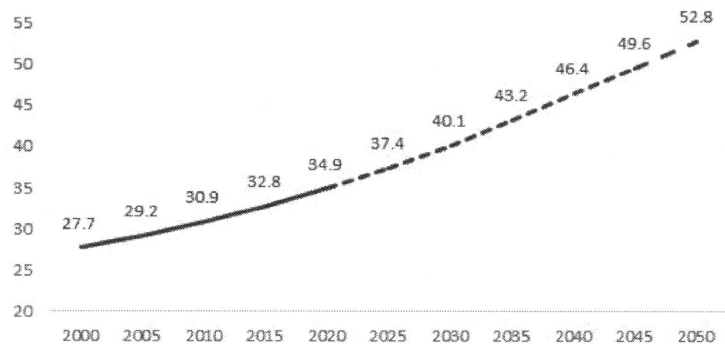

Chart 5: Projection of Urban Population (Percentage of Total)

Source: World Urbanization Prospects: The 2018 Revision.

suggests that productivity increases with city size. It has been estimated that in the US, for example, wages rise by six per cent as city density doubles.[19] Why does this happen? Mostly because of agglomeration economies. People benefit in many ways by being around other people; face-to-face contact is particularly important for both their personal lives as well as economic activities, despite modern technology enabling virtual face-to-face contact. Large cities have large labour markets, promoting flexibility for both employers and employees. Employees can shop for better jobs without having to change their residence because of the availability of many more choices in terms of jobs. With increasing female labour force participation, flexibility becomes even more important for working couples to manage their lives. Similarly, employers can find new employees more easily, both for expansion and the substitution of employees who leave. The availability of many people in one geographical area also enables many more service activities, including all kinds of business services, entertainment, restaurants, sports, and the like. The income generated from such activities increases demand for both manufactured goods and other services.

It is, therefore, possible that the general Indian policy of situating industries far away from urban centres since at least the 1970s may have reduced urban growth, caused by the loss of agglomeration economies for the economy as a whole. Thus, the ruralization of Indian industry may not be desirable. We need to devise policies so that manufacturing is encouraged to locate in towns and cities while, of course, taking care of pollution, harmful emissions, and the like.

Labour-intensive manufacturing can be encouraged to be based in large cities in India. Such sectors include apparels, toys, shoes, furniture, electronics assembly, most consumer goods for daily needs, and the like. In many East Asian countries, such light industries have constituted a major source of employment for women—which has been conspicuously lacking in India. Many of these sectors are also especially suited for backward and forward linkages with associated service activities. Much of the design services are necessarily located in cities, as are fashion and related services connected with clothing, especially for high-value items. Many light consumer goods are also suited for being moved by air, thereby promoting exports. Given the availability and cost of land, many such industries are also suitable for multistorey flatted factories which are rare in Indian cities, unlike in other Asian cities such as Dhaka, Hong Kong and Singapore. Hence, we need to shed our prejudices against the location of non-polluting industries in Indian cities.

Efficient and affordable transport facilities will also aid in promoting labour-using activities. The largest cities already provide extensive safe metro networks. In addition, there is need for frequent and comfortable bus services that are perceived as safe by women. Bus transport is much cheaper than metro services. It needs lower ex-ante capital investment and is also cheaper for passengers. This should be planned so that the walking time at both origin and destination is minimized, and they are deemed to be safe for women passengers.

Large cities also exist because of the agglomeration economies that arise from large transport hubs such as airports, ports, and bus and railway stations. These facilities create substantive demand for a whole host of services from other modes of transportation, accounting, financial services, hotels, restaurants, and the like. Similarly, large hospitals and other health facilities cannot exist outside large cities since they exhibit significant economies of scale. Medical specialties need an adequate number of patients on a regular basis, who can only be supplied within large cities and their environs. The same is true for entertainment centres like cinemas, theatres, bars and restaurants. In each case, economic activity begets economic activity, and that is the essence of agglomeration economies. The availability of all these services aids manufacturing activity as well.

Cities are centres of knowledge that give rise to new activities and innovation. Typically, large universities, medical schools, technology institutions, business schools, law schools, and others are located in and give rise to large vibrant cities. For example, the metropolitan area comprising Boston, Cambridge and other towns in the vicinity has arisen out of the location of many educational institutions. Within India, Pune, Ahmedabad, Chennai, Bengaluru, Hyderabad, Chandigarh, Delhi, Mumbai, and possibly Lucknow or Kanpur are similar in terms of the existence of large educational institutions, hospitals and other significant facilities.

So our attitude should be to celebrate the existence of large cities and to concentrate on how we can make them more liveable and productive. For this to happen, the governance of our cities needs to improve substantially.

Governance of Cities

As mentioned before, we already have about 65 million-plus cities whose numbers will keep increasing in the time to come. Yet, the governance of even the largest of our cities continues to be very weak. The overall administrative system of the country is based on the delineation of districts as the basic units of administration which are governed by officers of the All India Services, the Indian Administrative Service (IAS) and the Indian Police Service (IPS). Hence, there is some overlap between the jurisdiction of the general district administration, municipal governments and municipal corporations. The smooth development and administration of large cities need a much stronger and unified system of governance, as is the case in some large cities in other countries. But introducing unified systems of governance for metropolitan areas remains a challenge in many countries—both developing and developed.

The mayor or mayor equivalent is the chief executive in charge of these cities, much as the chief minister oversees a State and the prime minister the country. In India, however, the mayor is essentially a ceremonial head and much of the administrative responsibility is shouldered by the municipal commissioner, who is appointed by the State government from among the IAS or provincial service officers. Thus the chief administrator of the city has no connection with the city that he or she serves, and can be transferred at frequent intervals.

The provision of basic services in the city involves the universal supply of clean water, sanitation, solid waste disposal, power, roads for mobility, convenient modes of transportation, facilitation of housing, and the like. Many of these must be provided as public goods by some level of government, although some are private goods amenable to user charges. These are the key urban basic services that must be provided by the city for the welfare of its citizens. Since they are largely public goods, the city government should be empowered and competent enough to supply or facilitate these services for their citizens. Hence, there is a need for adequate resources to be available for city governments.

The absence of the universal availability of these essential public services at affordable costs is among the reasons for slow rural-urban migration, leading to an inadequate urban transformation in India. Liveable cities must provide these so that residents of all income levels have access to these. In many cases, the better-off have privatized their access to these services, be it water supply, electricity, education, health, security services or others, leaving the poor without similar access.

Large Indian cities, particularly the largest ones, have budgets that are larger than those of some of the smaller States in India, and also of many countries in the world. Of the ten largest cities in the world by population, two are in India, Delhi and Mumbai. But the administrative capacity as well as the powers of our city governments are very weak. The technical competence of much of the staff is also very low. The governance of such large cities leaves much to be desired—much greater competence and powers are needed to administer the city well and to have a vision for their development over time. Such a change could effectively make the mayors of some of the largest cities competitors of State government leaders such as senior ministers, and even the chief minister. Similarly, the chief administrators of restructured municipal corporations would also be effective competitors to senior IAS officials. Hence, there has been no appetite for major city government reforms and restructuring in the country.

However, if we are to have cities that are dynamic, vibrant, responsive to their citizens' concerns, and more liveable, city governments must be restructured urgently and made more powerful, competent and accountable. There really is not much choice. But this discussion has not even begun in our country. We must strengthen our municipal corporations at all levels.

City governments suffer from poor reputation and prestige among our young. Thus, even with high unemployment among the educated youth, the chances of young, competent graduates wanting to join city government are low. This is a real pity since shaping and managing cities should be very exciting work. Hence, the rejuvenation of city governments must include a major campaign to increase their prestige.

To increase competence within local governments, they need to be staffed with a whole set of professionals from different areas, such as financial experts, accountants, urban planners, architects, engineers, lawyers, and the like. In view of the huge expansion in education that has taken place over the last couple of decades at the college level, along with the proliferation of professional schools, there is no dearth of talent available for all these professions. Urban management and urban development must also be included in the syllabi of universities, business schools, law schools, schools of architecture and planning, and others. The increased use of IT in governance and in the functions of cities can help in the better governance thereof. This indicates the need for IT professionals to have a significant role in the administration of cities.

Working in municipal corporations should be seen as exciting and rewarding enough to attract the youth to shape the future of the cities. If municipal corporations are to be made more powerful and responsible for providing public services, their sources of revenue must be expanded considerably. Local government revenue in India, as a proportion of the GDP, is among the lowest among the major countries in the world. Inexplicably, the property tax is not used to its fullest potential. The huge expansion of formal housing, commercial spaces, malls, and a host of other structures is clearly visible to all of us. There is no reason why all such use of land should not be taxed appropriately. With the use of information technology, the enumeration of all such properties and the levying of property tax on them have become very simple. The current levels are either negligible or extremely low—so many of us do not even know how much property tax we pay. If municipal corporations provide a whole host of services, many of such services can be subject to the levy of appropriate user charges. If all this is done, cities would be less dependent on the devolution of resources from higher levels.

As the income streams of city governments become clearer, it would also be possible for them to float municipal bonds to raise resources for the required capital investment. That, of course, would require much better accounting and transparency in municipal finances so that these municipal corporations can be credit-rated for appropriate signalling to the markets. If this is found to be difficult, other structures for borrowing at low cost can be considered, such as the pfandbriefe system in Germany.[20]

The objective of city governments must be to make their cities economic engines, havens of productivity, centres of knowledge, centres of art and creativity, centres of entertainment, and, in general, easy and comfortable to live in.

Some Reflections on the Future of Indian Urbanization

A great deal of emphasis has been laid on the need for large cities and their productivity-enhancing nature—attributed to the advantages arising from agglomeration economies. The Covid-19 pandemic and its associated lockdowns necessitated a great deal of work from home. Many people moved away from their places of work to remote locations. Questions are therefore being raised on the necessity of people commuting to work, and if there is a real need for face-to-face contact in many activities. It is reported that in some of the key cities in the world, many office buildings have been vacated by large corporations, which are either moving to locations outside big cities or allowing their employees to work remotely. This phenomenon will no doubt have significant effects on the pattern of both employment and residential location in urban areas, and hence on the evolving structure of cities.

With the proliferation of streaming services for all kinds of content, what used to be a shared experience of entertainment is now becoming a solitary one. Similarly, it is being said that education at all levels can also be delivered remotely and more efficiently, precluding the need for students and teachers to congregate at schools, colleges and universities. Business in the law courts could also potentially be done remotely, as is now being enabled through new legislation. E-commerce is also changing the face of commercial retail business, to the extent that many shopping malls in the United States and other countries are being shut down—while in our country, shopping malls are still in their infancy and are spreading. We can already see the future in what is happening elsewhere. Food delivery services are substituting the experience of eating at restaurants with friends and family. With a substantial proportion of books, journals and other publications having been digitized, there is also no need for people to visit libraries. Cafés are the new working places in lieu of libraries.

Time alone will tell whether this kind of technology-induced change will alter behaviour in the manner described above, leading to unprecedented changes in urbanization and the structure of cities in the future. We must remind ourselves, however, that work from home, e-commerce, delivery of food, and other such facilities are possible only because of a host of workers providing such services in person. These also involve the existence of large warehouses, kitchens and other service facilities where workers must congregate. So it is not clear what kind of urban patterns will result from this technological change. One view is that human beings are social animals and that, after some initial enthusiasm for such isolated activities, the demand for face-to-face contact and shared community activities will rise again. Many post-Covid evaluations have revealed a significant loss in learning during the virtual schooling period. It is also reported that absenteeism in many school districts in the US has expanded significantly in the post-Covid period, to around 20–25 per cent. There are also reports of increasing loneliness, which is said to lead to significant mental health issues. At the same time, many office-goers are resisting any mandated returns to office.

There is no doubt that there will be changes in behaviour that will lead to the evolution of urban structures, which may still be difficult for us to imagine. But we need to keep thinking about this and design the evolution of our cities accordingly. It is possible that such changes may take more time in India because of its low income levels, making it difficult for people to work from home, especially due to poor conditions there.

The other literally earthshaking phenomenon is that of imminent climate change. Indian cities are already suffering from the ills of widespread pollution caused by various kinds of urban activities, from both industrialization and the wide distribution of emission-causing transportation. However, there are some reasons for hope. London, for example, now exhibits consistently high levels of air quality. It was not always so, even as late as the 1960s and 70s. Similarly, it was Beijing that topped the charts of the most polluted cities in the world until recently. That is no longer so since Indian cities have taken their place. The transformation of London, other cities in advanced economies, and more recently cities such as Beijing in terms of the reduction of pollution suggests that technology can help to cope with such emerging problems. But things may get worse before they get better in India.

Unprecedented high temperatures in summer are another aspect of climate change that is particularly relevant for India with respect to urban planning for the future. We must adapt the design of housing, the urban form, and transportation in a way that is more suited to these new conditions.

Urban structures must change to implement effective mitigation measures along with adaptation. This would involve transformative changes in patterns of urban transportation, building design, methods of cooling and warming, industrial pollution and emission-reducing technologies. The fact that India is still only 35–36 per cent urbanized suggests that we may be better placed to reorder our pattern and structure of urbanization in comparison to many countries that are more advanced than we are.

I believe that despite the many ills that bedevil the living experience in Indian cities and the upcoming challenges of the future, it is within our capability, imagination and strength of purpose to look forward to much more liveable cities—places where citizens can walk around safely, interact with others for both social and economic purposes, have access to parks for recreation, experience easy mobility, and have generally fulfilling urban lives.

Such change will enable greater growth of Indian urbanization and manufacturing, which are essential for achieving our overall aspirations for accelerated growth and development.

Appendix

Table A.1: Urban Population in India, 1901–2011

Census Year	Number of UAs/Towns	Total Population (in millions)	Rural Population (in millions)	Urban Population (in millions)	Urban Population (% of total population)
1901	1,830	238	213	26	10.8
1911	1,815	252	226	26	10.3
1921	1,944	251	223	28	11.2
1931	2,066	279	246	34	12.0
1941	2,253	319	275	44	13.9
1951	2,822	361	299	62	17.3
1961	2,334	439	360	79	18.0
1971	2,567	548	439	109	19.9
1981	3,347	683	524	160	23.3
1991	3,769	846	629	218	25.7
2001	4,378	1,027	742	285	27.8
2011	6,171	1,211	834	377	31.1

Note: 1) Urban agglomerations (UAs) which constitute a number of towns and their outgrowths have been treated as one unit.

2) The total population and urban population of India for the year 2001 includes the estimated population of those areas of Gujarat and Himachal Pradesh where the census could not be conducted due to natural calamities.

3) The total population and urban population of India for the year 1991 include the interpolated population of Jammu and Kashmir where the census could not be conducted.

4) The total population and urban population of India for the year 1981 include the interpolated population of Assam where the census could not be conducted.

Source: Census of India, 2011.

Table A.2: Share of Rural/Urban in Total Manufacturing GVA

Year	Rural	Urban
1950–51	56.0%	44.0%
1970–71	25.8%	74.2%
1980–81	31.8%	68.2%
1993–94	29.8%	70.2%
1999–2000	41.5%	58.5%
2004–05	42.5%	57.5%
2011–12	51.2%	48.8%

Source: MoSPI.

Table A.3: GDP Growth Performance

Five-Year Plans		Target (% GDP Growth)	Actual (% GDP Growth)
First	1951–56	2.1	3.6
Second	1956–61	4.5	4.2
Third	1961–66	5.6	2.7
Fourth	1969–74	5.7	2.1
Fifth	1974–79	4.4	4.8
Sixth	1980–85	5.2	5.5
Seventh	1985–90	5.0	6.0

Five-Year Plans		Target (% GDP Growth)	Actual (% GDP Growth)
Eighth	1992–97	5.6	6.7
Ninth	1997–2002	6.5	5.4
Tenth	2002–07	8.0	7.6
Eleventh	2007–12	9.0	8.0*
Twelfth	2012–17	8.0	7.1

Note: The growth targets for the first three plans were set for national income. In the fourth plan, it was the net domestic product. In all plans thereafter, the gross domestic product has been used at factor cost. The eleventh plan targeted the average GDP growth of the order of nine per cent for the plan period 2007–11, which implied that it would have had to increase gradually from 8.5 per cent in 2007–08 to 10 per cent in 2011–12.

*GDP growth for 2007–12 is 6.5 per cent as per 2011–12 prices.

Source: Five-Year Plan Reports, MoSPI.

Table A.4: Projections of Urbanization for the Next 30 Years

	2000	2005	2010	2015	2020	2025	2030	2035	2040	2045	2050
Total Population in Million	291	334	381	429	483	543	607	675	744	812	877
Urban Population in Million		1,144	1,231	1,309	1,383	1,452	1,513	1,565	1,605	1,636	1,659
Per cent Urban	27.7	29.2	30.9	32.8	34.9	37.4	40.1	43.2	46.4	49.6	52.8

Source: World Urbanization Prospects: The 2018 Revision.

Deepak Mishra and Mansi Kedia

Digitalization and Development: India's Journey from the Backwaters to the High Seas of Digital Revolution[1]

On a Personal Note

The readers of Dr Acharya's memoir *An Economist at Home and Abroad* would be well aware that he excelled at maintaining contact with friends and family around the world. This was at a time when international telephone calls cost an arm and a leg. With technological innovation and investments in communication infrastructure, Dr Acharya's options to stay connected have dramatically expanded, as is the case with billions of Indians. From standing at a public call office (PCO) booth late in the night just to make a one-minute call to another city, internet-enabled voice and video calls are now ubiquitous and virtually free. With the lowest price of data services in the world, Indians also have the distinction of being the largest generator of data and voice traffic globally. In recent times, Aadhaar—India's digital identity programme—has become the world's envy. Also notable is its success in the use of digital payments. This chapter tells the story of how a relatively poor country with a non-existent information technology and communication industry went on to become the third largest digitalized country in the world. While digitalization can be a worthy goal in itself, can it also become a means to achieve broader objectives—catalyzing growth, creating jobs and improving the quality of services? This essay argues that while digitalization has enormous potential for accelerating the pace of achieving developmental goals, their realization is neither assured nor automatic. This is because many of the analogue foundations that complement the digital revolution in India—for example, greater digital literacy, an improved business climate, and transparent and accountable governance—are in need of further reinforcement.

▪

Productivity Paradox Meets India's Digitalization

In 1987, Robert Solow famously quipped, 'You can see the computer age everywhere but in the productivity statistics.' Solow was pointing to the mismatch between massive investment in information and communication technology (ICT) by American companies that did not translate into a commensurate increase in productivity—an idea that came to be known as the Solow paradox.[2] While productivity eventually increased in the 1990s, studies showed that the causes of the productivity boom were not the investment in ICT, but competition and innovation.[3][4] For example, while both retail and banking sector companies made significant investments in ICT, productivity increased for retail but not for banks. Studies in other countries have found similar results, thereby making the quest to understand the productivity paradox an enduring one.

India today exhibits many characteristics of Solow's America of the 1980s. Not just Indian businesses, but government departments have also invested in digitalization with massive upgrades to infrastructure—including high-speed connectivity, cloud services, computing power for new technologies such as artificial intelligence (AI) and others. For businesses, India is among the biggest markets for online services including payments, retail trade, travel, food delivery, health and education—increasingly substituting for traditional brick-and-mortar options. The government has made a decisive bet by investing in population-scale, open-standards, low-cost and interoperable digital systems called digital public infrastructure (DPI), thereby building the foundation of India's digital economy using an approach that is not commonplace among other countries. Initial evidence suggests that DPI-led digitalization has greatly enabled India's ability to deliver welfare benefits and improve financial inclusion among the marginalized.

But unlike in the US, India's bet on digitalization seems to be translating into higher growth and accelerated development (see Box 1).[5] In other words, India may be able to overcome Solow's productivity paradox. We unpack this issue by breaking down our analysis into three parts.

Box 1. Defining Digitalization: One Size Does Not Fit All

While digital technologies have completely transformed our lives, there is no globally agreed-upon definition for many of the terms associated with them. According to the *Oxford Dictionary*, 'digitalization' means to change data into a digital form that can be easily read and processed by a computer. The OECD (2018) refers to digitalization as the use of digital technologies and data as well as their interconnection that result in new activities or changes in existing ones. We define digitalization as the process of adopting digital technologies and data for everyday use, not only to maximize economic and social gains, but also to minimize the risks associated with them.

In the first section, we demonstrate that digital technologies are now everywhere in India—most of its people, businesses and governments are now digitally connected, propelling India to the status of the third largest digitalized country in the world after the United States and China. In the second section, we trace India's historical journey—from laying the foundation of telecommunication services in the 1980s, to the Y2K-led ICT boom in the early 2000s and the Digital India 2.0 we see today—and delve into factors that have contributed to the rapid diffusion of digital technologies. In the third section, we examine whether the adoption of digital technologies has accelerated India's development in terms of higher economic growth, job creation and efficient service delivery—i.e. has it overcome the paradox or not? The final section brings it all together—highlighting the current risks and suggesting the way forward for digitalization to trigger the larger goal of growth and development.

India's Rapidly Growing Digital Footprints

In recent years, India has made remarkable strides in digitalizing its economy. It has the world's second largest mobile and internet network going by the number of users. It has rolled out 5G faster than all other countries in the world. Few countries witness volumes of data traffic per smartphone which are as high as that in India. Its digital identity network is among the largest in the world. India also tops the world in terms of the volume of digital transactions and export of ICT services. In the field of emerging technologies, India has become the largest contributor to global GitHub AI projects, and ranks third with respect to the number of homegrown unicorns (see Box 2). During its G20 presidency, India was recognized as the champion of digital public infrastructures (DPIs), a new approach to population-scale delivery of public services.

Box 2. India's Digital Stride

Mobile Subscription: Of the estimated 8.36 billion mobile cellular subscriptions worldwide, 1.78 billion are in China, followed by 1.14 billion in India and 372 million in the US.

Internet Traffic: Saudi Arabia has the highest average monthly data traffic at 35 GB, followed by Russia and India that have 18.4 GB and 16.9 GB, respectively.

5G Deployment: The proportion of Indian users with 5G-capable devices that are using 5G network increased 55 times within four months—from 0.1 per cent in September 2022 to 5.5 in January 2023—making it the fastest case of 5G deployment in any country.

Digital Identity: India has given out over 1.3 billion biometric ids as of 8 January 2024.

Digital Payments: Over 83 billion UPI transactions took place in India in FY2022–23—the highest volume for any country in the world. China is in the second place with 41.3 billion transactions (July 2023), and is marginally ahead of Brazil with 41 billion transactions in 2023.

ICT Service Exports: India is the second largest exporter of ICT services in the world (at 15.8 per cent in 2022), behind Ireland (22.5 per cent in 2022).

> **AI Projects:** India's contribution to GitHub for AI projects is the highest in the world at 23 per cent, followed by the US (14 per cent).
>
> **Unicorns:** As of October 2023, the third highest number of homegrown unicorns by country were from India, following the US and China.
>
> *Source*: SIDE 2024 (IPCIDE, ICRIER).[6]

The world now has its eyes on India's rapid digitalization. *The State of India's Digital Economy (SIDE) 2024 Report* by ICRIER shows that India is ranked third at an aggregate level, and twelfth at the user level among the G20 countries. It uses a new approach to measure digitalization that is better suited for developing countries.[7] It finds that when compared by their aggregate levels of digitalization, India ranks as the third largest digitalized country in the world—behind the US and China and ahead of the UK, Germany and Japan. When measured in terms of digitalization of the average user, India ranks 12th among G20 countries, with the top five spots taken by the US, the UK, Australia, Canada and Germany respectively (see Table 1).

Table 1: India's Rank in Digitalization among the G20 Countries

India is the Third Largest Digitalized Country in the G20		Indians are the 12th Most Digitalized out of G20 Country Users	
Country	CHIPS (Economy) Score	Country	CHIPS (User) Score
United States	65.1	United States	64.6
China	62.3	United Kingdom	57.7
India	39.1	Australia	55.8
United Kingdom	28.8	Canada	54.1
Germany	23.8	Germany	50.8
South Korea	21.9	China	50.3
Australia	20.7	South Korea	49.7
Indonesia	20.6	France	46.4

India is the Third Largest Digitalized Country in the G20		Indians are the 12th Most Digitalized out of G20 Country Users	
Japan	20.4	Saudi Arabia	46.1
France	19.9	Japan	41.6
Canada	19.8	Argentina	40.9
Saudi Arabia	19.7	India	39.4
Turkey	19.4	Italy	39.0
South Africa	19.4	Turkey	37.9
Brazil	18.6	South Africa	35.7
Mexico	18.2	Brazil	35.6
Italy	17.6	Mexico	32.6
Russia	16.5	Russia	32.6
Argentina	14.9	Indonesia	30.6

Source: SIDE 2024 (IPCIDE, ICRIER).

Digitalized People

When it comes to connecting people, India has the advantage not only of scale, but also of rapid growth. For example, India has the second highest number of mobile and internet users as well as one of the fastest growth rates in the world (see Figure 1). Indians also enjoy the second cheapest data prices out of all the G20 countries.[8]

While India has the second largest number of internet users in the world, it also has the largest number of non-users—the classic duality of a very large and developing economy. Nearly 48 per cent of Indians do not access the internet and the quality of fixed-line internet services does not match up to that of other G20 countries.[9] The unconnected are those on the margins (women, the rural population, the disabled, the aged and children). However, while gaps in internet access between rural and urban areas, and between men and women, continue to exist, they are declining (see Figure 3). The gender gap in internet access in India narrowed between 2020 and 2022, with significant improvements in access for rural women. The highest growth is in the 35+ age group, and from the northern and eastern regions of the country. The reason for this sharp rise is attributed to greater sharing of devices by women in households where men tend to be the primary users. The fall in the gender gap in rural areas, however, varied significantly across the country, with some States like Jharkhand recording an increase. Uttar Pradesh and Madhya Pradesh—two States with relatively low internet access among rural women—saw large reductions in the gender gap.[10]

India is also the second largest market after China for the adoption of a variety of digital services, including online retail, digital health, digital education, online food delivery, and such others. According to a recent survey, India is not only the second largest market for big social media companies, but 43.6 per cent of the users surveyed use social networks for business.[11]

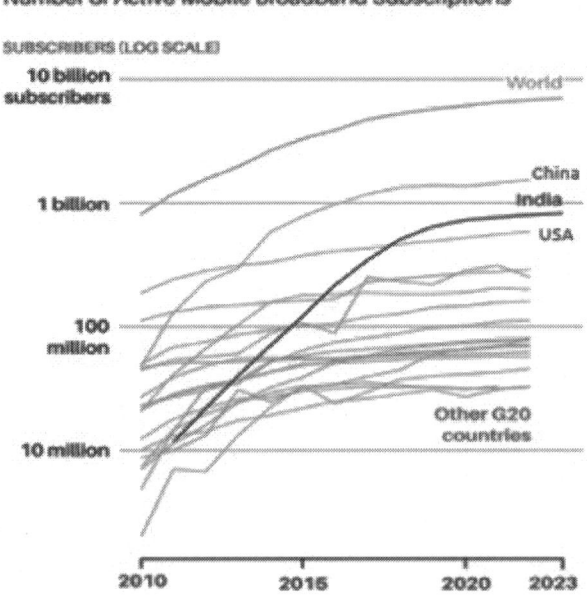

Figure 1: *India is one of the Fastest-Growing Mobile Internet Networks in the World*
Source: SIDE 2024 (IPCIDE, ICRIER).

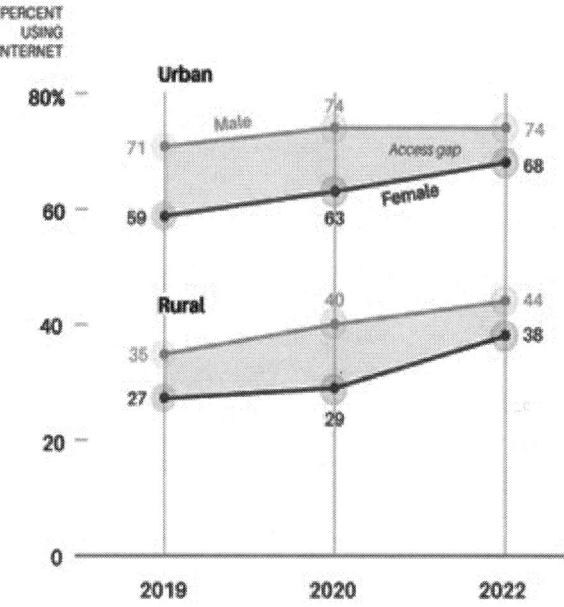

Figure 2: The Narrowing of India's Gender Gap between 2020 and 2022
Source: SIDE 2024 (IPCIDE, ICRIER).

Digitalized Businesses

India has also done reasonably well in connecting its businesses. In 2022, nine out of every 10 Indian businesses were connected to the internet, which is almost at par with developed countries like France and Canada (see Figure 3). The number of businesses with websites has increased across all sizes between 2021 and 2022, with the sharpest jump for large industries. In comparison to other G20 countries, this level of internet adoption is still considerably low, especially for small and medium businesses. The adoption of other digital tools like corporate email IDs and social media presence by Indian businesses has improved from 41 per cent and 35 per cent, respectively, to 49 per cent. WhatsApp is the main communication tool among smaller firms. An estimated 73 per cent and 75 per cent of firms with 1–10 and 11–100 employees, respectively, use the messaging service for business purposes. This is opposed to only 45 per cent and 56 per cent of the enterprises using corporate email IDs. Most importantly, online marketing and selling have also increased across firms of all sizes (see Figure 4). Almost 65 per cent of all manufacturing and services firms are now selling their products online in India.[12]

A survey conducted by DBS and Financial Times (FT) Longitude also highlights supply chain procurement, sales and marketing as areas with further potential to be digitized.[13] As per the survey, while the top 20 per cent of the firms lie close to the global frontier in terms of technological sophistication, the average firm lags behind.

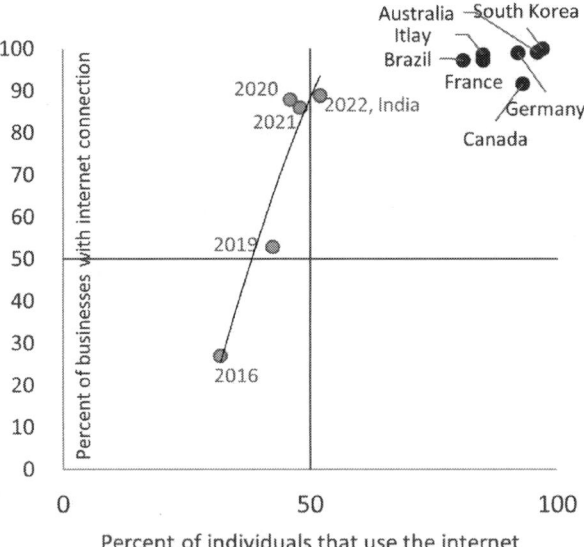

Figure 3: More Businesses than Individuals (per cent) in India are Connected to the Internet

Source: SIDE 2024 (IPCIDE, ICRIER).

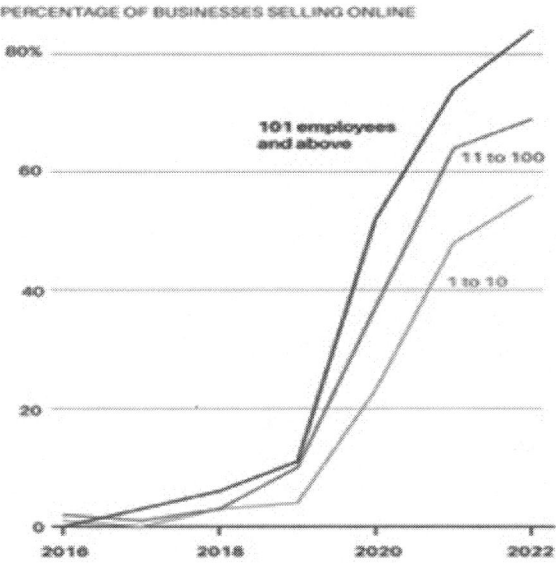

Figure 4: Steady Increase in the Share of Businesses Marketing and Selling Products Online

Source: SIDE 2024 (IPCIDE, ICRIER).

Digitalized Government

With the launch of the Digital India programme in 2015, the government rolled out a plethora of programmes to fast-track the digital availability of government services including citizen entitlements.[14] It was built upon the earlier efforts of the National e-Governance Plan (NeGP) rolled out in 2006, and integrated several other government initiatives—including the Digital Villages programme and common service centres—for the provisioning of digital services at the grassroots level. The Jan Dhan-Aadhaar-Mobile (JAM) trinity accelerated financial inclusion, closing the gender gap in bank account ownership which was more than 20 percentage points in 2014.[15] The Direct Benefit Transfer (DBT) scheme implemented through Aadhaar-linked Jan Dhan accounts enables welfare disbursement of over 314 government schemes across 53 ministries.[16] According to the finance minister's budget speech of February 2024, the DBT scheme—through the disintermediation of welfare distribution—resulted in savings worth ₹2.7 lakh crore while disbursing benefits worth ₹34 lakh crore.[17] The government is working towards a whole-of-government approach for digital service delivery, which includes taxation (GSTN and IT portal), public procurement (GeM), social protection (e-Shram), education (DIKSHA), vaccination (CoWIN), transportation (Parivahan and Sarathi) and document management (DigiLocker). More than 4,200 e-government services were provided across the country, recording 160 billion e-transactions in 2023–24.[18]

The government has also strengthened the implementation of its national broadband plan, recently christened Digital Bharat Nidhi. Now in its third phase, the programme aims to not only connect all the gram panchayats in India, but also include unconnected villages. The government is also promoting village-level entrepreneurship for the operation, maintenance and monetization of infrastructure.

The success in connecting public institutions is reportedly mixed. The average connectivity of schools and hospitals is low and varies significantly across States (see Figures 5 and 6). Fewer than 20 per cent of all schools in Odisha, West Bengal, Meghalaya, Madhya Pradesh, Bihar and Assam have a computer facility, and fewer than 10 per cent schools in Tripura, Odisha, Mizoram, Meghalaya, Bihar, Assam and Arunachal Pradesh have broadband connections.[19] The average share of hospitals with broadband connections across the country is about 16 per cent.[20] Building the digital backbone of social sector institutions will be critical to harness the potential of mass digitalization in the country.

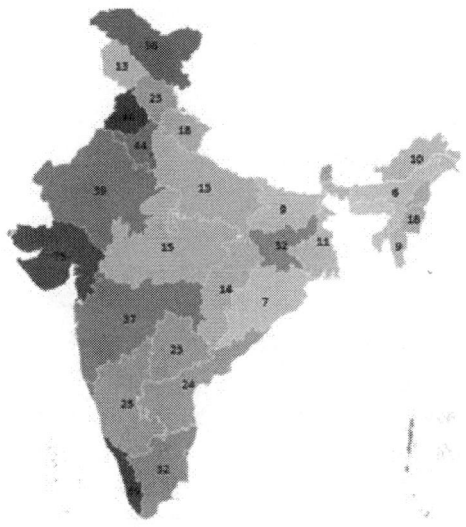

Figure 5: Percentage (%) of Schools Connected to the Internet
Source: SIDE 2023 (IPCIDE, ICRIER).

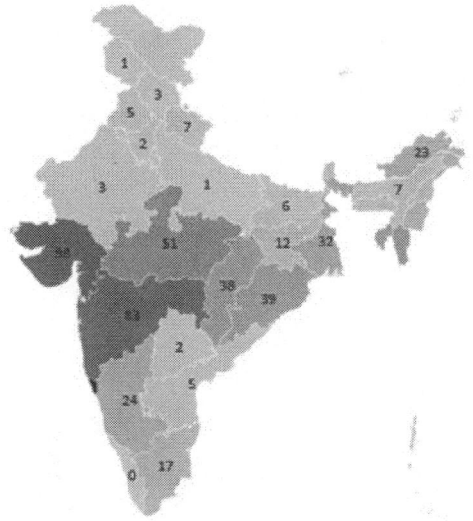

Figure 6: Percentage (%) of Public Hospitals with Broadband Connections
Source: SIDE 2023 (IPCIDE, ICRIER).

India's Digital Economy Has Been Decades in the Making

Past industrial revolutions have mostly bypassed India. The steam engine came to India 81 years after it was invented. By the time electricity arrived, it had been in use for 78 years. Passenger cars took 71 years, computers 22 years, and smartphones four to seven years. CoWIN, an app for making online appointments to get vaccinated and store certificates digitally, beat history—for the first time, an average Indian resident enjoyed the fruits of technological progress (a digital vaccination certificate) before her counterparts in the West. How did India—a country with poor resources and lacking in technological championship—become a global digital powerhouse? We examine this transition through four interrelated and overlapping phases.

Phase 1: The Liberalization of the Telecommunication Sector (1980s and 1990s)

India boasts of one of the largest and cheapest telecommunication networks in the world. Starting with the liberalization in 1981, India's telecom industry got transformed from a stodgy state monopoly to a hypercompetitive marketplace in two decades. The 1980s saw the separation of the Department of Telecommunication (DoT) from the Indian Post and Telecommunication Department, followed by the unbundling of DoT into Mahanagar Telephone Nigam Limited (MTNL), Bharat Sanchar Nigam Limited (BSNL), and Videsh Sanchar Nigam Limited (VSNL) to operate in metros, the rest of the country, and internationally, respectively. The 1990s witnessed the entry of domestic and foreign private players, the introduction of the National Telecommunications Policy (NTP 1994 and NTP 1999), and the establishment of the Telecom Regulatory Authority of India (TRAI). The subsequent two decades witnessed several key changes in licensing and spectrum assignment, tariff regulation, interconnection and liberalization of foreign direct investment (FDI) that led to rapid and robust growth in the subscriber base.

Phase 2: Back Office of the World (1990s and 2000s)

The initial success of India's ICT sector owes a great deal to the global market. A big breakthrough came at the end of the last millennium when millions of computer codes had to be fixed, and India, with its large pool of software engineers, could do this at a fraction of the cost compared to its Western counterparts (see Box 3). This gave birth to a new industry called information technology enabled services (ITeS) and business process outsourcing (BPO). The establishment of several software and technology parks of India (STPI), the investment in submarine cables, and strengthening the internet backbone, including the creation of the National Internet Exchange of India (NIXI) in 2003, helped India's nascent ICT industry experience unprecedented growth. The export of ICT services experienced a tenfold increase and grew from $5 billion in revenue in 2000 to $50 billion by 2008, and $152 billion in 2023 (see Figure 7). Large volumes of ICT services exports helped India gain valuable foreign exchange earnings and keep the current account deficit in check. The ICT sector was one of the few that generated high-paying jobs in large numbers, albeit from a modest base. According to NASSCOM, the IT-BPM sector employed 2 million people in 2009, which has increased to 5.4 million in 2023. This period also witnessed the rapid growth of cities like Bengaluru, Hyderabad, Mumbai and Gurugram (a suburb of Delhi), which are now globally recognized as important ICT hubs.

Box 3: Digitalization in Disguise

A technical glitch at the turn of the twenty-first century created an unanticipated opportunity for India's software industry. Due to what was popularly known as the Y2K bug (existing software that read years in two digits had to be recoded to distinguish the year 2000 from 1900), projects were outsourced to Indian companies that offered competitive rates and quality services. This opened up India's domestic industry to newer markets and expanded opportunities for India's ICT industry. Indian ICT services exports began to grow, and after more than two decades, India still continues to lead as the second largest exporter of IT services in the world. While the growth was completely led by big private companies in India, the government played an important role by introducing enabling policies that lowered the cost of imports for computer systems, setting up the Electronics and Computer Software Export Promotion Council (ESC) and software technology parks (STPs), and expanding vocational and technical education institutions providing diploma in coding and computer science to harness the growing potential of the sector.

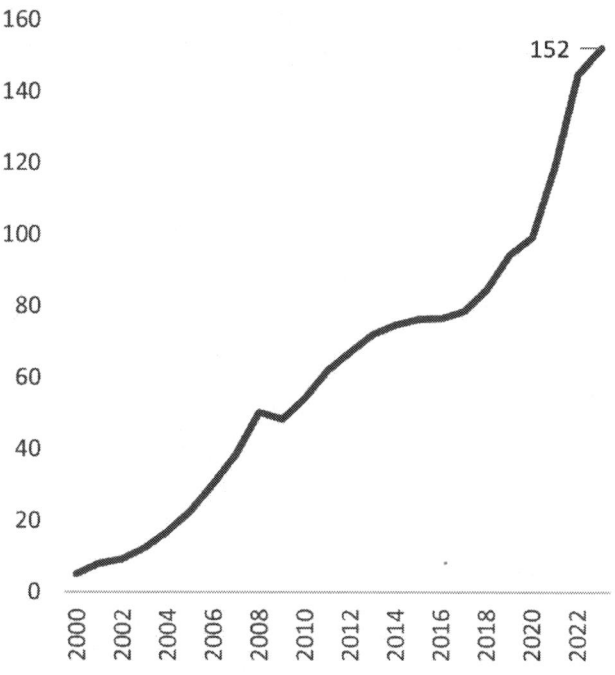

Figure 7: ICT Services Exports from India, in Billions ($) (2000–23)

Source: Compiled from RBI DBIE.

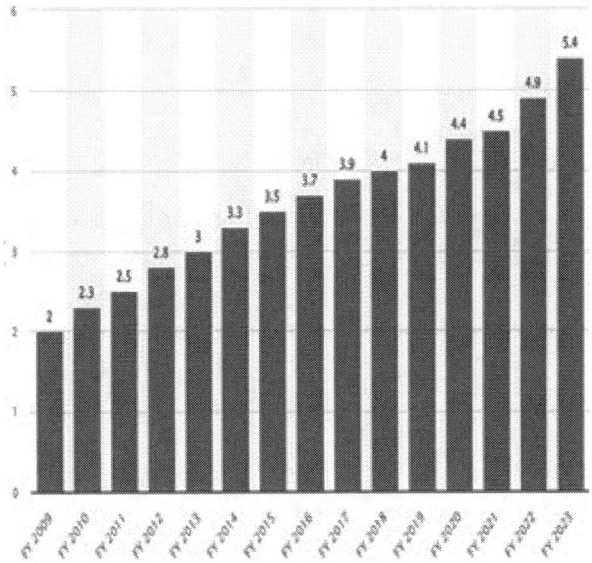

Figure 8: Employment in the IT-BPM Industry in India

Source: Compiled from Statista.

Phase 3: The Entry of the Big Techs (2005–15)

Like in most other countries, the initial years of the internet in India were confined to connecting important government departments, educational institutions and public sector enterprises. With the entry of private telcos (discussed in Phase 1) and improving access to internet services, many foreign internet companies—now referred to as 'Big Tech'—entered India, providing enterprise services, emails and chatrooms. Gmail was launched in 2004, YouTube in 2005, Facebook in 2006, Twitter (now X) in 2006, and Yahoo introduced local language chat rooms in 2006. Microsoft was already in the market offering the Windows OS along with its bundled Internet Explorer and email service. While India's ICT sector was gaining global competitiveness, the domestic market was largely served by the big American internet companies. In the next round of foreign entry—Amazon in 2012, Uber in 2013 and Netflix in 2016—Indian consumers got access to a variety of new digital services. Some Indian startups—the unicorns of today—also found pockets of success, but were no match to the rising scale and dominance of the Big Tech companies for whom India was rapidly becoming the largest market.

Phase 4: Digital India—A Path Less Travelled (2015–Present)

The Digital India programme of 2015 put digitalization at the centre of the government's policy efforts. Many existing programmes were revamped and strengthened, and by 2019, before the pandemic struck, digitalization had made its way to rural areas and several governance programmes. What set the Indian model apart was its championing of the development and deployment of digital public infrastructures (DPIs). A prominent example was the 'India Stack', a globally accepted reference to digital public infrastructure (DPI)—a new paradigm for digital service delivery that is now being tested and adopted in other countries, especially the Global South.

The path of digitalization pursued by India started to deviate from others in the post-Aadhaar period. The United States has given primacy to Big Tech and the Silicon Valley, while the European Union has put citizens' rights and privacy at the centre, and China has blurred the line between public and private. India, on the other hand, is trying to take a more nuanced path that brings together the public and private sectors, balancing regulation with innovation. The DPI-led approach to digitalization has also been endorsed by the G20 during India's presidency (see Box 4). This approach has yielded strong dividends for India, with many homegrown digital services seeing a user base of a 100 million-plus (see Figure 9).

India's push towards DPI-led digitalization is not just domestic; the aspiration is to internationalize the idea of DPIs for economic transformation. This is already manifesting through the adoption of MOSIP, the underlying open-source foundation for Aadhaar which is currently under use in other countries including Sri Lanka, Morocco, Philippines, the Republic of Guinea, Ethiopia and Uganda.[21] UPI linkages have been established with digital payment networks of seven other countries including Nepal, Bhutan, Sri Lanka, Singapore, UAE, France and Mauritius.[22] With the momentum around DPI, India has firmly established its position as a digital powerhouse of the future.

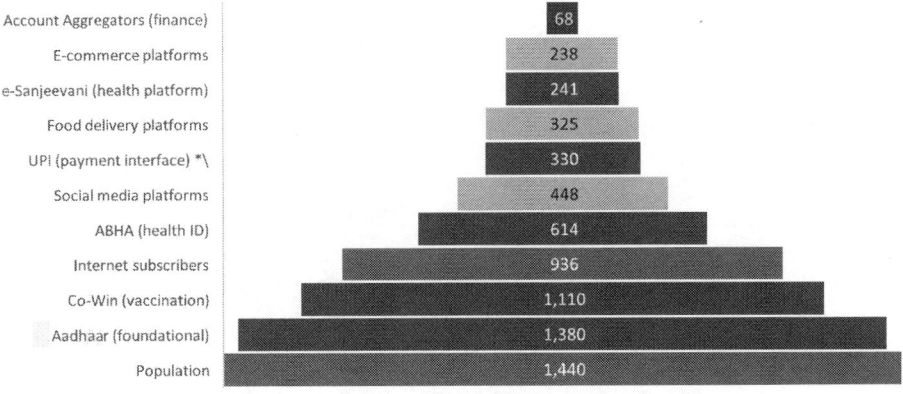

Figure 9: India Has Several Homegrown Public and Private Digital Infrastructure and Platforms with Million-Plus Users (2023)

Source: SIDE 2023 (updated) IPCIDE, ICRIER.

Box 4. Understanding DPIs

DPI was defined by the G20 as 'a set of shared digital systems which are secure and interoperable, built on open standards and specifications to deliver and provide equitable access to public/private services at societal scale and are governed by enabling rules to drive development, inclusion, innovation, trust, and competition and respect human rights and fundamental freedoms'.

According to the Centre for DPI, there are five foundational DPI categories: (i) identities and registries, (ii) payments, (iii) data sharing, (iv) trust infrastructure, and (v) discovery and fulfilment.[23] As a pioneer in the area, India has examples of thriving applications in each of these categories. Aadhaar is the world's largest biometrics-based identification system; the Unified Payments Interface (UPI) boasts of the highest number of transactions in the world; the data empowerment protection architecture (DEPA)—of which Account Aggregators are an application—is a growing use case of consent-based sharing of financial information. The slowly expanding open network for digital commerce (ONDC)—a network for matching buyers and sellers to facilitate commerce across sectors including grocery, mobility, food ordering, hotel booking, and such others—is already in operation across

1,000 cities, with Tier 2 cities driving 65 per cent of the orders on the network.[24] The government is in various stages of developing other sectoral DPIs—agriculture, education and skilling, health, and such others.

Apart from DPIs, the acceleration in the adoption of digital technologies in recent years has come on account of the Covid-19 pandemic. Long phases of lockdown led many businesses, especially those in the services industry, to go contactless. This required more investments in digital infrastructure and the adoption of online operations. One cannot rule out an initial overshooting—there is some evidence of a reversal in firm behaviour vis-à-vis digitalization—but by and large, the economy is at a new normal of digitalization. During the pandemic, the government not only leveraged its existing infrastructure and platforms to deliver digital services, it also reinforced the objective of 'digital only'. Pandemic-related shutdowns also increased the demand for connectivity in India. A LIRNEasia survey in the State of Tamil Nadu found that 23 per cent of the users that came online in 2020 did it due to the Covid-19 pandemic.[25] As the graphs presented in previous sections show, it was also an inflection point for business.

Digitalization: An End in Itself or a Means to Greater Goals?

The impact of digitalization on development can be studied at three levels.

The *first level* is digitalization as a goal in itself. As digital technologies become integral to our lives and businesses and governments increasingly offer their services only through digital channels, making the internet universally accessible, affordable and safe should become a national priority. In other words, access to digital technologies, especially the internet, can be seen as a basic human right to which every citizen is entitled.[26] The internet, like other utilities, such as water, electricity and sanitation, must be made available universally without necessarily assessing its impact on growth and productivity.

The *second level* is the microeconomic view—the impact of

digitalization on individuals and firms. There are several studies beginning from Robert Jensen's seminal paper on how the use of mobile phones increased consumer and producer welfare for fisheries in Kerala.[27] We demonstrate these micro-level impacts using the framework of inclusion, efficiency and innovation that was adopted in the World Bank Development Report of 2016.[28] Using Aadhaar, one of the many digital applications that are operating at scale in India, we provide some evidence of how India's digitalization process has become more inclusive, efficient and innovative.

Aadhaar's Impact through the Lens of Inclusion, Efficiency and Innovation

Boost to Inclusion: Besides serving its primary objective of providing an identity to every Indian, Aadhaar has given a massive boost to financial inclusion. The government's initiative of linking Aadhaar, mobile numbers and Jan Dhan bank accounts—also known as the JAM trinity—greatly improved account ownership among hitherto neglected sections of the society. By 2021, India reached significantly high levels of account ownership, closing the gaps between the rich and poor as well as men and women. These accounts were used to disburse welfare benefits at scale. For financial inclusion and social protection of unorganized workers, the government introduced the Aadhaar-linked e-Shram portal. Launched in August 2021, e-Shram is a national database of unorganized workers (NDUW) aged between 16 and 59. As of December 2023, there were over 290 million registrations, though varying significantly from State to State.

Push for Efficiency: The Direct Benefit Transfer (DBT) scheme was launched by the government in 2013 to minimize duplication and frauds in the disbursement of government benefits. The scheme was actualized through the Aadhaar Payments Bridge (APB) that facilitated timely payments to beneficiaries both in urban and rural areas. One good example is the Direct Benefit Transfer for LPG known as DBTL or Pratyaksh Hanstantrit Labh (PAHAL), launched in 2015. The scheme replaced the direct sale of LPG at subsidized prices and plugged leakages in the transfer of government benefits (see Table 2). In her latest budget speech, the finance minister announced that the Aadhaar-enabled Direct Benefit Transfer system led to savings worth ₹2.7 lakh crore while disbursing benefits worth ₹34 lakh crore. These savings have been redeployed into the government's Garib Kalyan programme.

Triggering Innovations: One of the key design principles of a DPI is to enable innovation atop the digital frame provided. Aadhaar is a foundational DPI for identities, which is now being leveraged for different purposes. For instance, Aadhaar-based electronic verification has become the norm in the provisioning of private sector services— telecom, banking and other financial services. The government has adopted its use in the attendance systems for beneficiaries of the MGNREGA scheme.[29] UIDAI, the authority governing Aadhaar, recently presented its roadmap for innovation, especially in the fintech space, providing a sandbox environment in a dedicated innovation lab at the UIDAI Tech Centre.[30]

Table 2: Estimated Savings Due to Direct Benefit Transfer (DBT) and Other Governance Reforms

Department	Scheme	Expenditure on the Scheme 2020–21 (in Cr)	Estimated Savings 2020–21 (in Cr)	Savings as a Percentage of Expenditure
Department of Rural Development	MGNREGS	111,170	7,803	7%
Department of Rural Development	NSAP	42,617	6.4	0.02%
Ministry of Petroleum and Natural Gas	PAHAL	35,195	1,609	5%
Department of Food and Public Distribution	PDS	541,330	34,700	6.4%

The *third level* is defined by impacts on the overall economy. This is where the Solow paradox becomes relevant. Following Solow, other economists also argued against techno-optimism.[31] Estimating the macroeconomic impact of a specific technology, say smartphones, broadband, AI or 5G, on indicators such as productivity, GDP growth or employment is not as straightforward as micro-level impacts. This is why economists are often sceptical about establishing a causal relationship between a specific technology and economic prosperity, even if they generally agree that technological progress is a driver of economic growth—the point with which we started this chapter. At the micro-level, impacts are both observable and measurable. However, there are challenges associated with finding quantitative evidence for the impact of digitalization at the macro-level. These include:

- First, digitalization brings benefits (creates new jobs, new modes of services delivery) and risks (destroys jobs through automation, frauds and security), and it happens over different points in time, across different geographies, and affects individuals and businesses differently. Therefore, estimating the net impact of digitalization over time, across the country, and over the entire labour force can be an exceedingly complicated exercise.

- Second, the way we estimate our national accounts, especially GDP, doesn't fully capture activities and digital transactions. The reporting of the national accounts captures the value-added of different industries, while the digital economy cuts across different industries (see Box 5).

- Thirdly, while technology saves time and hence expands leisure, it may not necessarily lead to higher growth, at least in the short run. An average Indian spends more than three hours daily on social media—made possible by time-saving technologies. There is very little addition to GDP from this, except the revenue of the social media companies and the income of influencers. Expectedly, in the long term, new occupations and more productive ways to use social media will emerge, contributing to higher growth and more jobs.

- Additionally, the impacts of digitalization at the micro and macro levels are not always complementary. Consider the case of a retail firm that adopts online sales and grows rapidly. If this growth substitutes for the sale of the brick-and-mortar firm, leaving aggregate retail sale unchanged at the macro-level, the impact of digitalization would be zero. So while a techno-optimist showing firm-level data may argue that digitalization has led to growth, the economist will point to aggregate data to make the exact opposite claim, namely that digitalization had no impact on the retail sector's growth. That's why, for any meaningful analysis on productivity and growth, careful analysis at the micro and macro levels will be necessary—which constitutes the agenda for future research work.

- Finally, for developing countries like India, the substitution effect may be dwarfed by an income effect. In the presence of a large informal sector, digitalization is likely to help expand the pie rather than end in a zero-sum game. Here, the micro and macro impacts might co-exist. Since many studies on the Solow paradox are based on developed economies, customizing an analysis on the macroeconomic impacts of digitalization in developing countries is required. Many more studies must be carried out to verify the possibility of different results.

Box 5. Estimating the Size of the Digital Economy

Whether or not it is observable in national statistics, the scale and speed of digitalization in India is undeniable. To begin with, the design of the national accounts and the GDP estimation is not one that easily allows for the isolation of the size of the digital economy. What it captures, at best, is the size and growth of ICT goods and services. Digitalization has transformed the way in which businesses operate and deliver. Physical goods and services are now ordered, delivered and consumed digitally. Accordingly, the OECD is proposing new methods of estimating the size of the digital economy—the digital supply-use table is both novel and complex. Many countries including the US, Canada, Australia and Netherlands that have undertaken this exercise explain the challenges associated with the estimation, primarily the absence of firm-level data on the nature of business activity. India's MoSPI is yet to officially undertake the measurement of the digital economy.

Navigating the Tides in the High Sea of Digitalization

This chapter highlights several reasons—both conscious and accidental—that led to India's current state of digitalization, which, by global standards and compared to its own stage of development, is quite impressive. As also argued in the previous section, despite massive digitalization, the impacts on productivity and growth are not easy to determine. But there are many examples that are indicative of potential growth. It is also well accepted that digitalization itself is a worthy goal and can make the development process more inclusive, efficient and innovative. And since India has charted its own course of digitalization and has taken advantage of the tailwinds, it should also be well prepared to navigate the high tides by universalizing connectivity and strengthening the analogue complements of digital technologies.

The unconnected and underconnected are mostly marginalized individuals including the very poor, women, the disabled and people living in the remote parts of the country.[32] While mobile networks are now ubiquitously available (99 per cent, as per the latest data), the number of people using the internet are at less than 70 per cent.[33] This gap is explained by challenges of affordability, literacy, digital skills and relevance. Solving for the usage gap will require an ecosystem approach that includes policies both on the supply and the demand sides. On the supply side, not only does infrastructure have to be taken to every government institution, school, hospital and gram panchayat, it also has to be upgraded to a minimum speed. With a de facto duopoly (Jio and Airtel currently account for 72 per cent of the market share), the future of India's telecom industry is mired in uncertainty.[34] Further, low average revenue per user (ARPU), changing technology and demands on network upgradation will require policy intervention to ensure that India's telecom infrastructure is prepared to operate in a world marked by industrial internet and a high-performance computing environment.

On the demand side, both data connections and devices have to be made affordable, applications more intuitive, and content relevant. Needless to say, communications have to be secure at all times. These elements collectively constitute the idea of meaningful connectivity—proposed recently by the International Telecommunication Union (ITU)—to build strong foundations for the digital economy. In this chapter, we don't discuss detailed policy recommendations on how this can be achieved, but it is important to highlight that a piecemeal approach or a one-off Pradhan Mantri Gramin Digital Saksharta Abhiyaan (PMGDISHA) to address digital literacy will not solve the usage gap that has consistently remained over 30 per cent.[35]

For a comprehensive and resilient growth of the digital economy, India's big IT companies must come to the fore. So far, they have focused on expanding their existing business and not enough on increasing digitalization within the country. The ICT boom has largely been confined to the educated youth living in many urban centres. Even more worryingly, many Indian IT firms continue to operate in the traditional areas of enterprise network and mainframes while the world has rapidly moved to high-speed internet, cloud computing and mobile technology.

Finally, digitalization has created new risks of privacy breaches, data misuses and other cyber-related financial crimes. The DPI approach is defined by three key pillars: (a) open, interoperable technology, (b) robust governance, and (c) resilient local systems. While the first has been templatized in all applications in India, the latter two need greater attention—building complementary regulatory institutions and communities of practices that involve the participation of the private sector, civil society and academia will be important to build safe, inclusive and secure delivery mechanisms.

For example, while UPI is the largest real-time payment system in the world with over 89.5 billion transactions in 2022, surveys also find that among the G20 countries, India has the highest payment fraud rate—45 per cent of the sampled population reported being a victim of a payment fraud in the last four years.[36] UPI constitutes 47 per cent of all cybercrime and 61 per cent of all online financial frauds in India.[37] According to the RBI's *Report on Trend and Progress of Banking in India* (2023–24), internet and card frauds (of ₹1 lakh and above) increased from 1,191 instances amounting to ₹40 crore in 2015–16, to 29,082 instances amounting to ₹1,457 crore in 2023–24. The absence of an effective grievance redressal mechanism and reduced trust can constrain the uptake of UPI. Additionally, as highlighted in the other sections, connectivity infrastructure needs to be strengthened to minimize frictions in the provisioning of essential services. Building effective guardrails and a strong analogue backbone is going to be crucial to harness the true potential of DPI-led digitalization in India.

Digitalization in India will continue to need steering to avoid risks that can result in counterproductive outcomes for the economy. Building strong analogue foundations—literacy, infrastructure and institutions—will certainly lead to growth dividends at scale. Challenging the productivity paradox will then become an easy possibility for India.

S. Mahendra Dev

Priorities for Indian Agriculture: A Case for Cooperative Federalism to Improve Incomes and Livelihoods

I have known Dr Shankar Acharya for the last three and a half decades, and benefitted immensely from his contributions as economist, policymaker, banker and columnist. He was India's longest-serving chief economic adviser, a key insider in framing macroeconomic policies, particularly in undertaking economic reforms. I got to know him much more closely when we were together on the Board of Kotak Mahindra Bank during 2013–18. As the chairman of the bank, Dr Acharya steered it with his vast experience and provided strategic direction to this financial institution from 2006 to 2018. In the course of my interactions with him at the bank, I learnt a great deal about macroeconomic and financial issues at the domestic and the global levels as well as geopolitical matters. His presentations on India's growth and macroeconomic policies at the annual meetings of the bank were very useful. I also enjoyed several dinners with him at the Trident Hotel in BKC, Mumbai. He is a wonderful human being with intellectual and personal integrity. It is indeed a privilege to contribute an essay to this volume in honour of Dr Shankar Acharya.

∎

Role, Goals and the Need for Reforms in Agriculture

Agriculture plays a pivotal role in the Indian economy and this sector's better performance is vital for growth and inclusive development.

Although it contributes towards less than one-fifth of the gross domestic product (GDP) now, it provides employment to 46 per cent of the Indian workforce. There are significant linkages between farm and non-farm sectors.[1] [2] [3]

The structural reforms and stabilization policies introduced in India in 1991 initially focused on industry, tax reforms, foreign trade and investment, and banking and capital markets. The economic reforms did not include any specific package especially designed for agriculture. It was deemed that protection granted to the industry in the form of import-substitution policies—like tight import controls and high import duties—hurt agriculture till 1991. Dis-protection to industry since 1991 (i.e. the lowering of tariffs leading to lower industrial prices, thereby helping agriculture improve its terms of trade) was supposed to correct this bias and improve the terms of trade for agriculture. Manmohan Singh put it in this way: 'This would create a potentially more profitable agriculture, which would be able to bear the economic costs of technological modernization and expansion.'[4] The reforms improved the terms of trade for agriculture and opened up new opportunities, such as benefits from trade and specialization, and widening choices in new technology, including biotechnology. It may be true that the liberalization of the non-agriculture sector indirectly had a positive impact on agriculture, but the latter has not undergone any major direct reforms since Independence. Agricultural markets witnessed only limited reforms. The need for direct reforms in agriculture is obvious.

In addition to domestic policies, the performance of the agriculture sector also depends on global economic and geopolitical developments. There are many challenges at the global level such as climate change, urbanization, migration, technologies like automation, and increased inequality. Furthermore, geopolitical challenges like the present conflicts in Russia-Ukraine, the Israel-Gaza war, and anti-globalization contribute to the changing context for agriculture.

There are three broad goals for agricultural development in India. These are: (a) achieve four per cent growth per annum in agriculture and raise the incomes of farmers, (b) facilitate inclusiveness, and (c) maintain the sustainability of agriculture by focusing on environmental and climate change concerns. It may be noted that all three goals are interconnected.

Repurposing and reforms in agriculture are important to achieve the above-mentioned goals. Raising productivity and incomes, diversification, using technology, promoting inclusiveness, including food and nutrition security, and developing climate resilience are priorities for India's agricultural development.

In the above context, this article examines (a) the performance of Indian agriculture, and (b) the challenges and policies for achieving the above development goals. It also discusses priorities and the reforms needed for agriculture.

The Performance of Indian Agriculture

In terms of growth, the performance of agriculture in the post-Independence era has been impressive as compared to the pre-Independence period. India's agricultural transformation from being a food-deficit country in the 1960s to attaining food self-sufficiency is well known, with achievements like the Green Revolution, the White Revolution, the growth in the cultivation of maize and breeding of poultry, the cotton revolution and the high growth in horticulture and livestock. India is the largest producer of milk, cotton and pulses, and the second largest in rice, wheat, fruits and vegetables. It is also the largest exporter of rice, bovine meat and spices.

Agricultural Growth

In the 1960s, the agricultural growth rate was around one per cent per annum (Table 1). In other periods, the growth rates ranged from 2.2 per cent to 4.3 per cent per annum. The highest growth rate of the GDP from agriculture was 4.3 per cent per annum in two periods: 2009–14 and 2018–23.

Table 1: Growth Rates in Agriculture GDP/GVA (per cent)

	Agriculture
1960–61 to 1968–69	1.04
1968–69 to 1975–76	2.24
1975–76 to 1988–89	2.47
1988–89 to 1995–96	2.76
1995–96 to 2004–05	2.28
2004–05 to 2014–15	3.72
2009–10 to 2013–14	4.30
2014–15 to 2022–23	3.93
2018–19 to 2022–23	4.32

Note: GVA: gross value-added

Source: GOI (2017) up to 2014–15; calculated from National Accounts Statistics for the period from 2014–15 to 2022–23.

Indian agriculture is undergoing a structural transformation as the composition of agricultural output has changed dramatically. The share of the crop sector in the value of output from agriculture and allied sectors in the GDP/GVA ratio has declined from 79.2 per cent in triennium ending (TE) 1971–72 to 59.7 per cent in TE 2021–22, while the share of the livestock sector has increased from 18 per cent to 33.5 per cent, and that of fisheries from 2.8 per cent to 6.8 per cent during the period under consideration (Figure 1).

The historical experience of different countries shows that a structural transformation from low-productive to high-productive sectors led to higher economic growth and the creation of greater productive employment. In India, the share of agriculture in the GDP in current prices has declined from 53.2 per cent in 1950–51 to 18.2 per cent in 2022–23, while the share of agriculture in total employment declined from 69.2 per cent to 45.8 per cent over the same period (Table 2). As a result, the ratio of the income of an agriculture worker to that of a non-agriculture worker declined from 0.51 in 1950–51 to 0.21 in 2022–23.

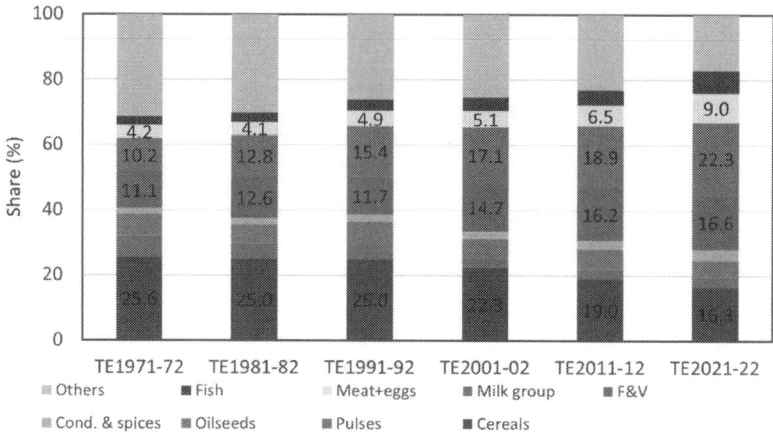

Figure 1: The Changing Composition of the Value of Output from Agriculture and Allied Sectors in India

Source: Sharma, 2023.[5]

Table 2: The Share of Agriculture and Allied Sectors in National Income and Employment—1950–51 to 2022–23

Year	Agriculture's Share in the Workforce	Agriculture's Share in GDP (%)		Ratio of Income of Agriculture Workers to That of Non-Agriculture Workers
		At Constant Prices	At Current Prices	
1950–51	69.2	61.7	53.2	0.51
1970–71	69.7	49.6	43.1	0.33
1990–91	59.0	35.1	29.8	0.29
2010–11	54.6	18.3	18.4	0.19
2022–23	45.8	15.4	18.2	0.21

Source: Chand and Singh:[6] up to 2010–11; author's estimates for 2022–23, based on PLFS (Periodic Labour Force Survey) and NAS (National Accounts Statistics) data.

Total Factor Productivity in Indian Agriculture

Using KLEMS (capital, labour, energy, materials and services) data, a study by Krishna and Meenakshi[7] estimates the total factor productivity (TFP) in Indian agriculture for the period from 1980–81 to 2018–19. The growth rate of the total factor productivity for the entire period was only 0.89 per cent per annum, while it was relatively high at 2.2 per cent in the last decade. TFP growth accounted for nearly one-third of agricultural growth over 38 years, but its contribution in the decade from 2010–11 to 2018–19 was the highest at nearly 58 per cent, driven largely by the decline in labour input. A recent study by Sengupta and others[8] shows that TFP growth was 0.8 per cent per annum between 1980 and 2019 without accounting for land. It accelerated to 2.0 per cent and 1.8 per cent per annum with the inclusion of land and land quality, respectively.

Income of Farmers

The Situation Assessment Surveys of the NSS (National Sample Survey) show that the average monthly income of agricultural households in current prices increased from ₹2,115 in 2003 to ₹10,218 in 2018–19 (Table 3). The share of cultivation in total income was the highest at 46 per cent in 2003 and 48 per cent in 2013. But the share declined to 37 per cent in 2018–19. The shares of income from animals and wages increased. The income from cultivation between 2013 and 2018–19 declined if we adjust with inflation. In fact, the average annual growth rate of the total income of farmers in real terms declined from 3.39 per cent between 2002–03 and 2012–13, to 2.37 per cent between 2012–13 and 2018–19.[9]

Table 3: Average Monthly Income of Agricultural Households in Current Prices—NSS Surveys 2003, 2013 and 2018–19

	Income (₹) Current Prices			Share in Total Income (%)		
	2003	2013	2018–19	2003	2013	2018–19
Cultivation	969	3,081	3,798	45.8	47.9	37.2
Animals	91	763	1,582	4.3	11.9	15.5
Wages	819	2,071	4,063	38.7	32.2	39.8
Non-Farm Business	236	512	641	11.2	8.0	6.3
Leasing out of Land	–	–	134	–	–	1.3
Total	2,115	6,426	10,218	100.0	100.0	100.0

Source: Situation Assessment Surveys of the NSO (National Statistical Office).

Inclusive Development in Agriculture

The second goal of agricultural development is sharing growth and achieving equity. Inclusiveness in agriculture should focus on inequalities with regard to regions, women and youth, disadvantaged social groups, small vs. large farmers, and irrigated vs. rainfed areas. The shrinking size of farms is a major problem. The share of marginal and small farmers increased from 70 per cent in 1980–81 to 86 per cent in 2015–16. The average size of farm holdings declined from 2.3 hectares in 1970–71 to 1.08 hectares in 2015–16. The viability of marginal and small farmers is a major challenge for Indian agriculture.[10]

A Convergence Hypothesis for Agricultural Per Capita Income across 20 Major States: 2000–01 to 2019–20

The analysis on regional convergence or divergence gained importance with the development of the neoclassical growth literature based on the Solow model[11] which predicted that poorer economies grew faster than richer economies.

Dev[12] indicated a divergence in per capita GSDP across States for the period from 2000–01 to 2019–20. Here, we examine whether States are converging in terms of agricultural per capita SDP for the longer period from 2000–01 to 2019–20 as well as subperiods. We estimated β convergence using the following equation:

$$ln \left(\frac{Y_{it}}{Y_{i,t-T}} \right) = \alpha_i + \beta \ ln \ (Y_{i,t-T}) + \varepsilon_{i,t}$$

Where, Y_{it} is per capita agricultural SDP for a State i at time t.
t-T is the length of the time period.
α_i is the steady growth rate of State i.
β is the beta convergence.
$\varepsilon_{i,t}$ is the error term.

The estimates on unconditional convergence for agricultural per capita GSDP reveal that the coefficient of initial income level is negative but not significant for the longer period in all but one subperiod (Table 4). It shows that per capita GSDP for agriculture is neither converging nor diverging across States. It is positively significant for the subperiod from 2014–15 to 2019–20, indicating the divergence of States.

Table 4: The Regression Equation of Convergence [Dependent Variable is Per Capita AGSDP, ln $(Y_{it}/Y_{i, t-T})$]

Period	Constant	Initial Income Level ln $(Y_{i, t-T})$	Adjusted R^2	F
2000–01 to 2019–20	0.1218 (1.4714)	-0.0106 (-1.1852)	0.0209	1.4047
2000–01 to 2005–06	0.1793 (1.0226)	-0.0173 (-0.912)	-0.0089	0.8317
2006–07 to 2019–20	0.0301 (0.3085)	-0.0006 (-0.0553)	-0.0554	0.0031
2006–07 to 2011–12	0.1524 (1.7794)	-0.0138 (-1.5095)	0.0631	2.2787
2011–12 to 2019–20	-0.1105 (-0.8596)	0.0144 (1.0601)	0.0065	1.1239
2014–15 to 2019–20	-0.3126 (-1.8862)	0.036** (2.0705)	0.1475	4.2869*

Notes: 1) Figures in parenthesis represent t values of the regression coefficients.
2) *, ** and *** indicate the significant at 1%, 5% and 10% levels respectively.

Source: Author's estimates.

Figure 2 provides the weighted and unweighted coefficient of variation (CV) for per capita agricultural GSDP. It shows that the CV declined during 2002–03 to 2012–13, and increased during 2014–15 to 2019–20. One has to examine the reasons for the increasing disparities in per capita agricultural SDP across States for this subperiod.

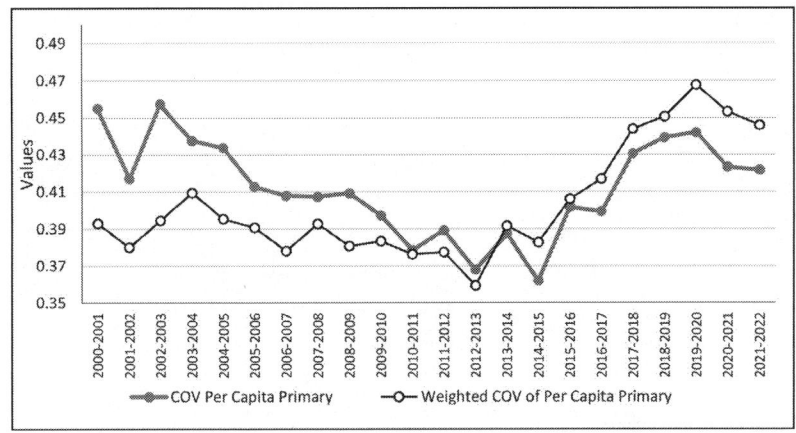

Figure 2: Interstate Disparities (Coefficient of Variation, CoV) in Per Capita Agriculture SDP

Source: Estimated from the data obtained from EPWRF (Economic and Political Weekly Research Foundation), which collected data from the RBI, *Handbook of Statistics on Indian Economy.*

Sustainability in Agriculture and Climate Change

The third goal of agricultural development is sustainability. We have to look at issues such as energy, the environment, natural resources and climate change. Waterlogging, soil erosion and groundwater depletion are some of the problems leading to the unsustainability of agriculture. M.S. Swaminathan appealed to the farmers as early as 1968 not to harm the long-term production potential for short-term gain.[13]

Climate change is a reality. Agriculture is the sector most vulnerable to climate change due to its high dependence on climate and weather. Agriculture is part of both the problem and the solution. Using district-level data on temperature, rainfall and crop production, the Economic Survey 2017–18[14] shows the following: (a) the impacts of the climate factors are significantly more adverse in unirrigated areas compared to irrigated areas, and (b) extreme temperature shocks reduce yields by 4 per cent and 4.7 per cent for kharif and rabi crops, respectively, while extreme rainfall shocks reduce yields by 12.8 per cent and 6.7 per cent for kharif and rabi crops, respectively.

Challenges and Policy Priorities for Achieving Higher Growth, Inclusion, Sustainability and Climate Resilience

Despite significant achievements, there are several challenges for Indian agriculture. The Economic Survey 2023[15] called for a reorientation due to challenges like climate change, rising input costs, fragmented landholdings, suboptimal farm mechanization, low productivity, and disguised unemployment. The RBI (2022) said, 'the agriculture sector suffers from low capital formation, declining R&D, low crop yields, inadequate crop diversity and intensity, with excessive dependence on subsidies and price support schemes.'[16]

The challenges and policy priorities for achieving the goals of agricultural development in the next two decades are discussed below.

A change in the narrative, repurposing and reforms in agriculture are needed in the new context: Basically, we have to repurpose and change the narrative of agriculture towards more diversified high-value production, better remunerative prices and farm incomes, marketing and trade reforms, and nutrition-sensitive, inclusive, environment-friendly and climate-resilient practices.

Global Developments and Challenges Have Implications for Indian Agriculture

There are many challenges at the global level, such as climate change, inequalities, protectionism, geopolitical issues and urbanization. The recent conflicts in Ukraine-Russia and Israel-Gaza had some impact on Indian agriculture and global supply chains. For example, attacks on vessels in the Red Sea area reduced traffic through the Suez Canal—the shortest maritime route between Asia and Europe. As a result, several shipping companies diverted their ships around the Cape of Good Hope. This increased delivery time by 10 days or more on average, hurting companies and supply chains.

Negotiations at the WTO have an impact on Indian agriculture. In the recent 13th WTO Ministerial Conference held in February 2024, India took a strong stand against the lobby of developed countries demanding a reduction in domestic support for agriculture. In fact, agricultural support is very high in advanced countries. At the global level, government support to agriculture is massive at more than $800 billion per annum in 2019–21.[17] Total agricultural support as a percentage of the agricultural GDP is 42 per cent in the OECD countries; 23 per cent is the world average; it stands at 22 per cent in China and is less than 10 per cent in India.[18] An analysis of different scenarios shows that shifting subsidies to R&D and incentives for green innovations will improve productivity and lower carbon emissions.[19]

Technological developments at the global level can help Indian agriculture positively. A study on 'achieving agricultural breakthrough' (CGIAR, 2023)[20] indicates seven agricultural breakthrough technologies. These are (1) reduced emissions from fertilizers, (2) alternative proteins, (3) reduced food loss and waste, (4) crop and livestock breeding, (5) reduced methane emissions from livestock, (6) agro-ecological approaches, and (7) digital services.

Agricultural Reforms for Higher Growth and Farm Incomes in India

(1) Marketing Reforms

Diversification and marketing reforms are needed for the transformation of Indian agriculture. The cropping patterns should be based on demand. Marketing reforms are needed to raise the incomes of farmers.

The Central government had to repeal the three farm laws because of opposition from some sections of the farmers. These market reforms were important and provided greater choice to farmers. Although the recent farm laws were repealed, States should continue reforms for higher agricultural growth and faster increases in farmers' income.

A recent survey by Suganthi and others[21] found that the average share of farmers in output value varied between 33 and 70 per cent across various crops. The survey findings suggested that the further development of agricultural markets, warehouses, pre-processing facilities, ripening units and cold storage was critical for efficient supply chain management.

It may be noted that despite MSP and subsidies, the Indian farmer is net-taxed as compared to farmers of other countries. An OECD and

ICRIER study showed that producer support estimates (PSEs) were negative to the tune of 14 per cent on average during the period from 2000–01 to 2016–17.[22] In other words, distorted policies are hurting Indian farmers.

(2) Price Policy

Remunerative price is the most important factor for farmers. The price factor, along with technology, was important even during the time of the Green Revolution. One of the instruments of price policy is fixing minimum support prices for 23 crops. Currently, a few farmer organizations are agitating to demand legally guaranteed MSP for 23 crops. There is, of course, a reason for such a demand for MSP with legal backing. When output increases well beyond the market demand at a price that is remunerative to producers, market prices decline and farmers are faced with a loss of income.

The MSP scheme has been in existence for several decades and it is particularly effective for rice and wheat crops. There are a few issues which need to be clarified with respect to legalizing the MSP. In the case of wheat and rice, the MSP has been combined with the procurement of all the grains offered at that price and a public distribution system through which the procured grains are distributed. Thus, it protects both producers and consumers. The public distribution system sale revenue is far less than the costs borne by the Central government. According to the latest budget (FY25), food subsidies amounted to ₹2 lakh crore. In this context, two questions arise. First, do we need to extend such a scheme to all crops? Second, in the context of a legalized MSP—which means that nobody can buy produce at a price lower than the MSP—what is the precise interpretation of the minimum support price?

In fixing the MSP, we need to consider two types of costs: A2 costs and C2 costs. A2 includes all paid-out costs (out-of-pocket expenses), while C2 covers paid-out costs as well as imputed costs which are the imputed value of family labour (FL), the imputed rental value of owned land, and the imputed interest on the value of owned fixed assets. At present, the government provides the MSP, which is equal to 50 per cent of A2+FL. Farmers are demanding that the MSP should be above the 50 per cent profit margin over the comprehensive cost (C2). This price will be unsustainable.

It may also be noted that the reach of the MSP is limited at the national level. The Situation Assessment Survey (SAS) of Agricultural Households for 2018–19 shows that only 8.8 per cent of all households see any crop at MSP. Gulati and Roy[23] show that this percentage goes down further to 5.5 per cent if one uses the data of the National Accounts Statistics.

(3) Subsidies and Investments in Agriculture

One major reform needed in the agriculture sector relates to the reduction in subsidies and an increase in investments. Agricultural subsidies are fiscally unsustainable and encourage the misuse of resources, leading to environmentally malignant developments. There is a trade-off between subsidies and public investment in agriculture.

Subsidies constitute around seven per cent of the GVA in agriculture, while public investment is only a little more than two per cent (Table 5). In other words, subsidies are more than three times the volume of public investment. Fertilizer and power subsidies constitute the bulk of the overall subsidies in agriculture. These subsidies lead to soil degradation and ground water exploitation.

Table 5: Public Investment and Subsidies in Agriculture, 2011–12 to 2020–21

Year	Public Investment (₹ Crore)	Subsidy Including Power (₹ Crore)	Public Investment as Percentage of GVA, Agriculture and Allied	Subsidies as Percentage of GVA, Agriculture and Allied
1	2	3	4	5
2011–12	35,576	118,063	2.37	7.86
2012–13	39,617	131,996	2.37	7.88
2013–14	40,467	127,600	2.10	6.62
2014–15	47,004	138,689	2.25	6.62

Year	Public Investment (₹ Crore)	Subsidy Including Power (₹ Crore)	Public Investment as Percentage of GVA, Agriculture and Allied	Subsidies as Percentage of GVA, Agriculture and Allied
2015–16	55,870	164,130	2.51	7.37
2016–17	66,362	158,994	2.63	6.31
2017–18	66,786	194,689	2.36	6.88
2018–19	79,473	205,678	2.63	6.82
2019–20	72,696	220,666	2.16	6.57
2020–21	76,852	250,195	2.13	6.93

Source: Chand and Singh.[24]

(4) Reform Agriculture, Introduce an Agriculture Food Marketing Council (AFM Council), and Raise Direct Benefit Transfers (DBTs)

There is a view that in the context of the changing landscape of Indian agriculture, we do not need agricultural produce marketing committees (APMCs), MSPs or subsidies. Instead, the focus has to be on basic income support, remunerative prices, and environmental concerns.[25] There will be negative externalities on the farmers' expected incomes due to climate change. In order to address these market failures, it is suggested that an AFM (agriculture and food marketing) council be established on the lines of the GST Council.[26] The AFM council can play a major role in substituting the MSP and the APMCs with DBT (Direct Benefit Transfer) provisions. This will include compensation for the loss of *mandi* fees, production-linked DBT to change the cropping pattern, and DBT to farmers to assure basic income.[27]

(5) Technology, Research and Extension

The average yield of most crops in India is low relative to most of the major producer countries in the world, and there are very large variations in yields across States. The average productivity of rice in India (41.4 quintal per hectare) is lower than the world average (47.2 quintal per hectare), and even less than 60 per cent of the yield in China (70.4 quintal per hectare), which is the largest producer of rice in the world.[28]

The new agricultural technologies on the horizon are largely biotechnologies. There has been a revolution in cotton production due to the success of BT cotton. India has conditionally approved genetically modified (GM) mustard crop. An analysis of hybrid DMH-11 shows that it gives a yield advantage of 37 per cent with the same level of inputs.[29] The study also shows that the farming community will get 99 per cent of the additional monetary gains, leaving only one per cent to the seed companies. The use of many such hybrids—which are safe—can be encouraged for raising farm incomes and improving food security.

Public sector investment in agriculture research and development in India is only 0.3 per cent to 0.5 per cent of the agricultural GDP—which is much lower than China, Israel and USA. This needs to be raised to at least 1.0 per cent, as is being invested by most developing countries. The returns to investment on research and extension will be much higher with respect to agricultural growth as compared to other investments.

Frontier technologies—offering immense benefits available for ready application in agriculture—can be classified as: (i) biotechnology, (ii) digital technology, (iii) nanotechnology, (iv) space science and global positioning system (GPS) tools, and (v) advance engineering technologies including sensors and unmanned aerial vehicles (UAV).[30] Breakthroughs in these fields have immense potential for application in agriculture and allied activities, as well as agri-business.

Digital technology and the use of modern technology such as artificial intelligence, machine learning, blockchain technology, drones, sensors, and others can enhance agricultural growth and farmers' incomes. This technology would help in getting reliable information for better crop planning, crop estimation, improved access to farm inputs and services, market intelligence, supply planning and such others.

There have been new-generation startups coming up in agriculture. The startups have brought about several innovations in products, processes, marketing and organization.[31] These startups have been cutting down the length of the value chain. They can complement the digital public infrastructure for agriculture.

(6) Increase and Diversify Exports

India's exports have increased significantly over the last three years and reached $53 billion in 2022–23 (Table 6). However, as imports increased in tandem, the trade surplus of recent years has not reached the 2012–13 and 2013–14 levels. We do not see consistent policies regarding international trade. There is no long-term policy to address exports. Export bans are imposed frequently, which hurts the farmers the most. There is a need for predictability and stable export policies. The diversification of exports is also necessary.

Table 6: Agricultural Exports and Imports in India ($ billion)

Year	Exports	Imports	Trade Surplus
2012–13	41.7	19.0	22.7
2013–14	43.3	15.5	27.7
2014–15	39.1	21.2	17.9
2015–16	32.8	22.6	10.2
2016–17	33.7	25.6	8.1
2017–18	38.9	24.9	14.0
2018–19	39.2	20.9	18.3
2019–20	35.6	21.9	13.7
2020–21	41.9	21.7	20.2
2021–22	50.2	32.4	17.8
2022–23	52.5	35.7	16.8

Source: Damodaran[32] up to 2021–22; Sharma[33] for 2022–23.

(7) Water Management

Water is the leading input in agriculture and a major policy issue in the twenty-first century. It is clear that better and efficient management of water resources is necessary for India to achieve 'more crops per drop'.

According to a Niti Aayog report, 'India uses two–three times the water used to produce one tonne of grain in countries like China, Brazil and USA. This implies that with water use efficiency of those countries India can at least double irrigation coverage or save 50 per cent water currently used in irrigation.[34] The procurement, subsidies and water policies are biased towards rice and wheat. Three crops— rice, wheat and sugarcane—corner 75 to 80 per cent of all irrigated water. There is a need to shift from rice and wheat to millets and non-cereals for an equitable sharing of water. Interstate disputes and conflicts on water at the farm level are expected to increase over time. The problem is not due to the shortage of water resources but is caused by inefficient management. Water management should be given number one priority when it comes to policies on agriculture.

Food Systems Approach for Increase in Demand, Incomes, Food and Nutrition Security, Sustainability and Climate Change Resilience

In September 2021, the UN secretary-general convened the Food Systems Summit which aimed for a global food systems transformation to achieve the Sustainable Development Goals (SDGs) by 2030. It also aimed to harness science and technology to raise the levels of nutrition and protect the environment. There were five action tracks to achieve the objectives. These were: (a) ensure access to safe and nutritious food for all, (b) shift to sustainable consumption patterns, (c) boost nature-positive production, (d) advance equitable livelihoods, and (e) build resilience to vulnerabilities, shocks and stress.[35]

According to the FAO,[36] 'food systems encompass the entire range of actors and their interlinked value-adding activities involved in the production, aggregation, processing, distribution, consumption and disposal of food products that originate from agriculture, forestry or fisheries, and parts of the broader economic, societal and natural environments in which they are embedded.' In many countries, the food systems approach is being followed to improve farmers' incomes, attaining inclusive and sustainable growth. In this context, it would be useful to look at challenges and policy priorities across food systems in India.

(a) Policies for Inclusive Development

Increasing the viability of small and marginal farmers, reducing social, gender and regional inequalities, women's empowerment, and improving rainfed areas are some of the goals of equity in agriculture.

The viability of small and marginal farmers should be boosted. Around 86 per cent of agricultural holdings belong to small and marginal farmers. There are many technological and institutional innovations which can enable small farmers to increase incomes through diversification and benefit from value chains. Small farmers require special support, public goods and links to input and output markets. Farmer producer organizations (FPOs) can help in raising their incomes. The e-Choupal initiative of ITC is an example of technology benefitting small farmers. One of the more successful examples of value chains that helped smallholders, women and consumers is Anand Milk Union Limited (Amul), created by the Father of the White Revolution in India, Verghese Kurien. These types of innovations are needed in other food systems activities. We need to have policies for land consolidation, along with land development activities, to tackle the challenge of the low average size of holdings.[37]

Agriculture is becoming increasingly feminized as men migrate to the rural non-farm sector and urban areas. Nearly 76 per cent of rural women work in agriculture as compared to 49 per cent of rural men in agriculture in 2022–23. Agricultural policies should correct the gender bias in the functioning of institutions and support systems, including property rights for women.

Another issue is hunger and malnutrition in India. There are five challenges on this issue, as listed below:

(a) According to the FAO,[38] 16 per cent of the Indian population (234 million) still suffer from undernourishment.

(b) Despite the decline over the period from 2015–16 to 2019–21, 35 per cent of Indian children suffer from stunting as of 2019–21.

(c) The percentage of anaemic women between 15 and 49 years of age was 57 per cent in 2019–21, having increased from 53.1 per cent in 2015–16.

(d) The FAO[39] indicated that around 75 per cent of the Indian population—around 104.3 crore people—could not afford a healthy diet which cost $3.066 (in purchasing power parity) per capita per day in 2021.

(e) At the same time, obesity increased between 2015–16 and 2019–21 as shown below:

(i) The percentage of overweight children under five years increased from 2.1 per cent to 3.4 per cent.

(ii) The percentage of overweight or obese women rose from 20.6 per cent to 24.0 per cent.

(iii) The percentage of overweight or obese men increased from 18.9 per cent to 22.9 per cent.

Apart from other factors, safe and healthy diversified diets are needed for tackling the above challenges. Several women and children suffer from deficiencies of micronutrients such as iron, iodine, zinc, vitamin A and vitamin B12. Biofortification is one way of providing access to micronutrients. We should also promote naturally biofortified crops such as sweet potato, moringa (drumsticks), breadfruit and various berries which are rich in micronutrients.[40] Dev and Pandey[41] provide nine pathways for safe and healthy diets for achieving nutritional security in India. These are: (a) improving dietary diversity, (b) reducing post-harvest losses, (c) biofortification of staples, (d) empowerment of women, (e) enforcing standards of foods safety, packaging and labelling, (f) improving WASH (water, sanitation and hygiene), (g) food safety awareness and nutrition education, (h) implementing food safety and nutrition programmes, and (i) using ICT.

Inclusive food systems need strong social protection programmes. India has a long experience of these programmes. Strengthening India's National Rural Employment Guarantee Act, public distribution system (PDS), nutrition programmes like ICDS and mid-day meal programmes can improve livelihoods and nutrition for the poor. In the PDS, there is a need to offer millets for better nutrition.

(b) Sustainability and Climate Resilience

Agro-ecology, the sustainability of agriculture, and climate change issues are becoming much more important now than ever before.[42]

A review of water, energy and fertilizer subsidies that encourage unsustainable resource use is needed.

According to Swaminathan, there are two major pathways towards fostering an evergreen revolution. The first one is organic farming. The second pathway is green agriculture wherein 'ecologically sound practices like conservation farming, integrated pest management, integrated nutrient supply and natural conservation and enhancement, are promoted.'[43]

Agriculture and Climate Resilience

In the COP26 meeting in Glasgow, India announced that it would aim to attain net-zero emissions by 2070, draw 50 per cent of its consumed energy from renewable sources by 2030, and cut its carbon emissions by a billion tonnes by the same year. India wants commitments from developed countries to providing finance, the transfer of technology and emission reductions, given their historically high consumption patterns. Climate justice is another issue. A multi-pronged action plan covering all major carbon-emitting sectors can help accelerate India's progress towards the net-zero goal.

The agriculture sector is the most vulnerable to climate change. Agriculture is part of the problem and the solution. It alone contributes 13 per cent of global emissions—amounting to 30 per cent if we add deforestation. India needs more adaptation measures while developed countries want more mitigation measures.

Climate-smart agriculture is being discussed throughout the world to reduce GHG emissions and increase resilience. The FAO[44] has discussed strategies needed for climate-smart agriculture. It is defined as agriculture that sustainably increases productivity resilience (adaptation), reduces or removes GHGs (mitigation), and enhances the achievement of national food security and development goals. The FAO[45] also says that there is a need for raising the technical capacity of farmers, particularly smallholders, to enable them to adopt climate-smart agricultural practices.

Conservation agriculture and zero budget natural farming are some of the methods that have to be used as part of adaptation and mitigation measures to tackle climate change. Of course, they are not complete substitutes for chemical-based farming.

Zero Budget Natural Farming (ZBNF)

Subhash Palekar has promoted ZBNF. It only uses natural resources like soil, water, air and cow urine. Andhra Pradesh has become the first State to adopt ZBNF. The State has targeted covering the entirety of its agricultural land under natural farming by 2027. A study by Das and others[46] examines the benefits of natural farming. This study shows that yields are lower under ZBNF compared to the method of integrated crop management (ICM). The study cautions that there may be an adverse impact on food security if ZBNF is implemented on a large scale. It recommends a large-scale assessment of the natural farming method before recommending it for wider adoption in the country.

The *Global Food Policy Report 2022* prepared by the International Food Policy Research Institute (IFPRI) recommends the following on climate change and food systems: (a) R&D for climate-resilient, resource-efficient and sustainable innovations in food systems, (b) holistic, inclusive governance and management of water, land, forest and energy resources, (c) promoting healthy diets and the increased sustainability of food production, (d) improving value chain efficiency, facilitating trade, and reducing food loss, (e) inclusion and social protection, and (e) reorienting financial flows and attracting new finance.[47]

Institutions and Governance

Strengthening institutions and governance is crucial for achieving growth, equality and sustainability in agriculture. Institutions throughout the agricultural value chains and food systems are important for better governance and effective implementation of policies. There are several examples of best practices in institutions relating to alternative markets, contract farming, self-help groups, farmer-producer companies, women's collectives like the Kudumbashree Mission in Kerala, institutions relating to canal and groundwater irrigation and natural resource management. We have to scale up some of these successful institutions for improving agricultural development.

Macro Policies and Non-Agriculture

(a) Macro Policies are Equally Important for Indian Agriculture

Agricultural scientists and economists generally restrict themselves to policies related to the farm sector. However, there is a need to look at macro policies and the non-agriculture sector while analyzing issues on agriculture. Policies on fiscal, monetary, trade, the exchange rate, and industry and services have an impact on agricultural development.

(b) The Solution for Agriculture Lies in Non-Agriculture

Finally, the role of non-agriculture is equally important for sustainable agriculture and food systems. We have to invest in agriculture for raising livelihoods, but simultaneously, shift the population from agriculture to non-agriculture over time. NABARD's All India Rural Financial Inclusion Survey (NAFIS) in 2015–16 indicated that only 23 per cent of rural income was from agriculture (cultivation+livestock) if we considered all rural households. It also revealed that agricultural households did not depend only on farm income but on multiple sources for their livelihoods. Some economists like Srinivasan[48] argue that agricultural policies may be important, but a fundamental factor for low productivity in agriculture lies in non-agriculture. Non-agriculture is not absorbing labour force from agriculture. The lack of labour reforms is considered one of the reasons for the non-absorption of labour in manufacturing.[49] This is similar to the views put forward by Arthur Lewis, who produced a model of 'economic development with unlimited supplies of labour', which envisaged capital accumulation in the modern industrial sector so as to draw labour from the subsistence agricultural sector.[50] Therefore, labour-intensive manufacturing and services can reduce pressure on agriculture. The income from agriculture is not sufficient for smallholders and informal workers. Strengthening rural MSMEs and food processing is part of the solution.

The Way Forward

There have been significant achievements in Indian agriculture since Independence. However, it faces many challenges in achieving the goals of agricultural development, viz. growth, inclusion and sustainability. The 'deficit' mindset of the 1960s has to be changed. India is no longer a country with food shortages. The structural reforms and stabilization policies introduced in India in 1991 did not undertake reforms for agriculture. It was thought that the reforms in industry would help agriculture indirectly. There is a need for direct reforms in agriculture to improve growth and farmers' incomes.

Repurposing and reforms in agriculture are necessary in the changing landscape. Global economic and geopoliticial developments will impact India. The new context and priorities for Indian agriculture are the diversification and modernization of agriculture which is demand-based—raising productivity and incomes for farmers, promoting exports, focusing on post-harvest activities and value chains, improving food and nutrition security, sustainability and climate resilience.

The elements of the new narrative are: increasing total factor productivity, marketing reforms, providing remunerative prices to farmers, reducing subsidies and increasing investments, promoting startups for innovations, developing digital technology, and promoting water management. For inclusion, boosting the viability of small holdings, women's empowerment in agriculture, and accessible and affordable healthy diets are needed. Sustainability includes an evergreen revolution with climate-resilient agriculture, precision farming, encouragement to organic and zero-based natural farming in a gradual manner, inclusive governance, and the effective management of water, land, forest and energy resources. Agriculture and food systems are important as India has to feed its population of 1.66 billion by 2050, with inclusion and sustainability.

There are suggestions to replace the MSP, input subsidies and APMCs with direct benefit transfers. It is also advocated that India should institute an agriculture and food marketing council (AFM) on the lines of the GST Council to discuss Centre-State issues on food and agriculture.

To conclude, agriculture is a State subject according to the Indian Constitution. States in India allocate significant amounts of funds to agriculture in their State budgets. The States spend 60 per cent of total government expenditure, 70 per cent of education and health spending, and a larger share in public capital expenditure. The Centre has to work closely with States in a spirit of cooperative federalism for improving the incomes and livelihoods, promoting inclusive growth and sustainability in agriculture. Achieving high growth is important, but growth without inclusiveness and sustainability will not be useful.

A.K. Bhattacharya

Waiting for Consensus: How India's Political Economy Impacts Its Economic Reforms

Economic reforms do not take place in a political vacuum. This may sound like a truism. But ignoring it may result in us not recognizing that the quality and pace of economic reforms have an intricate relationship with the prevailing political environment. And this relationship is not as simple as a linear equation between cause and effect. A stable political environment may not always necessarily encourage economic reforms as it resets the terms of engagement that a political system has with its citizens, and thereby influences the ruling establishment's commitment to reforms in various ways. Governments enjoying the benefit of strong political capital may not always be encouraged to experiment with such economic reforms that can impair their vote-winning capability.

Conversely, the path towards effective economic reforms does not always get smoother if there is political instability. Yet, there is the much-celebrated instance of a reform-minded ruling establishment in India, implementing policy changes to unshackle the economy despite a dangerous mix of fraught politics, a fragile government and an economic crisis. In brief, the chemistry between politics and economic reforms is complex and often unpredictable. How and under what political circumstances can a government implement economic reforms without any backlash has been a subject of close examination by scholars.

A recent paper from the International Monetary Fund (IMF) has argued that reforms 'do not lead to electoral costs when implemented in a way that internalises political economy considerations.'[1]

The IMF paper presents three possibilities. One, reforms incur significant electoral costs only when these are implemented in the run-up to the elections. And if these reforms are undertaken earlier in the tenure of the ruling party, their electoral prospects are not in jeopardy. Two, reforms could become a political liability if these are implemented during a phase of weak economic activity, but their consequences are benign if they are carried out in good times. And three, reforms which give rise to adverse 'distributional effects—notably some types of financial deregulation and external capital account liberalization under some conditions' can be electorally costly for the ruling party.

The IMF paper, therefore, recommends only those reforms that are well crafted, well timed, transparently framed with proper communication, and are carefully implemented. This is easier said than done. However, the paper suggests four strategies in this respect. One, governments should act on implementing reforms soon after an electoral victory, before their 'political honeymoon' with the electorate begins to fade out. Two, there are greater chances of a success in implementing reforms when economic conditions are favourable. Three, reforms should be politically savvy in that they must take care of the adverse effects on income distribution in the early stages of their implementation. Reforms work better when complemented with the creation of social safety nets or job training or retraining programmes. And finally, reforms must enjoy the support and commitment of the top political leadership and they must secure prior support of business and civil society.

How relevant are these prescriptions for the Indian reforms experience? To be sure, the IMF paper relies on the experiments and lessons from reforms in only two countries—Peru and Spain. But it would appear that Latin America or Europe is, in many ways, different from Asia. At the same time, those lessons—recounted in the IMF paper—may also have a strong resonance with the Indian experiments with reforms, in particular the years after 1991. What those experiments with reforms in the last three decades bring out eloquently, therefore, is a highly uncertain and unstable relationship between the political establishment of the day and the nature of economic policymaking.

This essay attempts an exploration of that relationship in India and how it has evolved since the country's Independence. This assessment is divided into four sections, with the first phase of assessment beginning in 1947 and covering the next four decades till 1991. It explores the manner in which governments under different political dispensations and different prime ministers defined their approach to economic policymaking during this period.

The second phase of assessment covers five years from 1991 to 1996—when the country, under the prime ministership of P.V. Narasimha Rao, witnessed the first burst of economic reforms before they lost steam. The third phase covers the years from 1996 to 2014 when different coalition governments dealt with the reforms agenda in their own ways.

The fourth and final phase covers 10 years from 2014 to 2024 when Prime Minister Narendra Modi ran a single-party majority government with the Bharatiya Janata Party at the helm, and redefined the pace and dimension of economic reforms. Among the key questions this essay tries to answer are: Do stable governments at the Centre provide greater sustenance to economic reforms? How has political consensus on economic reforms developed in India over the years? Finally, what needs to be done to ensure that its political economy becomes more conducive to a steady pace of economic reforms?

From Independence to 1991

About two years before India gained freedom from British rule in 1947, an important document was produced by leading industrialists, economic policymakers and bankers to provide an outline of an investment programme and policy priorities that the country should adopt after Independence. The document—'A Brief Memorandum Outlining a Plan of Economic Development for India'[2]—was also known as the Bombay Plan, providing an overall perspective on the economic planning that would be needed for 15 years after India became independent. While underlining the need for investing in education and healthcare facilities—in addition to reforming agriculture through the consolidation of small landholdings and reducing the huge debt burden on farmers—the document noted that the government would have to find the resources for setting up basic industries, even as small and large private-sector companies could be free to take up the manufacture of consumption goods. Among the eminent industrialists who contributed to this document were Purshottamdas Thakurdas, J.R.D. Tata, G.D. Birla, Kasturbhai Lalbhai and Lala Shri Ram. But a more important contributor was John Matthai, an economist who would become the finance minister of India in 1948.

The Bombay Plan, to be sure, was a source of great comfort for Indian industrialists as well. They were assured that while the government would be focused on setting up basic industries, the private sector would be encouraged to enter the manufacturing sector to produce consumption goods and meet the growing demand in a newly independent country. However, things changed slowly but steadily in about a decade. The turn towards a socialistic model of economic development became evident soon after the Planning Commission was set up to assist the government's economic policymaking in 1950. In the next six years, the shift in India's economic policy was completed.

By 1953, the winter session of Parliament decided to adopt a socialistic model of economic development. At around the same time, a handful of private airlines were nationalized and the state-owned Indian Airlines was born, while simultaneously, the Tata-owned Air India was taken over by the Jawaharlal Nehru government even though it embittered the prime minister's relations with J.R.D. Tata, who led the group at that time and, ironically, was one of the authors of the Bombay Plan. Two years later in 1955, the country's largest private bank—the Imperial Bank of India—was nationalized and rechristened the State Bank of India. And a year later, over 245 privately owned life insurance companies were merged into the Life Insurance Corporation (LIC) and the government became its new owner. This was just around the time that the Nehru government unveiled its Industrial Policy Resolution of 1956, which strengthened the licensing regime and mandated that the commanding heights of the economy would be under the control of state-owned enterprises.[3]

The Nehru government, during these years, was enjoying a majority in Parliament that was robust and unchallenged. The government had the political capital to bring about necessary factor-market reforms and allow the private sector a free play in the manufacturing sector or bring about agricultural reforms. The Bombay Plan had indeed outlined such a course of policy action for the first 15 years after Independence. To be sure, the first two finance ministers appointed by Nehru did indicate a path towards liberalization. But they had relatively short tenures. R.K. Shanmukham Chetty quit in the wake of a minor controversy over following a parliamentary protocol,[4] and John Matthai resigned over his differences with Nehru on the question of setting up the Planning Commission.[5] And Nehru was apprehensive that his third finance minister C.D. Deshmukh may not approve of the turn his government's economic policies were taking towards a socialistic pattern of development. So when asked, Deshmukh gave his green signal to Nehru's socialistic economic policies. Thus, the political economy of the 1950s endorsed a turn away from a free-enterprise economy. Nehru accepted the Bombay Plan's recommendation on the state setting up basic industries, but made little effort to encourage the private sector to play a larger role in the manufacturing sector. Instead, controls on private industries were made more stringent through its industrial policy and steps were taken to nationalize the country's largest private bank, all aviation companies including one that was led by one of India's leading industrial houses, and life insurance companies. A strong government, ironically, was working against reformist economic policies.

What happened in the latter half of the 1960s and the 1970s was a little different. After Nehru's demise in May 1964, a seemingly weak leader Lal Bahadur Shastri took charge of the government for about 18 months. But in outlining his economic policy plans, he showed how strong and committed his government was to reforming the Indian economy. Assisted by his principal advisor L.K. Jha, Shastri outlined an economic liberalization strategy that included reforms of trade and industrial policies, in addition to an exchange rate adjustment by devaluing the Indian rupee.[6] Many industry leaders were unhappy and Shastri even had to let go his finance minister T.T. Krishnamachari, who was not comfortable with the devaluation proposal. But Shastri died prematurely in January 1966. His devaluation proposal was implemented by his successor Indira Gandhi six months later, along with marginal trade liberalization measures. But those policies were gradually reversed under the newly appointed prime minister, who used such a reversal to assert her leadership and to steer policymaking in a different direction.[7] Drought and a war with Pakistan in 1965–66 had also taken a heavy toll on the Indian economy. A weak prime minister in 1964–65 had shown the courage to initiate bold economic reforms, but another prime minister, in her bid to strengthen her hold on the Congress and the government, decided to turn away from reforms. This is how unstable and complex the equation between India's political economy and its economic reforms has been.

In 1966, Indira Gandhi's government was threatened from within because of dissension in the Congress party. Gandhi was trying hard to assert her independence from the Congress old guard, popularly described as the Syndicate, and led by leaders like former Madras chief minister K. Kamaraj, Andhra Pradesh leader Neelam Sanjiva Reddy, chief minister of Mysore S. Nijalingappa, and the chief of the West Bengal Congress Committee Atulya Ghosh. It was as a part of her political strategy to assert her leadership without being subjugated by the Syndicate that Gandhi embarked on an economic policy drive that, from 1969 to 1971, saw the nationalization of 14 banks in the teeth of opposition from her own finance minister Morarji Desai, the imposition of draconian monopoly laws to keep large industries and their growth under check, and the nationalization of a host of sick textile companies.

The Congress was a substantially weakened political force after the general elections in 1967 saw the party winning only 283 seats out of a total Lok Sabha seat strength of 516. In the election of 1962 which the Congress fought under Jawaharlal Nehru's leadership, it had won 361 seats. Indira Gandhi had to struggle hard to gain full control of the party by sidelining the powerful Syndicate leaders. But it was a weak government with fewer seats in the Lok Sabha, and the ruling party was facing internal leadership struggles. And yet the government took some bold decisions. Those decisions were not reformist in spirit, but they changed the contours of economic policymaking in India. A weak government did take bold decisions even though they were not reformist in the truest sense of the term—raising questions about the thesis that it is only a strong and stable government that makes decisive policy moves.

The correlation between a strong government and bold decisions, however, was seen once again when Indira Gandhi returned to the Lok Sabha after the 1971 general elections with a greater number of seats for the Congress faction that she was leading—she won 352 out of the 441 seats that her party fought. She doubled down on the kind of socialistic economic policies that she had initiated from 1969 to 1971. She nationalized coal and general insurance industries, repealed the old Foreign Exchange Regulation Act and introduced a new one to impose curbs on companies with more than 40 per cent foreign equity, and abolished the special privileges and financial benefits that were assured to the princely states at the time they acceded to the Union of India in 1947. Once again, it was a strong and stable government that was taking bold economic policy steps without worrying about the political consequences of those decisions.

After a brief interlude that saw the Janata Party government in power between 1977 and 1979, when reforms made no major movement either way, the 1980s saw the advent of slow and halting steps towards economic liberalization. The gradual relaxation of the industrial licensing policy or the introduction of a long-term fiscal policy were steps taken by governments led by strong leaders, enjoying undisputed support in Parliament. To tide over its balance of payments challenges caused partly by the two successive oil price shocks, the Indira Gandhi government took a loan of over $5.7 billion from the IMF under its Extended Fund Facility (EFF). The loan amount was the largest sanctioned by the Bretton Woods institution to any one of its members till then.

There was political resistance from the Opposition parties and even from within the ruling Congress party, but the Indira Gandhi government went ahead and negotiated a loan with reform conditionalities, which, however, avoided hard steps like the devaluation of the currency or a reduction in its tariffs. Notably, the decision to take an IMF loan indicated how a government appeared to be willing to use its political capital to take hard policy decisions. That was a Congress government under Indira Gandhi which had returned to power with a decent majority in 1980, barely three years after its banishment from New Delhi in the wake of the excesses it perpetrated on people and Opposition politicians during the Emergency from 1975 to 1977.

A new facet of the equation between reforms and the political economy was noticeable in 1984. Even as the Indira Gandhi government had initiated the process of gradual relaxations in industrial policy, a bump in export earnings improved India's external sector significantly by 1984. This helped the Indira Gandhi government forgo the remaining instalments of the IMF loan. The negotiations for the IMF loan and the announcement of giving up the claims on the remaining instalments thereof highlighted the contrasting styles that arose out of how the political economy was geared towards dealing with ushering in any hard policy reforms, and that too at the behest of an international organization. The IMF loan was negotiated in utmost secrecy, while the decision to forgo the last few instalments of the loan (about $1.16 billion) was announced by Indira Gandhi's finance minister in his budget speech as a vindication of its freedom from any influence of an international organization.

The experience of reforms was somewhat different during the Rajiv Gandhi government that was formed at the end of 1984 when the Congress, under him, won the general elections by winning a record number of 414 seats in the Lok Sabha. In the first couple of years, the Rajiv Gandhi government did unveil a moderate dose of economic reforms including the further liberalization of the industrial licensing regime and the launch of the long-term fiscal policy. And yet, when a controversy erupted over an alleged payment of bribes by the Rajiv Gandhi government in a deal for purchasing guns for the Indian Army, the promised economic policy reforms took a backseat despite the fact that the Congress still retained its political strength at the Centre. The huge political firepower enjoyed by the Rajiv Gandhi government soon lost both its fire and its power. The government continued to take a few important steps to liberalize trade and industrial policies, but it appeared to be rudderless in the wake of the bribery scandal over payments to the Swedish gun manufacturer Bofors. Soon, the Rajiv Gandhi government began relying more on borrowing to finance investments, which did boost growth but also drove the Indian economy to two related problems—fiscal indiscipline with a rapidly rising fiscal deficit, and a balance of payments crisis with its current account deficit widening to unsustainable levels.

The equation between India's political economy and economic reforms during the first 44 years after Independence shows that a government with strong political capital did bring about major economic policy shifts, but most of those changes were not in favour of economic reforms. Instead, these changes were to move India towards a socialistic pattern of economy with the state gaining control of major economic activities through nationalization and state-controlled planning. The pace of such changes sped up when the ruling establishment's political survival came under threat.

In contrast, the move towards economic reforms took place under three different sets of circumstances. Under the seemingly weak leadership of Shastri, reforms gained momentum but ran out of steam. With the formation of a strong government with a single-party majority, reforms did get a boost, but these were planned almost on the sly and there was hardly any public justification for these. And finally, once a strong government came under political attack from Opposition parties, there was even less focus on reforms. The liberalization of economic policies suffered, even though the economy hurtled towards a fiscal and balance of payments crisis. A common factor during these four decades was the absence of a powerful lobby for economic reforms, either within these governments or outside.

The Reforms Era: From 1991 to 1996

India's economic reforms in 1991 were executed at a rapid pace not just in the wake of an unprecedented economic crisis, but also against the backdrop of an uncertain political situation. Understandably, this spawned an assumption that the dramatic changes in fiscal, trade and financial-sector policies as part of India's famous economic reforms in 1991 could not have taken place without the accompanying political crisis of that time. How true is this assumption?

Two factors need to be kept in mind. Politically, the Congress party did not have the required number of seats in the Lok Sabha to command a majority on its own after the elections in 1991. Its seat strength was only 232—well short of a majority. But with the support of Janata Dal from the outside, it formed a minority government. With two general elections having already been held—one in 1989 and the other in 1991—the political parties were not very keen on forcing another general election. They also realized that the Indian economy was in a perilous situation and needed to be steered by a government for at least a few years without any political disruption.

Thus, even though many of the political parties in the Opposition benches were not in complete agreement with the bold reforms that were being implemented by the Congress government in 1991, they did not muster the political courage to escalate their opposition to a point that could plunge the government into another political crisis leading to its fall, and pushing the country into another general election. The fact of the matter is that when those bold reforms were being undertaken in the first 100 days after the formation of the Rao government in June 1991, neither Prime Minister P.V. Narasimha Rao nor his finance minister Manmohan Singh were elected members of Parliament yet. Rao became a member of the Lok Sabha a few months later after winning a by-election in Nandyal in Andhra Pradesh, and Singh became a Rajya Sabha member representing Assam.

The second factor at play was the choice made by Narasimha Rao in appointing a technocrat, Singh, as his finance minister. That decision helped substantially blunt any political targeting that the Opposition leaders could have planned against a minority government for having taken such major economic policy decisions. Singh was seen to be a finance minister who was not in politics and was taking those steps as a technocrat in the interest of the Indian economy—to rescue it from an unprecedented crisis. If Narasimha Rao had chosen a professional politician to be at the helm of the finance ministry, it is likely that the Opposition parties would not have been so benign or mild in their response to the many decisions that dramatically altered the country's economic laws. Not only was industrial licensing scrapped for most industries except a few strategic ones, but monopoly laws and export subsidies were also abolished.

What is often not recognized is that the political economy of 1991 was not that receptive to the hard economic reforms that were initiated by Rao and Singh. There were many hiccups and bumps on the way. Even the process of depreciating the Indian currency against the US dollar in two stages—by about 9 per cent on 1 July and then again by about 12 per cent on 3 July—faced many uncertain moments. After the first round of devaluation, the reaction was sharp and adverse. Recall that the finance minister took a politically astute decision. He chose not to go to the Union Cabinet for its endorsement or to Parliament for its approval before devaluing the currency, on the grounds that this decision was in the domain of the country's apex bank the Reserve Bank of India, and did not require an assent from the country's top political leadership in charge of governance or the legislature. Prime Minister Narasimha Rao had agreed with this approach. But after the hue and cry about how the Indian government had allowed itself to be dictated to by international financial institutions like the World Bank and the International Monetary Fund, Rao developed cold feet. On the morning of 3 July, the prime minister asked his finance minister to hold back the second round of devaluation of about 12 per cent that was scheduled to take place that day. The finance minister used a clever ploy. After checking with the Reserve Bank of India, Singh told his prime minister that the process of devaluation had already begun and it would not be possible to stall it at that time. To be sure, this was a tactical reply and not the whole truth. The first round of devaluation had been completed and technically, the second round of the currency adjustment could have been held back. Of course, this would have substantially set back the potential gains from the devaluation exercise and stymied the other trade policy and exchange rate policy changes that Singh had planned. But the reality of the kind of political economy that prevailed at that time could not be missed. If only the economic policy team at the helm had not held firm on its reforms agenda, the political economy could have halted the reform process at a very early stage.

Such dangers lurked even when the Narasimha Rao government ventured into ambitious industrial policy reforms that scrapped licensing for most industries. Preparations for a new-look industrial policy had begun much earlier. A draft of a liberalized industrial licensing policy had been prepared when the V.P. Singh government was formed in 1989.[8] But that government did not get an opportunity to implement the changes as it fell, paving the way for the short-lived Chandra Shekhar government which also fell prematurely, even before it could present the budget for 1991–92 in February 1991. The P.V. Narasimha Rao government formed in June 1991 dusted off that policy paper and considered it after minor changes.

However, after the devaluation experience, political opposition to the kind of reforms Rao and Singh were bringing in began to grow roots. Indeed, there were serious political reservations about how Singh was rewriting Nehruvian economic policies with little regard for the Congress and its economic heritage. When the proposal for revising the industrial policy was taken up by the Cabinet, the prime minister had no option other than referring the proposed industrial policy to a high-level ministerial committee for its review. This was yet another example of how the political economy in India would react to proposals for major economic reforms. In the end, what helped were some cosmetic changes in the industrial policy proposal—some clever introduction of phrases that extolled the virtues of Nehruvian economic policies, and a reiteration that the new industrial policy was not opposed in spirit to the economic philosophy of the Congress.[9]

Another clever ploy was to let the new industrial policy be tabled as a statement just before the presentation of the budget for 1991–92. Thus, the new policy was not even read out in Parliament and its tabling was immediately followed by Singh's budget speech, diverting the attention of parliamentarians and political parties to the proposals in the budget, instead of the dismantling of the industrial licensing regime. It was economic reforms on the sly and this became necessary because of the nature of India's political economy that would not allow reforms to be introduced through a big-bang announcement.

What helped the government roll out economic reforms in 1991 was also its success in convincing industry organizations and prominent industry leaders about the need for the kind of changes in trade and industrial policies that it was bringing about. Using the influence that Tarun Das, director-general of the Confederation of Engineering Industry (which later became the Confederation of Indian Industry), wielded among its members and other industry leaders, the Rao-Singh duo succeeded in implementing many reforms with muted resistance and relative ease. This too was an important factor that facilitated reforms in 1991.

But even during the heady days of economic reforms, not every decision could be implemented without any political hitch. Singh's bold decision to increase fertilizer prices by 40 per cent and align them to market-linked principles met with a major political pushback.[10] Within weeks of the decision on a fertilizer price hike, farmers' organizations supported by many political parties in Punjab, Haryana and Andhra Pradesh raised a banner of revolt against the P.V. Narasimha Rao government. So shrill were the protests that the Congress Parliamentary Party was forced to hold a meeting in early August 1991 to discuss the fertilizer price increase move.

Singh had expected that his prime minister would support the reform which would have saved as much as ₹1,800 crore of subsidies a year (or almost a sixth of the total subsidies bill of the government). But Singh was seen to be the fall guy. Many Congress leaders argued that Singh did not understand the political costs of his move and his decision had to be reviewed. Singh decided to quit in protest, but Rao dissuaded him on the grounds that the finance minister should not be deserting his prime minister at a time when he was under such a severe political attack. Singh took back his resignation and rolled back the fertilizer price increase to only 30 per cent. Protests by farmers had been brought under control, and a partially reduced increase in fertilizer prices went through. Two steps forward followed by one step backward did represent some forward movement, even though the progress was achieved through a compromise. Singh's experiments with reforms on fertilizer prices were something similar and reflective of the fraught nature of India's political economy prevailing at that time.

It is important to recognize that even as the Narasimha Rao government inched towards acquiring a reasonable degree of political stability with more support for the Congress in the Lok Sabha, the fervour for further economic reforms cooled off significantly. The pace of reforms, unfortunately, was inversely proportional to the government's political stability—the greater the strength of the ruling party in Parliament, the lower was the desire to push through more economic reforms. The urgency for reforms was also on the wane as the Indian economy improved with steady fiscal consolidation, rising foreign exchange reserves, and a declining current account deficit.

What also shifted the government's focus away from economic reforms were two major developments. In December 1992, a frenzied mob of Hindu fanatics demolished the Babri Mosque in Ayodhya, egged on by leaders of the Bharatiya Janata Party. This was followed by riots in different parts of the country including Mumbai. No sooner had the political upheaval after the mosque's demolition subsided than a major stock market scandal rocked the government. The securities scam masterminded by stock market operator Harshad Mehta scarred Singh's reputation as well. Singh decided to quit after the Joint Parliamentary Committee probing the securities scam made uncharitable comments about his conduct. Rao and Singh's focus on the government's economic reforms agenda got diluted significantly. So it was not just a question of the Rao government gaining in political strength and the economy's health improving, but the government also had to douse many other political and economic fires before it could refocus on implementing the remaining reforms to which it was committed.

Lessons from Coalition Governments: From 1996 to 2014

The era of coalition governments at the Centre—which began in the late 1980s after the end of the Rajiv Gandhi regime—continued till 2014. During this period, governments were not ruled by any single political party. Of course, these coalitions were led by a political party like the Janata Dal from 1988 to 1990, the Samajwadi Janata Party from 1990 to 1991, the Congress from 1991 to 1996, the Bharatiya Janata Party from 1996 to 2004, and the Congress again from 2004 to 2014. But these parties were supported by other groups to help them gain a majority in the Lok Sabha. In most cases, the alliance partners were part of the government. The lone exception was the government of Chandra Shekhar from 1989 to 1990, where the Congress party supported it from the outside. Thus when the Congress withdrew its support in February 1991, the Chandra Shekhar government also fell, forcing the country into another general election just about three years after the previous one and at a time when the Indian economy was facing its worst crisis.

But what stands out in terms of political economy impacting the reforms process was how India's economic policies were held to ransom by political crises. Even international financial institutions like the World Bank and the IMF would decline any Indian request for assistance till such time a stable government was in place after the elections.[11] Delegations of senior Indian government officials were sent to Washington to hold consultations with the IMF for a structural loan linked to India implementing the much-needed economic reforms. However, all that India got was a small amount of a short-term loan, while the requests for a larger loan were kept pending till the Indian government could return to them after the elections. Talks for such loans were indeed resumed after July 1991, when the Rao-Singh duo took bold reformist measures and presented a budget that secured the confidence of the Bretton Woods institutions.

But once the immediate economic crisis was overcome, the pace of implementing subsequent reforms slowed considerably. This was the most striking in two sectors—insurance and trade. Reforming the insurance sector was one of the last proposals that Singh, as finance minister, had mooted. In 1994, a year after Singh set up a committee to restructure the insurance industry in line with the way the changes in the financial sector were introduced, the Rao government embarked on a difficult path that would eventually allow the private sector and foreign capital to enter the sector, but not before some politically trying and uncertain moments. The recommendations of the committee, headed by R.N. Malhotra, a former governor of the Reserve Bank of India, were accepted by Singh. The committee's recommendations were fundamentally reformist as it wanted the private sector to enter the insurance industry (the private sector was barred from the life insurance sector in the 1950s by the Nehru government, and from the general insurance sector in the 1970s by a government run by his daughter, Indira Gandhi). More importantly, the committee suggested that foreign companies be allowed to enter the insurance sector by floating Indian companies, preferably a joint venture with Indian partners—a suggestion that turned out to be a bone of contention.

Behind it all was the question of fixing a cap on the foreign equity participation in insurance companies, which soon snowballed into a major political controversy. Should foreign companies be given a majority control of an Indian company operating in a key financial services sector like providing insurance? There were views that without majority control being ceded to the foreign company, no significant insurance player would like to enter the Indian market. Alternative suggestions were to place a 26 per cent or a 49 per cent cap on foreign equity in the insurance sector. When the Congress or the succeeding United Front government in the mid-1990s wanted to push for such reforms, the opposition came from the Bharatiya Janata Party. And when the Bharatiya Janata Party came to power after 1998, its proposal on allowing foreign companies to operate in the insurance sector met with similar opposition from the Congress party, which was then in the Opposition.

Clearly, the political economy of reforms was witnessing a different phase in India. Scoring a political point by creating hurdles in the government's plans on such reforms became an instrument used by almost all major political parties when they were in the Opposition. They were neither worried nor embarrassed by the fact that they had mooted the same proposal earlier when they ran the government. It was political opportunism at its worst and economic reforms were the casualty. This went on for a few years. It was only in 1999 that the BJP government could manage to get Parliament to pass a law to set up the Insurance Regulatory and Development Authority of India (IRDAI) as an autonomous body to regulate and develop the insurance industry.

By April 2000, IRDAI was incorporated as a statutory body. Note that the cap on foreign equity in insurance companies could be set only at 26 per cent—a level that would not be tinkered with till 2015 when the BJP government would raise it to 49 per cent, and to 74 per cent in 2021. Equally notable is the fact that for almost 15 years, 10 of which were ruled by the Congress-led United Progressive Alliance with Singh as prime minister (who, as the finance minister, had liberalized policy and relaxed curbs on foreign investment in the 1990s), the foreign equity cap in the Indian insurance sector remained unchanged. It is also a comment on the political economy prevailing in the UPA era of 10 years—when the government that was powerful enough to have brought in a series of rights-based laws to guarantee rural jobs, food and information, could not move on relaxing the foreign investment cap in either the insurance sector or even the retail industry.

It was only the BJP government formed in 2014 which raised the foreign equity cap. Note that 2014 also marked the return of a single-party majority rule at the Centre after two and a half decades. It was a majority government, there was no major economic crisis either, and yet the insurance sector liberalization got a welcome fillip under the Modi government in 2015 and again in 2021, although the latter phase of liberalization could be attributed partly to the reforms that got pushed during the Covid pandemic when parliamentary scrutiny was a little relaxed. Insurance reforms in India, therefore, bore the impact of political opportunism. Instead of a strong political resistance scuppering economic reforms, it was political opportunism that came in the way of furthering liberalization. The absence of an economic crisis also contributed to the lack of momentum.

Trade policy reforms also experienced a rocky ride, though not as politically turbulent as witnessed by the insurance sector. Trade policy suffered from a few rollbacks after a big-bang approach under a crisis situation had ushered in major reforms in 1991. For the next five years, tariffs were brought down. Against a peak import tariff of over 300 per cent, they were reduced to just about 50 per cent by February 1995. The reduction in the peak rate of customs duty between 1991 and 1995 was gradual and phased through Finance Minister Singh's five budgets—from over 300 per cent before the reforms to 150 per cent in 1991, 110 per cent in 1992, 85 per cent in 1993, 65 per cent in 1994 and 50 per cent in 1995. The import duty on capital goods for general projects and machinery—which was 85 per cent before the reforms—was unified and reduced to 25 per cent for almost 80 per cent of all machinery items. The customs duty on power projects and related machinery was cut to 20 per cent, and the duty on fertilizer projects was slashed to nil, along with the lowering of duties on ferrous and non-ferrous metals to 35–40 per cent by 1995. Equally significant was the slashing of the number of customs duty rates to just 12. In the next two years, even though there was a change of government with the United Front coalition at the helm, the peak rate of customs duty was brought down further to 40 per cent.[12]

A new coalition government at the Centre—led by the right-wing Bharatiya Janata Party—showed that the political beliefs of the ruling party were a critical factor in the pursuit of economic reforms. This was effectively captured by a conversation between the newly appointed finance minister of the Atal Bihari Vajpayee government Yashwant Sinha and his chief economic adviser Shankar N. Acharya (who was among the senior officials instrumental in bringing down the import tariff under the previous two regimes). Sinha asked Acharya whether the economist would be comfortable working under a BJP government, implying that he might not be comfortable with the party's political beliefs in Swadeshi economic policies (essentially implying self-reliance). Acharya's frank response ('Sir, I am a civil servant; it's my duty to offer the best economic advice I can to whoever is my minister') seemed to have settled the issue for the moment. But the conversation underlined the deep undercurrents of how a changing political economy was beginning to influence the course of India's economic reforms.[13]

Not surprisingly, Sinha's budgets unveiled a set of measures that temporarily changed the direction of import tariff reforms. His first budget in 1998 did endorse the idea of a gradual reduction in the customs duty on a wide range of industrial raw materials, machinery and goods, effected over the last few years. Referring to them, he said: 'These measures have enhanced the competitiveness of Indian industry.' But springing a surprise, he said that even as the domestic industry was responding favourably to the restructuring of customs duties and had shown resilience, it also needed to improve its competitive efficiency to meet the challenges of global competition. Since concerns over the reduction in the customs duty could not be ignored, the path of transition had to be calibrated to ensure that the adjustment process for the Indian industry was orderly, without leading to any serious disruption. For adopting this approach, Sinha put the onus on the

Indian industry, a cross-section of which had expressed concern over its health as a consequence of the sharp reduction in import duties. Sinha's argument was that while indigenous goods were subjected to sales tax and other local taxes, imported goods were free from such a burden. Thus, Sinha, in order to provide 'a level playing field to the domestic industry', levied an eight per cent tax on imports, which he believed was approximately equal to the burden of local taxes on domestic producers of goods.

The template of India's political economy that had influenced its economic reforms since the 1990s changed. It was a regressive move as far as import tariff reforms were concerned. But Sinha did not present the move to either industry or the political classes as a protectionist measure. His explanation was to justify the eight per cent special additional duty (SAD) on all imports—barring a few classified goods—as a response to a legitimate demand for a level-playing field. It was not a convincing justification. But such a justification would be used by subsequent BJP governments as well while raising import tariffs.

A reflection of that era—when import tariff reductions had been by and large accepted—was the sharp reaction evoked by the move to levy the eight per cent special additional duty. It was criticized by many and welcomed by only a few. Many industrialists feared that the new duty would trigger cost-push inflation and throw industrial activity out of gear at a time when it was facing a slowdown. So intense was the pushback that less than 15 days after that move, Sinha had to partially roll back the levy by reducing SAD to four per cent. Industry responded with relief and welcomed the rollback. It was perhaps because of such an environment and a vocal lobby still actively demanding more reforms that Sinha returned to the path of trade policy reforms by 2001, when he announced the government's intention to progressively reduce the peak rate of the customs duty to 20 per cent within three years. An inter-ministerial working group had been set up to suggest the modalities, and according to its recommendations, the government was advised to create a road map. Sinha's new road map for customs duty reduction was to cut, by 2004–05, the number of basic customs duty rates to only 2 to 10 per cent for raw materials, intermediates and components, and 20 per cent for final products. Simultaneously, he cut the peak customs rate from 35 per cent to 30 per cent. The goals set by Sinha in 2002 were mostly achieved as indicated in his road map, until this trajectory was reversed in 2018 with tariffs for many items being raised.

What changed after 2014 was significant. Import licensing had been virtually eliminated by 2014 and the peak import duty rate for non-agricultural goods had been reduced to 10 per cent by 2007. And this was possible for a combination of political economy factors. At one level, the overall environment was still reform-friendly. It was under some pressure from industry that a BJP government and its finance minister were persuaded in 1998 to reduce the level of the additional tariff by half.

This environment was missing during the tenure of the Narendra Modi government when import tariffs began to be raised once again, but neither was there any industry outcry nor any sign of the government's inclination to reconsider its protectionist steps. The second factor was the effective pressure being put by policy commentators. Arvind Panagariya, a well-regarded trade economist, and many other leading policy commentators kept up the pressure on the government for sustained trade policy reforms through periodic commentaries in various media publications. They bemoaned the problematic reversal of tariff liberalization between 1998 and 1999.[14] These commentators would question the increase in tariffs or India's increasing recourse to using anti-dumping steps under provisions of the World Trade Organization and a policy preference for import-substitution measures. Such critical comments against the reversal in the government's trade policy were made almost as forcefully by the same set of commentators during the Modi regime, but their impact on actual government policy was hardly felt or seen. The political economy under the Modi regime had become less responsive to public criticism or commentary, striking a blow against economic reforms, although it must be conceded that the Union budget in July 2024 raised hopes for some reform in import tariffs and factor-market reforms. How soon or how speedily these reforms get implemented, only time will tell.

The Modi Years: From 2014 to 2024

The installation of the Narendra Modi government in 2014 raised hopes of speedier economic reforms, not the least because the BJP held a simple majority in the Lok Sabha on its own strength—an advantage it enjoyed for over ten years. Apart from the political capital the BJP enjoyed, the party was also seen as committed in principle to the idea of economic reforms. It was an ideal situation of the political economy becoming supportive of reforms. Not surprisingly, therefore, one of the earliest decisions the Modi government took was to promulgate an ordinance to relax the norms for acquisition of land for setting up industrial projects across the country. Industry hailed the decision, but the Opposition political parties were fundamentally critical of the move and raised a banner of protest. There were murmurs of concern over the ordinance even among a few of BJP's party leaders. The ordinance had to be converted into a piece of legislation after getting the assent of both houses of Parliament. But this became difficult with growing political opposition to it and the Modi government decided to let the ordinance lapse. It was ironic that a majority government with political intent to reform laws met with a serious setback as far as implementing its first major economic reform initiative was concerned.

A similar fate awaited a few other major reforms that the Modi government had mooted. These included reforms of farm sector laws to give farmers the freedom to sell their produce outside their village markets or *mandi*s, relax stock-holding norms for agricultural commodities and to facilitate the entry of companies into farming. But these reforms were opposed by a large section of farmers, mainly in Punjab, Haryana and western Uttar Pradesh. So intense was their long agitation that the new farm sector laws passed by Parliament in 2020 during the Covid pandemic had to be rolled back by December 2021. Just as the changes in the land acquisition law, the farm sector reforms too were put in cold storage.

Arguably, the Modi regime's handling of key reforms in the areas of land acquisition and the farm sector revealed yet another facet of India's political economy. Even a majority government may be unable to implement bold economic reforms if these are changes sought to be brought about in areas that belong to the State List of the Indian Constitution, or which are in the Concurrent List, governed by both the Centre and the States. It is not enough for the political party to enjoy a majority in the Lok Sabha. Equally important is how well the political parties in power in the States are convinced about the need for reforms in areas where they would have a decisive say. This underlines the need for even a ruling party—with a majority in the Parliament—to consult with different Opposition political parties and particularly those running governments in the States in order to take them on board before bringing about such key reforms. With respect to reforms in land acquisition and the farm sector, the Modi government took the support of the Opposition parties and the State governments for granted and did not consult them adequately before promulgating those ordinances. The well-intended reforms of labour laws faced a similar problem. The labour reforms were passed by Parliament, but their notification faced hurdles as some States were not on board and many labour unions also entertained serious reservations.

The Modi government's experiments with major changes in economic laws thus offer yet another insight into the interplay between India's political economy and reforms: the government at the Centre must not only enjoy a majority in the Lok Sabha to ensure the smooth implementation of major economic reforms, it must also take the Opposition and State governments on board before proposing them. India's political economy demands a consensus approach for implementing reforms, particularly with respect to reforms of laws where both the Centre and the States enjoy concurrent powers. Also missing was an engagement with industry to convince its leaders of the need for economic reforms.

Indeed, the success of the Modi government in implementing a few reforms in key areas reiterates the same principle of a need for a consensus approach and prior engagement with industry to bring it on board. The major reforms of the Modi government, like the launch of the goods and services tax (GST) and the institution of a system for resolving insolvency and regulatory reforms in the real estate sector, showed how the government involved the States and other stakeholders in implementing these key reforms. If a spirit of cooperation with States in reforming these laws had been missing, it is likely that these changes too would have met a fate similar to what happened to the proposed reforms of land, labour and farm sector laws. This is a new lesson on the importance of political economy in the effective implementation of economic reforms. As the developments during the first ten years of the Modi government showed, even with strong political capital, the tasks of implementing reforms do not become smooth unless there is a cooperative and consensus-making approach. Why and how the GST became a reality (this, in principle, was as contentious as the land or the farm sector reforms) in spite of the States' fears that they would lose their unilateral power to tax goods and services is a lesson on reforms. Chances of reforms are brighter even for a majority government which adopts a consultative and cooperative approach instead of an attitude of 'Ekla Chalo Re' or going your own way alone.

The Takeaways

So what are the key lessons on India's reforms story from a political economy standpoint? The presence of a political and economic environment supportive of reforms is a key attribute that enables the political economy to make a meaningful impact on the roll-out of the desired economic policy changes. This is amply brought out in the developments in the first four decades after India's Independence. Governments during this period enjoyed a decent majority in Parliament, but there was a complete absence of a political climate that encouraged economic reforms. Instead, the political environment encouraged a bigger role of the government in the business of running businesses and deciding for businesses what services or goods they should be providing or producing.

When the Indian economy was in trouble from the late 1980s, the response of the political economy to the need for reforms underwent a reassuring change. The willingness to consider pursuing some of the long overdue reforms in industrial policies became evident in the late 1980s. And when the economy was in dire straits facing its worst crisis, the political establishment went along with the reforms even when they were implemented by a minority government. That was in 1991.

Ironically, however, the fervour for reforms slowed considerably as the Indian economy averted the crisis and was back on the growth path. The major reform steps that were taken during the crisis years were continued, but the appetite for fresh and decidedly more difficult reforms was missing. It was not a question of providing compensatory benefits for sections of industry or people to withstand the early pains of reforms. The National Renewal Fund—created to help workers who lost jobs as a result of reforms or closure of industries—could hardly facilitate the launch of an exit policy for labour, a move that Finance Minister Singh had to abandon in the mid-1990s. The Vajpayee government did show its firm commitment to reforms by privatizing several state-owned enterprises, but its track record was sullied because it also presided over a temporary increase in import tariffs.

The ten years of coalition rule of the United Progressive Alliance saw no major economic reforms, apart from a steady reduction in import tariffs. And when the Narendra Modi government was formed with a single-party majority in 2014, hopes of accelerated reforms revived. But nothing much happened apart from a flawed roll-out of the goods and services tax (GST) regime, strengthening the digital public infrastructure for payments, launching real estate sector reforms, introducing an insolvency resolution mechanism, and establishing a monetary policy system with inflation targeting. Instead, there were disruptive moves like demonetization, a gradual increase in import tariffs (though there has been a marginal course correction on this front since 2024), and the reintroduction of import-substitution policies like the production-linked incentive (PLI) scheme. Opening up the economy by joining a regional trading bloc like the Regional Comprehensive Economic Partnership (RCEP) was rejected on the specious grounds that its farm sector would be affected and industry would face the adverse consequences of dumping by China. And when it moved ahead with reforms of land, labour and farm sector laws without adequate consultation and consensus-building, the results were disappointing.

India's political economy is yet to become so mature as to recognize the importance of economic reforms and encourage their implementation with serious commitment. There is plenty of lip service paid to reforms by all governments post-1991. But they take place mostly when a crisis grips the economy and the political establishment sees no way out other than reforms to bail the economy out. In that seminal sense, India's political economy continues to suffer from a serious flaw as it is yet to embrace economic reforms as an article of faith.

The only way to take the process of economic reforms forward is not to underestimate the importance of building an environment for reforms. This is because even a political majority is not a guarantee for economic reforms. Without building an environment conducive to reforms and political consensus, reforms that do not hurt industries or segments of the population may still be implemented. But if hard reforms or the much-talked-about second generation of reforms have to be implemented without a crisis and in spite of having a political majority, India's political economy must learn the importance of consensus-building involving Opposition political parties, State government representatives and industry leaders.

List of Contributors

1. *Montek Singh Ahluwalia,* Former Deputy Chairman, Planning Commission, and former Finance Secretary, Government of India
2. *Ajay Chhibber,* Distinguished Visiting Scholar, IIEP, George Washington University, and former Assistant Secretary-General, UN
3. **Sajjid Chinoy,** Chief India Economist and Managing Director, J.P. Morgan
4. *S. Mahendra Dev,* Former Vice-Chancellor, IGIDR, and former Chairman, Commission for Agricultural Costs & Prices, Government of India
5. *Manish Gupta,* Associate Professor, National Institute of Public Finance and Policy
6. *Emmanuel Jimenez,* Director General, Independent Evaluation, Asian Development Bank
7. *Radhicka Kapoor,* Senior Employment Specialist, Decent Work Team for South Asia, International Labour Organization
8. *Mansi Kedia,* Senior Fellow, ICRIER
9. *Uday Kotak,* Founder of the Kotak Bank Group and its former Managing Director and CEO
10. *Deepak Mishra,* Director and CE, ICRIER
11. *Rakesh Mohan,* Former Deputy Governor, RBI, and former Secretary, Department of Economic Affairs, Government of India
12. *Sudipto Mundle,* Chairman, Centre for Development Studies and Member, 14th Finance Commission
13. *Michael Debabrata Patra,* Former Deputy Governor, Reserve Bank of India
14. *Shyam Saran,* Former Foreign Secretary and PM's Special Envoy on Climate Negotiations and US-India Civil Nuclear Deal, Government of India
15. *Martin Wolf,* Associate Editor and Chief Economics Commentator, *Financial Times.*

16. **Roberto Zagha**, Former Director-India, World Bank, and former Secretary, Commission on Growth and Development
17. **Amita Batra**, Professor, School of International Studies, JNU
18. **A.K. Bhattacharya**, Editorial Director, *Business Standard*

Notes

Whither the World Economy? Implications for India, by Martin Wolf

1. See Wolf, Martin, *India's Exports*, Oxford University Press for the World Bank, London and New York, 1982.
2. The analyses of growth trends in this chapter are based on the averages of the growth rates over 10 years, placed in the final year in a series of 10. GDP figures are measured at purchasing power parity.
3. These data are from the International Monetary Fund, *World Economic Outlook Database April Edition*, https://tinyurl.com/4jeywjwb. Accessed on 13 February 2025.
4. The defect of GDP per head as an indicator of productivity is that it ignores the impact of changes in the share of the population that is of working age.
5. See IMF, *World Economic Outlook*, April 2024, Chapter 1, pp. 15–16, and Chapter 3, https://tinyurl.com/mr2dzwta. Accessed on 9 December 2024.
6. For a discussion on the earlier slowdown, see Wolf, Martin, *The Crisis of Democratic Capitalism*, Penguin, London and New York, 2023, pp. 122–27 (especially Figure 26, p. 124).
7. See Gordon, Robert, *The Rise and Fall of American Growth: The U.S. Standard of Living since the Civil War*, Princeton University Press, Princeton, New Jersey, 2016.
8. Wolf, Martin, 'The tricky judgements on when to loosen', *Financial Times*, 23 April 2024, https://tinyurl.com/3sb957yk. Accessed on 9 December 2024.
9. See Haldane, Andy, 'Why an uncertain world needs to take on more risk', *Financial Times*, 18 May 2024, https://tinyurl.com/3udpzwnd. Accessed on 9 December, 2024.
10. See Chrimes, Tommy, et al., *The Great Reversal: Prospects, Risks, and Policies in International Development Association (IDA) Countries*, World Bank, 2024.
11. International Monetary Fund, *World Economic Outlook Database*, https://tinyurl.com/yc67axaw. Accessed on 13 February 2025.
12. See IMF, *World Economic Outlook Database April Edition*, https://tinyurl.com/4jeywjwb. Accessed on 13 February 2025 (Chapter 3 'Slowdown in Global Medium-Term Growth: What Will It Take to Turn the Tide?', pp. 65–85, especially Figure 3.4, p. 68).
13. See *Our World in Data: Fertility Rates*, https://tinyurl.com/mr2f59hj. Accessed on 9 December, 2024.
14. See Wolf, *Crisis of Democratic Capitalism*.

15. See Wolf, Martin, 'the world economy's story remains one of integration', *Financial Times*, 19 January 2024, https://tinyurl.com/34yvyfh2. Accessed on 9 December, 2024; Subramaniam, Arvind, and Martin Kessler, 'The Hyperglobalization of Trade and its Future', Peterson Institute for International Economics Working Paper No. 13–6, 25 July 2013, https://tinyurl.com/3wyycsvu. Accessed on 9 December 2024; Subramaniam, Arvind, Martin Kessler, and Emanuele Properzl, 'Trade hyperglobalization is dead. Long live…?', Peterson Institute for International Economics Working Paper No. 23–1, November 2023, https://tinyurl.com/2n5rukh4. Accessed on 9 December 2024; Aiyar, Shekhar, and Anna Ilyina, 'Charting Globalization's Turn to Slowbalization After Global Financial Crisis', International Monetary Fund, 8 February 2023, https://tinyurl.com/372ew2ea. Accessed on 9 December 2024.

16. This draws on the discussion in Wolf, 'the world economy's story…'

17. See 'The High Cost of Global Economic Fragmentation', *IMF Blog*, 28 August 1983, https://tinyurl.com/4whhwusx. Accessed on 9 December 2024; Kose, M. Ayhan, and Allen Mulabdic, 'Global trade has nearly flatlined. Populism is taking a toll on growth', *World Bank Blogs*, 22 February 2024, https://tinyurl.com/y23fet2v. Accessed on 9 December 2024.

18. See Patel, Dev, Justin Sandefur, and Arvind Subramaniam, 'A Requiem for Hyperglobalization: Why the World Will Miss History's Greatest Economic Miracle', *Foreign Affairs*, 12 June 2024, https://tinyurl.com/3mdyj7zx. Accessed on 9 December 2024.

19. Blanga-Gubbay, Michael, and Stela Rubinova, 'Is the Global Economy Fragmenting?', Staff Working Paper: Research ERSD-2023-10, World Trade Organization, https://tinyurl.com/4r5ee337. Accessed on 9 December 2024.

20. Ibid.

21. See Wolf , Martin, 'Tariffs are bad policy, but good politics', *Financial Times*, 11 June 2024, https://tinyurl.com/4dy5jm2r. Accessed on 9 December 2024.

22. The opportunity in services is a significant part of the argument in Chatterjee, Shoumitro, and Arvind Subramanian, 'India's Inward (Re)Turn: Is it Warranted? Will it Work?', Policy Paper No. 1, Ashoka Centre for Economic Policy, October 2020.

23. See WTO, *World Trade Statistical Review 2023*, Table A3, p. 57.

24. Wolf, Martin, 'We need the G20—but what is it for?' *Financial Times*, 12 September 2024, https://tinyurl.com/8a2f8whp. Accessed on 9 December 2024.

25. Prime Minister's Office, 'English rendering of the Prime Minister, Shri Narendra Modi's address from the ramparts of Red Fort on the occasion of 77th Independence Day', 15 August 2023, https://tinyurl.com/4a8b65ra. Accessed on 9 December 2024.

26. See Hamadeh, Nada, Catherine Van Rompaey, and Eric Metreau, 'World

Bank Group country classifications by income level for FY24 (July 1, 2023–June 30, 2024)', World Bank, 30 June 2023, https://tinyurl.com/466xt2t6. Accessed on 9 December, 2024; IMF, *World Economic Outlook Database*, https://tinyurl.com/ycx53aa8. Accessed on 9 December 2024.

27. See WTO, *World Trade Statistical Review 2024*, Tables A7 and A8.
28. Ibid.
29. See Chatterjee and Subramanian, 'India's Inward (Re)Turn'.
30. See, on this, Baldwin, Richard, *The Globotics Upheaval: Globalization, Robotics, and the Future of Work*, Oxford University Press, 2020; Wolf, Martin, 'Globalisation is not dying, it's changing', *Financial Times*, 13 September 2022, https://tinyurl.com/5n6v7x7p. Accessed on 9 December 2024; Baldwin, Richard, Rebecca Freeman, and Angelos Theodorakopoulos, 'Deconstructing Deglobalization: The Future of Trade is in Intermediate Services', *Asian Economic Policy Review*, Vol. 19, No. 1, 2024, pp. 19–37.

The Global Trade Reset in the 2000s and India's Trade Policy Priorities, by Amita Batra

1. The first two sections partially draw from Batra, A., *India's Trade Policy in the 21ˢᵗ Century*, Routledge, London, 2022.
2. The exception in the trends evident for East Asia has been Korea, probably owing to its more vertically integrated industrial structure.
3. The multifiber arrangement (MFA) of 1974, a complex web of bilateral import quotas, was terminated with a 10-year transition period in the Uruguay Round of negotiations and as part of the Agreement on Textiles and Clothing. For China, the 10-year period that ended in 2005 was extended to 2008 owing to its accession to the WTO only in 2001. In the MFA period, the US and the EU were the largest importers with manufacturing countries in Southeast Asia including Korea, Taiwan and China.
4. Also referred to as Singapore issues, these include competition, government procurement, trade facilitation and investment.
5. Torsekar, Mihir P., and John VerWay, 'East Asia-Pacific's participation in Global Value Chain for Electronic Products', *Journal of International Commerce and Economics*, USITC, March 2019, https://tinyurl.com/ym7vjvvm. Accessed on 13 February 2025.
6. Alternative perspectives on the increase in DVA in China are discussed in detail in a forthcoming paper, Batra, Amita, 'Evolving Contours of Global Trade: Way Forward for India', CSEP Discussion Paper, 2025, (forthcoming).
7. Cyrill, Melissa, 'What is Made in China 2025 and Why Has it Made the World so Nervous?', *China Briefing*, 28 December 2018, https://tinyurl.com/r8khatyr. Accessed on 3 March 2025.
8. Ironically, these provisions are making a comeback, selectively or more broadly, in the industrial-policy-led third decade as member economies, as

'national security' and economic security become increasingly overlapping goals for the US and other economies around the world.

9. Crawford, Jo-Ann, and Barbara Kotschwar, 'Investment Provisions in Preferential Trade Agreements: Evolution and Current Trends', Staff Working Paper ERSD-2018-14, 2018.

10. Mattoo, A., Nadia Rocha, and Michele Ruta, *Handbook of Deep Trade Agreements*, World Bank, 2020, p. 220.

11. In 1957, the EU Treaty of Rome was the first to include a general provision prohibiting or restricting the import or export of commodities on grounds of protection to plant or animal life.

12. The general belief being that developing countries have less stringent environmental regulations. Drawing upon this logic, the pollution haven and emission arbitrage hypotheses are proposed for the high possibility of a shift of investment to the less developed economies.

13. Mattoo, A., et al., *Handbook of Deep Trade Agreements*, p. 599.

14. 'USMCA: Labor provisions', Congressional Research Service, 20 January 2022, https://tinyurl.com/4vdkdxm9. Accessed on 3 March 2025.

15. The underlying perception being that China had been flouting the multilateral rules to its advantage.

16. Australia, Brunei, Canada, Chile, Japan, Malaysia, Mexico, New Zealand, Peru, Singapore, the United States, Vietnam.

17. EU FTA with New Zealand.

18. Global Trade Alert, https://tinyurl.com/3j5swubp. Accessed on 3 March 2025.

19. WTO, 'Global Trade Outlook and Statistics', April 2024, https://tinyurl.com/5b3x62kn. Accessed on 10 March 2025.

20. Dahlman, A., and M.E. Lovely, 'US led effort to diversify Indo-Pacific supply chains away from China runs counter to trends', Peterson Institute of International Economics, 2023; Freund, C., et al., 'Is US Trade Policy Reshaping Global Supply Chains?', World Bank Policy Research Working Paper 10593, October 2023.

21. The share of manufactured exports in India's total merchandise exports has declined from almost 78 per cent in 2000 to about 64 per cent in 2023 (*Source*: World Development Indicators, World Bank Database).

22. See Batra, Amita, 'India in the GVC diversification strategy: A reality check', *Business Standard*, 5 January 2023.

Climate Change in India: An Agenda for the Next 10 Years, by Montek Singh Ahluwalia

1. This paper draws heavily from a more detailed earlier paper, 'How India can reach Net Zero: A strategy for 2025–35', by Montek S. Ahluwalia and Utkarsh Patel, which was published in the *Oxford Review of Economic Policy*, Vol. 40, No. 2, Summer 2024, pp. 350–65, https://tinyurl.com/aadhfym7.

Accessed on 13 February 2025. Some of what was said in the earlier paper is updated to reflect recent developments. I am grateful to Utkarsh Patel for many helpful suggestions on this paper.

2. This is due to the sterling work of the Intergovernmental Panel on Climate Change (IPCC), an international group of about 4,000 scientists located in research institutions all over the world. It was established in 1988 by the World Meteorological Organization (WMO) and the United Nations Environment Programme (UNEP). The group systematically reviews the latest findings on climate change and what it implies for the earth's ecosystem.

3. There is evidence that this is happening, with previously arid regions getting more rainfall while some of the agriculturally important areas are getting less.

4. The US never ratified it, Canada withdrew from the Agreement in 2011, and Japan, New Zealand and Russia did not make further commitments beyond the first commitment period. One of the problems was the reluctance of developed countries to accept the proposition that developing countries should not have any obligations when China was classified as a developing country and had expanded its emissions very rapidly.

5. China and Indonesia agreed to reach net zero in 2060 and India agreed to do it by 2070.

6. UNFCC, 'Outcome of the first global stocktake. Draft decision -/CMA.5. Proposal by the President', United Nations Climate Change, 13 December 2023, https://tinyurl.com/4vnrjspe. Accessed 12 December 2024.

7. One approach would be to distribute the available carbon budget according to the size of the population, thus giving all countries an equal per capita entitlement. This will obviously be seen as favouring larger countries such as China and India. It also does not take into account the historical inequity arising from early industrializers taking up carbon space. There could be other variations, but this aspect was never considered.

8. The voluntary nature of the commitments is underscored by the fact that they are described as Intended Nationally Determined Contributions (INDCs). In other words, unlike commitments undertaken in trade agreements, they are not negotiated among the signatories. Each country offers what it can.

9. Although written as an equation, it is actually an identity since the two GDP terms and the two En terms cancel out.

10. If 'developed country status' is interpreted as graduating out of what the World Bank calls 'middle income group of countries', it would call for a growth rate of the GDP of about 8+ per cent per year on average up to 2047.

11. India's Mission LiFE (Lifestyle for Environment) promotes sustainable choices which individuals can make to contribute towards climate change mitigation.

12. The IEA has estimated that improvements in energy efficiency can reduce

total emissions by about 30 per cent from the baseline.

13. Ahluwalia, Montek S., and Utkarsh Patel, 'How India can reach net zero: a strategy for 2025–35', *Oxford Review of Economic Policy*, Vol. 40, No. 2, Summer 2024, pp. 350–65, https://tinyurl.com/4y7phyc7. Accessed on 12 December 2024.

14. See in this context, Fischer, Carolyn, Chenfei Qu, and Lawrence H. Goulder, 'Rate-Based Emissions Trading with Overlapping Policies: Insights from Theory and an Application to China (English)', Policy Research working paper, PLANET Washington D.C., World Bank Group, 2024, https://tinyurl.com/4wdftbum. Accessed on 12 December 2024.

15. More sophisticated electricity markets which allow for wide variations in electricity prices to reflect the supply of RE will incentivize the creation of storage capacity to absorb excess generation during certain hours of the day. For example, the market clearing price (MCP) in the day-ahead market on IEX on Sunday, 1 September 2024, 1.15–1.30 p.m., fell to ₹0.3/kWh. Prices are expected to fall further as flexible generators will be pushed to the technical minimum capacity factor during peak RE generation periods, triggering negative system-level marginal prices.

16. The low speed of these vehicles is not a constraint since speed is not possible in crowded cities in any case, and the range is also not an issue as battery replacement or charging is relatively easy.

17. PIB, '12,146 public EV charging stations operational across the country', 6 February 2024, https://tinyurl.com/4ejhnmj2. Accessed on 12 December 2024.

18. Many medium and large industries use coal-fired furnaces or boilers to produce heat for various processes. It is possible to replace furnaces with electrical heaters to achieve temperatures up to 1,200°C and eliminate coal use.

19. The price charged for canal water is also very low. This would not affect an efficient allocation of water if it could be rationed across farmers, but farmers upstream have an immense incentive to grow highly water-intensive crops. This has prevented the canal system from being extended over a larger area which could have been irrigated on the basis of a tighter rationing of water.

20. Mathur, et al., estimate the annual financial requirement for achieving an additional 2.5–3 billion tonnes of CO_2 sequestration from the forestry sector to be ₹60,000 crore or 0.3 per cent of the current GDP. This is five times the currently estimated annual expenditure on state and centrally sponsored forest conservation schemes. See Mathur, Ajay, et al., 'Will India Attain Its Forestry NDC Target of Achieving 2.5–3 Billion Tonnes of CO_2 Equivalent Through Additional Forest and Tree Cover by 2030?', The Energy and Resources Institute, January 2021, https://tinyurl.com/mr3wmusp. Accessed on 12 December 2024.

People Power: Human Capital Development in India and Other Asian Economies, by Emmanuel Jimenez

1. Acharya, Shankar, 'Prospects for India's Youth: Cloudy with High Chance of Thunder and Lightning', *Rediff.com*, 6 October 2022, https://tinyurl. com/4ukcb6mm. Accessed on 2 December 2024.
2. Bloom, David E., and Jeffrey G. Williamson, 'Demographic Transitions and Economic Miracles in Emerging Asia', *The World Bank Economic Review*, Vol. 12, No. 3, 1998, pp. 419–55.
3. Yusuf, Shahid, 'Growth Performance of Middle-Income Countries: East Asia vs. Latin America', Center for Global Development, CGD Notes, January 2023.
4. Hassan, Mohammad Izhar, 'Demographic Dividend in India: A Missed Opportunity', *Transactions of the Institute of Indian Geographers*, Vol. 43, No. 1, 2021, pp. 135–45.
5. Acharya, Shankar, 'Can India Grow without Bharat?', *Business Standard*, 25 November 2003, https://tinyurl.com/5n8dtyza. Accessed on 13 February 2025.
6. World Bank, 'School enrollment, secondary (% gross)—East Asia & Pacific', 30 September 2024, https://tinyurl.com/48pcnect. Accessed on 22 October 2024.
7. Dattani, Saloni, et al., *Life Expectancy, Our World in Data*, 2023, https:// tinyurl.com/cshuuwz6. Accessed on 22 October 2024.
8. Ravallion, Martin, 'Mashup Indices of Development', Policy Research Working Paper 5432, World Bank, 2010, https://tinyurl.com/yrske798. Accessed on 12 December 2024.
9. The harmonized learning outcomes provide internationally comparable global learning data using achievement test scores across countries. See 'Harmonized Learning Outcomes (HLO) Database', World Bank Group, https://tinyurl.com/mtra5hen. Accessed on 12 December 2024.
10. The actual formula is: HCI = Survival x School x Health, where Survival = (1–Under-5 Mortality Rate)/1, School = $e\Phi$[Expected years of school x (harmonized test score/625) – 14] Health = $e\Phi$[γASR x (Adult Survival Rate – 1) + γStunting x(Not stunted rate – 1)].
11. The source of Table 2 is World Bank, *The Human Capital Index 2020 Update*, 2022.
12. Raj, J., V. Gupta, and A. Shrawan, 'Economic Growth and Human Development in India—Are States Converging?', Centre for Social and Economic Progress Working Paper 51, 2023, https://tinyurl.com/yvd2hzsv. Accessed on 12 December 2024; Asian Development Bank, *Human Capital Development in South Asia Achievements, Prospects, and Policy Challenges*, 2017, https://tinyurl.com/283xannz. Accessed on 12 December 2024.
13. International Initiative for Impact Evaluation Development Evidence Portal,

https://tinyurl.com/3j5t6cxh. Accessed on 2 December 2024.

14. Kapoor, R., et al., 'How is India Doing on Malnutrition and Non-Communicable Diseases? Insights from the National Family Health Surveys (2005 –06 to 2019 –21)', POSHAN Data Note No. 92, International Food Policy Research Institute, 2023, https://tinyurl.com/84b46kvb. Accessed on 12 December 2024.

15. Avula, R., et al., 'Reducing Childhood Stunting in India: Insights from Four Subnational Success Cases', *Food Security*, Vol. 14, 2022, pp. 1085–97, https://tinyurl.com/55ckazt6. Accessed on 12 December 2024.

16. OECD/WHO, 'Health at a Glance: Asia Pacific 2022', https://tinyurl.com/53raac6x. Accessed on 12 December 2024.

17. UNESCO, 'Out-of-School Children and Adolescents in Asia and the Pacific', https://tinyurl.com/bdcwb3zn. Accessed on 22 October 2022.

18. Snilstveit, Birte, et al., 'The Impact of Education Programmes on Learning and School Participation in Low- and Middle-Income Countries', International Initiative for Impact Evaluation, Systematic Review Summary 7, 2016.

19. Innovations for Poverty Action, *Best Bets: Emerging Opportunities for Impact at Scale*, 2023, https://tinyurl.com/3hjrfzwn. Accessed on 13 February 2024.

20. World Bank, *World Development Report 2018: Learning to Realize Education's Promise*, 2018, https://tinyurl.com/mteb83j5. Accessed on 12 December 2024.

21. Ibid.

22. Heckman, James, 'Invest in Early Childhood Development: Reduce Deficits, Strengthen the Economy', *Heckman Equation*, 2012, https://tinyurl.com/5b393dh4. Accessed on 12 December 2024.

23. Central Square Foundation, *Building Strong Foundations: Examining Early Childhood Education in India*, 2023, https://tinyurl.com/3jys3vbp. Accessed on 12 December 2024.

24. World Bank, *World Development Report 2018: Learning to Realize Education's Promise*, 2018, https://tinyurl.com/mteb83j5. Accessed on 12 December 2024.

25. World Bank, *The Human Capital Project*, 2018, https://tinyurl.com/ydxees39. Accessed on 12 December 2024.

26. Innovations for Policy Action, *Best Bets: Emerging Opportunities for Impact at Scale*, 2023, https://tinyurl.com/3hjrfzwn. Accessed on 13 February 2025.

27. Ibid.

28. World Health Organization, 'Disability-adjusted life years (DALYs)', The Global Health Observatory, https://tinyurl.com/2cpafr7x. Accessed on 12 December 2024.

29. Thomas, Arya Rachel, Umakant Dash, and Santosh Kumar Sahu, 'Illnesses and Hardship Financing in India: An Evaluation of Inpatient and Outpatient Cases, 2014-18', *BMC Public Health, 2023*, pp. 23–204.

30. International Initiative for Impact Evaluation Development Evidence Portal, https://tinyurl.com/56fdph32. Accessed on 22 October 2024.

31. Gizaw, Z., T. Astale, and G.M. Kassie, 'What Improves Access to Primary

Healthcare Services in Rural Communities? A Systematic Review', *BMC Primary Care*, Vol. 23, 2022, p. 313, https://tinyurl.com/jdjxbrd6. Accessed on 13 February 2025.

32. Fritz, Manuela, and Hanna Frommel, 'How to Dampen the Surge of Non-Communicable Diseases in Southeast Asia: Insights from a Systematic Review and Meta-Analysis', *Health Policy and Planning*, Vol. 37, 2022, pp. 152–67.

33. Innovations for Policy Action, *Best Bets: Emerging Opportunities for Impact at Scale*, 2023, https://tinyurl.com/3hjrfzwn. Accessed on 13 February 2025.

34. WHO, *Global Spending on Health: Global Spending on the Rise?*, 2021.

35. National Health Authority, 'About Pradhan Mantri Jan Arogya Yojana', https://tinyurl.com/3ve2txh2. Accessed on 22 October 2024.

36. Thomas, Arya Rachel, Umakant Dash and Santosh Kumar Sahu, 'Illnesses and Hardship Financing in India: An Evaluation of Inpatient and Outpatient Cases, 2014–18', *BMC Public Health*, Vol. 23, 2023, p. 204.

37. Jain, Neetu, 'Indian-origin CEOs Ruling World', *LinkedIn*, 2023, https://tinyurl.com/y4w6m8af. Accessed on 12 December 2024.

38. Bajaj, Niti, 'Indians are Taking over Corporate America—and Tech Layoffs Won't Stop Them', *Forbes*, 17 December 2022, https://tinyurl.com/3z6symbv. Accessed on 12 December, 2024.

39. World Bank, *World Development Report 2019: The Changing Nature of Work*, 2019, https://tinyurl.com/3u439tse. Accessed on 12 December 2024.

40. Jimenez, Emmanuel, and Elizabeth M. King, 'The Skills of "Tigers"', *Human Capital Formation and Economic Growth in Asia and the Pacific*, Wendy Dobson (ed.), Routledge, Oxford, 2013.

41. Lee, Jihyun, 'Non-Cognitive Characteristics and Academic Achievement in Southeast Asia Countries based on PISA 2009, 2012 and 2015', OECD Working Paper No. 233, OECD, October 2020, https://tinyurl.com/yedmt8pf. Accessed on 12 December 2024.

42. Glewwe, Paul, Qiuquiong Hong, and Albert Park, 'Cognitive Skills, Noncognitive Skills, and School-to-Work Transitions in Rural China', IZA Discussion Paper 10566, 2017, https://tinyurl.com/yc4en4p2. Accessed on 12 December 2024.

43. Montenegro, Claudio E., and Harry Anthony Patrinos, 'A Data Set of Comparable Estimates of the Private Rate of Return to Schooling in the World, 1970–2014', *International Journal of Manpower*, 2021, https://tinyurl.com/45pa39wr. Accessed on 12 December 2024.

44. Jimenez, Emmanuel, Vy Nguyen, and Harry Patrinos, 'Human Capital Development and Economic Growth in Malaysia and Thailand: Stuck in the Middle?', *Human Capital Formation and Economic Growth in Asia and the Pacific*, Wendy Dobson (ed.), Routledge, Oxford, 2013.

Latin America's Failure to Catch Up: The Examples of Argentina and Brazil, by Roberto Zagha

1. The paper benefitted from comments by Mike Spence, Patricia Clarke Annez, Edmar Bacha, Uri Dadush, Stephen Howes, Danny Leipziger, Francisco Vidal Luna, Andre Lara Resende, Simao Silber, and Carlos Antonio Luque.
2. Myrdal, Gunnar, *Asian Drama: An Inquiry into the Poverty of Nations*, Random House, New York, 1972.
3. Meade, James, *The Economic and Social Structure of Mauritius*, Routledge, New York, 1961.
4. 'Income Inequality, Indonesia, 1992 –2019', World Inequality Database, https://tinyurl.com/mvas99d4. Accessed on 9 December 2024.
5. Dorfman, Ariel, 'Defending Allende', *The New York Review of Books*, 21 September 2023.
6. Bevins, Vincent, 'Make The Economy Scream', *The Nation*, 27 November 2023, https://tinyurl.com/3xyyyxef. Accessed on 9 December 2024.
7. World Bank, *The Growth Report: Strategies for Sustained Growth and Inclusive Development*, World Bank Publications, 23 July 2008, https://tinyurl. com/4ur99z6k. Accessed on 9 December 2024.
8. Bacha, Edmar, Guilherme Tombolo, and Flavio Versiani, 'Reestimating Brazil's GDP Growth from 1900 to 1980', *Revista Brasileira de Economia,* March 2023.
9. Alejandro, Carlos Dias, 'No Less of Hundred Years of History, Plus some Comparisons', January 1982; Luque, Carlos Antonio, et al., *Valor Econômico*, 12 May 2020; 'Ascenção e Queda da Argentina, and Luque et alia', *Business Standard*, 27 February 2020. Argentina's Crisis.
10. Krueger, Anne, 'Meant Well, Tried Little, Failed Much: Policy Reforms in Emerging Market Economies', International Monetary Fund, 23 March 2004. https://tinyurl.com/3cwyypw4. Accessed on 9 December 2024.
11. 'How Did Argentina Pull Off a 100-Year Bond Sale?', *Financial Times*, 20 June 2017, https://tinyurl.com/3hk8yv8a. Accessed on 9 December 2024.
12. IMF, 'Statement by David Lipton, First Deputy Managing Director of the IMF, at the Conclusion of His Visit to Argentina', Press Release no. 17/120, April 2017, https://tinyurl.com/5n7xx8xr. Accessed on 9 December 2024.
13. Sturzenegger, Federico, 'Macri's Macro: The Meandering Road to Stability and Growth', Brookings, 5 September 2019, https://tinyurl.com/44ww5y2z. Accessed on 9 December 2024.
14. Guzmán, Martín, 'Argentina's Unseen Fragility', *Project Syndicate*, 4 May 2018, https://tinyurl.com/7fh5rwyy. Accessed on 9 December 2024.
15. Cardoso, Eliana, 'A Inflação no Brasil. Escola de Economia São Paulo', Fundação Getúlio Vargas and IMF, Article IV, 2005.
16. IMF, 'Brazil: 2024 Article IV Consultation-Press Release; Staff Report; and Statement by the Executive Director for Brazil', 11 July 2024, https://tinyurl. com/y2y2428. Accessed on 17 March 2025.

17. Klein, Herbert, and Francisco Luna, *Feeding the World: Brazil's Transformation into a Modern Agricultural Economy,* Cambridge University Press, Cambridge, 2018.

18. Resende, André Lara, 'Juros, moeda e ortodoxia', Portfolio Penguin, São Paulo, 2017; Bacha, Edmar, 'Brazil's Plano Real: A View from the Inside', *Development Economics and Structuralist Macroeconomics,* Amitava Dutt and Jaime Ros (eds.), Edward Elgar Publishing, Cheltenham, 2003; Arida, Persio, *Essays of Brazilian stabilization programs,* 2005, Massachusetts Institute of Technology, PhD thesis.

19. Cardoso, Fernando Henrique, *A Arte da Política,* Civilização Brasileira, 2006, p. 413.

20. Brazil, Russia, India and South Africa.

21. Bacha, Edmar, *Alem da Triade: Ha Como Reduzir os Juros?,* Casa das Garças, Rio de Janeiro, 2010.

22. Giavazzi, Francesco, and Marco Pagano, 'Can Severe Fiscal Contractions Be Expansionary? Tales of Two Small European Countries', *NBER Macroeconomics Annual,* Vol. 5, 1990, pp. 75–111.

23. Resende, André Lara, *Consenso e contrassenso: Por uma economia não dogmática,* Portfolio Penguin, 2020; Resende, André Lara, *Camisa de Forca Ideológica,* Portfolio Penguin, 2022; Several articles published in *Valor Economico.*

24. *Valor Economico,* 9 and 25 January 2017.

25. Methodological Note of April 2015 and inflation report of May 2015, Brazil Central Bank; IMF, 'May 2015 Brazil Report'; BIS Memorandum, October 2014.

26. *Valor Economico,* 2 February 2017; Blanchard, Olivier, and Julien Acalin, 'What Does Measured FDI Actually Measure?', Policy brief, Peterson Institute for International Economics, October 2016.

27. Kose, M. Ayhan, and Eswar Prasad, 'Capital Accounts: Liberalize or Not?', *Finance & Development,* IMF, https://tinyurl.com/48kyfxea. Accessed on 9 December 2024.

28. Bhagwati, Jagdish, 'Why Free Capital Mobility Can Be Hazardous to Your Health', NBER, Conference on Capital Controls, 1998; Jeanne, Olivier, Arvind Subramanian, and John Williamson, 'Who Needs to Open the Capital Account?', Peterson Institute Press, 2012; Stiglitz, Joseph, 'Capital Market Liberalization, Economic Growth and Instability', *World Development,* Vol. 28, 2000; Stiglitz, Joseph, *Globalization and its Discontents,* W.W. Norton, New York, 2002; Stiglitz, Joseph, 'Capital-Market Liberalization, Globalization, and the IMF', *Oxford Review of Economic Policy,* Vol. 20, 2004, pp. 57 –71; IMF Independent Evaluation Office, 'The IMF Approach to Capital Account Liberalization: Issues Paper/Terms of Reference for an Evaluation by the Independent Evaluation Office', 2004, https://tinyurl.com/5585rtrd. Accessed on 14 February 2025.

Moving China from the Margins to the Centre of Global Finance, by Shyam Saran

1. Garcia-Herrero, Alicia, 'Can Chinese Growth Defy Gravity', *Bruegel*, 20 June 2023, https://tinyurl.com/3kdn6muf. Accessed on 13 November 2024.
2. 'Project mBridge reached minimum viable product stage', BIS, 11 November 2024, https://tinyurl.com/3yb6xj5m. Accessed on 13 November 2024.

Reforming the Bretton Woods Institutions for the Twenty-First Century, by Ajay Chhibber

1. An earlier version of this paper was prepared for the Atlantic Council's Bretton Woods 2.0 project.
2. Poverty has surged due to various crises. The latest—the Ukraine crisis—has pushed an additional 50 million into extreme poverty according to UNDP. 'Global cost-of-living crisis catalyzed by war in Ukraine sending tens of millions into poverty, warns UN Development Programme', United Nations Development Programme. The World Bank had earlier estimated that about 90 million people had fallen into extreme poverty due to the Covid pandemic. Covid-19 leaves a legacy of rising poverty and widening inequality. But hopefully these are temporary setbacks, and poverty will revert to its long-term decline by 2030.
3. Especially the access to vaccines, which some have termed 'vaccine apartheid'.
4. Average global temperatures are now more than one degree higher than the 1951–80 average.
5. Graham, Niels, 'Emerging markets need new engines of growth', Atlantic Council, 13 July 2022, https://tinyurl.com/y74vb9hd. Accessed on 14 February 2024; Derviş, Kemal, 'The Future of Economic Convergence', Project Syndicate, 12 February 2018, https://tinyurl.com/yhckmwkx. Accessed on 9 December 2024.
6. The issue of governance structure and voting shares, and the leadership selection process is taken up in a separate paper. But broadly, a shift of voting shares from the EU countries towards China, India and other emerging economies in Africa is needed.
7. Between the start of the pandemic in March 2020 and March 2022, the IMF granted funding equivalent to $171 billion to 90 developing economies. This drops to a mere $75.4 billion—a figure similar to the $75 billion in IMF funding commitments between January and September 2009, during the global financial crisis—when the amount for flexible credit lines is excluded (Table 2). However, the overall financing needs of developing countries were estimated at $2.5 trillion as of March 2020. Current needs may be higher when the additional financing needs imposed by the pandemic are taken into account. Nevertheless, even the conservative estimate exceeds the IMF

lending capacity, estimated at a total of $1 trillion; 'Special Drawing Rights (SDRs) and the COVID-19 crisis', ECLAC, 25 April 2022, https://tinyurl.com/3k4kueay. Accessed on 14 February 2025.

8. But these are largely restricted among the advanced economies.

9. The Chiang Mai initiative and the BRICS Contingent Facility.

10. Coulibaly, Brahima Sangafowa, and Eswar Prasad, 'The international monetary and financial system: How to fit it for purpose?', *Brookings*, 17 November 2020, https://tinyurl.com/f76bmabh. Accessed on 9 December 2024; Data also from the Shanmugaratnam-Brookings Project.

11. Reinhart, Carmen M., and Christoph Trebesch, 'The International Monetary Fund: 70 Years of Reinvention', *Journal of Economic Perspectives*, Vol. 30, No. 1, pp. 3–28, 2016. Accessed on 9 December 2024.

12. To date, about 27 such banks exist.

13. Author's own proposed structure.

14. Heldt, E.C., and H. Schmidtke, 'Explaining coherence in international regime complexes: How the World Bank shapes the field of multilateral development finance', *Review of International Political Economy*, Vol. 26, No. 6, 2019, pp. 1160–86, https://tinyurl.com/y7nebrkv. Accessed on 9 December 2024.

15. ADB, et al., Joint Report on Multilateral Development Bank's Climate Finance, June 2021 (rev. August 2021), https://tinyurl.com/yc5f9sp4. Accessed on 9 December 2024.

16. 'A WAR IN A PANDEMIC', Migration and Development Brief 36, May 2022, https://tinyurl.com/3w6pvajp. Accessed on 9 December 2024.

17. 'From Billions to Trillions: MDB Contribution to Financing for Development', World Bank Document, https://tinyurl.com/m7h9rjv8. Accessed on 9 December 2024.

18. And even the way aid is counted in DAC has been criticized. See Cutts, Stephen, 'Inflated rates means overseas aid statistics are not credible', *Financial Times*, 15 June 2022 .

19. Livingston, J., 'Their Great Depression and Ours', *Challenge*, Vol. 52, No. 3, 2009, pp. 34–51, https://tinyurl.com/5nmrcxjn. Accessed on 9 December 2024.

20. Rogoff, Kenneth, 'Why Is the IMF Trying to Be an Aid Agency?', *Project Syndicate*, 3 January 2022, https://tinyurl.com/24z73zwf. Accessed on 9 December 2024.

21. Ghosh, Atish R., et al., 'When Do Capital Inflow Surges End in Tears?', *The American Economic Review*, Vol. 106, No. 5, 2016, pp. 581–85, https://tinyurl.com/mue9766d. Accessed on 9 December 2024; Ostry, Jonathan D., Prakash Loungani, and Davide Furceri, 'Neoliberalism: Oversold?', *F&D*, Vol. 53, No. 2, June 2016, https://tinyurl.com/3byyrf3p. Accessed on 9 December 2024; Goldstein, Steve, 'Here's the alternative to U.S. dollar dominance — and it's not a rival currency, gold or bitcoin', *MarketWatch*, 13 July 2022, https://tinyurl.com/bdcvdhhy. Accessed on 9 December 2024.

22. Stiglitz, Joseph E., 'Capital-market Liberalization, Globalization, and the IMF', *Oxford Review of Economic Policy*, Vol. 20, No. 1, March 2004, pp. 57–71, https://tinyurl.com/bdd6vbdn. Accessed on 9 December 2024.

23. In November 2012, the IMF issued a revised position on capital market liberalization, but how much of this led to change in actual IMF advice remains to be assessed, see 'The liberalization and management of capital flows: an institutional view', IMF, November 2012, https://tinyurl.com/yc74xmj5. Accessed on 9 December 2024.

24. Reinhart, Carmen M., and Kenneth S. Rogoff, 'Financial and Sovereign Debt Crises: Some Lessons Learned and Those Forgotten', IMF, https://tinyurl.com/2p8yyvhe. Accessed on 9 December 2024.

25. Schenk, Catherine, 'The IMF Remains the Lender of Last Resort – Literally', Chatham House–International Affairs Think Tank, 3 March 2022, https://tinyurl.com/yc6zpvev. Accessed on 9 December 2024.

26. In some cases, the reserve build-up was due to other factors, such as in China due to exchange targeting. See also 'Here's the alternative to U.S. dollar dominance — and it's not a rival currency, gold or bitcoin', MarketWatch, 16 July 2022, https://tinyurl.com/3ybr7x87. Accessed on 14 February 2025.

27. Lombardi, Domenico, and Ngaire Woods, 'The Political Economy of IMF Surveillance', CIGI Working Paper No. 17, 25 February 2007, https://tinyurl.com/mp23r48u. Accessed on 9 December 2024; Dhar, Sanjay, 'IMF Performance in the Run-Up to the Financial and Economic Crisis: Bilateral Surveillance of the United States', IMF, 9 December 2010, https://tinyurl.com/3f8hmtzr. Accessed on 9 December 2024; Dhar, Sanjay, and Shinji Takagi, 'IMF Surveillance of the Euro Area: From Conception Through Crisis', IEO Background Paper BP/10/04, https://tinyurl.com/4fjd9t3k. Accessed on 9 December 2024.

28. Pisani-Ferry, Jean, André Sapir, and Guntram B. Wolff, 'An Evaluation of IMF Surveillance of the Euro Area', Bruegel Blueprint 14, 31 October 2011, https://tinyurl.com/595frzen. Accessed on 9 December 2024.

29. Arora, Vivek, 'Five Lessons from a Review of Recent Crisis Programs', IMF Blog and Crisis Program Review, 11 July 2016, https://tinyurl.com/ykeu3zn8. Accessed on 9 December 2024.

30. Breen, M, 'IMF conditionality and the economic exposure of its shareholders', *European Journal of International Relations*, Vol. 20, No. 2, 2014, pp. 1–21, https://tinyurl.com/2vs9t5az. Accessed on 9 December, 2024; Andresen, Lena Lee, 'The Influence of Financial Corporations on IMF Lending: Has it Changed with the Global Financial Crisis?', SUERF Policy Brief, SUERF—The European Money and Finance Forum, https://tinyurl.com/w6s8ukbx. Accessed on 9 December 2024; 'Unlocking Development Finance: Market Finance for Development: Taking Stock', Discussion Draft Note #1, 25 October 2023.

31. Four countries—Albania, Armenia, Georgia, and Mozambique—have been

under IMF programme for over 80 per cent of their membership years and Haiti, Mali, Malawi and Romania for over 70 per cent of their membership years. Bulgaria and Argentina have been under programmes for more than 60 per cent of their membership years. These chronically sick patients, so to speak, probably need a different approach than just ever-continuing IMF programmes, as their problems are more structural and governance-related for which the IMF may not be the right institution to help out.

32. Reinhart, Carmen M., and Christoph Trebesch, 'The International Monetary Fund: 70 Years of Reinvention', *Journal of Economic Perspectives*, Vol. 30, No. 1, Winter 2016, pp. 3–28, https://tinyurl.com/4m4mkamh. Accessed on 9 December 2024.

33. Guild, James, 'Why the World Bank Torched its "Ease of Doing Business" Ranking', *The Diplomat*, 7 October 2020, https://tinyurl.com/2a5exwts. Accessed on 9 December 2024; Broome, André, 'Doing Business: How Countries Gamed the World Bank's Business Rankings', British Politics and Policy at LSE, 6 January 2022, https://tinyurl.com/mr22kvet. Accessed on 9 December 2024.

34. Parks, Bradley, Ani Harutyunyan, and Matt DiLorenzo, 'What Makes the World Bank So Influential—Its Money or Its Ideas?', *Brookings*, 19 May 2020, https://tinyurl.com/3h3sdbvp. Accessed on 9 December 2024.

35. Broome, André, 'Doing Business: How Countries Gamed the World Bank's Business Rankings', British Politics and Policy at LSE, 6 January 2022, https://tinyurl.com/mr22kvet. Accessed on 9 December 2024.

36. In FY21, the WBG could only claim to have leverage in $23.4 billion of private finance in all its operations.

37. As of 2019, 48 guarantee transactions utilizing $7.4 billion in IBRD/IDA commitments supported the mobilization of $30.2 billion of commercial financing plus $20 billion of public financing. Since its inception, MIGA has provided more than $27 billion in guarantees (PRI) for more than 700 projects in over 100 developing countries. MIGA currently has an outstanding guarantees portfolio of over $10 billion.

38. Kotecha, Mahesh K., 'Rising Role of Preferred Creditor Status in Ratings of Multilateral Development Banks', Bretton Woods@75 Compendium, 2019, https://tinyurl.com/4aabd728. Accessed on 9 December 2024.

39. Emergency projects in response to disasters were found to be as successful as projects which took much longer to prepare according to IEG, the evaluation department of the WBG.

40. Hans Singer pointed out in 1956 that because of fungibility, external aid only financed the marginal projects. Therefore, it is better to assess overall country outcomes rather than individual projects—but this is not easy to attribute to MDBs, especially as their role in overall financing has diminished over time.

41. Chhibber, Ajay, 'Festering global problems require more globalized financing',

Brookings, 29 January 2016, https://tinyurl.com/nfjvr8vr. Accessed on 17 March 2025.

42. Fraga, Arminio, 'Bretton Woods at 75', *Project Syndicate*, 18 March 2019, https://tinyurl.com/5cf5p3da. Accessed on 9 December 2024.

43. Some limits must be set for how often a country can get IMF assistance—especially when there is not a balance of payments crisis.

44. Mazzucato, Mariana, and Alan Donnelly, 'How the G7 Could Help the Debt-Distressed', *Project Syndicate*, 23 June 2022, https://tinyurl.com/2h3epkxx. Accessed on 9 December 2024.

45. The European Investment Bank (EIB) already informally calls itself the European Carbon Bank.

46. Some suggest the regional MDBs focus more on country and regional issues and the World Bank on global issues. Birdsall, Nancy, 'MDBs: Why Governance Matters', Bretton Woods@75 Compendium. Accessed on 9 December 2024; World Bank Group, 'Enhancing the Effectiveness of the World Bank's Global Footprint', Independent Evaluation Group (IEG) Approach Paper, 11 April 2022, https://tinyurl.com/44ntvzt4. Accessed on 9 December 2024.

47. MIGA provides political risk guarantee, but once a project in a country takes a political risk guarantee, it could become a stigma and require political risk guarantees on all future projects with market financing.

48. Both the borrower and the lender have a disincentive to use a guarantee instead of a loan, as the borrower who takes the guarantee is precluding a loan of the same amount and the lender makes money on the loan.

49. Coulibaly, Brahima Sangafowa, and Eswar Prasad, 'The International Monetary and Financial System: How to Fit It for Purpose?', *Brookings*, 17 November 2020, https://tinyurl.com/f76bmabh. Accessed on 9 December 2024.

50. Sullivan, Arthur, 'World Bank Warns of Crisis for Developing Nations', *DW–Business, Economy and Finance News*, 15 February 2022, https://tinyurl.com/yc4ha7x7. Accessed on 9 December 2024; Maki, Sydney, 'Why There's a Looming Debt Crisis in Emerging Markets: QuickTake', *Bloomberg*, 5 May 2020, https://tinyurl.com/mwknxhyu. Accessed on 9 December 2024.

51. Such an increase will also make it easier to adjust quota shares.

52. World Bank, 'Protecting the Poorest Countries: Role of the Multilateral Development Banks in Times of Crisis', Explanatory Note, 7 July 2020, https://tinyurl.com/5hbjzpss. Accessed on 9 December 2024.

53. Some argue that the MDBs must make better use of existing capital base and show their willingness to leverage in private capital before giving them a capital increase.

54. Humphrey, Chris, 'All Hands on Deck', ODI, April 2020, https://tinyurl.com/jb3x5762. Accessed on 9 December 2024.

55. Chakrabarti, Suma, Mandeep Bains, and Annalisa Prizzon, 'Future Directions for the World Bank and the Broader MDB System: Some Reflections',

ODI: Think Change, 14 April 2022, https://tinyurl.com/3vwhx4rx. Accessed on 9 December 2024; Settimo, Riccardo, 'Higher multilateral development bank lending, unchanged capital resources and triple-A rating. A trinity after all?', Occasional Paper 488, Bank of Italy, 2019; See also, the G20 Capital Adequacy Framework (CAF) Report for ideas on these.

56. Ben-Artzi, Ruth, Regional Development Banks in Comparison: Banking Strategies versus Development Goals, Cambridge, Cambridge University Press, 2016, https://tinyurl.com/3zja489v. Accessed on 9 December 2024.

57. Sweden, for example.

58. González Durántez, Miriam, and Calli Obern, 'The EU's Carbon Border Tax Could Hurt Developing Countries', Project Syndicate, 24 June 2022, https://tinyurl.com/4afz9bsa. Accessed on 9 December 2024.

59. US Secretary Janet Yellen, in a speech at the Atlantic Council in April 2022, made the case for a Bretton Woods 2.0 and raised the issue of whether this was the right time for such a major reform, by stating, 'The discussion for the Bretton Woods which culminated in 1944 started in 1941 when the USA had not even yet formally entered WWII.' She argued there was no better time to start such a discussion than now.

60. World Bank Group, 'Bretton Woods after 75 Years: Perspectives from the Board', 16 October 2019, https://tinyurl.com/4xybj924. Accessed on 9 December 2024.

61. Nagarajan, G., and V.A. Nageswaran, 'Harnessing Private Capital for Global Public Goods: Issues, Challenges and Solutions', CSEP Working Paper 57, October 2023, https://tinyurl.com/y9jvjzmm. Accessed on 9 December 2024.

62. Asian Development Bank has updated its Capital Adequacy Framework and come up with ideas to increase its lending capacity by $10 billion per year without impairing its credit rating. This includes the Innovative Finance Facility for Climate in Asia and the Pacific (IF-CAP), which allows donors to guarantee parts of the existing sovereign loan portfolio on ADB's balance sheet to free up capital to invest in new climate projects.

Getting Rich before Getting Old: India's Macroeconomic Imperatives in a Post-Pandemic World, by Sajjid Z. Chinoy

1. Chinoy, S., T. Jain, and D. Sood, 'India's growth dynamics: separating signal from noise', J.P. Morgan India Economics Research Note, 2023.

2. Sood, D., S. Chinoy, and T. Jain, 'India: The State of State Finances', J.P. Morgan India Economics Research Note, 2024.

3. This assumes the central deficit is pegged at 4.4 per cent of GDP and state deficits at three per cent of GDP. However, the combined deficit is lower than the sum of the two deficits because the Centre's capex loans to the States are shown as state borrowing rather than revenues. These, therefore, need to be netted out to avoid double counting.

4.   Bloom, D.E., D. Canning, and J. Sevilla, 'Population Aging and Economic Growth in Asia', NBER, 2010.

5.   Kelley, A.C., and R.M. Schmidt, 'Evolution of recent economic-demographic modeling: A synthesis', *Journal of Population Economics*, Vol. 18, 2005, pp. 275–300, https://tinyurl.com/4ra87a8v. Accessed on 5 March 2025.

6.   UNFPA, 'China: The Economic Miracle and Demographic Dividend in China', 2017.

7.   Bloom, D.E., D. Canning, and J. Sevilla, 'The Demographic Dividend: A new perspective on the economic consequences of population change', RAND Corporation, 2003.

8.   Chinoy, S., T. Jain, and D. Sood, 'India in 2024: Growth, Stability, Duality', J.P. Morgan India Economics Research Note, 2024.

9.   Taken literally, the survey would suggest the compound annual real per capita consumption growth between 2011 and 2023 was very soft, with rural at 3.2 per cent and urban even lower at 2.6 per cent. That said, there has always been a difference in levels between the CES and GDP data. The latter show a CAGR of about five per cent. In the previous survey, GDP data showed a CAGR of 6.8 per cent even as the CES showed a growth of 4.5 per cent for rural and 4.3 per cent for urban consumption. Therefore, there is always a level difference in the surveys vis-à-vis private consumption estimates in the GDP accounts. Therefore, the survey is more useful to assess directional changes.

10.   Penn World Table version 10.01 Database, Groningen Growth and Development Centre, https://tinyurl.com/4xnuj3rw. Accessed on 10 March 2025.

11.   PWT last available data is from 2019. KLEMS is from 2021–22. For growth accounting, both PWT and KLEMS use investment data from CSO for estimating capital input. Labour input differs between PWT and KLEMS as the latter does not include working hours per worker. Both PWT and KLEMS rely on the official labour force survey to estimate the employment level, but PWT uses ILO estimates from 2017 to 2019. KLEMS captures the quality of labour by considering the earnings of five educational groups, while PWT captures this concept by estimating human capital based on average years of schooling for those aged 25 and above, according to Shinya Kotera and Teng Teng Xu.

12.   Alonso, Christian, and Margaux MacDonald, 'Advancing India's Structural Transformation and Catch-up to the Technology Frontier', IMF Working Paper (WP/24/138), 2024.

13.   The Labour contribution for various countries in the exhibit is from Penn World Table (PWT) for cross-country comparability. For India, even if one considers KLEMS data for labour contribution, the conclusion does not differ.

14.   To be sure, this could be because either people have stopped looking for work

(fall in labour force participation) or are unable to get a job (unemployed). However, the former sometimes includes 'discouraged' workers who stop looking for work because they cannot find any.

15. IMF, 'Drivers of Growth in India', India: Article IV Consultations, 2023.
16. Chatterjee, S., and A. Subramanian, 'Has India Occupied the Export Space Vacated by China? 21st Century Export Performance and Policy Implications', Peterson Institute for International Economics, 2023.
17. NASSCOM, 'India's Tech Industry Talent: Demand Supply Analysis', 2022.
18. Panagariya, Arvind, 'India: The Emerging Giant. New York', Oxford University Press, IMF, 2018.
19. Chinoy, S., and T. Jain, 'What Drives India's Exports and What Explains the Recent Slowdown? New Evidence and Policy Implications', India Policy Forum, 2018.

Monetary Policy Challenges and Choices in Heightened Uncertainty, by Michael Debabrata Patra

1. Paulos, John A., *A Mathematician Plays the Stock Market*, Basic Books, 2003.
2. Knight, Frank H., *Risk, Uncertainty and Profit*, Vol. 31, Houghton Mifflin, 1921.
3. Ozturk, E.O., and X.S. Sheng, 'Measuring Global and Country-specific Uncertainty', *Journal of International Money and Finance*, Vol. 88, 2018, pp. 276–95.
4. Patra, Michael Debabrata, et al., 'Measuring Uncertainty: An Indian Perspective', *RBI Bulletin*, October 2023, https://tinyurl.com/5n8mbf43. Accessed on 9 December 2024.
5. Ibid.
6. Patra, Michael Debabrata, Joice John, and Asish Thomas George, 'Are Food Prices the "True" Core of India's Inflation?', *RBI Bulletin*, January 2024, https://tinyurl.com/uvmb3uw2. Accessed on 9 December 2024.
7. Ball, L., and N.G. Mankiw, 'Relative Price Changes as Aggregate Supply Shocks', *The Quarterly Journal of Economics*, Vol. 110, No. 1, 1995, pp. 161–93.
8. Patra, Michael Debabrata, Joice John, and Asish Thomas George, 'Are Food Prices the "True" Core of India's Inflation?', *RBI Bulletin*, January 2024, https://tinyurl.com/uvmb3uw2. Accessed on 9 December 2024.
9. Pesaran, M.H., Y. Shin, and R.J. Smith, 'Bounds Testing Approaches to the Analysis of Level Relationships', *Journal of Applied Econometrics*, Vol. 16, No. 3, 2001, pp. 289–326.
10. Patra, Michael Debabrata, Joice John, and Asish Thomas George, 'Are Food Prices the "True" Core of India's Inflation?', *RBI Bulletin*, January 2024, https://tinyurl.com/uvmb3uw2. Accessed on 9 December 2024.
11. Ibid.
12. Patra, Michael Debabrata, et al., 'Flexible Inflation Targeting (FIT) in India,

Chapter I in the Report on Currency and Finance 2020–21', Reserve Bank of India, 2021, https://tinyurl.com/yj9bywvw. Accessed on 9 December 2024.

13. Patra, Michael Debabrata, Joice John, and Asish Thomas George, 'Are Food Prices the "True" Core of India's Inflation?' *RBI Bulletin*, January 2024, https://tinyurl.com/uvmb3uw2. Accessed on 9 December 2024.

14. Patra, Michael Debabrata, and B.B. Bhoi, 'Quelling the Post-pandemic Inflation Surge: The Indian Experience', *Monetary Policy Responses to the Post-Pandemic Inflation*, B. English, K. Forbes, and A. Ubide (eds.), CEPR Press, 2024.

15. Patra, Michael Debabrata, I. Bhattacharyya, and J. John, 'Pushing Back Post-Pandemic Price Pressures: A Monetary-Fiscal Symphony', *Economic and Political Weekly*, Money Banking and Finance Special Issue, Vol. LIX, No. 21, 25 May 2024, https://tinyurl.com/yrdxfp5x. Accessed on 9 December 2024.

16. Ibid.

17. Friedman, M., 'The Role of Monetary Policy', *American Economic Review*, Vol. LVIII, No. 1, March 1968, https://tinyurl.com/2kde73ms. Accessed on 9 December 2024.

18. Friedman, M., *Perspective on Inflation, There's No Such Thing as a Free Lunch*, Open Court, Illinois, 1975, pp. 113–15.

19. Borio, C., et al., 'The Two-regime View of Inflation', BIS Papers, No. 133, 2023, https://tinyurl.com/235mtch2. Accessed on 9 December 2024.

20. Hamilton, J.D., 'A New Approach to the Economic Analysis of Nonstationary Time Series and the Business Cycle', *Econometrica*, Vol. 57, No.2, 1989, pp. 357–84, https://tinyurl.com/2rvjs97y. Accessed on 9 December 2024.

21. Patra, Michael Debabrata, Joice John, and Asish Thomas George, 'Recent Regime Reversal in Inflation: The Indian Experience', *RBI Bulletin*, April 2023, https://tinyurl.com/2pvdssft. Accessed on 9 December 2024.

22. Patra, Michael Debabrata, et al., 'Anatomy of Inflation's Ascent in India', *RBI Bulletin*, December 2022, https://tinyurl.com/nhkmb3xu. Accessed on 9 December 2024.

23. Patra, Michael Debabrata, et al., 'Flexible Inflation Targeting (FIT) in India, Chapter I in the Report on Currency and Finance 2020–21', Reserve Bank of India, 2021, https://tinyurl.com/yj9bywvw. Accessed on 9 December 2024.

24. Ibid.

25. Benes, M.J., et al., 'Inflation Forecast Targeting for India: An Outline of the Analytical Framework', RBI Working Paper Series No. 7/2016, 2016.

26. Benes, M.J., et al., 'Quarterly Projection Model for India: Key Elements and Properties', RBI Working Paper Series No. 8/2016, 2016.

27. John, J., et al., 'A Recalibrated Quarterly Projection Model (QPM 2.0) for India', *Reserve Bank of India Bulletin*, February 2023.

28. Patra, Michael Debabrata, I. Bhattacharyya, and J. John, 'Pushing Back Post-Pandemic Price Pressures: A Monetary-Fiscal Symphony', *Economic and Political Weekly*, Money Banking and Finance Special Issue, Vol. LIX,

No. 21, 25 May 2024, https://tinyurl.com/yrdxfp5x. Accessed on 9 December 2024.

29. John, J., et al., 'A Recalibrated Quarterly Projection Model (QPM 2.0) for India', Reserve Bank of India Bulletin, February 2023.

30. King, M., 'The Institutions of Monetary Policy', Lecture by the Governor of the Bank of England at the American Economic Association Annual Meeting, San Diego, 4 January 2004, https://tinyurl.com/bdeftdc8. Accessed on 9 December 2024.

31. Greider, W., *Secrets of the Temple: How the Federal Reserve Runs the Country*, Reprint edition, Simon and Schuster, 1989.

32. Goodfriend, M, 'Monetary Mystique: Secrecy and Central Banking', Federal Reserve Bank of Richmond Working Papers, No. 85–7, August 1985, https://tinyurl.com/2tnbtszr. Accessed on 9 December 2024.

33. Corrigan, Gerald E., 'Statement before the United States Senate Committee on Banking, Housing, and Urban Affairs', Bulletin of the Federal Reserve Bank of New York, 1990.

34. Bernanke, Benjamin S., 'Inaugurating a New Blog', *Brookings Commentary*, The Brookings Institution, 30 March 2015.

35. Draghi, M., 'Speech by President of the European Central Bank at the Global Investment Conference in London', 26 July 2012.

36. Gorodnichenko, Y., Tho Pham, and O. Talavera, 'The Voice of Monetary Policy', *American Economic Review*, Vol. 113, No. 2, February 2023, pp. 548–84, https://tinyurl.com/543yufhc. Accessed on 9 December 2024.

37. Haldane, A., A. Macaulay and M. McMahon, 'The 3 E's of Central Bank Communication with the Public', Bank of England Staff Working Paper No. 847, January 2020, https://tinyurl.com/425637kt. Accessed on 9 December 2024.

38. BIS, *Annual Economic Report*, June 2018.

39. Ahmed, F., M. Binici, and J. Turunen, 'Monetary Policy Communication and Financial Markets in India', IMF Working Papers, WP/22/209, 2022, https://tinyurl.com/bdfrtkv4. Accessed on 9 December 2024.

40. Powell, J., 'Remarks by Chairman of the Federal Reserve of the United States', Panel Discussion, Thomas Laubach Research Conference, 19 May 2023.

41. Das, S., 'Central Banking in Uncertain Times: The Indian Experience', Opening Plenary address delivered at the Summer Meetings organized by Central Banking, London, 13 June 2023, https://tinyurl.com/3yp7xscv. Accessed on 14 February 2025.

42. Patra, Michael Debabrata, J. John and I. Bhattacharyya, 'When Circumspection is the Better Part of Communication', *RBI Bulletin*, July 2023, https://tinyurl.com/mr2zbu9p. Accessed on 14 February 2025.

Fiscal Performance in a Soft State: A Review of Central and State Government Finances in India, by Sudipto Mundle and Manish Gupta

1. Myrdal, G., *Asian Drama: An Enquiry into the Poverty of Nations*, Penguin Press, London, 1968.
2. Mundle, S., and S. Sikdar, 'Subsidies, Merit Goods and the Fiscal Space for Reviving Growth: An Aspect of Public Expenditure in India', *Economic and Political Weekly*, Vol. 55, No. 5, February 2020.
3. Falling short of an absolute majority, the BJP now depends on two key regional parties from Bihar and Andhra Pradesh to stay in power. The INDIA alliance, consisting of the Indian National Congress and several regional parties, is now a strong opposition with a large number of seats in Parliament, in addition to being in power in several States.
4. Bhattacharya, R., et al., 'Year End Macroeconomic Review FY 2023–24', NIPFP Policy Brief, May 2024.
5. This remark is subject to the caveat that social services such as health are primarily subjects under the State list in the 7th schedule of the Constitution.
6. Bhattacharya, R., et al., 'Year End Macroeconomic Review FY 2023–24'.
7. Finance Commission, 'Finance Commission in Covid Times: Report for 2021–26', Fifteenth Finance Commission Vol. 1: Main Report, October 2020.
8. Mundle, S., 'The Economic and Political Geography of Development Divergence among States: Challenges and Opportunities', Inaugural Address, Regional Science Association National Conference on Regional Development, Pune, 22–23 December 2023.
9. Sen, A., *Development as Freedom*, Oxford University Press, Oxford, 1990.
10. Sen, A., 'Mortality as an Indicator of Economic Success and Failure', *Economic Journal*, Vol. 108, No. 446, 1998, pp. 1–25.
11. Mundle, S. 'The Economic and Political Geography of Development Divergence among States: Challenges and Opportunities', Inaugural Address, Regional Science Association National Conference on Regional Development, Pune, 22–23 December 2023.
12. The lack of any clear relationship between fiscal performance and development orientation, seen through the bivariate lens, has been verified through regression analysis. It confirms the absence of any statistically significant relationship between the capex ratio and the economic development indicator (per capita income), the social expenditure ratio and the social development indicator (life expectancy), and per capita income and the fiscal deficit. However, consistent with the bivariate picture on the receipts side described above, per capita income is significant at the one per cent level of confidence when regressed against per capita own revenue receipts, with an R-square value of 0.82 (Appendix table A1).

India's Quest for Productive Employment and the Role of MSMEs, by Radhicka Kapoor

1. Periodic Labour Force Survey (2022–23).
2. International Labour Organization, *India Employment Report 2024: Youth employment, education and skills*, https://tinyurl.com/2jmf78zz. Accessed on 9 December 2024; Basole, Amit, 'Structural Transformation and Employment Generation in India: Past Performance and the Way Forward', *The Indian Journal of Labour Economics*, Springer, The Indian Society of Labour Economics (ISLE), Vol. 65, No. 2, pp. 295–320, https://tinyurl.com/yuek9n3b, Accessed on 9 December 2024; Ghose, Ajit, 'India Employment Report 2016: Challenges and the Imperative of Manufacturing-Led Growth', *OUP Catalogue*, Oxford University Press, number 9780199472574, https://tinyurl.com/3vnhdsbn. Accessed on 9 December 2024.
3. Kapoor, Radhicka, 'A Big Push for Labour Intensive Manufacturing', *A New Reform Paradigm: Festschrift in Honour of Isher Judge Ahluwalia*, Radhicka Kapoor (eds.), Rupa Publication, New Delhi, 2022, pp. 159–97.
4. OECD/ILO, 'MSME Productivity, Inclusive Growth and Decent Work Creation', 2022, https://tinyurl.com/4mhyvamd. Accessed on 9 December 2024.
5. Although our analysis is for the period till 2015–16, it is worth noting that the government of India has recently revised the definition of MSMEs to one based not just on investment in plant and machinery but also on the annual turnover.
6. Kapoor, Radhicka, 'Stylized Facts on the Evolution of the Enterprise Size Distribution in India's Manufacturing Sector', ICRIER Working Paper No. 409, 2022, https://tinyurl.com/snx57xkh. Accessed on 9 December 2024.
7. 'Enterprises by business size', OECD, https://tinyurl.com/phhc62jx. Accessed on 14 February 2025.
8. Nagaraj, R., 'Of "Missing Middle", and Size-based Regulation: A New Frontier in the Labour Market Flexibility Debate', CSE Working Paper 2018-7, Azim Premji University, 2018.
9. Referring to them as entrepreneurs in the traditional sense of the word (i.e. those who undertake a venture, organize it, raise capital to finance it, assume the whole or major part of the risk of business, sell output in the market, pays workers' wages with the sales proceeds, repay the loan with interest, and claim what is left as profit) is, in fact, not correct.
10. Hsieh, Chang-Tai, and Benjamin A. Olken. 'The Missing "Missing Middle"', *Journal of Economic Perspectives,* Vol. 28, No. 3, 2014. pp. 89–108, https://tinyurl.com/4kh6knxy. Accessed on 14 February 2025.
11. Kapoor, Radhicka, and P.P. Krishnapriya, 'Understanding Changes in the Distribution of Employment in India's Manufacturing Sector', (forthcoming).
12. This fraction decreases as we look at previous years, since the number of years preceding that year also decreases.

13. Hasan, Rana, and Karl Robert Jandoc, 'The Distribution of Firm Size in India: What Can Survey Data Tell Us?', Asian Development Bank Economics Working Paper Series No. 213, 2010.

14. Kapoor, Radhicka, and P.P. Krishnapriya, 'Explaining the contractualisation of India's workforce', ICRIER Working Paper No 369. 2019, https://tinyurl.com/56vvvvda. Accessed on 9 December 2024.

15. Kapoor, Radhicka, 'Stylized Facts on the Evolution of the Enterprise Size Distribution in India's Manufacturing Sector', ICRIER Working Paper No. 409, 2022, https://tinyurl.com/snx57xkh. Accessed on 9 December 2024.

16. Schoar, Antoinette, 'The Divide between Subsistence and Transformational Entrepreneurship', NBER Chapters, *Innovation Policy and the Economy*, Vol. 10, 2010, pp. 57–8.

17. Herrera, Ana María, and Eduardo Lora, 'Why So Small? Explaining the Size of Firms in Latin America', *The World Economy*, Vol. 28, No. 7, 2005, pp. 1005–28.

18. Nageswaran, Venkatraman Anantha, and Gulzar Natarajan, 'India's Quest for Jobs: A Policy Agenda', Carnegie Endowment for International Peace, 2019, https://tinyurl.com/2z2szk6t. Accessed on 9 December 2024.

19. This is referred to as the productivity ecosystem approach (ILO & OECD, 2022) and the following discussion draws from this approach.

20. OECD/ILO, 'MSME Productivity, Inclusive Growth and Decent Work Creation', 2022, https://tinyurl.com/4mhyvamd. Accessed on 9 December 2024.

21. Nagaraj, Rayaprolu (ed.), *Industrialisation for Employment and Growth in India: Lessons from Small Firm Clusters and Beyond*, Cambridge University Press, Cambridge, 2021.

22. The heterogeneity in the evolution of the employment distribution across states of India underscores the importance of locational factors in determining the growth performance of firms (Kapoor, 2022).

23. Bloom, Nicholas, and John Van Reenen, 'Why Do Management Practices Differ across Firms and Countries?', *Journal of Economic Perspectives*, Vol. 24, No. 1, pp. 203–24, 2010, https://tinyurl.com/38c74sr6. Accessed on 9 December 2024.

24. Parker, Storey, and van Witteloostuijn, 'What happens to gazelles? The importance of dynamic management strategy', *Small Business Economics*, Vol. 35, No. 2, 2010, pp. 203–26, https://tinyurl.com/yeytnvaz. Accessed on 14 February 2025.

25. OECD/ILO, 'MSME Productivity', https://tinyurl.com/4mhyvamd. Accessed on 9 December 2024.

26. OECD, 'The Digital Transformation of SMEs', *OECD Studies on SMEs and Entrepreneurship*, 2021, https://tinyurl.com/2rs983h6. Accessed on 9 December 2024.

27. Goyal, Tanu, and Radhicka Kapoor, 'Annual Survey of Micro, Small, and Medium Enterprises (MSMEs) In India: Leveraging E-commerce for the

Growth of MSMes', ICRIER Report 23-r-06, ICRIER, 2023, https://tinyurl.com/4fscztme. Accessed on 9 December 2024.

28. OECD/ILO, 'MSME Productivity', https://tinyurl.com/4mhyvamd. Accessed on 9 December 2024.

29. Unemployment rates among the educated youth are roughly three times those among uneducated youth.

30. Grimm, Michael, Peter Knorringa, and Jann Lay, 'Constrained Gazelles: High Potentials in West Africa's Informal Economy', *World Development*, Vol. 40, No. 7, 2012, pp. 1352–68, https://tinyurl.com/23b278as. Accessed on 10 March 2025.

31. Boston, T.D., and L.R. Boston, 'Secrets of gazelles: The differences between high-growth and low-growth business owned by African-American entrepreneurs', *The Annals of the American Academy of Political and Social Science*, Vol. 613, No. 3, 2007, pp. 227–36.

Indian Urbanization Is Slowing Down: What Can Be Done about It?, by Rakesh Mohan

1. I am deeply indebted to Divya Srinivasan for her help in compiling this article, and to Greg Ingram for his usual deeply insightful comments.

2. Acharya, Shankar, and Rakesh Mohan, 'An Analysis of Projected Urban Infrastructure Investment Costs in India', *Review of Urban and Regional Development Studies*, Vol. 2, No.1, January 1990.

3. Acharya, Shankar, and Rakesh Mohan (eds.), *India's Economy: Performance and Challenges*, Oxford University Press, New Delhi, 2010.

4. 'Urbanization Takes on New Dimensions in Asia's Population Giants', Population Reference Bureau, 1 October 2001, https://tinyurl.com/mppamumx. Accessed on 9 December 2024.

5. Ministry of Finance, Government of India, *Economic Survey 2016-17*, Volumes 1 and 2, 2017, p. 221.

6. Mathur, Om Prakash, 'Whither Indian Urbanisation?', *Changing Paradigms of Urbanisation*, Om Prakash Mathur (ed.), Academic Foundation, 2024, p. 204.

7. India's definition has been consistent over time, so intertemporal comparisons are appropriate. However, there is no uniformity in the definition of 'urban' across countries. The United Nations takes each country's definition as given.

8. United Nations, Department of Economic and Social Affairs, Population Division, *World Urbanization Prospects: The 2018 Revision* (ST/ESA/SER.A/420), 2019.

9. Mohan, Rakesh, and Chandrashekar Pant, 'The Morphology of Urbanization in India, Some Results from the 1981 Census', *Economic and Political Weekly*, Vol. XVII, Nos 38 and 39, 18 and 25 September 1982.

10. Mathur, Om Prakash, 'Whither Indian Urbanisation?', pp. 199–218.

11. Jharkhand was split off from Bihar in 2000, thereby taking away some of the more industrialized and urbanized areas of the former undivided state. The level of urbanization of undivided Bihar was 13.1 per cent in 1991, but after the division it was only 11.3 per cent in 2011, while Jharkhand's level was 24.05 per cent in 2011.

12. Chan, Kam Wing, 'China's Hukou Reform Remains a Major Challenge to Domestic Migrants in Cities', *World Bank Blogs*, 17 December 2021, https://tinyurl.com/3phj3zps. Accessed on 9 December 2024. It is reported that there is some ongoing discussion now to reform the hukou system.

13. Harris, John R., and Michael P. Todaro, 'Migration, Unemployment and Development: A Two-Sector Analysis', *American Economic Review*, Vol. 60, No. 1, 1970, pp. 126–142.

14. I am grateful to Greg Ingram for sensitizing me to this issue.

15. Also shown in Table 1.9, in Mathur, Om Prakash, 'India's Urban Transition', *Changing Paradigms of Urbanisation*, Om Prakash Mathur (ed.), Academic Foundation, 2024, p. 77.

16. Personal communication. Paper yet to be published.

17. Ghani, Ejaz, A.G. Goswami, and W.R. Kerr, 'Is India's Manufacturing Sector Moving Away from Cities?', Working Paper No. 17992. National Bureau of Economic Research, Cambridge, US, 2012, https://tinyurl.com/mryf6wrt. Accessed on 9 December 2024.

18. Saikia, Dilip, 'Industrial Location in India under Liberalization', Institute for Financial Management and Research, Munich Personal RePEc Archive, 1997; Sekhar, A. Uday, 'Industrial Location Policy: The Indian Experience', World Bank Staff Working Papers Number 620, 1983, https://tinyurl.com/34ndp9ns. Accessed on 9 December 2024.

19. Glaeser, Edward, and Abha Joshi Ghani, 'Rethinking Cities', World Bank Publications, 2013, pp. 1–14.

20. A set of highly credit-rated German mortgage banks issue bonds known as *pfandbriefes* to raise funds at low cost. These funds are then lent to individual local governments, who otherwise would not have high credit ratings.

Digitalization and Development: India's Journey from the Backwaters to the High Seas of Digital Revolution, by Deepak Mishra and Mansi Kedia

1. This paper draws on our previous research work, especially ICRIER's flagship annual publication called *State of India's Digital Economy* (SIDE) *Report*, 2023 and 2024; Deepak, M., et al., *State of India's Digital Economy (SIDE) Report*, IPCIDE, ICRIER, 2024, https://tinyurl.com/4mecuwvw. Accessed on 9 December, 2024.

2. Solow, R.M., 'Growth Theory and After', *The American Economic Review*, Vol. 78, No. 3, 1988, pp. 307–17, https://tinyurl.com/yc723pnz. Accessed on 9 December 2024.

3. McKinsey Global Institute, *U.S. Productivity Growth, 1995-2000*, 2001, https://tinyurl.com/yctywhc6. Accessed on 9 December 2024.
4. Nevens, T.M., and G. Morse, 'The Real Source of the Productivity Boom', *Harvard Business Review—Forethought*, 2002, https://tinyurl.com/r4z6w866. Accessed on 9 December, 2024.
5. World Bank Group, *World Development Report 2016: Digital Dividends*, 2015, https://tinyurl.com/y5has7m6. Accessed on 9 December 2024.
6. Deepak, M., et al., *State of India's Digital Economy*, 2024.
7. The new approach has three properties. First, it uses a much wider definition of digitalization through its Connect-Harness-Innovate-Protect-Sustain (CHIPS) framework, capturing both the opportunities and risks created by digitalization. Second, it recognizes the scale of the network, and the depth of the use of technology at the economy-wide level, by proposing two separate indices—CHIPS (Economy) and CHIPS (User). Finally, it is estimated almost entirely using outcome indicators.
8. 'The cost of 1GB of mobile data in 237 countries', *Cable.co.uk.*, https://tinyurl.com/5y4y799r. Accessed on 9 December 2024.
9. Deepak, M., et al., *State of India's Digital Economy*, 2024.
10. Ibid.
11. 'Social Media Usage & Growth Statistics', *Backlinko*, 10 February 2025, https://tinyurl.com/2xn92ccm. Accessed on 9 December 2024.
12. The results of the World Bank's Technology Adoption Survey for India shows that firms are most likely to use technology for payments, followed by sales, and much less likely for quality control, sourcing, production planning and business administration.
13. '65% of Indian Businesses have seen a positive outcome from digital transformation, finds DBS and FT Longitude Survey', DBS, 14 February 2023, https://tinyurl.com/mf73yy7x. Accessed on 9 December 2024.
14. PIB, 'Achievements Made under Digital India Programme', 23 December 2022, https://tinyurl.com/2eh64esd. Accessed on 9 December 2024.
15. Deepak, M., et al., *State of India's Digital Economy (SIDE) Report, 2023*, IPCIDE, ICRIER, 2023, https://tinyurl.com/3fpkhpwt. Accessed on 9 December 2024.
16. Government of India, 'DBT Schemes', https://tinyurl.com/mr2fb492. Accessed on 9 December 2024.
17. Government of India, 'Interim Budget 2024–25, Speech of Nirmala Sitharaman, Minister of Finance', 1 February 2024.
18. Ministry of Electronics and Information Technology, GOI, *eTaal Dashboard*, https://tinyurl.com/327ur2kw. Accessed on 14 February 2025.
19. UDISE+, *Report on Unified District Information System For Education Plus (USIDE+)*, Ministry of Education, GOI, 10 October 2022.
20. Deepak, M., et al., *State of India's Digital Economy*.

21. MOSIP, 'Identifying a Billion', 4 September 2022, https://tinyurl.com/d6muc7w7. Accessed on 9 December 2024.

22. European Payments Council, 'UPI: revolutionising real-time digital payments in India', 26 June 2024, https://tinyurl.com/383x4zwt. Accessed on 9 December 2024.

23. Centre for Digital Public Infrastructure, *DPI Overview*, https://tinyurl.com/5n7ydykz. Accessed on 9 December 2024.

24. Choudhury, D., 'Tier 2 cities drive 65% of retail orders on ONDC in April', *Money Control*, 6 May 2024, https://tinyurl.com/mr2tr6uf. Accessed on 9 December 2024.

25. LIRNEasia, 'Internet use at 53% of 15+ population in Tamil Nadu: COVID-19 pandemic boosted internet uptake among the marginalised, but a significant digital divide remains (Press Release)', 25 November 2021, https://tinyurl.com/bdfhr2xu. Accessed on 9 December 2024.

26. In 2019, the Kerala High Court held 'Right to Internet Access' as a fundamental right. The court declared that the right to have access to the internet becomes the part of right to education as well as right to privacy under Article 21 of the Constitution of India.

27. Jensen, R., 'The Digital Provide: Information (Technology), Market Performance, And Welfare In The South Indian Fisheries Sector', *The Quarterly Journal of Economics*, Vol. 122, No. 3, August 2007, pp. 879–924, https://tinyurl.com/2fb958er. Accessed on 9 December 2024.

28. The World Bank Group, *World Development Report: Digital Dividends*, 2016, https://tinyurl.com/4swp4p44. Accessed on 9 December 2024.

29. Asian News International, 'UIDAI unveils Aadhaar innovations at Global Fintech Festival 2023', *Economic Times*, 7 September 2023, https://tinyurl.com/3yjma9pr. Accessed on 9 December 2024.

30. PIB, 'UIDAI comes back to Global Fintech Fest with the theme "Reimagine Aadhaar"', 6 September 2023, https://tinyurl.com/mvma8axw. Accessed on 9 December 2024.

31. Acemoglu, D., et al., 'Return of the Solow Paradox? IT, productivity, and employment in US manufacturing', *American Economic Review*, Vol. 104, No. 5, 2014, pp. 394–99, https://tinyurl.com/48t3ezes. Accessed on 9 December 2024.

32. GSMA refers to this as the usage gap in connectivity.

33. GSMA, 'The State of Mobile Internet Connectivity 2022', 2022, https://tinyurl.com/yn8jb6fx. Accessed on 9 December 2024.

34. Kant, K., 'Market concentration of telecom sector leaders rises to 72% in FY23', *Business Standard*, 12 June 2023, https://tinyurl.com/3y9mrhuu. Accessed on 9 December 2024.

35. Shanahan, M., and K. Bahia, 'The State of Mobile Internet Connectivity 2023', GSMA, October 2023, https://tinyurl.com/kzknrdsn. Accessed on 9 December 2024.

36. ACI Worldwide, *2023 Prime Time for Real-Time Report*, 2023, https://tinyurl. com/ndvdrh6y. Accessed on 9 December 2024.

37. Future Crime Research Foundation (FCRF), 'A Deep Dive into Cybercrime Trends Impacting India', 2023.

Priorities for Indian Agriculture: A Case for Cooperative Federalism to Improve Incomes and Livelihoods, by S. Mahendra Dev

1. Kaldor, N., *Strategic Factors in Economic Development*, Cornell University Press, Ithaca, 1967.

2. Kuznets, S., *Toward a Theory of Economic Growth with Reflections on the Economic Growth of Nations*, Norton, New York, 1968.

3. Mellor, J.W., *The New Economic Growth: A Strategy for India and the Developing World*, Cornell University Press, Ithaca, 1976.

4. Singh, Manmohan, 'Inaugural Address', *Indian Journal of Agricultural Economics*, Vol. 50, No. 1, 1995, pp. 1–8.

5. Sharma, Vijay Paul, '*Transforming Indian Agriculture: Emerging Trends, Challenges and Policy Options*', Presidential Address delivered at the 37th Annual Conference of the Indian Society of Agricultural Marketing, Tamil Nadu Agricultural University, Coimbatore, 14 September 2023.

6. Chand, Ramesh, and Jaspal Singh, *From Green Revolution to Amrit Kaal: Lessons and Way Forward for Indian Agriculture*, NITI Aayog Working paper 02/2023, 2023, https://tinyurl.com/4zxd3ar5. Accessed on 9 December 2024.

7. Krishna, K.L., and J.V. Meenakshi, 'Agricultural Productivity Growth and Structural Transformation in Rural India: Some Recent Evidence', *Journal of Quantitative Economics*, Vol. 20, No. 1, Supplement in honour of Prof. C.R. Rao, 2022, pp. 277–302, https://tinyurl.com/4tk4k3tr. Accessed on 9 December 2024.

8. Sengupta, S., D. Suganthi, and B. Goldar, 'Total factor productivity growth in Indian Agriculture: Accounting for Land Quality', *RBI Occasional paper*, Vol. 44, No. 1, 2023, pp. 22–51.

9. Narayanamoorthy, A., and Chandra S. Nuthalapati, 'Decelerating Farmers' Incomes: New Evidence from SAS Data and Ways Forward', *Economic and Political Weekly*, Vol. 58, No. 49, 2023, pp. 13-17.

10. Dev, S. Mahendra, 'Transformation of Indian Agriculture? Growth, Inclusiveness and Sustainability', *Indian Journal of Agricultural Economics*, Vol. 74, No. 1, 2019, pp. 9–61.

11. Solow, R.M., 'A contribution to the theory of economic growth', *Quarterly Journal of Economics*, Vol. 70, No. 1, 1956, pp. 65–94.

12. Dev, S. Mahendra, 'Regional Dimensions in India: Economic Growth, Inclusive and Sustainable Development', Presidential Address delivered at the 58th Annual Conference of the Indian Econometric Society, Agartala, February 22–24, 2024.

13. Swaminathan, M.S., *From Green to Evergreen Revolution, Indian Agriculture: Performance an Challenges,* Academic Foundation, 2010.
14. Ministry of Finance, GOI, *Economic survey 2017-18,* 2018.
15. Ministry of Finance, GOI, *Economic survey 2022-23,* 2023.
16. RBI, *Report on Currency and Finance,* 2022.
17. Martin, Will, 'The 800 billion dollar question: Repurposing Agricultural Support for People, Planet and Prosperity', Presentation made at IFPRI, 2024, https://tinyurl.com/8vrdsd27. Accessed on 9 December 2024.
18. Fan, Shenggen, 'Agriculture Support Policy Reform, Experience from China', Presentation made at International Food Policy Research Institute, Washington, D.C., 2024, https://tinyurl.com/2dp2wv5j. Accessed on 17 March 2025.
19. Martin, Will, 'The 800 billion dollar question: Repurposing Agricultural Support for People, Planet and Prosperity', Presentation made at IFPRI, 2024, https://tinyurl.com/8vrdsd27. Accessed on 9 December 2024.
20. CGIAR, *Achieving Agricultural Breakthrough: A deep dive into seven technological areas,* 2023, https://tinyurl.com/2dbn24mw. Accessed on 9 December 2024.
21. Suganthi, D., Rishabh Kumar, and Monika Sethi, 'Agriculture Supply Chain Dynamics: Evidence from Pan-India Survey', *RBI Bulletin,* January 2024, pp. 121–35.
22. Gulati, A., and C. Cahill, 'Resolving farmer-consumer binary', *Indian Express,* 9 July 2018, https://tinyurl.com/5n7cerb8. Accessed on 9 December 2024.
23. Gulati, A., and R. Roy, 'From Plate to Plough: The Reach and Depth of MSP', *Financial Express,* 3 January 2022, https://tinyurl.com/4kexv6r7. Accessed on 9 December 2024.
24. Chand, Ramesh, and Jaspal Singh, 'From Green Revolution to Amrit Kaal, Lessons and Way Forward for Indian Agriculture', NITI Aayog Working Paper 02/2023, 2023, https://tinyurl.com/4zxd3ar5. Accessed on 9 December 2024.
25. Deodhar, S.Y., and Vijay Kelkar, 'Making a New Beginning on Farm Reforms', *Economic and Political Weekly,* Vol. 59, No. 16, 2023, pp. 43–50.
26. Ghanwat, A., A. Gulati, and P. Joshi, 'Report of The Supreme Court Appointed Committee on Farm Laws', 21 March 2022, https://tinyurl.com/hntzsrkn. Accessed on 9 December 2024.
27. Deodhar, S.Y., and Vijay Kelkar, 'Making a New Beginning on Farm Reforms', *Economic and Political Weekly,* Vol. 59, No. 16, 2023, pp. 43–50.
28. Sharma, Vijay Paul, 'Transforming Indian Agriculture: Emerging Trends, Challenges and Policy Options', Presidential Address delivered at the 37th Annual Conference of the Indian Society of Agricultural Marketing, Tamil Nadu Agricultural University, Coimbatore, 14 September 2023.
29. Nuthalapati, Chandra S., et al., 'Hybrid Mustard and Biotechnology: Pathways for Doubling Farmers' Incomes and Nutritional Security', *Economic and Political Weekly,* Vol. 58, No. 43, 2023, pp. 47–54.

30. Chand, Ramesh, and Jaspal Singh, 'From Green Revolution to Amrit Kaal: Lessons and Way Forward for Indian Agriculture', NITI Aayog Working Paper 02/2023, 2023, https://tinyurl.com/4zxd3ar5. Accessed on 9 December 2024.

31. Rao, N. Chandrasekhara, R. Sutradhar, and T. Reardon, 'Disruptive Innovations in Food Value Chains and Small Farmers in India', *Indian Journal of Agricultural Economics*, Vol. 72, No.1, 2017, pp. 24–48.

32. Damodaran, H., 'What India's latest farm exports data show', *Indian Express*, 14 February 2023, https://tinyurl.com/msvaz6mt. Accessed on 9 December 2024.

33. Sharma, Vijay Paul, 'Transforming Indian Agriculture: Emerging Trends, Challenges and Policy Options', Presidential Address delivered at the 37th Annual Conference of the Indian Society of Agricultural Marketing, Tamil Nadu Agricultural University, Coimbatore, 14 September 2023.

34. NITI Aayog, 'Rising Agricultural Productivity and making farming Remunerative for farmers', An Occasion paper', 2015.

35. Von Braun, Kaosar Afsana, Louise O. Fresco, and Mohamed Hassan, 'Seven Priorities to end hunger and protect the planet', *Nature,* Vol. 597, No. 7874, 2021, pp. 28–30.

36. FAO, *Sustainable Food systems, Concept and Framework*, 2018, https://tinyurl.com/5357smj4. Accessed on 9 December 2024.

37. Rangarajan, C., and S. Mahendra Dev, 'Removing the Roots of Farmers' Distress', *The Hindu*, 28 January 2019, https://tinyurl.com/2x24srra. Accessed on 9 December 2024.

38. FAO, *The State of Food Security and Nutrition in the World 2023*, 2023.

39. Ibid.

40. Swaminathan, M.S., and P.C. Kesavan, 'Achieving the Sustainable Development Goals', Guest Editorial, *Current Science*, Vol. 110, No. 2, 2016, pp. 127–8.

41. Dev, S. Mahendra, and V.L. Pandey, 'Dietary Diversity, Nutrition and Food Safety', *Indian Agriculture Towards 2030: Pathways for Enhancing Farmers' Income, Nutrition Security and Sustainable Food and Farm Systems*, R. Chand, P. Joshi, and S. Khadka (eds.), Springer, New Delhi, 2021, pp. 39–82.

42. Rao, C.H.H., *Agriculture, Food security, Poverty and Environment*, Oxford University Press, New Delhi, 2005.

43. Swaminathan, M.S., *From Green to Evergreen Revolution, Indian Agriculture: Performance an Challenges*, Academic Foundation, New Delhi, 2010.

44. FAO, '"Climate-Smart" Agriculture: Policies, Practices and Financing for Food Security, Adaptation and Mitigation', 2010, https://tinyurl.com/zjukfbsx. Accessed on 9 December 2024.

45. FAO, 'Sustainable food systems: Concept and framework', 2018, https://tinyurl.com/5357smj4. Accessed on 9 December 2024.

46. Das, S., M. Khurana, and A. Gulati, 'Zero Budget Natural Farming:

Implications for sustainability, profitability and food security', NABARD Research Study no. 43, 2024.

47. IFPRI, *Global Food Policy Report, 2022*, 2022.

48. Srinivasan, T.N., 'Development Strategy: The State and Agriculture since Independence', Valedictory Address at the 10th Annual Money and Finance Conference, Indira Gandhi Institute of Development Research, 18–19 January 2008.

49. Acharya, Shankar, *An Economist at Home and Abroad*, HarperCollins Publishers, Uttar Pradesh, 2021.

50. Lewis, W. Arthur, 'Economic development with unlimited supplies of labour', *The Manchester School*, Vol. 22, No. 2, 1956, pp. 139–91.

Waiting for Consensus: How India's Political Economy Impacts Its Economic Reforms, by A.K. Bhattacharya

1. Ciminelli, Gabriele, et al., 'The Political Costs of Reforms: Fear or Reality?', IMF Staff Discussion Note, October 2019, p. 4.

2. Thakurdas, Purshotamdas, et al., 'Memorandum Outlining a Plan of Economic Development for India', Penguin, London, 1944, pp. 1–6.

3. Bhattacharya, A.K., *The Rise of Goliath: Twelve Disruptions That Changed India*, Penguin, New Delhi, 2019, pp. 34–54.

4. Bhattacharya, A.K., *India's Finance Ministers: From Independence to Emergency (1947-1977)*, Penguin, New Delhi, 2023, pp. 2–19.

5. Ibid., pp. 20–38.

6. Kudaisya, Medha, *The Life and Times of G.D. Birla*, Oxford University Press India, New Delhi, 2003, pp. 339–49.

7. Bhattacharya, A.K., *India's Finance Ministers: From Independence to Emergency (1947-1977)*, Penguin, New Delhi, 2023, pp. 307–12.

8. Mohan, Rakesh, *India Transformed: 25 Years of Economic Reforms*, Penguin, New Delhi, 2017, pp. 3–10.

9. Bhattacharya, A.K., *India's Finance Ministers: Stumbling into Reforms (1977-1998)*, Penguin, New Delhi, 2024, p. 317.

10. Agha, Zafar, 'Under attack, Narasimha Rao Govt lowers hiked fertiliser prices and compromises on the issue', *India Today*, 31 August 1991, https://tinyurl.com/4ymh24f8. Accessed on 14 February 2025.

11. Sinha, Yashwant, *Confessions of a Swadeshi Reformer: My Years as Finance Minister*, Penguin, New Delhi, 2007, p. 10.

12. Bhattacharya, A.K., *India's Finance Ministers: Stumbling into Reforms (1977-1998)*, Penguin, New Delhi, 2024, pp. 424–6.

13. Acharya, Shankar, *An Economist at Home and Abroad: A Personal Journey*, HarperCollins, New Delhi, 2021, p. 176.

14. Panagariya, Arvind, *India's Trade Policy: The 1990s and beyond*, HarperCollins, New Delhi, 2024, pp. 35–39 and 51–58.

Index

5G, 297, 315
14th Five-Year Plan, 31

A2 costs, 332
Aadhaar, 294, 303, 310, 311, 313,
    314, 399
Aadhaar Payments Bridge (APB),
    313
Account Aggregator (AA), 259
adaptation, xviii, 13, 48, 49, 53, 72,
    140, 289, 340, 402
Addis Ababa Action Agenda, 140,
    148
African Development Bank, 130
All India Rural Financial Inclusion
    Survey (NAFIS), 342
Allende, Salvador, 95, 381
allyshoring, 35, 43
Alves Branco Tariff, 104
Anand Milk Union Limited
    (Amul), 338
Annual Survey of Industries (ASI),
    184, 243, 244, 245, 246, 248,
    249, 251, 252, 253, 255, 274
Argentinian Central Bank/
    Banco Central de la República
    Argentina (BCRA), 101, 102,
    103
Asian Development Bank, 121,
    130, 254, 370, 378, 388, 394
Asian Infrastructure Investment
    Bank (AIIB), xxii, 121, 131, 136

Association of Southeast Asian
    Nations (ASEAN), 26, 40, 42, 43,
    44, 45, 46, 130, 131
autoregressive conditional
    heteroskedastic (ARCH) model,
    210
auto regressive distributed lag
    (ARDL), 200
Ayushman Bharat, 89

Baldwin, Richard, 22
Banga, Ajay, 151
Bank for International Settlements
    (BIS), 121, 124, 126, 127, 131,
    132, 135, 136, 382, 383, 391, 392
Bank Indonesia, 132
Bank of Thailand, 126
Baotou Rare Earth Products
    Exchange, 134
Belt and Road Initiative (BRI), 121
Bharat Sanchar Nigam Limited
    (BSNL), 306
Bharatiya Janata Party, 347, 358,
    360, 361, 362, 363, 364, 365, 393
Biden, Joe, 38, 51
Bilateral Investment Treaty (BIT),
    44
Biofortification, 339
Birla, G.D., 348, 403
BIS Innovation Hub, 126
Bloom, David, 164
Bolsonaro, Jair, 106

Bombay Plan, 347, 348, 349
Brent, 123, 133, 134, 135
Bretton Woods, v, xxiii, 130, 137,
    139, 144, 145, 152, 351, 359,
    383, 386, 387, 388
BRICS, 110, 121, 130, 131, 132,
    384
BRICS Development Bank, 121
business process outsourcing
    (BPO), 307

C2 costs, 332
Carbon Border Adjustment
    Mechanism (CBAM), 35, 36, 44
carbon tax, 59, 60, 148
Cardoso, Fernando Henrique, 108,
    109, 382
Cavallo, Domingo, 99
central bank digital currency
    (CBDC), 125, 126
Central Bank of Brazil (BCB), 105,
    106, 110, 113
Central Bank of the United Arab
    Emirates, 126
Central Electricity Authority
    (CEA), vii, xiv, 64, 262
Central Electricity Regulatory
    Commission (CERC), 64
Chatterjee, Shoumitro, 21
Chetty, R.K. Shanmukham, 349
Chiang Mai Initiative
    Multilateralisation (CMIM), 131
Chicago Mercantile Exchange, 122,
    134
China Financial Futures Exchange
    (CFFEX), 133
China Interbank Bond Market, 129
China International Payment

System (CIPS), xxii, 127, 128,
    131, 135, 136
China National Offshore Oil
    Corporation (CNOOC), 134
China-Plus-One, xvii, 22, 24, 35,
    42, 43, 159, 188, 189
China Securities Regulatory
    Commission, 129
climate-smart agriculture, 340
Collor de Mello, Fernando, 107,
    108
common but differentiated
    responsibilities and respective
    capabilities (CBDR-RC)
    principle, 36
Communist Party of China (CPC),
    122
Companhia Vale do Rio Doce, 105
compound annual growth rate
    (CAGR), 160, 167, 389
Confederation of Engineering
    Industry/Confederation of
    Indian Industry, 356
Conference of the Parties (COP),
    49, 51, 54
Congress, xiv, 103, 149, 152, 350,
    351, 352, 353, 354, 356, 357,
    358, 360, 393
constrained gazelles, 260
Consultative Group for
    International Agricultural
    Research (CGIAR), 140, 331, 401
consumer price index (CPI), 195,
    199, 201, 204
Container Corporation of India
    Limited (ConCor), 67
COP21, 50
COP26, 51, 52, 55, 58, 340

COP28, 51, 54
COP29, 52, 53, 54
Corrigan, Gerald, 207

da Silva, Luiz Inácio Lula, 110
Dalian Commodity Exchange, 133
Dashing Protocol, 126
Das, Tarun, 356
data empowerment protection
   architecture (DEPA), 311
deindustrialization, 109, 114
demographic dividend, xx, 77, 78,
   82, 90, 91, 92, 164, 181
demonetization, xii, xxxi, 368
Department of Telecommunication
   (DoT), 306
Desai, Morarji, 350
Deshmukh, C.D., 349
Development Committee (DC),
   145
Development Evidence Portal, 82,
   88, 378, 379
development finance institutions
   (DFIs), 139
Digital Bharat Nidhi, 304
Digital Currency Research Institute
   (DCRI), 125, 126, 127
Digital India 2.0, 296
digitalization, xvi, xxix, 294, 295,
   296, 298, 304, 310, 312, 313,
   315, 316, 317, 318, 319, 398
digital public infrastructure (DPI),
   295, 297, 310, 311, 312, 314,
   318, 319, 398
Direct Benefit Transfer (DBT), 303,
   304, 313, 314, 334, 398
disability-adjusted life years
   (DALYs), 87, 379

dispute settlement mechanism
   (DSM), 34, 37, 38, 46
distribution companies (DISCOM),
   59, 60, 61, 62, 65
Doha Development Agenda
   (DDA), xvii, xviii, 28, 31, 34
domestic value addition (DVA),
   30, 374
Don Pedro II, 104
Dutch disease, 96

Earth Summit, 49
Ease of Doing Business Index, 143
e-CNY, 125, 126
Electronics and Computer Software
   Export Promotion Council
   (ESC), 308
Embraer, 105
emerging market economy (EME),
   42, 192
emissions trading system (ETS),
   60, 63
environment and sustainable
   governance (ESG), 32, 33
environment-related provisions
   (ERPs), 32, 33
e-Shram, 304, 313
European Bank for Reconstruction
   and Development, 130
European Central Bank, 126, 392
Evolution Roadmap, 151

Farmer producer organizations
   (FPOs), 338
Federal Reserve Bank of New York,
   126, 392
female labour force participation
   rate (FLFPR), 186

Fernández, Alberto, 103
flexible inflation targeting (FIT),
203, 207, 208, 390
foreign direct investment (FDI),
28, 112, 113, 141, 147, 189, 306,
382
foreign portfolio investment (FPI),
141
foreign value addition (FVA), 30
free trade agreement (FTA), 33, 36,
37, 39, 43, 44, 46, 375
friendshoring, 35, 36, 40, 43

G20, 18, 137, 145, 149, 150, 151,
152, 297, 298, 299, 301, 310,
311, 318, 373, 388
Gandhi, Indira, 349, 350, 351, 352,
359, 402
Gandhi, Rajiv, xii, 352, 358
Ganzhou Rare Metal Exchange,
134
García-Herrero, Alicia, 120
GATT, 28, 31, 34
GDP per head, xvi, 5, 6, 8, 10, 13,
19, 20, 23, 372
Ghosh, Atulya, 350
Global Alliance for Vaccination
(GAVI), 140
Global Capability Centres, 159, 173
Global Environmental Fund (GEF),
140
global financial crisis (GFC), xxiii,
24, 27, 29, 33, 138, 139, 208
Global Fund to Fight AIDS,
Tuberculosis and Malaria
(GFATM), 140
global public goods (GPGs), 140,
148, 149

global value chains (GVCs), xvii,
xviii, 24, 25, 26, 27, 28, 29, 30,
31, 32, 34, 35, 39, 40, 41, 43, 188
Goldman Sachs, vii, 110
goods and services tax (GST), xxx,
192, 216, 334, 343, 366, 367, 368
Gore, Al, 143
Green Climate Fund, 140, 151
greenhouse gases (GHGs), 12, 48,
49, 340
Green Revolution, 322, 332, 400,
401
gross value-added (GVA), 245, 246,
256, 273, 291, 323, 333
Gupta, Shishir, 269
Guzmán, Martín, 103

Heckman, James, 85, 379
Hong Kong Monetary Authority,
122, 126, 132
Household Consumption
Expenditure Survey (HCES), 175
Hoz, Martínez de, 99
hukou, 267, 397
Human Capital Index (HCI), xix,
78, 79, 80, 81, 83, 90, 378
hyperglobalization, xvi, 4, 14, 16,
373
hyperinflation, 99, 103, 104, 107

Ibrahim, Anwar, 132
ICRIER, vii, xiv, 298, 299, 300,
301, 302, 303, 305, 311, 332,
370, 394, 395, 397, 398
IMF, i, xxiii, 4, 5, 6, 7, 9, 10, 11,
12, 14, 15, 19, 20, 23, 98, 99,
100, 101, 102, 103, 109, 110,
112, 113, 115, 116, 117, 124,

125, 126, 130, 131, 138, 139,
140, 141, 142, 144, 145, 146,
147, 148, 149, 178, 193, 345,
346, 351, 352, 359, 372, 373,
374, 381, 382, 383, 384, 385,
386, 387, 389, 390, 392, 403
Imperial Bank of India, 348
import-substitution, xxxi, 31, 114,
321, 364, 368
Independent High-Level Expert
Group (IHLEG), 52, 53, 54
Indian Airlines, 348
Indian Institute of Management
(IIM), 90
Indian Institute of Technology
(IIT), 90
Indian Oil Corporation, 67
Indo-Pacific Economic Framework
(IPEF), 38, 39
Industrial Policy Resolution, 348
inflation expectations, 103
Inflation Reduction Act (IRA), 35,
36, 37, 71
information and communication
technology (ICT), 295, 296, 297,
307, 308, 309, 316, 318, 339
information technology enabled
services (ITeS), 307
Innovations for Poverty Action
(IPA), 85
Insurance Regulatory and
Development Authority of India
(IRDAI), 360
integrated crop management
(ICM), 341
intellectual property (IP), 32
intellectual property rights (IPR),
32

intended nationally determined
contributions (INDCs), 51, 55,
58, 73, 376
Inter-American Development
Bank, 130
International Bank for
Reconstruction and
Development (IBRD), 144, 147,
386
International Energy Agency
(IEA), 64
International Finance Corporation
(IFC), 143
International Food Policy Research
Institute (IFPRI), 84, 341, 401,
402
International Initiative for Impact
Evaluation, 82
International Monetary and
Finance Committee (IMFC), 145
International Telecommunication
Union (ITU), 318
investor-state dispute settlement
(ISDS), 32

Jalan, Bimal, xiii
Jan Dhan, 303, 313
Jan Dhan-Aadhaar-Mobile (JAM),
303, 313
Jensen, Robert, 313
Jha, L.K., 349
Jinping, Xi, 16, 123
Jose, Ashley, 269
J.P. Morgan, 125, 130, 157, 158,
159, 161, 163, 167, 168, 172,
177, 184, 189, 193, 370, 388, 389
Juncker, Jean-Claude, 76

Kamaraj, K., 350
Kaya identity, 56
Kessler, Martin, 14, 373
Kissinger, Henry, 95
Krishnamachari, T.T., 349
Kubitschek, Juscelino, 105
Kudumbashree Mission, 341
Kurien, Verghese, 338
Kyoto Protocol, 50

Lalbhai, Kasturbhai, 348
Lewis, Arthur, 342
Life Insurance Corporation (LIC), 348
local content requirements (LCR), 36
Logistics Performance Index (LPI), 44, 45
London Metal Exchange, 122

Macri, Mauricio, 100
Made in China 2025, 31, 374
Mahanagar Telephone Nigam Limited (MTNL), 306
Malhotra, R.N., 359
Markov switching model, 203
Mastercard, 126
Matthai, John, 348, 349
Meade, James, 94
Mehta, Harshad, 358
Melo, Collor de, 107
Menem, Carlos, 99
MGNREGA, 182, 215, 314
microenterprises, 244, 246, 248
Micro, Small and Medium Enterprises Development (MSMED) Act, 243
micro, small and medium

enterprises (MSMEs), vi, xxvii, 242, 243, 244, 247, 253, 255, 256, 257, 258, 259, 260, 342, 393, 394, 395
Milei, Javier, 103
minimum support price (MSP), 331, 332, 333, 334, 343, 401
Mission Creep, 142, 146
mitigation, xviii, 13, 36, 48, 49, 50, 52, 53, 54, 125, 140, 289, 340, 341, 376
Mode 4 liberalization, 44
Modi, Narendra, 18, 20, 21, 347, 361, 364, 365, 366, 367, 368, 373
MODVAT (modified value added tax), xiii
Monetary Policy Report (MPR), 205
Monroe Doctrine, 95
most favoured nation (MFN), 32, 36, 37, 42
multilateral development banks (MDBs), 52, 139, 140, 142, 144, 147, 148, 150, 151, 152, 386, 387
Multilateral Investment Guarantee Agency (MIGA), 143, 144, 386, 387
Myrdal, Gunnar, 94, 212

National e-Governance Plan (NeGP), 303
National Family Life Survey, 82
National Internet Exchange of India (NIXI), 307
National Renewal Fund, 368
National Rural Employment Guarantee Act, 339
National Security Council, 95

National Telecommunications
  Policy, 306
nearshoring, xvii, 24, 36
Nehru, Jawaharlal, ix, 348, 350
Nepal Rastra Bank, 126
net-zero, xviii, 340
new collective quantified goal
  (NCQG), 52, 53
Nijalingappa, S., 350
NITI Aayog, 75, 400, 401, 402
non-governmental organization
  (NGO), 86, 88
North American Free Trade
  Agreement (NAFTA), 33
NSSO, 181, 243, 244, 245, 246,
  248, 251, 271
Nuclear Power Corporation of
  India Limited (NPCIL), 63

obesity, 339
official development assistance
  (ODA), 139, 140, 151
open network for digital commerce
  (ONDC), 311, 399
Organisation for Economic Cooperation and Development
  (OECD), 81, 116, 139, 244, 296,
  316, 331, 379, 380, 394, 395
original design manufacturer
  (ODM), 27
original equipment manufacturer
  (OEM), 27
own account enterprises, 244
own revenue receipts (ORR), 216,
  220, 223, 228, 229, 231, 232,
  233, 234, 235, 236, 237
own tax revenue (OTR), 216, 229

Palekar, Subhash, 341
panda bonds, 122
Paris Agreement, 36, 50, 51, 52,
  54, 74
Patel, Dev, 16
Pedro II, Don, 104
People's Bank of China (PBOC),
  124, 125, 126, 129, 132, 136
Periodic Labour Force Survey
  (PLFS), 173, 181, 183, 271, 324
Perón, Juan, 98
Petrobras, 105
pfandbriefe, 287
Phillips curve, 199, 206
Planning Commission, 262, 275,
  348, 349, 370
Plano Real, 108, 109, 110, 112, 382
Plaza Accord, 26
plurilaterals, 46
power purchase agreements
  (PPAs), 61
Pradhan Mantri Gramin Digital
  Saksharta Abhiyaan, or
  PMGDISHA, 318
Pratham, 86
preferential trade agreements
  (PTAs), xviii, 31, 32, 33
premiumization, 171, 173
producer support estimates (PSE),
  332
production-linked incentive (PLI),
  xxxi, 42, 368
productivity ecosystem approach,
  242, 243, 257, 395
Programme for International
  Student Assessment (PISA), 91,
  380

Project mBridge, 122, 126, 127, 135, 136, 383
public distribution system (PDS), 314, 339
public sector borrowing requirement (PSBR), 168
purchasing power parity, 9, 19, 20, 339, 372

Qualified Foreign Institutional Investor (QFII) Scheme, 128, 129
qualified foreign institutional investors (QFIs), 134
quarterly projection model (QPM), 205, 206, 207, 391

Ram, Lala Shri, 348
Rao, P.V. Narasimha, xiv, 118, 347, 354, 355, 356, 357, 403
Ravallion, Martin, 78
Reddy, Neelam Sanjiva, 350
Regional Comprehensive Economic Partnership (RCEP), 41, 43, 44, 46, 121, 368
renewable energy (RE), 53, 55, 58, 59, 60, 61, 62, 64, 68, 69, 70, 71, 74, 377
renewable purchase obligations (RPOs), 59, 60
Renminbi Liquidity Arrangement (RMBLA), 132
Renminbi Qualified Foreign Institutional Investor (RQFII) scheme, 129
renminbi (RMB), xxii, 119, 121, 122, 123, 124, 125, 127, 128, 132, 133, 134, 135, 136

Report on Currency and Finance (RCF), 209
reshoring, xvii, 24, 40
Resilience and Sustainability Trust facility, 143
Rousseff, Dilma, 111
rules of origin (ROOs), 37, 41, 44

Sandefur, Justin, 16, 373
Sen, Amartya, 219
Shanghai Futures Exchange, 133
Shanghai International Energy Exchange, 133, 134, 135
Shastri, Lal Bahadur, 349
Shekhar, Chandra, 356, 358
Singh, N.K., 18
Singh, Vishwanath Pratap, xiii, 355
Sinha, Yashwant, vii, 362
slowbalization, xvi, 4, 14, 16, 17, 18, 373
Society for Worldwide Interbank Financial Telecommunications (SWIFT), xxii, 124, 127, 128, 131, 135, 136
software and technology parks of India (STPI), 307
Solow paradox, 295, 315, 316
Solow, Robert, 295
South East Asian Central Banks Research and Training Centre, 130
sovereign wealth funds (SWFs), 139
special and differential treatment (S&DT), 36
special drawing rights, 124, 148, 149, 384

State Bank of India, 348
state-owned enterprise (SoE), 34
structural adjustment programmes
(SAPs), 143
Subramanian, Arvind, 14, 16, 21,
373, 382
Summers, Lawrence, 18
surveys of professional forecasters
(SPF), 197
Swaminathan, M.S., 329

tariffs, xxxi, 18, 25, 28, 32, 34, 35,
36, 38, 40, 42, 43, 45, 46, 62,
99, 104, 107, 108, 111, 321, 351,
361, 363, 364, 368
Tata, J.R.D., 348
Teaching at the Right Level
(TaRL), 86
Telecom Regulatory Authority of
India (TRAI), 306
Thakurdas, Purshottamdas, 348
time-of-day (TOD) metering, 61
TotalEnergies, 134
total factor productivity (TFP),
178, 325
trade and sustainable development
(TSD), 33
Trans-Pacific Partnership (TPP),
33, 34
TRIPS plus, 32
Trump, Donald, 18, 50, 54
Tsinghua University, 127

UNEP, 51, 376
Unified Payments Interface (UPI),
297, 310, 311, 318, 319, 398
Unincorporated Non-Agricultural
Enterprises (Excluding

Construction) in India survey,
243
United Fruit Company, 95
United Nations Framework
Convention on Climate Change
(UNFCCC), 49, 50, 51
United States-Mexico-Canada
Agreement (USMCA), 33, 375
Urban Agglomerations, 264
Urban Land (Ceiling and
Regulation) Act, 275
Uruguay Round, 28, 374
US-Canada Auto Pact, 31

Vajpayee, Atal Bihari, 362, 368
value-added, xiii, xxviii, 15, 29,
176, 245, 256, 267, 268, 269,
315
Vargas, Getúlio, 104, 381
VAT, xiii
Videla, Jorge Rafael, 99
Videsh Sanchar Nigam Limited
(VSNL), 306
Visa, 126
Volcker interest rate shock, 107

West Texas Intermediate (WTI),
123, 133, 134, 135
White Revolution, 322, 338
World Bank, xi, xii, xiii, xix, xxiii,
3, 12, 20, 23, 44, 45, 47, 78, 79,
80, 81, 85, 86, 93, 101, 106, 111,
112, 116, 121, 126, 130, 131,
136, 137, 138, 139, 140, 143,
144, 145, 146, 147, 148, 151,
152, 186, 212, 261, 262, 313,
355, 359, 371, 372, 373, 374,
375, 376, 377, 378, 379, 380,

381, 383, 384, 386, 387, 388, 397, 398, 399
World Development Report 2018, 85, 86, 379
World Trade Organization (WTO), xvii, xviii, 12, 17, 18, 25, 26, 28, 31, 33, 34, 36, 37, 38, 41, 46,

330, 373, 374, 375

Xiachouan, Xhou, 117

zero budget natural farming, 340
zero-Covid policy, 35
Zhengzhou Commodity Exchange, 133

Made in the USA
Monee, IL
15 May 2026

6c29ae73-1c6b-457a-a6ca-85c412f131b4R01